Continental Philosophy

D1427228

Continental Philosophy

An Introduction

David West

Polity

First published in 2010 by Polity Press
Reprinted in 2011 (twice), 2012, 2013, 2014

Polity Press
65 Bridge Street
Cambridge CB2 1UR, UK

Polity Press
350 Main Street
Malden, MA 02148, USA

ISBN-13: 978-0-7456-4581-0
ISBN-13: 978-0-7456-4582-7(pb)

A catalogue record for this book is available from the British Library.

Typeset in 10.5 on 12 pt Sabon
by Toppan Best-set Premedia Limited
Printed and bound in the USA by Edwards Brothers, Inc.

The publisher has used its best endeavours to ensure that the URLs for external websites referred to in this book are correct and active at the time of going to press. However, the publisher has no responsibility for the websites and can make no guarantee that a site will remain live or that the content is or will remain appropriate.

Every effort has been made to trace all copyright holders, but if any have been inadvertently overlooked the publisher will be pleased to include any necessary credits in any subsequent reprint or edition.

For further information on Polity, visit our website: www.politybooks.com

Contents

Preface to the Second Edition

This book is a revised and substantially expanded edition of *An Introduction to Continental Philosophy*, which was first published in 1996. Apart from a number of minor changes, there are two major additions. The first is a new section, in chapter 4, focusing on Hannah Arendt and, to a lesser extent, Carl Schmitt, both of whose ideas are increasingly influential in both continental and Anglophone political philosophy. The second major addition is a completely new chapter (chapter 8), which considers some 'radical departures' in continental philosophy at the onset of the twenty-first century. It includes extended discussion of Giorgio Agamben, Jean-Luc Nancy, Slavoj Žižek and Alain Badiou. These thinkers are by no means new – they were born either during or just after the Second World War. But the strong political inflection of their ideas has helped them to gain considerable prominence in the aftermath of the events of 11 September 2001 and the ensuing 'war on terrorism'. What is more, their shared emphasis on, and contrasting understandings of, the nature of 'the political' relate in interesting ways to the ideas of Schmitt and Arendt (discussed in chapter 4). The broader or lasting philosophical significance of these thinkers is, however, in the absence of the benefits of historical hindsight, still uncertain.

Apart from these textual additions, each chapter now starts with a brief 'Outline' and ends with a guide to further reading. Suggestions for further reading include both primary sources – or what amount to some of the key texts of continental philosophy – and a selection of guides and commentaries. Some additional and more specific references are provided in relevant endnotes. These new sections are designed to make the book more accessible and user-friendly to both students and general readers who want to deepen their knowledge of continental philosophy. For helpful comments on the new edition, I would like to thank Norman Abjorensen, David Eden, Leonard Lawlor, Michael Leininger-Ogawa, Matthew Sharpe and Ryan Walter. I am also grateful for the constructive criticisms and suggestions of one anonymous reviewer and the less constructive comments of another from whom, nevertheless, I was able to learn.

David West
Canberra, 2010

Preface to the First Edition

One of the most important and persistent features of continental philosophy, as we shall see, is its emphasis on the social, cultural and historical conditions of thought and existence. Continental philosophy is self-consciously historical. On the other hand, a major complaint against an Enlightenment too impressed by natural science is its wilful ignorance of history. Not surprisingly, any adequate understanding of contemporary thinkers in the continental tradition requires at least some knowledge of the history of that tradition. Thus, although the emphasis in what follows is on the ideas of currently influential thinkers and schools, their ideas are presented within a broad historical account. Whereas analytical philosophers of the twentieth century can be regarded as the Enlightenment's reasonably direct heirs, continental philosophy is the outcome of a series of critical responses to dominant currents of modern Western and Enlightenment philosophy. Of course, it is impossible given the scope of this work to provide any reasonably complete account of even the major contributors to continental philosophy. Rather, the aim here is to describe only the most important ideas of some of the tradition's most influential representatives.

In this spirit, the first chapter briefly characterizes continental philosophy in terms of the opposition between continental and analytical philosophy and the historical and philosophical roots of this opposition. It seems inevitable that some statement of the distinctiveness of continental philosophy must, in this way, come first. But, as Hegel recognized, such (and perhaps also these) prefatory remarks are more likely to be understood at the end than at the beginning.

Chapter 2 presents a somewhat more detailed account of modernity, modern and Enlightenment philosophy and some of the continental critics of these tendencies. This chapter acts as a kind of hub for the rest of the book. Subsequent continental thinkers and schools of thought are considered as developments of, or reactions against, the ideas of these continental critics. Later chapters aim to provide succinct introductions to major philosophical approaches and thinkers, including Marxism and the Frankfurt School, hermeneutics and phenomenology, existentialism, structuralism and poststructuralism. Finally, postmodernism can be seen as the most determined attempt yet to escape the fundamental assumptions of modern Western philosophy. Unavoidably, there are overlaps and sideways connections between some of the chapters. For example, Heidegger is surely best understood in the context of hermeneutics and phenomenology, in the company of Husserl and Gadamer (chapter 4). But Heidegger also exerted a major influence on Sartre, who is discussed in chapter 5. Again, Nietzsche, discussed here in the company of Kierkegaard and Sartre, was a major contributor both to the thought of the Frankfurt School and to Heidegger and the poststructuralist critique of humanism, and so also to postmodernism.

It remains for me to acknowledge the invaluable contributions of colleagues and friends. Philip Pettit and Robert Goodin commissioned an extended chapter for Blackwell's *Companion to Political Philosophy* on the 'Continental Contribution', which was the germ of the present project. John Thompson and Gill Motley, my editors at Polity Press, offered enthusiastic and patient support throughout its completion. Sue Fraser provided frequent and valuable assistance with research and referencing. An anonymous reader gave me a number of very helpful and timely comments for which I am very grateful. Finally, I would like to thank all those who read and commented on earlier drafts of individual chapters and in some cases, heroically, the whole manuscript, in particular: Nils Bubandt, Terrell Carver, Bruin Christensen, Tom Clarke, Frances Daly, Penelope Deutscher, Moira Gatens, John Hart, Barry Hindess, Peter McCarthy, Paul Patton, Philip Pettit, Scott Simon, Andrew Vincent, Caroline West, Glenn Worthington and Norbert Zmijewski.

David West
Canberra, 1995

1

Introduction: What is Continental Philosophy?

Outline

There is considerable agreement about which major thinkers and philosophical approaches belong to the continental tradition of philosophy. There is much less agreement, however, about what *defines* continental philosophy – what criteria allow us to identify these thinkers and approaches. As an analytical philosopher might say, the reference or extension of the term 'continental philosophy' is much clearer than its sense or 'intension'. In part, this reflects the problematic origins and motives of the distinction between continental and analytical philosophy. Most helpfully, the continental tradition of philosophy can be understood as the outcome of a series of critical responses to the dominant currents of modern European philosophy and, in particular, the Enlightenment's championing of science and scientific rationality.

Before engaging with at least some of the complexities and controversies that surround the term 'continental philosophy', it is helpful to give a more straightforward definition. Continental philosophy includes a range of thinkers and philosophical approaches usually contrasted with the 'analytical philosophy' that has dominated academic philosophy in the English-speaking world for most of the twentieth century. Continental philosophy in this sense includes such thinkers as Hegel, Marx, Kierkegaard, Nietzsche, Husserl, Heidegger, Arendt, Sartre, Beauvoir, Gadamer, Adorno, Derrida, Foucault,

Lyotard, Kristeva, Irigaray and Badiou. It involves philosophical approaches that include Hegelian idealism, Marxism, the 'critical theory' of the Frankfurt School and Habermas, existentialism, hermeneutics, phenomenology, structuralism, poststructuralism, postmodernism and some forms of feminism. This description should at least make clear, even at this early stage, that there is no single, homogeneous continental tradition. Rather, there is a variety of more or less closely related currents of thought. There are thinkers who, in one way or another, work in an identifiably continental mode.[1]

For the purposes of this book, the identification of a distinctly continental array of approaches in philosophy will be made primarily in historical terms. It will be useful not only to identify a group of thinkers who bear certain family resemblances to one another, but also to trace some of the more obvious lines of descent, to sketch an intellectual family tree. Thus a number of contrasts of both substance and style will be traced to the emergence of distinctively continental currents of thought in response to the main direction taken by modern European philosophy and, in particular, the Enlightenment. The dominant temper of that intellectual upheaval combined scepticism about the claims of traditional metaphysics, religion and morality with considerable (and, in the opinion of some, inordinate) admiration for the methods of the natural sciences. If science is nonetheless exposed to scepticism or doubt, then it is challenged as the most convincing example of human knowledge.[2] In comparison with natural science, other claims to knowledge seem insecure to the characteristic philosophers of the Enlightenment, who typically seek to place artistic, moral and even religious truths on more rationally defensible, more scientific and thus more secure foundations.

For a number of continental critics of the Enlightenment, however, the efforts of these thinkers were doomed from the start. The failures and difficulties they met with in their attempts to provide secure, rational foundations for the moral, religious and artistic dimensions of human knowledge were not so much signs of an uncompleted project as the inevitable consequences of a distorted, one-sided philosophical approach. The Enlightenment's critics saw the need for a very different response to questions which neither scientific method nor Enlightenment philosophy appeared equipped to answer. The result was a number of novel intellectual approaches, which together make up what we are here calling continental philosophy. The main contours of this continental critique can be traced to the writings of Kant, Rousseau and German Romantics and idealists like Herder, Novalis, the Schlegel brothers, Hölderlin and Schelling. It is expressed most systematically and ambitiously, though, in the philosophy of

Hegel. Subsequent contributors to the continental tradition are almost invariably 'post-Hegelians', in the sense that they either develop or react against, but rarely simply ignore, the thought of Hegel. Their ideas bear the marks of the Hegelian system, even when they vigorously oppose or reject it. In what follows, we shall examine some of the most important of these ideas.[3]

However, before going on to this task, it is perhaps necessary to ward off a possible objection to our whole enterprise.[4] Even if we set aside straightaway those objections habitually raised against any attempt to express a large subject in relatively few words or to make difficult ideas more accessible, we are left with a more substantial worry. This is that the isolation of a separate tradition of continental philosophy is contentious or even perverse. The project may seem particularly odd to readers from continental Europe itself – Europe, that is, considered apart from those mainly English-speaking islands at its western extremity. After all, the various currents of Western philosophy share a common history from the pre-Socratics, Plato and Aristotle, through the significant influence of Christianity, Judaism and Islamic scholarship to such central figures of modern European philosophy as Descartes, Locke, Hume, Leibniz, Spinoza and Kant. With some justice, the term 'continental philosophy' can even be accused of ethnocentrism, since evidently only the European continent is intended. Continental philosophy can only be a variant of Western philosophy.

In fact, continental philosophy began life as a category of exclusion. Until recently the analytical philosophy prevailing within the English-speaking countries of the West, including the United States, Britain, Australia, Canada and New Zealand, has almost completely ignored philosophical work produced on the continent of Europe since Kant – or, in other words, continental philosophy. As recently as the 1970s, a course in philosophy that failed to mention Hegel or Nietzsche, Husserl, Heidegger or Sartre was not considered in the least deficient. In this respect, Kant, whose significance is acknowledged within both analytical and continental traditions, represents a decisive point of transition or even rupture. His philosophy was, in part, a response to the radical scepticism of David Hume, one of the central figures of the Scottish Enlightenment and a significant influence on analytical philosophy. Kant's response is still taken very seriously by analytical philosophers. But the work of Hegel, whose most important ideas arise directly from his critical response to Kant, has been largely ignored. So it is with and after Hegel that it begins to make sense to speak of continental and analytical rather than simply of European or Western philosophy. A whole series of subsequent nineteenth- and twentieth-century continental thinkers, usually either directly influenced by or reacting against Hegel or Hegelian ideas, have either been ignored altogether by analytical philosophers or, like Sartre and Camus, valued mainly for their literary works.

The genealogy of continental philosophy can, then, be traced to Hegelian and associated responses to Kant. But, as a category of exclusion, continental philosophy was first identified as a distinct tradition from the perspective of an emergent analytical philosophy. The latter development was given major impetus around the start of the twentieth century by such figures as Gottlob Frege, Bertrand Russell and G. E. Moore, who were engaged at the time in a protracted battle with what was then, both in Britain and the rest of the English-speaking world, an overwhelmingly idealist and Hegelian (or in other words, 'continental') ascendancy.[5] The rise of analytical philosophy dates from this time. Whitehead and Russell's *Principia Mathematica* was an important watershed.[6] Ironically, continental Europe was then dominated by positivist and neo-Kantian philosophies, both much closer in spirit to analytical than to contemporary continental philosophy.

In effect, analytical philosophy revived the sceptical, scientific spirit of the Enlightenment with the help of technical developments in symbolic logic and the foundations of mathematics. The resulting principles and techniques were deployed, initially with great enthusiasm, against the 'usual suspects' or, at least, their direct descendants: the claims of 'continental' metaphysical idealism, traditional religion and dogmatic morality. At its most rigorous (or rigid), analytical philosophy applies what is sometimes called Hume's fork. Hume claims: 'All the objects of human reason or enquiry may naturally be divided into two kinds, to wit, *Relations of Ideas*, and *Matters of Fact*.' The former include principally the truths of mathematics and logic, which are 'discoverable by the mere operation of thought, without dependence on what is anywhere existent in the universe'. The latter are contingent truths about the world which 'seem to be founded on the relation of *Cause and Effect*'.[7] Of course, Hume has in mind those truths most systematically expressed in the natural sciences of his day. Anything that belongs to neither category, including scholastic philosophy or 'metaphysics' and religion, is revealed *ipso facto* as worthless from the point of view of reason or genuine knowledge. Although analytical philosophers relax this principle somewhat in practice – if only to make sense of their own activity, which itself does not fall clearly into either category – they continue to work very much in its spirit. Since philosophy is neither a branch of logic or mathematics nor a natural science comparable to physics or biology, it must restrict itself austerely to the careful analysis of concepts. The only scientifically respectable philosophy is henceforth analytical. According to the 'linguistic turn' taken by twentieth-century philosophers more generally, this task is then interpreted as involving first and foremost the analysis of language. Michael Dummett's statement is representative: '[T]he goal of philosophy is the analysis of the structure of *thought*' and 'the only proper method for analysing thought consists in the analysis of *language*.'[8]

Continental philosophers, on the other hand, can be regarded as the distant relatives of those metaphysicians, moralists and religious believers so caustically dismissed by Hume, at least in the sense that they are unwilling to abandon the concerns and insights intimated by these modes of experience. Similarly, they continue to address questions which ordinary common sense has never ceased to regard as important elements of the philosopher's task. These are, above all, existential, moral or ethical and aesthetic questions: questions about the nature of existence and the meaning of life, questions of right and wrong or of the meaning of art and beauty. In other words, they share the concern of traditional philosophers with wisdom rather than mere knowledge.[9] From the point of view of analytical philosophy, however, continental philosophers continue to employ dubious metaphysical methods, which have been superseded by their own more precise, rigorous and scientific tools of conceptual analysis. In these terms, the continental approach has been subjected to frequent criticism, from 'logical positivist' diatribes against the 'senseless' utterances of 'metaphysics' to the continuing, though recently abating, concern to demarcate 'science' from 'nonsense'. When A. J. Ayer reiterates Hume's complaint that metaphysics comprises neither verifiable statements of fact nor analytical or logical truths, and should therefore be dismissed as nonsense, he chooses the eminently continental figure of Heidegger as his target.[10] There is some irony again here, since Heidegger, as we shall see, was also preoccupied with the need to overcome metaphysics, albeit in a very different sense.[11]

In other words, 'continental philosophy' is no innocent, and for that matter not just a boring, classificatory label, but rather begins life as something closer to a term of abuse. The opposition between continental and analytical philosophy thus resembles that other, more worldly and now increasingly obsolete opposition between East and West. The observer of politics soon realizes that 'East' and 'West' are ideological rather than geographical terms. The West is free, capitalist and prosperous, and celebrates human rights and the American way.

The East has been totalitarian, stagnant and oppressive. Despite their geographical locations, Japan and Australia are, for most purposes, regarded as belonging to the West, whereas Cuba belongs to the East. Similar anomalies beset any straightforwardly geographical interpretation of the distinction between analytical and continental philosophy.

Thus Frege played a significant role in the development of analytical philosophy despite being German, as did the logical positivists of the Vienna Circle and Ludwig Wittgenstein, who were Austrian.[12] On the other hand, there are obvious affinities between such nineteenth- and twentieth-century British idealists as T. H. Green, Bradley, Collingwood and Oakeshott and their idealist contemporaries across the Channel. Even John Stuart Mill, an honoured figure within the analytical tradition, was deeply influenced by the ideas of Wilhelm von Humboldt, a friend of Goethe and Schiller, and by German Romanticism. Gilbert Ryle, author of *The Concept of Mind* (a classic of analytical philosophy), studied for a time with Husserl. Contemporary English-speaking philosophers such as Richard Rorty, Alasdair MacIntyre and Charles Taylor, working mainly in North America, self-consciously develop continental themes, albeit in the idiom of analytical philosophy. Again, there are now thriving schools of analytical philosophy in France and Germany, where there have in the past also been periodic revivals of neo-Kantianism, which is not so very different in its fundamental claims. Logical and analytical approaches to philosophical questions, finally, have a long tradition in Poland (for example, the Lvov–Warsaw school) as well as in other East European countries.

Certainly, then, a straightforwardly geographical basis for the identification of two mutually isolated traditions in Western philosophy cannot be found and, in any case, would be unlikely to be philosophically interesting. To adapt Derrida's apt phrase, the continent is 'the nonempirical site of a movement'.[13] On the other hand, although there is evidence that the distinction between analytical and continental philosophy is the product of antagonism between distinct philosophical camps, it is not easy to identify clear and substantial doctrinal differences or to define the two approaches reliably in terms of divergent methods, topics, styles or even moods. Certainly, it would be premature to attempt a firm distinction at this stage. Like all ideologically tinged oppositions, the distinction between analytical and continental philosophy has served as much to prevent serious intellectual engagement as to identify genuine differences. Intellectual traditions reflect social and historical allegiances as much as strictly intellectual considerations. It will surely prove more fruitful, therefore, to go on directly to a consideration of continental philosophy and the intellectual approaches and thinkers with which it is associated.

Further Reading

Simon Critchley, *Continental Philosophy: A Very Short Introduction* provides an alternative (though related) definition of continental philosophy. On developments in individual countries, see G. Gutting, *French Philosophy in the Twentieth Century*, A. Bowie, *Introduction to German Philosophy: From Kant to Habermas* and S. Benso and B. Schroeder's edited collection, *Contemporary Italian Philosophy*. For introductory accounts of major philosophers and schools within the continental tradition, covering similar ground to this book, but with a different approach, see W. R. Schroeder, *Continental Philosophy: A Critical Approach* or Andrew Cutrofello, *Continental Philosophy: A Contemporary Introduction*.

2

Modernity, Enlightenment and their Continental Critics

Outline

The West's self-conscious modernity – its understanding of itself as rational, socially advanced and therefore modern – accelerated rapidly in the period from 1500 AD as a result of a series of interrelated developments, which included the Renaissance and the revival of humanism, voyages of discovery and important advances in the natural sciences, Protestant Reformation, the rise of capitalism and the emergence of the modern system of nation-states. From the seventeenth century, modern philosophers like Francis Bacon and René Descartes began to dismantle the monolithic worldview of the Middle Ages – a combination of Christianity and Ancient philosophy. By the time of the eighteenth-century European Enlightenment, science and scientific rationality had become the ultimate arbiters of knowledge, morality and politics. Immanuel Kant's attempt to define the *limits* of scientific knowledge in order to 'make room' for morality, freedom and faith, was a crucial watershed for subsequent philosophers in the continental tradition. The tensions within Kant's system provoked a number of critical responses from Romantics, metaphysical idealists, theologians and political conservatives. Hegel's ambitious attempt to reconcile both Enlightenment and 'counter-Enlightenment' perspectives – by means of an embodied, historical, socialized and dialectical conception of reason – soon fell apart. The dissolution of Hegel's system, however, gave rise to a number of further responses and reactions, which provide the disparate sources of a distinctively continental tradition in philosophy.

From modernity to Enlightenment

Continental philosophy is a significant and continuing strand of Western philosophy. It can be traced to a series of reactions to what have become known as modernity and Enlightenment. The Enlightenment was a philosophical as well as a more broadly intellectual and cultural movement of the eighteenth century, but it can also be regarded as the culmination in the intellectual sphere of a series of events and developments transforming European society, particularly from the onset of the 'modern' period around 1500 AD. As we shall see, these social, economic and cultural developments were interwoven both with longer-term processes of 'modernization' and with the emergence of the West's self-consciousness as 'modern'. By the time of the Enlightenment, the West had formed a strong, though not uncontested, belief in the superiority of its own thought, institutions and values. It boasted the successful completion of a number of modernizing processes of development, including the emergence of the modern state and the rise of a capitalist market economy. Intellectually, autonomous scientific, artistic and moral spheres were demarcated from what had previously been an overwhelmingly religious worldview that made no such clear distinctions. The West had come to see itself as modern.

In its own eyes at least, then, Western society was modernized by a series of social and cultural developments, which can be traced back to ancient Greece and Rome and which continue into modern times. The characterization of these apparently unplanned, or at least uncoordinated, developments as processes of modernization, rather than simply as change, relies on the role allegedly played in them by rationality. Western society is more modern because it is more rational. This is brought out clearly in Max Weber's sociological account of the evolution of Western society as a process of 'formal' rationalization.[1] Rationalization, in Weber's sense, involves the abandonment or reform of traditional practices in favour of procedures designed to achieve more efficiently the goals identified with these practices. The result is what has also been described as the 'instrumental' rationalization of society: institutions are fashioned into more effective *means* for the realization of particular *ends*. In this sense, for example, Roman law significantly rationalized the legal and administrative systems of the Empire. Legislators produced a more ordered and consistent legal code, removing anomalies and incoherencies inherited from traditional practice and the precedents of the common law. Roman law then served as a model for the reform of many of the legal systems subsequently adopted in continental Europe.[2]

Significantly, although Roman law itself was far from secular in the contemporary sense, rationalization in the West was increasingly associated with processes of secularization, or what Weber calls 'disenchantment'.[3] The reform of traditional institutions and practices in the interest of greater efficiency disrupts the authority of religious beliefs and values.[4] For the rationalizing spirit, tradition and religion are no longer sufficient reasons for acting in a particular way. In this spirit, throughout the medieval period the gradual separation of state from church freed both laws and decision-making from the restrictions of religious belief and traditional morality, producing states and the political sphere in their modern sense for the first time. The secularization of the state allowed a politics and an administration more pragmatically attuned to temporal 'reasons of state' or, in later democratic variants, the secular interests of the community. Machiavelli's *The Prince* is a notoriously unsentimental exploration of the implications of the separation of politics from morality. What is more, alongside the development of a relatively autonomous politics and state, the mode of operation of the state could also be rationalized. Traditional arts of government were displaced by a more systematically organized administration or 'bureaucracy'. The bureaucratic state is run by officials, who are selected according to criteria to do with professional expertise rather than family ties or wealth. Decisions are made according to fixed and predictable rules rather than at the discretion of trusted individuals. Each case must be recorded in a detailed and systematic manner. The rationalization of politics and state advanced throughout the medieval period, despite its subsequent characterization by a later and self-consciously more enlightened time as the 'Dark Ages'. William the Conqueror's 'Domesday Book' of 1086, a systematic record of the land for purposes of taxation, is just one example.[5]

Similar processes of formal or instrumental rationalization occurred in the economic sphere, with the gradual spread of capitalist relations of production. Capitalism, a mode of economic organization that allows the free circulation and unlimited private accumulation of capital, begins to emerge with the rise of free cities from the thirteenth and fourteenth centuries. Capitalism, too, erodes traditional ways of organizing production and challenges the customary regulation of prices and wages. An increasingly free market intensifies competition between enterprises and unleashes the profit motive, creating a dynamic mechanism for greater productive efficiency and accelerating rates of economic growth. At the same time, broader social transformations are set in train. Traditional ties of authority are weakened as large numbers of peasants are displaced from country to town. New wealth provides a powerful base for the political and intellectual aspirations of the 'bourgeoisie' – the rising, middling classes of traders and merchants, small manufacturers, bankers and moneylenders, lawyers and accountants. This class will eventually play a significant role in subsequent cultural, intellectual and political developments associated with modernity and Enlightenment.

This rationalization of state and economy sets the scene for a significant transformation of thought and culture. What has been described as the arrival of an explicit and self-conscious 'discourse of modernity' marks a further stage in the evolution of the West.[6] From around 1500, there is a recognizable break from the past and, for the self-consciousness of the West, a new sense of time. One aspect of the new consciousness is that the chauvinism by which Hellenes, Jews and then Europeans had regarded themselves as superior is reinterpreted in world-historical terms. The West claims henceforth that its institutions and thought bear a privileged relation to a uniquely valid rationality, markedly reinforcing pretensions to universal truth already present in Epicurean and Stoic thought. Europeans come to see themselves as more modern, more advanced or more developed than peoples they now describe as traditional, backward or primitive – and whom they sometimes even see as being incapable of such development. A number of historic events contributed to the appearance of this self-conscious modernity and 'openness to the future'. In Habermas's words, 'The discovery of the "new world", the Renaissance, and the Reformation – these three monumental events around the year 1500 constituted the epochal threshold between modern times and the middle ages.'[7] Although, according to Habermas's account, the self-consciousness of modernity is not fully articulated until the eighteenth century with the Enlightenment, the moment of transition is then fixed in the past: 'Only in the course of the eighteenth century did the epochal threshold around 1500 become conceptualized as this beginning.'[8] The Enlightenment, as its name intimates, understands this threshold as the first dawning of an age of reason and light.

Voyages of discovery, Renaissance and Reformation, these 'monumental events' helped trigger a profound transformation of the social, cultural and intellectual life of Europe. In the process, the view of the world still dominant at the end of the Middle Ages, essentially a synthesis of Christian doctrine and classical Greek science and cosmology, was unravelled. By the sixteenth century, philosophers, moralists and political thinkers had begun to cast doubt on traditional beliefs and religious authority in search of surer, more rational foundations for our knowledge of nature, our moral beliefs and the political order. The voyages of discovery had put Europeans into contact with previously unknown and (to them) evidently primitive peoples. Travellers' tales of encounters with 'uncivilized' or 'savage' natives were popular and would continue to figure in the fictions and moral treatises of the Enlightenment.[9] The interest of these encounters was heightened by the evident contrast between these peoples and what was being learned of the civilizations of ancient Greece and Rome. The rediscovery of these cultures, made possible in part by the contributions of Islamic scholars who had translated and so preserved many of the texts of classical antiquity, inspired a 'renaissance', a rebirth or reawakening, of both arts and sciences. Artists and architects imitated ancient temples and sculptures, and revived classical subjects, techniques and literary genres. The revival of these forms encouraged the flourishing of humanism, which placed greater emphasis on human interests, capacities and concerns and less on the supernatural or divine. The art of the Renaissance paid more attention to secular themes and, in the works of Michelangelo or Leonardo da Vinci, unashamedly celebrated the perfection of the human form. Even the religious art of the Renaissance accorded greater space to human experience and emotion. Humanism was also associated with a more realistic employment of artistic techniques – sometimes to the advantage of the newly developing sciences, for example with the more accurate anatomical representation of the human body – and the systematic application of linear perspective for the representation of objects in three-dimensional space.[10]

Parallel to the humanism of the cultural and artistic spheres were developments in philosophy and science that opened ever-deeper fissures in a hitherto overwhelmingly religious worldview. Philosophical humanism helped to legitimate what Francis Bacon (1561–1626) termed 'learning' as opposed to the 'wisdom' of traditional morality and religion. Still, Bacon's defence of unaided human knowledge of 'God's works' depends on theological premises:

> let no man upon a weak conceit of sobriety or an ill-applied moderation think or maintain, that a man can search too far, or be too well studied in the book of God's word, or in the book of God's works; divinity or philosophy: but rather let men endeavour an endless progress or proficience in both . . .[11]

Achievements in the natural sciences provided an important spur to this new self-confidence. From now on there was less emphasis on the limitations of human knowledge, more on its actual or potential achievements. Human beings can investigate the world unaided. They no longer need to reconcile their findings with either revealed religion or established authority. Even the appropriation of classical Greek and Roman texts had to be critical. Ideally, the pursuit of knowledge should 'begin anew from the very foundations'.[12] With philosophers such as Bacon, the modern conception of science as a systematic, critical and unconditional enterprise is clearly formulated for the first time.

Not surprisingly, knowledge produced on this humanist basis soon came into conflict with the teachings of established religion. A notable example is the confrontation of Galileo Galilei (1564–1642) with the Catholic Church. Galileo's astronomical observations led him to support the 'heliocentric hypothesis' of Copernicus that the sun rather than the earth is at the centre of the universe. Copernicus' hypothesis would eventually greatly simplify calculations of the movements of the planets.[13] Heliocentrism was in sharp conflict with the orthodox view of the Church, adopted from the second-century Egyptian, Ptolemy, that the home of God's most important creature must be the centre of the universe. The Church refused to separate the moral and religious issue of the importance of 'man' and 'his' earth from more purely scientific questions of astronomical calculation and prediction. In a striking scene of Bertolt Brecht's play, dramatizing this historic confrontation, senior figures of the Church are invited to confirm Galileo's revolutionary observations with the help of his telescope, but they simply refuse to look. The Inquisition shows Galileo the instruments of torture and he recants. Although Galileo was condemned by the Inquisition in 1616 and remained in confinement for the rest of his life, his ideas could not be contained so easily, and the victory of the Church was to prove short-lived. Galileo is able to arrange for a copy of his *Dialogue on Two World Systems* to be smuggled across the border to safety in Holland.[14] The events described in Brecht's play are representative of the broader historical transformation. The scientific discoveries of 'natural philosophers' like Galileo and Newton eroded the worldview of medieval Christendom. Constructed under the domination of the Catholic Church, this worldview was a complex synthesis of classical and Christian doctrine. Perhaps at the heart of the medieval picture is a view of the world as an ordered and meaningful cosmos – a very old idea already present in the thought of Pythagoras and other pre-Socratics. All the elements of nature, including humanity, are understood according to their place in a coherent, ordered and meaningful universe. The Church reconciled this cosmology with Christian doctrine. The world is seen as God's creation and as the expression of his will, as something visibly imbued with both meaning and purpose. Similarly, evidence for the existence and power of God is to be found throughout a natural world whose perfection and complex interdependence so clearly seem to be the product of intelligent and beneficent design. This view also accorded well with Aristotle's 'teleological' biology, which explained the development of plants and animals by the final goal or form, the *telos* that they strive to achieve.[15]

For the medieval worldview, then, the central categories are purpose, meaning and divine will. By contrast, the world that comes into view with the science and philosophy of the modern period is radically disenchanted. The world is no longer a meaningful order replete with moral and religious significance but, as Charles Taylor puts it, 'a world of ultimately contingent correlations to be patiently mapped by empirical observation'.[16] The dualist philosophy of René Descartes (1591–1650) is one important source of this picture of the physical world. For Aristotle, *psyche* ('breath', 'life' or 'soul') is what makes a body alive and so is essentially embodied. There is no strict separation between mind and matter; therefore, what seem to us almost animistic explanations of biological development, as 'striving' or 'aiming' for a final goal, are not clearly ruled out. Descartes's dualism of mind and matter, on the other hand, serves to drive a wedge between the scientific explanation of bodies in space and what become strictly 'mental' categories of purpose and will. A purely mechanical model of the material world as matter extended in space is combined with a picture of mind as essentially immaterial and disembodied.[17] Although God is invoked as the ultimate guarantor of the truth of our experience of the external world, he plays no substantive role in the explanation of events within it. The sufficient reason for every event in nature can be found within nature itself.

The revised view of the external world of nature also implies a novel account of the human 'subject'. In the terms of Descartes's dualism, the self is conceived as a non-physical subject of experience, essentially distinct both from its physical embodiment and its place in a meaningful order of nature. The self is no longer defined or constrained by an essential purpose, bound simply to realize an intrinsic nature or *telos*. The characteristic self of modern philosophy is an abstract and disembodied subject of consciousness. Descartes's account of this self emerges from the attempt to find indubitable foundations for knowledge. He pursues his famous method of radical scepticism or doubt, confident only of those beliefs that it is impossible to doubt. By this method Descartes soon arrives at the conclusion that the only thing that is certain is that 'I am, I exist'. I can doubt the evidence of my senses, the existence of an external world, even the existence of my own body. But when I doubt that I exist, it seems that I unavoidably presuppose my own existence. When I am doubting, I am thinking, and if I am thinking then I must exist. This train of reasoning delivers the famous *cogito ergo sum* or 'I think, therefore I am' of Cartesian philosophy. Descartes proceeds apace to the more controversial conclusion, that what I am 'essentially' is a thing that thinks. An essential property or attribute of a thing is one that is indispensable to its being that thing. An 'accidental' or 'contingent' property, on the other hand, is one that a thing may or may not have and still be the thing that it is. In this specific philosophical sense, whales are essentially marine mammals but only accidentally victims of human aggression. Descartes reasons that if I can doubt the existence of my body, then my physical attributes cannot be essential ones. I could be who I am without my body. The self is only accidentally physical, but essentially mental: 'I am not more than a thing which thinks, that is to say a mind or a soul, or an understanding, or a reason.'[18] If I am essentially a thing that thinks, then the connection between my self and my body can only be a non-essential or accidental one. Those features of a human being deriving from its physical embodiment are merely accidental or contingent features of a self that is essentially disembodied. By implication, purpose and meaning can no longer be derived from our place in an ordered cosmos. In future, the self must find its purpose, the meaning of its existence, from within itself. The self must become, in Taylor's terms, a 'self-defining subject'.[19]

This disembodied, self-defining subject corresponds to a very different picture of the nature of human knowledge. For the most influential currents of modern philosophy the goal of knowledge is no longer to decipher meanings woven into the fabric of the world, in order either to fulfil God's design or to live more in harmony with the purposes of nature. Rather, the value of knowledge is principally instrumental. Knowledge is something that makes our lives more certain, and perhaps more comfortable, by improving our ability to predict and control nature. Bacon expresses this view of knowledge in the clear, but explicitly patriarchal, terms of a relationship between man and a female nature: 'that knowledge may not be, as a curtesan, for pleasure and vanity only, or as a bondwoman, to acquire and gain to her master's use; but as a spouse, for generation, fruit, and comfort.'[20] The ambition, even arrogance, of these aspirations was encouraged by the combination of theoretical elegance and predictive success soon achieved by the natural sciences and, perhaps most impressively, in the mechanics and astronomy of Isaac Newton (1642–1727).[21] At the same time, less optimistic sub-currents of

European culture expressed fears at the excess of these ambitions. Expressions of this sentiment ranged from dramatizations of the Faust legend by Marlowe and Goethe to nineteenth-century Gothic tales about the potentially monstrous products of scientific hubris, like *Frankenstein*.[22] Still, the dominant currents of modern thought admire mathematics and natural science as the most impressive and most obviously useful examples of human knowledge.

A corollary of the modern view of knowledge is scepticism about other forms of human knowledge and experience. Religion, in particular, would suffer in the longer term. That said, early modern thought was not dominated by 'free thinkers', whether agnostic or atheist. Philosophers continued to profess belief in God, whether out of genuine conviction or fear of the consequences of unbelief. For Descartes an 'ontological' proof of the existence of God is necessary, if he is to escape from the predicament of 'solipsism' – the belief that we can only be certain of the existence of our own mind or consciousness and cannot know that anything or anyone else exists. We can trust the evidence of our senses only on the assumption of a benign deity, who would not allow us to be permanently deceived by an 'evil demon'.[23] Other thinkers maintain the compatibility of faith and reason or, like Bacon and Locke, insist on the value of religious 'wisdom' or 'revelation' as opposed to mere human 'learning'.[24] Still, the world of the modern period is significantly disenchanted. Nature is essentially nothing more than a mechanistic system of extended matter without religious or moral significance. By the same token, our knowledge of this disenchanted world no longer provides unequivocal or immediate support for either morality or religion.

The culmination of the tendencies implicit in modern philosophy is reached with the Enlightenment in the eighteenth century. Most notably in France, the so-called 'Encyclopaedists', including such figures as d'Alembert, Diderot, Voltaire, Helvétius and d'Holbach, produced an influential dictionary or 'encyclopaedia' of contemporary arts and sciences. These Enlightenment figures argued for liberal and anticlerical views, which found dramatic expression in the French Revolution of 1789. In Germany, Kant espoused the Enlightenment as the transition from 'immaturity' and dependence to the 'spirit of freedom' and autonomy, the ability 'to use one's understanding without guidance from another'.[25] Enlightenment thinkers conducted a more confident and open assault on the Church and traditional morality. However, the typical profession of these thinkers is still a form of deism, a religious faith shorn of 'superstitious' elements unacceptable to reason. A mature and rational humanity no longer requires either the distraction of miracles or the crude motivation of visions of hell and damnation.[26] At the same time, Enlightenment thinkers are even more convinced of the value of science. After the Enlightenment, scepticism about science carries the hint of bravado previously attached to atheism.

A rather different 'Scottish Enlightenment' is associated with the more conservative, sceptical philosophy of David Hume (1711–76) and the moral and economic writings of Adam Smith (1723–90). Hume, about a century after Descartes was writing, brings out the full implications of the Cartesian view of nature. He ridicules the medieval worldview's conception of nature as a teleological system of entities propelled by inner necessity to fulfil their essential purpose or goal. Even if such essential purposes or 'powers' existed, we could never have knowledge either of them or of the 'necessary connection' between events that they are supposed to imply. Knowledge of reality can only be derived from a careful observation of the 'constant conjunction' between contingent events. Where such a constant conjunction is observed, we are inclined (though for Hume not necessarily entitled) to attribute a causal relationship between events designated 'cause' and 'effect'.[27] The recent successes of natural scientists can only be accounted for in these terms. Scientific knowledge depends on the conscientious observation of the regularities of nature. Hume, like Hobbes some 100 years earlier, also seeks to apply the method of science to the 'science of man', to what are now known as human or social sciences.[28]

Certainly, scientific knowledge has nothing to do with either knowledge of canonical texts (whether Aristotle or the Bible) or a sensitive reading of nature considered as the manifestation of God's will. Hume challenges all attempts to base religious belief on our experience of the world, whether in the form of the argument from design or from the alleged evidence of miracles.[29] He directs some of his most biting irony at religion, in particular its dogmatic morality and the high-flown claims of theology. But Hume's scepticism also challenges the claims of moral and aesthetic judgement more generally. His classic statement of the distinction between facts and values announces that 'virtue is not founded merely on the relations of objects'.[30] There can be no derivation of an 'ought' from an 'is'; no collection of facts, however exhaustive, implies an evaluative conclusion. Judgements of value, whether of good and evil or of 'beauty and deformity', simply reflect our sentiments, our inclinations or taste.[31] Morality and aesthetics are based not on reason or knowledge but on feelings of pleasure and pain: 'Pleasure and pain, therefore, are not only necessary attendants of beauty and deformity but constitute their very essence. . . . An action, or sentiment, or character is virtuous or vicious; why? because its view causes a pleasure or uneasiness of a particular kind.'[32] A variety of different accounts of moral and aesthetic value are provided by Enlightenment thinkers. But characteristically, value is something that must be added by human subjects to an evaluatively neutral world. Morality might be explained in terms of feelings of pleasure and pain or the impressions of a 'moral sense', as it is with Hume. Utilitarians like Jeremy Bentham developed Hume's picture of moral and aesthetic judgement as a projection of human desire or the capacity for pleasure and suffering. Moral laws are explained by Kant as the decrees of self-legislating rational beings.[33] With subjectivism, values are regarded, in desperation, as the unchallengeable expressions of arbitrary will. In general, the self-defining subject must seek moral guidance from within. Values, previously manifest in every facet of a meaningful world, must now be justified. Values must be provided with foundations.

The critical philosophy of Immanuel Kant

There are, of course, many variants of Enlightenment philosophy within the broad constellation of ideas just described; the philosopher Immanuel Kant (1724–1804) occupies a pivotal position in their development.[34] He is respected as a major figure by later philosophers from both analytical and continental traditions, though different aspects of his works are highlighted and differing interpretations favoured within them. Kant's 'critical philosophy' seeks to establish the limits and underlying structure of human knowledge and experience, a project that has, from the outset, both negative and positive intentions, reflecting the dilemma faced by human reason in its relation to philosophical or 'metaphysical' questions: 'Human reason has this peculiar fate that in one species of its knowledge it is burdened by questions which, as prescribed by the very nature of reason itself, it is not able to ignore, but which, as transcending all its powers, it is also not able to answer.'[35] Kant's critical philosophy is able to play a pivotal role in the subsequent development of European philosophy, because it draws together most of the central issues of Enlightenment thought in a suggestive way. Most influentially, his critique of 'pure reason', which concerns the kind of knowledge of the external world most clearly demonstrated in the natural sciences, provides an imaginative synthesis of empiricism and rationalism, opposing camps in what was perhaps the central philosophical dispute of the period.[36] Both empiricism and rationalism are characteristically modern philosophies, seeking to place human knowledge on firm and indubitable foundations and to resist spurious claims to religious knowledge. Of course, this stance was not incompatible with a religious belief purified of unjustifiable pretensions and superstitious remnants. Sceptical empiricists, who regarded human knowledge as a very inadequate instrument, were sometimes open to alternative sources of wisdom.

Empiricists such as John Locke (1632–1704), George Berkeley (1685–1753) and David Hume hold that all human knowledge is ultimately based on experiences – on our 'impressions' or 'sensations' or observations of the external world. In the technical terms associated with the dispute between empiricists and rationalists, empiricists hold that all worthwhile knowledge is a posteriori, or something we can only achieve *after* having the appropriate experiences. Our knowledge is not based on any innate ideas: when we are born the mind is a blank slate or *tabula rasa*. By contrast, rationalists maintain that important, possibly the most important, instances of human knowledge are available to us prior to or independently of our experience. Rationalists are closer to the Platonic tradition in philosophy. Taking pure mathematics and logic rather than natural science as their favoured models, rationalists argue that such knowledge can only be understood as something we have a priori or *before* experience. Already Plato's dialogues contained arguments for this position. In the dialogue *Phaedo*, Socrates defends the view that 'what we call learning is just recollection' in order to prove the immortality of the soul.[37] In the *Meno* he uses the example of proofs in geometry to portray the process of learning as a kind of recollection or remembering of what we must have already known before.[38] The truths of mathematics and logic can be demonstrated without appeal to experience and could never be contradicted by it. No number of observations could ever persuade us that '2 + 2 = 5' or that 'It is raining and it is not raining' is ever true. Abstract mathematical entities, such as perfectly straight lines, points that occupy no space or perfect circles and triangles, are never met with in experience. So how can we have knowledge of these entities, the kind of knowledge demonstrated in Euclid's geometry, unless it is somehow innate? Rationalists are unconvinced by empiricist attempts to explain this knowledge in some other way, whether as the product of generalization from experience or as comprising ultimately contentless truths by definition.

Kant seeks to combine the insights of both empiricism and rationalism. He agrees with the rationalists that there are important truths we can know a priori, but he seeks to provide a more adequate explanation for the possibility of such knowledge than any provided by rationalism. He agrees with empiricists that much of our knowledge depends on experience but, according to Kant, empiricists neglect the 'formal' contribution which the mind makes to the empirical 'content' it receives from sensation or 'intuition'. Although we rely on experience, on 'receptivity' or intuition, for the particular contents of our knowledge, the structure or form of that experience is provided by the human mind or 'understanding'. Experience of an external world would not be possible at all without the form contributed by the mind. For Kant, in other words, the views of both rationalists and empiricists are equally one-sided. Rationalists undervalue the contribution of experience or intuition, which is essential for any genuine scientific knowledge. Empiricists realize this, but fail to recognize the importance of the formal structure, or 'concepts', by which our experience is organized. A famous remark sums up Kant's position: 'Thoughts without content are empty, intuitions without concepts are blind. It is, therefore, just as necessary to make our concepts sensible, that is, to add the object to them in intuition, as to make our intuitions intelligible, that is, to bring them under concepts.'[39] Experience is necessarily made up of a combination of 'thoughts' or concepts, which contribute the form of experience, and 'intuitions', which contribute its content. Kant's basic insight allows a distinctive solution to the problem of accounting for human knowledge. Self-consciously alluding to the impressive achievements of natural scientists such as Galileo, Torricelli and Stahl, Kant describes his contribution as a 'Copernican revolution' in metaphysics, a dramatic overturning of previous philosophical assumptions comparable to that achieved in astronomy by Copernicus:

> Failing of satisfactory progress in explaining the movements of the heavenly bodies on the supposition that they all revolved round the spectator, [Copernicus] tried whether he might not have better success if he made the spectator to revolve and the stars to remain at rest. A similar experience can be tried in metaphysics, as regards the *intuition* of objects. If intuition must conform to the constitution of the objects, I do not see how we could know anything of the latter *a priori*; but if the object (as object of the senses) must conform to the constitution of our faculty of intuition, I have no difficulty in conceiving such a possibility . . . experience is itself a species of knowledge which involves understanding; and understanding has rules which I must presuppose as being in me prior to objects being given to me, and therefore as being *a priori*.[40]

It is possible for us to have a priori knowledge of the form or structure of experience – the form that all experience must share, if it is to be possible experience for us – because it is our mind or understanding that contributes that form to experience. Kant calls this special kind of knowledge 'transcendental', because although it concerns the nature of our experience, it does not derive from it in the way that the empiricists had supposed.

Kant also expresses his claims about the necessary structure of our experience with a further distinction, which has become important for subsequent philosophy. The distinction, intended to cut across that between a priori and a posteriori knowledge, is between 'analytic' and 'synthetic' truths. Analytic truths, like straightforward definitions, can be found to be either true or false simply in virtue of the meanings of the terms they contain or, in other words, by analysis. For example, the proposition that 'A bachelor is an unmarried male' is, on at least one obvious interpretation of the terms it contains, simply true by definition. In Kantian terms, the concept of the predicate ('. . . is an unmarried male') is included in the concept of the subject ('a bachelor'). The truth of synthetic propositions, on the other hand, cannot be decided in this way. That 'No woman has ever been President of the USA' is a truth that can be known only synthetically. In this case, the concept of the predicate is clearly not included in the concept of the subject (being male is not part of the definition of a president). Analytic truths, which depend simply on the meanings of the terms we use and tell us nothing about the real world, are plausible examples of a priori knowledge. We don't find out that they are true by observation or experience. The most obvious examples of synthetic truths, on the other hand, appear to be factually informative and to depend on actual evidence or experience and therefore to be a posteriori truths. For Kant, crucially, transcendental knowledge of the basic form or structure of experience involves the less obvious possibility of truths that are both synthetic and a priori. Kant's philosophy, in other words, implies that we can have substantive or non-trivial knowledge of the structure of experience independently of all experience.

Kant describes his novel approach as 'transcendental idealism', a description that has often been misunderstood. In philosophical terms, idealism is usually associated with the belief that there is no external, material reality. There are only ideas. Empiricism provides an obvious sceptical route to this belief. If all our knowledge of the external world comes from sensations that are seemingly 'in the mind', how do we know that anything 'out there' corresponds to our sensations? After all, when we dream or hallucinate, we have similar sensations, but they prove to be merely illusory. The only way we can check the veracity of our experience is through other sensations, but the same problem applies to them as well. *Sceptical* idealists maintain that we can have no certain knowledge of the existence or nature of an external world; we can only have knowledge of our sensations. *Dogmatic* idealists, such as the 'good bishop' Berkeley, go one step further, claiming that they can know that reality is essentially mental, because the very idea of a material reality is incoherent or self-contradictory. In its contemporary version all our statements about reality are disguised statements about 'sense data'. For what is now usually called 'phenomenalism', statements about physical objects are logical constructs of statements about sense data. So when I make a statement about a tree, it can in principle be reduced to a complex series of statements about my sensations – what I see and what, under certain conditions, I would see. It is the latter series of statements that express what I *know* as opposed to what common sense usually asserts about an external material world.[41]

Kant's transcendental idealism has been misunderstood, particularly by philosophers of analytical persuasion, as a version of idealism or phenomenalism in the above senses. But in fact, Kant's *transcendental* idealism is designed to refute all forms of what he calls 'empirical' idealism. Briefly, Kant claims that the world as it appears to us, the 'world of appearances' or 'phenomenal world', is inevitably experienced as a material world of causally interacting objects in space and time. But we cannot know that the world as it is 'in itself' or the 'things in themselves' of the 'noumenal' world are actually organized in this way. We only have knowledge of the world of appearances; we cannot assume that the world really is exactly as it appears. But crucially, this does not mean that we only have knowledge of the contents of our minds or that there is no basis for a distinction between seeming and reality – the conclusion drawn by empirical idealists. As Allison points out, Kant maintains a distinction between mere 'semblance' (*Apparenz*) or 'illusion' (*Schein*) and reality.[42] That distinction is maintained *within* the 'world of appearances' (*Erscheinungen*), as it must be since that is the only possible object of human knowledge. In his own terms, Kant is, therefore, an *empirical* realist, because he believes that we can achieve an objective knowledge of reality. The point of Kant's transcendental distinction between appearances and reality is of a different order. As Allison puts it:

At the transcendental level . . . the distinction between appearances and things in themselves refers primarily to two distinct ways in which things (empirical objects) can be 'considered': either in relation to the subjective conditions of human sensibility (space and time), and thus as they 'appear', or independently of these conditions, and thus as they are 'in themselves.'[43]

The point of Kant's distinction is, in fact, to undercut what he sees as the source of much metaphysical confusion, including scepticism and empirical idealism, namely transcendental *realism*. The transcendental realist regards appearances as things in themselves or, in other words, as existing in that form independently of the 'universal, necessary, and, therefore, a priori conditions of human knowledge'.[44] In effect, the transcendental realist thus understands human knowledge as an inferior or confused imitation of the perfect and absolute knowledge available to an infinite intelligence or, in other words, God.[45] According to Kant, scepticism and empirical idealism are the inevitable results of attempting to understand human knowledge in this way.

Kant's rejection of transcendental realism thus also helps to make more sense of his Copernican revolution. Copernicus helped to overcome a cosmology, which insisted, essentially on religious grounds, that the earth must be at the centre of the universe because humanity is God's most important creation. Similarly, the essential task Kant sets for his critical philosophy is to expunge the ultimately religious sources of previous metaphysical confusion. Human knowledge must be understood in purely human terms rather than according to the misleading and unattainable standard of divine intuition. Kant's further demonstration of the usefulness of transcendental idealism lies in his discussion of the metaphysical paradoxes which result from a transcendentally realist perspective. The attempt to say something substantive about reality in abstraction from the inescapable conditions of human knowledge inevitably leads to the contradictions or 'antinomies' of previous or 'dogmatic' metaphysics. In the second part of the *Critique of Pure Reason*, the Transcendental Dialectic, Kant discusses the paradoxes which result from transcendentally realist assumptions. These include cosmological attempts to understand the world through 'an initially plausible but ultimately incoherent conception of the sensible world as a whole existing in itself'.[46] Kant also discusses theological arguments for the existence of God and claims of 'rational psychology' about the real nature of the human soul. In each case, he argues that opposed and seemingly irrefutable metaphysical positions stem from shared but mistaken assumptions of a transcendentally realist kind.

Kant's attempts to *prove* his claims about the necessary structure of our experience have, however, turned out to be a source of controversy. In particular, his 'transcendental deduction' of the 'categories' has been subjected to much scrutiny. The transcendental deduction is designed to establish the necessity of those basic features of our experience that Kant claims to be transcendental conditions of all possible experience. Briefly, it is designed to establish the necessity of space and time as 'forms of intuition' and the necessity of the 'pure concepts of the understanding', which define a material world of causally interacting objects and a unitary subject of experience, the 'I think' that must be able to 'accompany all our representations'. The difficulty of Kant's argument is notorious and I shall not attempt to reconstruct it here.[47] For the mainstream of analytical philosophy, though, it seems clear that Kant's transcendental arguments cannot amount to successful logical deductions. As arguments, they are either unconvincing or they can be reduced to analytical claims of no great significance.[48] Accordingly, for analytical philosophers Kant's crucial class of synthetic a priori truths turns out to be empty. Only analytical truths, which are ultimately contentless or 'tautological' truths by definition, can be known a priori. Analytical philosophy then sets out from an austere interpretation of Kant's critical philosophy, taking his strictures against traditional metaphysics to close off all further 'speculative' discussion of such questions. In effect, the analytical tradition reverts to Hume's claim that anything that cannot be understood as consisting either of 'matters of fact' (a posteriori and synthetic) or 'relations of ideas' (a priori and analytic) is not genuine knowledge but a species of nonsense. This tradition emphasizes the negative pole of Kant's dilemma, maintaining that philosophy should ignore those questions which 'it is not able to answer'. In this spirit, analytical philosophers have paid less attention to those fundamental questions that, according to Kant, human reason and, indeed, the living and acting human individual, 'is not able to ignore'.[49]

The continental tradition, on the other hand, places greater emphasis on Kant's recognition that there are nevertheless metaphysical, moral and aesthetic questions that we are unable to ignore. Continental philosophers have also been more sympathetic to Kant's transcendental deductions. From their perspective, it is not surprising that these arguments are not strict logical deductions. For Kant logical deduction and observation or experiment (corresponding to Hume's two legitimate categories of truth) are central features of theoretical reason in its normal empirical employment within the bounds of knowledge. His own critical philosophy, which is designed to establish the limits of 'understanding' (*Verstand*) in that sense, must itself inevitably venture beyond these limits. Philosophical reflection cannot be reduced to the more limited, and no doubt more reliable, methods of the understanding. Evidently, Kant did not understand his transcendental arguments as strict logical deductions either. Dieter Henrich has argued that a juridical paradigm and legal standards of proof were in fact uppermost in his mind. Philosophical explanations are never incontrovertible demonstrations but 'probations' (*probationes*), which are necessarily holistic and never as clear and rigorous as 'the forms of discourse for whose sake the justification is undertaken'.[50] Philosophical reflection, as an exercise of 'reason' (*Vernunft*), necessarily operates beyond the safe but limited confines of knowledge or understanding. Subsequent continental philosophers, in diametrical opposition to the tendency of empiricist and later analytical readings of Kant, place even greater value on philosophical reason as opposed to 'mere' understanding.

Accordingly, too, for the continental tradition Kant's second and third critiques, dealing with moral or practical reason and judgement, play a greater role. Certainly, moral and political questions are central to Kant's understanding of Enlightenment, which he defines as a process of maturation or escape from dependency: 'Enlightenment is man's emergence from his self-imposed immaturity. Immaturity is the inability to use one's understanding without guidance from another.'[51] He makes it quite clear, however, that he is not thinking only of the unfettered pursuit of factual or scientific understanding. Not only a 'book to serve as my understanding', but also 'a pastor to serve as my conscience' and 'autocratic despotism' are mentioned as obstacles to maturity. Freedom of public speech within responsible limits, freedom in religious matters and free discussion of legislation are all essential elements in the unfinished process of Enlightenment. 'Free thinking' is a 'kernel' which 'gradually reacts on a people's mentality' so that 'they become increasingly able to act freely'.[52] Those of Kant's successors who had a more critical stance towards the Enlightenment project tended to focus more on questions of morality and politics as well as artistic, aesthetic and religious areas of thought and experience.

Unlike some of his contemporaries, Kant was certainly aware that Enlightenment philosophy created a serious problem for morality and religion. Above all, a purely mechanistic view of the world as a concatenation of material causes and effects seems to undermine notions of freedom and moral responsibility. If, as a work like La Mettrie's (1709–51) *L'Homme machine* suggests, human beings are simply the playthings of causal forces, their actions the result of either biology or social conditioning, then it seems to make little sense to regard them as free and responsible agents.[53] It is also not obvious how the scientific rationality of the Enlightenment can support moral principles or imperatives at all (in Hume's terms, how an 'ought' can be derived from an 'is'). Any basis for the objective moral evaluation of human actions is apparently undermined.[54] Kant's response is a dual strategy designed to establish a secure basis for moral judgement independent of scientific reason. In the first place, the critique of pure reason sets limits to the pretensions of scientific rationality or understanding, not to rule out of court the claims of morality and religion (as some empiricist readings of Kant would suggest) but, precisely, to 'make room for faith'. In the Preface to the second edition, Kant remarks:

> I have therefore found it necessary to deny *knowledge*, in order to make room for *faith*. The dogmatism of metaphysics, that is, the preconception that it is possible to make headway in metaphysics without a previous criticism of pure reason, is the source of all that unbelief, always very dogmatic, which wars against morality.[55]

His own religious convictions were influenced by Pietism, a Lutheran movement that emphasized acts of worship rather than theological doctrine. The second, more positive part of Kant's strategy is to provide a firm foothold for morality and religion consistent with his critique of pure theoretical reason. In fact, he follows the same basic pattern of argument. His alternative account of the objectivity of moral judgement is based on an examination of the transcendental conditions of our *practical* experience. If we regard morality as a fact of human existence, then what are the necessary conditions for its possibility? What are the necessary 'postulates' of moral experience and judgement?

Kant's reply is that the fundamental postulate of morality is freedom, since, if we are not free, we cannot be held responsible for our actions, and moral judgements cannot be applied to them. But freedom must also be reconciled with causal necessity, which Kant has shown to be an essential feature of the physical world. To achieve this reconciliation, he exploits the distinction between phenomenal and noumenal realms. Freedom is understood as an attribute of the noumenal or intelligible self rather than the causally determined empirical or phenomenal self. Put another way, freedom is an essential feature of the way we understand ourselves as self-conscious persons, who are also *agents* in the world, even though we are at the same time physical and therefore causally conditioned entities. Kant takes his account of morality to imply that free or moral action must be something completely purified of the 'empirical' motivations, the desires and impulses, of particular human individuals or phenomenal selves. A moral action must be motivated purely by the intention to do what is right, not by any particular interest or desire of the individual. The 'synthetic a priori' principles of morality must be derived, therefore, from the abstract notion of a rational will or agent, from which all distinguishing individual features have been expunged. The individual acts freely and morally when he or she acts purely in obedience to a universal moral law that is the product of reason alone.

Accordingly, Kant's famous 'categorical imperative' invites agents to 'universalize' the maxim of their actions: 'Act only on that maxim through which you can at the same time will that it should become a universal law.' This is Kant's version of the more familiar 'golden rule', that you should do to others what you would have them do to you. The examples Kant uses to illustrate the categorical imperative are designed to show that immoral actions are self-defeating when they are considered as examples that everyone might follow. Thus, lying is effective (the lie is believed and the agent's ulterior motives are served) only if most people tell the truth. If everyone lies (the hypothesis we entertain if we universalize the maxim of this action), then no one is believed, and both the purposes served by the institution of truth-telling and the purposes of the liar are inevitably frustrated. In another of Kant's formulations, intended to be equivalent to the first, the categorical imperative is expressed as the injunction never to treat others merely as means but always as ends in themselves:

> [M]an, and in general every rational being, *exists* as an end in himself, *not merely as a means* for arbitrary use by this or that will: he must in all his actions, whether they are directed to himself or to other rational beings, always be viewed *at the same time as an end*.[56]

We should never use other people merely as instruments to our own ends (though we can, of course, enter into voluntary and mutually advantageous transactions, as long as these respect the autonomy of both parties). To act morally is to treat others as intelligible or rational beings and therefore as moral ends.

Some of Kant's most suggestive and, unfortunately, also most obscure remarks are contained in the third of his critiques, *The Critique of Judgement*, which contains the interrelated critiques of aesthetic and teleological judgement. As well as making an influential contribution to the philosophy of art, Kant provides what has been described as a bridge between the critiques of pure and practical reason. In Stuart Hampshire's words, 'there is a bridge that conducts us from unreclaimed nature to rational freedom'.[57] Aesthetic experience mitigates the stark opposition between two seemingly incommensurable dimensions of human life: on the one hand, our bodily existence within the deterministic realm of physical nature (the object of our empirical or scientific knowledge) and, on the other, our existence as autonomous rational agents obeying the universal dictates of pure practical reason alone. Our aesthetic experience of natural beauty delivers an awareness of the meaningfulness or 'purposiveness' of nature, which mirrors the successful work of art's apparently natural inevitability – our sense that it could not have been otherwise, even though, as an 'end in itself', it serves no determinate function. As a result, we are more able to feel 'at home in nature':

> For the judgment of taste a beautiful work of art has the self-forming liveliness of a living organism in nature. The gap between the formative powers of nature, with their own indeterminate purposiveness, and the free, formative powers of human beings, has been closed. Human beings can to this extent feel at home in nature, in spite of the strain of their divided selves in moral endeavor.
> ... Closing the threatened gap between moral man and natural processes from the other side, we recognize natural beauty as involving a view of natural things 'after the analogy of art, and not as aimless mechanism'.[58]

Kant does not, at least after 1787, regard the purposiveness of nature as the actual product of God's intentional design.[59] But our aesthetic appreciation of the universe *as if* it were created or designed for some purpose makes it easier for us to reconcile the uncompromising demands of morality with the factual indifference of the material world. Kant's suggestive remarks are taken up by other thinkers in the continental tradition. Friedrich Schiller, for example, in his essay 'On the Aesthetic Education of Man', sees art as a means to the recovery of a harmonious, organic unity for humanity. Beauty is the path from the 'state of nature' (*Naturstaat*) to an ethical state (*sittlicher Staat*) more adequate to the needs of the moral as opposed to merely physical individual. Beauty is the path to freedom.[60] In that spirit, too, there would be affinities between Kant's third critique and the criticisms of Enlightenment and modernity expressed by Romanticism, by Hegel and by other continental thinkers.

Continental critics of Enlightenment

Kant's thought was an important point of departure for a number of influential critics of modernity and Enlightenment. But some of the sources of what has been called the 'counter-Enlightenment' also predate Kant's critical philosophy.[61] The intellectual and cultural movement we have talked about as the Enlightenment was opposed almost from the beginning. Its sober and often moralistic 'free thinkers' were condemned as atheists and corrupters of society. There were, of course, many who defended traditional morality, orthodox religion and the absolute state. From the modernizing perspective of the Enlightenment, these defenders of the old order were dull conservatives or even benighted reactionaries, struggling in vain against the inevitability of historical 'progress' and 'improvement'.[62] But other critics could not be categorized or dismissed so straightforwardly. Although they rejected some of the central tenets of Enlightenment thought, they also appreciated the value and force of its attacks on superstition, dogma and arbitrary authority. They did not wish to return to the world that had existed before, but they also recognized one-sidedness and even dangers in the quickening tide of modernization. Their criticisms sought to divert rather than to reverse or halt this social and intellectual movement.

Jean-Jacques Rousseau (1712–78) was a complex and contradictory figure who made a fertile contribution to the continental critique of Enlightenment. He also exerted a considerable influence on Kant, especially his moral philosophy and conception of autonomy. Rousseau was vividly aware of the ongoing social and cultural transformation of Western society, but he was strongly critical of the direction of 'civilization', of what we are calling modernity. Some of his most powerful passages concern the degraded existence of 'civilized' as opposed to 'savage man':

> The savage and the civilised man differ so much in the bottom of their hearts and in their inclinations, that what constitutes the supreme happiness of one would reduce the other to despair. The former breathes only peace and liberty; he desires only to live and be free from labour; even the *ataraxia* of the Stoic falls far short of his profound indifference to every other object. Civilised man, on the other hand, is always moving, sweating, toiling, and racking his brains to find still more laborious occupations: he goes on in drudgery to his last moment, and even seeks death to put himself in a position to live, or renounces life to acquire immortality. He pays his court to men in power, whom he hates, and to the wealthy, whom he despises; he stops at nothing to have the honour of serving them; he is not ashamed to value himself on his own meanness and their protection; and, proud of his slavery, he speaks with disdain of those, who have not the honour of sharing it.[63]

'Savage' or natural man is healthy and vigorous, has little foresight or fear of death and has no command, because little need, of language. He also exists without morality, for 'having no moral relations or determinate obligations one with another', 'men in a state of nature . . . could not be either good or bad, virtuous or vicious.'[64] The natural man has a healthy 'love of self' (*amour de soi*), the 'natural feeling which leads every animal to look to its own preservation, and which, guided in man by reason and modified by compassion, creates humanity and virtue'.[65] The natural love of self is contrasted with the more competitive and destructive concern with one's position in comparison to others. The characteristic *amour propre* of man in civilized society is 'a purely relative and factitious feeling, which arises in the state of society, leads each individual to make more of himself than of any other, causes all the mutual damage men inflict one on another, and is the real source of the "sense of honour" '.[66] The evils of 'society' flow inexorably and, as Rousseau significantly admits, irreversibly from economic and demographic trends associated with the development of society. As population increases and more intensive forms of agriculture become possible, human beings come into closer and more frequent contact with one another. Language develops, because it is useful to this intercourse. People start to compare themselves with one another and develop 'ideas of beauty and merit'. Alongside love and friendship develop their opposites, 'jealousy', 'discord' and 'impetuous fury'.[67] With settled agriculture, private property becomes inevitable, and from private property, with equal inevitability, arise ever greater economic and political inequalities and ultimately despotism.

Rousseau's condemnation of the evils of civilized existence is forceful and unambiguous. It stands in sharp contrast to the universalistic pretensions of uncritical partisans of Enlightenment and modernity. Where the ancient Greeks formed their sense of themselves in contrast to the inferiority of 'barbarians', and his contemporaries were imposing the 'benefits' of civilization on the inhabitants of newly discovered or newly accessible regions of the globe, Rousseau celebrates the simpler and healthier existence of the peoples colonized or enslaved. Indeed, a double slavery was involved. Colonized peoples were often literally enslaved by representatives of a civilization, which Rousseau regarded as itself little better than slavery. He makes considerable use of what we would now call anthropological reports about the 'Caribs of Venezuela', the 'Hottentots of the Cape of Good Hope' or the 'Oroonoko Indians' and the inhabitants of the Caribbean.[68] But significantly, Rousseau does not propose that we 'resume' an 'ancient and primitive innocence'. To advocate the abolition of private property or society and the 'return to nature', often associated with his name, would be 'a deduction in the manner of my adversaries'. For those, like Rousseau himself, 'whose passions have destroyed their original simplicity', there is no choice but to participate critically in their respective communities, mitigating where possible the deleterious effects of civilization.[69]

In this sense, it is misleading to associate Rousseau with the Romantic idea of the 'noble savage' – the view that humanity is naturally good and that we should return to nature.[70] In fact, Rousseau's 'conditional and hypothetical reasonings' are directed against any assumption of an original human nature, whether good or bad, altruistic or selfish.[71] The state of nature figures frequently in modern political philosophy as a hypothetical condition of human society prior to the institution of political authority. Thomas Hobbes (1588–1679) had exploited this device in pursuit of rational foundations for his newly scientific 'civil philosophy'. Hobbes assumes the natural selfishness and rapacity of individuals and reasons that only a sovereign or 'Leviathan', equipped with near-absolute powers, can impose order and prevent the destructive 'war of each against all'.[72] Political authority is justified, because the only alternative is chaos. But according to Rousseau, Hobbes, like other such philosophers, 'in speaking of the savage' has 'described the social man'.[73] Greed, pride and rapacity are products of society rather than attributes of the natural man. We are deceived if we believe we can ever make reliable statements about a state of nature. All we can ever hope to describe are forms of humanity corresponding to earlier or later stages of social development. The state of nature posited by philosophers like Hobbes is more accurately seen as such a stage in the development of society. Generalizations about a state of nature are impossible, because the life of human individuals depends not on a universal human nature but, rather, on the social, economic and cultural character of society. The individual is, as one jargon has it, socially constituted.

Rousseau's insight into the social constitution of individuality is reflected in the more constructive political philosophy of his *Social Contract* (1762). Rousseau regards the state's maintenance of order, which is Hobbes's prime justification of political authority, as a rudimentary achievement, which barely compensates for our loss of natural liberty. But although Rousseau is scathing about civilized society, he recognizes that the sacrifices individuals make on entering society also bring significant gains. What the individual loses in natural liberty, he gains in 'civil' and 'moral liberty':

> The passage from the state of nature to the civil state produces a very remarkable change in man, by substituting for instinct in his conduct, and giving his actions the morality they had formerly lacked. Then only, when

the voice of duty takes the place of physical impulses and right of appetite, does man, who so far had considered only himself, find that he is forced to act on different principles and consult his reason before listening to his inclinations.

Although this transition involves the loss of 'some advantages which he got from nature', in society the individual is compensated by a stimulation and extension of his faculties, an ennobling of feeling and an uplifting of the soul. It is only in society that the individual becomes a responsible moral agent as opposed to a creature of impulse; it is only in society that the individual is truly free. It is the individual's 'moral liberty' which 'alone makes him truly master of himself; for the mere impulse of appetite is slavery, while obedience to a law which we prescribe to ourselves is liberty'.[74] In other words, the loss of natural liberty, which is lamented (at least 'conditionally' and 'hypothetically') in the 'Discourse on Inequality', is now recognized as a necessary sacrifice, if we are to achieve a more fully human moral liberty. Significantly, Rousseau's idea of moral liberty is taken up in Kant's moral philosophy, in particular the notion of autonomy as the subjection of will to a rational law of its own making.[75]

Rousseau's distinctively social account of human individuality is also at the heart of his famous notion of the 'general will'. In common with modern philosophers such as Locke and Hobbes, Rousseau is not satisfied with 'unenlightened' justifications of the state by 'divine right' or tradition. Instead, he derives the sovereignty of the state from the people. Although he has little liking for actual democracies – preferring the more aristocratic rule of ancient Sparta or Livy's Rome – his justification of the state is, in an important sense, still a democratic one. In whatever way the government is constituted, whether democratically or aristocratically, it should act in accordance with the 'general will' of the citizens. But, for Rousseau, the general will is not simply equivalent to the 'will of all' or the sum of particular wills. It must express the general interest, which may be very different. That is why democratic political institutions may not be the best way of finding out what the general will is. Democratic institutions are only guaranteed to reflect the sum of all (or the majority's) particular wills. The general will, which represents the common interest of society as a whole, is likely to be in conflict with what some or even most members of society actually want – their subjective or particular wills. But the realization of the general will is nevertheless compatible with, indeed is a condition of, individual freedom, since genuine moral freedom (as opposed to merely 'negative' freedom) requires not the absence of interference by other individuals or by society, but, rather, the positive transformation of the individual within society. Critics of Rousseau have seen this equation of liberty with subjection to the general will as a large step towards totalitarianism. It has been seen as licence for the tyrannical view that individuals can, in Rousseau's words, be 'forced to be free'.[76] Many contemporaries saw his political philosophy as justification of the radical but authoritarian Jacobinism of the French Revolution and even of the Terror. For much subsequent political thought, however, Rousseau's ideas nevertheless contain the valuable insight that, whatever the defects of existing societies, it is only within society that individuals can exist as fully rational, purposive moral beings. It is only in society that individuals have access to a full range of values, interests and forms of life. The life of the human individual is consequently far richer than the meagre repertoire of instinctive responses and biological needs of the hypothetical 'natural man'.[77]

Other significant sources of counter-Enlightenment thought can be found in the vigorous and diverse critical reaction in Germany to Kant's critical philosophy.[78] Kant's sophisticated attempt to 'deny *knowledge*, in order to make room for *faith*' was challenged by a growing number of his contemporaries.[79] His dubious positing of an unknowable noumenal realm and the unhelpful abstraction of his conceptions of practical reason and categorical imperative failed to meet the demanding standard set by his own critical method and, as a result, tended to undermine both religion and morality. Friedrich Heinrich Jacobi (1743–1819), also an enthusiastic reader of Rousseau, coined the term 'nihilism' (*Nihilismus*) to describe what he saw as the destructive consequences of Enlightenment rationality for religion, morality and the authority of the state. With his provocative 'Letters on the Teaching of Spinoza' (1785), he is a major protagonist in the so-called 'pantheism controversy', which had an enormous impact on German intellectual life at the end of the eighteenth century. Spinoza's nominally religious metaphysical system appeared to avoid the problems of both Cartesian dualism and mechanistic materialism by positing a single metaphysical substance, which he dubs 'God or Nature' (*Deus sive Natura*). Jacobi argues that Spinoza's pantheist belief that nature and God are the same thing is really equivalent to atheism. The fatalist implications of Spinoza's determinist system, in which every event must have a reason or cause, are also deemed incompatible with genuine human freedom and moral responsibility. According to Jacobi, Kant's transcendental philosophy (which ironically gained further popularity as a result of the pantheism controversy) could provide no real defence against these nihilist implications, no convincing response to Hume's radical scepticism and solipsism.[80] However, Jacobi's only solution, like Pascal before him and Kierkegaard subsequently, is an ungrounded but nonetheless somehow unavoidable leap into faith (*Glaube*). Only faith can provide a reliable basis for religion and hence for individual freedom, morality and social order.

More promisingly, Johann Georg Hamann (1730–88) retained, in his critical response to Kant's philosophy, a role for rationality alongside religious faith. His 'Meta-Critique on the Purism of Pure Reason' (*Metakritik über den Purismum der reinen Vernunft*) (1784/1800) applies the critical standard proclaimed in Kant's philosophy to the assumptions of critical reason itself. Hamann attacks, in particular, the Platonic dualism of Kant's noumenal realm beyond mere appearances and the associated 'hypostasis' of reason, which imputes human reasoning to a universal and disembodied faculty. According to Hamann's more Socratic and Aristotelian principles, reason is recognized instead as always embodied in particular activities, always mediated by human language. By implication, reason is always dependent on some particular and changing social and historical context. Like Jacobi, Hamann's attack on Kant ultimately derives from his strong religious convictions and depends on the intuitive support of faith. Unlike Jacobi, though, Hamann sees reason, correctly understood and restricted to properly modest proportions, as compatible with the insights of faith. The path to faith is facilitated, however, not by reason but by art, which conveys a direct, intuitive experience of nature as God's Creation. Hamann's conception of art, expressed in his *Aesthetica in nuce* (1762), was a major spur to the Romantic 'Storm and Stress' (*Sturm und Drang*) movement emerging in German art and letters at the time. His belief that the Creation can be understood as a communication from God allows him to reconcile the seemingly inconsistent claims 'that art ought to imitate nature and reveal the word of God; and that art ought to express the innermost personality of the artist'.[81] The combination of these claims made an essential contribution to the considerable expressive and metaphysical ambitions of Romanticism.

Traces of Hamann's approach can be detected in the thought of his friend, Johann Gottfried von Herder (1744–1803), who also regards language as the essential medium of our humanity.[82] Language underlies the distinctively human powers of memory and anticipation implicit in consciousness or 'reflection'. These powers compensate for the relative paucity and weakness of human as compared to animal instincts. In place of the fixity and certainty of the animal's instinctual responses, human beings have greater freedom and an enhanced ability to cooperate with one another. For Herder, crucially, language, as the essential medium for human thought and consciousness, is not just a vehicle for the expression of thoughts or ideas, which might have existed without it. Language is what makes thought possible and, as such, is inseparable from it. By the same token, different languages are not simply alternative instruments for the expression of the same ideas, but, rather, correspond to different ways of thinking and feeling, different thoughts and feelings. One result of this is that it may sometimes be difficult or even impossible to translate satisfactorily from one language to another. This 'constitutive role' of language for human thought and culture is also incompatible with the idea of a universal human essence, whether natural, intellectual or spiritual, independent of particular societies, an implication which further undermines universalist assumptions of human nature or historical progress favoured by the Enlightenment. Herder's views argue, instead, for the importance of the specific histories of distinct peoples. They also provided inspiration for nationalism, which was to become perhaps the most powerful ideological force of the nineteenth century. The languages of different peoples or nations correspond to differences of culture and sensibility, defining a distinct national identity.

In fact, Herder represents an even more radical departure than Rousseau's from Enlightenment assumptions. Although Rousseau is sceptical of universal histories and notions of inevitable progress, he does not hesitate to offer sharply critical advice to his contemporaries. He is ambivalent about the apparent direction of social development and the benefits of modernity, but he does not think that this process of development could have been avoided or could now be reversed. Rousseau's social and political philosophy is explicitly, if not unambiguously, prescriptive. Herder's thought, on the other hand, tends towards relativism. His account of human society seems to imply the incommensurability of the values and 'qualities of character' of different peoples and cultures.[83] The unique way of life of a nation or people cannot be measured against any other, let alone definitively evaluated in terms of some universal human essence or single model of the ideal society. Even though Herder does suppose an underlying, shared 'humanity' (*Humanität*), it is overlaid by differences of language and culture. Other Enlightenment philosophers, such as Hume and Montesquieu, had acknowledged the diversity of human societies, but they saw the variety of laws and customs as alternative means to the satisfaction of common human wants.[84] Herder's account of the self, on the other hand, suggests that even human wants are inseparable from the concrete forms of life of particular communities. In other words, Herder's appreciation of national and cultural difference provides an alternative to the universalizing tendencies of the Enlightenment, and indeed with ambiguous implications. On the one hand, the recognition of diversity was liberating in a German-speaking world resentful of the dominance of French culture throughout the eighteenth century. Germans should look for their own way through the thickets of modernity. On the other hand, relativism remains only a few steps from nihilism. For if there is no universal moral standard, then, it seems, there might as well be no standard at all. Any value can be defended as an essential component of some discrete cultural tradition. As we shall see, the apparently short path from the social constitution of the individual through relativism to nihilism sets a stubborn and recurrent problem for subsequent thinkers in the continental tradition.

The ideas of Jacobi, Hamann and Herder emerged in the broader context of Romanticism and the 'Storm and Stress' movement in art and literature. German thinkers, in part motivated by nationalist resentment at a predominantly French Enlightenment, cultivated the more 'devout, inward vision of the German soul'.[85] There was a widespread concern to defend religion or, more modestly, the truths expressed by means of religion against the lifeless and homogenizing materialism of French thought.[86] Romanticism celebrated the emotional, spiritual and aesthetic qualities of humanity. Though sympathetic to Kant's message that moral life must be understood in terms other than the deterministic and reductive categories of natural science, Romantics were repelled by his austere conception of autonomy as the rational self's subjection to a universally valid moral law and independence from 'empirical' motives of desire or inclination. They valued sincerity, authenticity and self-expression instead, qualities manifest in Goethe's extremely popular epistolary novel, *The Sorrows of Young Werther* (1774). At the same time, Romantics were not simply sentimentalists. After all, the treatment of feeling and emotion in both thought and fiction was hardly something which began with the Romantic movement.[87] It was the uninspired nature of this treatment, particularly in what was seen as the exhausted classicism of the eighteenth century, which was objectionable. In terms congenial to the thought of Jacobi, Hamann and Herder, Romantics advocated originality and individuality, the defiance of artistic and sometimes also social norms, and a contempt for all merely conventional feeling and action. They were, in Isaiah Berlin's words, 'champions not of feeling against reason, but of . . . the proud, indomitable, untrammelled human will'.[88]

For Romanticism, value and beauty belong above all to the unique and the original. Like artists fashioning a work of art, individuals should cultivate their particular attributes, their individuality. Taylor describes the idea of the human subject implicit in the Romantic view as 'expressivism', which understands the subject in terms of categories of expression rather than mechanistic categories of natural science. Expressivism is identified with two ideals. It involves, first, the pursuit of self- as opposed to other-dependence – 'an inner force imposing itself on external reality' – an idea associated with Rousseau and Kant as well as with Leibniz and Spinoza. This ideal of autonomy combines, secondly, with the insight of Hamann and Herder that expression is an essential rather than merely an accidental feature of individual self-development. Just as language is inseparable from the thoughts it communicates, so expression more generally does not leave unchanged whatever is expressed. Expressivism involves, in other words, 'the notion that the realisation of a form clarifies or makes determinate what that form is'.[89] The analogy between the individual human life and the work of art encapsulates this conception:

> [M]an as a conscious being achieves his highest point when he recognises his own life as an adequate, a true expression of what he potentially is – just as an artist or writer reaches his goal in recognising his work as a fully adequate expression of what he wanted to say. . . . The specific property of human life is to culminate in self-awareness through expression.[90]

Life is like art and so art is crucially important for life. At the same time, it is important to remember that Romanticism in art is only one significant manifestation of a broader intellectual counter-Enlightenment, which laid the groundwork and set much of the agenda for subsequent philosophical innovation in the continental tradition.[91]

The Hegelian synthesis

The elaborate philosophical system of Georg Wilhelm Friedrich Hegel (1770–1831) attempts an ambitious synthesis of both Enlightenment and counter-Enlightenment themes.[92] It has been the inspiration or at least a significant reference point for most subsequent contributions to a distinctively continental tradition of philosophy. Hegel was influenced by Rousseau and Herder, by Goethe, Hölderlin and

Romanticism, but he was also deeply imbued with Greek culture and philosophy and the ideals of classicism. Kant's philosophy, too, is an important point of departure. Hegel takes much further Kant's distinction between 'reason' (*Vernunft*) and mere 'understanding' (*Verstand*). Hegel claims much greater scope for the fluid, synthesizing capacities of speculative and practical reason as against the more prosaic defining, fixing and ordering activities of the understanding. He associates the latter unflatteringly with the rigid categories and lifeless abstractions of Kant's philosophy. In the same spirit, Hegel recognizes the force of criticisms levelled at the abstractly rational principles of Enlightenment rationality by thinkers such as Rousseau and Herder, and shares their scepticism at attempts to found an adequate view of human life, particularly life's moral, political and aesthetic dimensions, upon them. On the other hand, he is equally hostile to any Romantic or irrationalist abandonment of the achievements of modernity. Like the Romantics, Hegel sees Kant's complex system of separate faculties of pure and practical reason and aesthetic judgement as ultimately dry and dehumanizing. He pursues the Romantic goal of an ultimate resolution of the divisions embodied in Kant's philosophy and, related to this, the recovery of the community, wholeness and harmony associated with classical antiquity. Hegel also appreciates the threat, vividly demonstrated in the excesses of the French Revolution, of the tyrannical rationalism that he regards as the political expression of the Enlightenment's limited and one-sided rationality. But Hegel is equally determined to preserve the characteristic gains of modernity, including individual freedom, the constitutional state and critical reason.

Hegel's philosophical synthesis is all-encompassing, but it can be introduced most pointedly in terms of his reaction to Kant's moral philosophy and what Hegel sees as its expression in the French Revolution. Hegel is sceptical about the possibility of deriving concrete moral judgements from the abstract commitment to universality alone. It has become a familiar criticism of Kant to point out that simply universalizing the maxims of one's actions does not enable us to distinguish between moral and immoral ones. The principle of universality does not by itself rule out the possibility of a consistently evil agent, since any action, even the most immoral, can be described in such a way that its maxim can be universalized without contradiction. A powerful and brazen individual might maintain the maxim that might is right without falling into inconsistency. These considerations suggest that the purely formal and abstract categorical imperative is without content.[93] A second problem concerns the motivation of the moral agent. We have already seen that Kant defines genuinely moral action as action performed not simply in accordance with duty but for the sake of duty alone: 'For if any action is to be morally good, it is not enough that it should *conform* to the moral law – it must also be done *for the sake of the moral law*.'[94] But he finds it difficult to explain how ordinary human beings can be motivated by the moral law as such, without support from, or even against, their desires and inclinations.

What is worse, finally, Hegel believes, the abstraction of Kant's account of morality is more likely to lead to evil than good. He sees the French Revolution as an historical demonstration of the dangers inherent in the purely abstract rationality of Kant's moral philosophy. Hegel describes how, when 'each individual consciousness rises out of the sphere assigned to it' and 'grasps itself as the notion of will', it finds that 'its purpose is the universal purpose, its language universal law, its work universal achievement'.[95] But universal consciousness finds itself unable to produce any positive content, and 'there is left for it only negative action; it is merely the rage and fury of destruction', which aims only for death.[96] The French revolutionary Terror is the characteristic manifestation of the 'absolute freedom' and abstract universality of Kant's moral philosophy. In fact, this outcome is similar to what might be expected from the irrationalism of the Romantic celebration of pure, unconstrained and defiant will. Indeed, Hegel sees both as variants of the same erasure of 'otherwise valid duties':

> Once self-consciousness has reduced all otherwise valid duties to emptiness and itself to the sheer inwardness of the will, it has become the potentiality of either making the absolutely universal its principle, or equally well of elevating above the universal the self-will of private particularity, taking that as its principle and realising it through its actions, i.e. it has become potentially evil.[97]

For Hegel, there are dangers in any account of morality that ignores the tissue of moral values, duties and social practices in existing communities. It is characteristic of Enlightenment rationalism, precisely, to ignore these established, merely traditional values and practices of society in order to start again from scratch and design new and more rational principles. Hegel suggests that Kantian universalization reconstructs the intersubjective dimension, the relationship to others which is obviously essential to any understanding of morality, only in an abstract and ultimately empty way. The categorical imperative is a reconstruction of universal 'morality' (*Moralität*), but cannot ground the concrete intersubjectivity of 'ethical life' (*Sittlichkeit*). For Hegel, as for both Rousseau and Herder, ethical life can only be sustained through involvement with the culture, values and practices of an existing community.[98] Again, it is worth emphasizing that from Hegel's perspective the individual autonomy celebrated in Kant's moral philosophy is not rejected, but reconciled with the values of organic wholeness and community. But genuine freedom – freedom that is not destructive for both individual and society – must be grounded in the ethical life of a community.

Hegel's account of the concrete intersubjectivity of ethical life also responds to the problem of the relationship between what is right and what is natural, between the 'moral' or 'rational' will on the one hand and what we want or desire as particular human individuals on the other. With Kant's view of morality, as we have seen, it is never clear why particular human individuals (as opposed to God or angels) would ever act in accordance with the moral law. There is an apparently unbridgeable gulf between nature and morality. For Hegel, on the other hand, the individual can only exist as such within particular communities. The individual is a product rather than a premise of the social order. As a result, not only will even the most rational reflections of the abstract individual never produce an adequate basis for ethical life, but without a concrete moral community there would be no individuals capable of such moral deliberation in the first place. But the social constitution of the individual also means that the moral or rational will is not so absolutely opposed to natural inclination. The moral will results from rationalizing or socializing rather than simply ignoring or overriding natural inclinations. The will, as opposed to mere impulse, is 'particularity reflected into itself and so brought back to universality, i.e. it is individuality'.[99] Whereas the 'wilful' impulses of the particular human organism bear no intrinsic relation to the interests of others, the socially constituted 'will' of the mature human individual reflects the demands of community, though, of course, this does not mean that the wills of all members of society will necessarily be in complete harmony. The rational will, like Rousseau's general will, is not equivalent to the will of all.

At first sight, Hegel's position, like that developed by Herder and the Romantics, seems to imply relativism. Without timeless and universal moral principles, it seems that we cannot criticize the values of different cultures or times, however repugnant they may seem. Enlightenment rationalism might lead to the revolutionary Terror, but without universal principles how can the Terror be condemned? Hegel seeks to avoid relativism with the help of an ambitious philosophy of history. The diversity of cultural forms is conceived as stages in a process of historical development, moments in an unfolding 'dialectic of spirit'. The term 'dialectic' derives from the Greek word for debate or discussion. Classically, in Plato's Socratic dialogues the argument advances through the opposition of conflicting points of view. For example, a particular answer to the question 'What is justice?' is proposed and then criticized. But criticism does not simply erase the initial proposal; rather, it leads to an alternative and presumably better suggestion. In Hegelian terms, it produces a determinate rather than a merely abstract negation of the original view. In parallel terms, Hegel understands particular historical societies and their associated worldview or 'spirit' (*Geist*) as dialectically transcending previous ones, incorporating their positive features while eliminating negative ones. The tensions within one way of thinking are left behind in the transition to a more adequate one, though the new way of thinking will have tensions of its own.[100] History can be reconstructed as a series of structures of consciousness or 'spirit', embodied in particular historical societies. Although history advances over the course of this series of worldviews, the advance is not one of *linear* progress, where each stage is deemed superior to the one that precedes it, but rather a complex and conflict-ridden process of development better understood as an ascending spiral.

Furthermore, Hegel thinks that the overall direction of the spirally ascending dialectic can be understood as the progress of freedom. 'The History of the world is none other than the progress of the consciousness of Freedom.'[101] Through the dialectic of history, according to Hegel, spirit – the concrete community considered as the embodiment of a particular worldview or conception of life – becomes increasingly rational and self-conscious. World history is boldly sketched in these terms. The 'stationary' civilization of the 'Orient', which allows freedom only to the despotic ruler, is eclipsed by the classical world and republican liberty of ancient Greece and Rome. Medieval Christendom enthrones a religion which assumes the equal worth of all before God and sets the stage for the further development of freedom. The 'Germanic' world of Protestantism asserts the rights of the individual conscience to a direct relationship with God.[102] At the same time, the spectre of relativism is exorcized. Hegel retains what amounts to a universal standard for the critical evaluation of societies without resorting to abstract arguments from nature or pure practical reason. Societies or cultures can be evaluated by locating them in the ascending series of dialectically unfolding forms. Significantly, Hegel's philosophy of history never questions the ultimate value of Western civilization or modernity. But his dialectical account of the historical development of the West is considerably more nuanced than conventional Enlightenment narratives. Modernization is reconstructed not as the uninterrupted, linear development of society, but as a sequence of one-sided but ultimately advancing manifestations of spirit.

Hegel's dialectical method is also applied in his early and most famous attempt to escape from the central conundrum of Enlightenment epistemology, *The Phenomenology of Mind*. The characteristic approach of the Enlightenment sees knowledge as a medium or instrument by which the subject, understood in Cartesian terms, gains access to an external reality. This approach faces a series of well-known and intractable difficulties. How can we overcome sceptical doubts about the reliability of this instrument or doubts whether the external world exists at all? How can we know that there are other minds? How, Hegel is inclined to add, do we know that this view of knowledge is itself accurate? If we adopt the stance of Cartesian radical doubt, then even this view must itself be questioned. According to Hegel, Kant's transcendental idealism relies on a similar view of mind or 'understanding' as the unavoidable funnel of our experiences of the outside world. The positing of an unknowable 'thing-in-itself' or 'noumenon' is an immediate and, for Hegel, unsatisfactory consequence of this picture of knowledge. Kant is forced into the embarrassing position of postulating the existence of something of which, by definition, we can know nothing at all. Hegel's radical alternative to the inherently problematic approach of modern epistemology is to begin from a position that is genuinely without presuppositions. He proposes 'an examination of consciousness from the inside as it appears to itself – in other words, a phenomenology of mind'.[103] The phenomenology aims to produce 'an exposition of knowledge as a *phenomenon*, as it actually *appears*, not insofar as it conforms to some preconceived model'.[104] Hegel's argument assumes that when the problem of knowledge is put to consciousness, consciousness itself will be able to provide the solution.

Starting with 'sense certainty', the most basic form of sensory consciousness, Hegel shows how consciousness evolves through a series of transformations towards increasingly developed forms. Each form of consciousness (like each stage of history) contains tensions or contradictions which render it incomplete and unstable, so that it is ultimately bound to give way dialectically to more adequate forms. The scope of Hegel's enterprise is daunting. He traces not only the development of sensory or empirical consciousness but also the emergence of self-consciousness and reason through a variety of forms of moral, religious and philosophical thought. In fact, he attempts to compress the entire history of morality, art, religion and philosophy into the stages of his phenomenology of mind. The ethical community of the modern state, art and religion are identified as stages on the way to 'absolute knowledge'. The dialectic culminates with the self-reflective appropriation of the whole process of spirit's dialectical development by philosophy or, more precisely, Hegel's own philosophy. Philosophy brings spirit to the fullest and most fully rational self-consciousness – a self-consciousness equivalent to the highest possible realization of freedom. Philosophical knowledge is absolute, because it is a form of consciousness without further internal contradiction or incompleteness: 'The terminus is at that point where knowledge is no longer compelled to go beyond itself, where it finds its own self, and the notion corresponds to the object and the object to the notion.'[105] In Hegel's terms, our knowledge of the world turns out to be just one moment in the unfolding self-consciousness of spirit in its manifold forms.

The outcome of Hegel's novel approach to philosophy is thus a form of idealism. Starting from the 'mind as it appears to itself' Hegel, perhaps not surprisingly, arrives at a view of reality as a whole as 'Mind as it appears to Itself'. Hegel's position is best understood as a radicalization of Kant's transcendental idealism. If the only world we can know is one that conforms to the form of our understanding, then it is not surprising that that world has features aligning it more with mind than with the 'merely material'. However, this does not mean that Hegel denies the existence of external or material reality any more than did Kant's transcendental idealism. Hegel's idealism has the rather different implication that what is rational is real or actual and what is real is rational. As Taylor puts it:

> Hegel's idealism, far from being a denial of external material reality, is the strongest affirmation of it; it not only exists but necessarily exists. . . . Absolute idealism means that nothing exists which is not a manifestation of the Idea, that is, of rational necessity. Everything exists for a purpose, that of the coming to be of rational self-consciousness, and this requires that all that exists be the manifestation of rational necessity.[106]

Reality is not 'merely ideal', as Berkeley's empirical idealism had implied, made up of Cartesian or Humean ideas without any underlying substance or materiality. Rather, reality is ideal in the sense that its elements are related in an intellectual or rational rather than a purely mechanical way. As Findlay puts it, Hegel's idealism is essentially teleological: reality can only be understood in terms of its ultimate purpose or goal, the realization of self-conscious spirit. It implies that 'nothing whatever in our world or our thought can have any meaning or function but to serve as a condition for the activities of self-conscious Spirit'.[107] At the limit of philosophical reflection, mind feels at home and at one with the world again.

Hegel's philosophy exerted considerable influence throughout the nineteenth century and beyond, at first mainly in Germany and then more widely. Hegelianism was the dominant philosophical school in Germany until the 1840s and gave rise to an influential movement of British idealists in the latter part of the century, including such philosophers as T. H. Green (1836–82), Bernard Bosanquet (1848–1923) and F. H. Bradley (1846–1924). In Italy, Giovanni Gentile (1875–1944) and Benedetto Croce (1866–1952) were both prominent Hegelians. More broadly, the Enlightenment's apotheosis of scientific reason was significantly qualified though not entirely reversed – Hegel also knew a great deal about the natural sciences of his day. Both Hegel's philosophical understanding of history and his historical understanding of morality, art, religion and philosophy as essential stages on the road to absolute knowledge encouraged a whole range of cultural developments and intellectual disciplines. But the Hegelian synthesis was to prove an unstable amalgam and, as a dominant philosophical school, it soon became a popular target of criticism. Ironically, the more faithful expositors of Hegel's ideas have had less impact on the subsequent history of thought than some of his harshest critics. Hegel would be attacked for his idealism and political conservatism, for his excessive rationalism and for the overweening ambition of his philosophical system. In Britain at the start of the twentieth century, the attacks of Bertrand Russell, G. E. Moore and others revived the empiricist approach and, in effect, founded analytical philosophy. Others, through their distinctive responses to what they were inclined to see as yet another manifestation of the distorted rationality of the Enlightenment, initiated a further series of approaches defining a distinctly continental tradition in philosophy.[108]

Further Reading

A major founding text of modern philosophy, both analytical and continental, is René Descartes, *Meditations on First Philosophy*. A characteristic expression of Enlightenment philosophy is David Hume, *Enquiries Concerning Human Understanding and Concerning the Principles of Morals*, which is more accessible than the longer *A Treatise of Human Nature*. Kant's short classic is *Groundwork for the Metaphysics of Morals*, but the indispensable keys to his mature system are the *Critique of Pure Reason*, *Critique of Practical Reason* and *Critique of the Power of Judgement*. The diverse currents of Romanticism are well represented by Jean-Jacques Rousseau's 'Discourse on the Origin of Inequality', Herder's *Discourse on the Origin of Language* and Friedrich Schiller's essay *On the Aesthetic Education of Man*. A first approach to Hegel's complex philosophical system is the Preface to *Phenomenology of Spirit*, the *Introduction to the Lectures on the Philosophy of History* and *Lectures on the History of Philosophy*.

There are many accounts of the emergence of 'modern' philosophy and the Enlightenment in the West. Charles Taylor's *Hegel* and *Sources of the Self* include useful and influential accounts of both. Bernard Williams's *Descartes: The Project of Pure Enquiry* is a succinct account of that philosopher. An authoritative introduction to Kant is provided by H. E. Allison, *Kant's Transcendental Idealism: An Interpretation and Defense*. F. C. Beiser, *The Fate of Reason: German Philosophy from Kant to Fichte* and Manfred Frank, *The Philosophical Foundations of Early German Romanticism* are good guides to the aftermath of Kant's critical philosophy. On Rousseau, see T. O'Hagan, *Rousseau*. For Hegel, read (in rough order of difficulty) Peter Singer, *Hegel*, Richard Norman, *Hegel's Phenomenology* and Charles Taylor, *Hegel*. A helpful guide to Hegel's language is Michael Inwood, *A Hegel Dictionary*.

3

Dialectics of Emancipation: Marx, the Frankfurt School and Habermas

Outline

One influential reaction to Hegel's synthesis of Enlightenment and counter-Enlightenment ideas leads to Marxism and 'critical theory'. Karl Marx adopted the position of Hegel's more radical 'Young' or 'Left Hegelian' followers, who saw his 'dialectic' of historical development as far from complete. Far from being manifest in existing philosophy, human emancipation requires further advances. But Ludwig Feuerbach's critique of religion helped to convince Marx that the fundamental causes of human alienation are not intellectual or philosophical but social and economic. With his friend Friedrich Engels, Marx came to the conclusion that the capitalist class or 'bourgeoisie' must be overthrown by proletarian revolution. Capitalism must be replaced first by socialism and eventually by the classless society of communism. Although many specific claims and predictions of Marxism proved wide of the mark, Marx's critical *method* is championed in the 'critical theory' of the Frankfurt School. Critical theorists from Theodor Adorno, Max Horkheimer and Herbert Marcuse to so-called 'second-generation' thinkers like Jürgen Habermas continue to pursue Marx's emancipatory intentions, but they do so at an ever-increasing distance from both orthodox Marxism and actual working-class struggles. At the same time, critical theory has exerted considerable influence on other philosophers and approaches within the continental tradition.

Feuerbach, Marx and Marxism

Hegel's philosophy was dominant in Germany at least until the 1840s, but a major division soon emerged, essentially over the question of whether the dialectic of history was substantially complete or incomplete.[1] The so-called 'Old Hegelians' were both politically and philosophically more conservative. They interpreted Hegel's philosophy as a sophisticated reconciliation of religion and philosophy, which overcame the destructive scepticism of the Enlightenment and established a new basis for faith. They saw both the existing political order in Prussia under Frederick William III and its intellectual expression in Hegelian idealism as the culmination of the dialectical unfolding of 'spirit' and, therefore, as moments of the Absolute. On the Old Hegelians' reading, Hegel's *Philosophy of Right* (1821) demonstrated, above all, the obligations of the individual to the community and the state. A variety of currents of continental and British idealism and conservatism continued to work essentially within this philosophical framework.[2] However, Hegel's 'Young Hegelian' successors were to have greater impact both on subsequent continental philosophy and on the world. They interpreted Hegel's writings rather differently, asserting the incompleteness of the historical process and the need for a further turn of the dialectical spiral. Both the existing political order and the prevailing philosophy and religion must be transformed or even abolished. Through radical social and intellectual criticism, philosophers could bring about intellectual and political revolution. Of the Young Hegelians, Ludwig Feuerbach (1804–72), in particular, was to exert long-lasting influence, mainly through his influence on the thought of Karl Marx (1818–83) and Friedrich Engels (1820–95). From these origins a series of important contributions to continental philosophy can be traced. These range from the ideas of Marx himself and the intellectual and ideological system of historical materialism and Marxism constructed in his name to a variety of critical renewals of Marxian thought, including the 'Western Marxism' of the Frankfurt School and Habermas. Finally, Marxism continues a somewhat subterranean existence as a prime object of postmodernist critique.[3]

The three influences which contributed most to the formation of Marx's ideas were described by his collaborator, Engels, as German idealist philosophy, French socialism and English economics.[4] The philosophy Engels had chiefly in mind was, of course, Hegel's, but his contribution was significantly mediated by Feuerbach.[5] The critical examination of religion plays a central role in Feuerbach's philosophy, but in a manner that was strongly influenced by Hegel. As a result, Feuerbach's critique of religion, presented in his most famous work *The Essence of Christianity* (1841), is more complex and nuanced than earlier expressions of Enlightenment rationalism. The Enlightenment's 'free thinkers' were mostly hostile to what they saw as the superstitious and unscientific elements of traditional Christianity. They also bemoaned the role played by the church in shoring up authoritarian regimes in Europe. But reactions to religion took a variety of forms. Relatively few espoused an openly atheist position, and even fewer explored the possibly radical, even nihilistic, moral and political implications of unbelief.[6] A more common response was an abstract deism, defended either as a rational religion purified of superstitious and dogmatic elements or, more pragmatically, as the only alternative to the social chaos, which seemed the most likely result of widespread atheism. As Voltaire remarked: 'If God did not exist, it would be necessary to invent Him.'[7]

By contrast, although Feuerbach denies the literal truth of religious belief, he still finds much truth in religion, indeed much truth even in the detail of doctrine and faith, which to the Enlightenment was indefensible. Feuerbach's critique of religion is dialectical, in the sense that he argues for a 'determinate' rather than a merely 'abstract' negation of religion. If religion is false, it is not *ipso facto* worthless. The negation of religion does not leave us with nothing, but rather suggests a positive, determinate outcome – in effect, a higher dialectical stage. According to Feuerbach, although religion is literally false, it is nevertheless deeply rooted in human needs. If religion is the product not of divine revelation but of humanity itself, then it must also reflect human needs and aspirations. Adapting Hegel's understanding of the process of human self-realization through history, Feuerbach understands the divine as an externalization or 'objectification' of human nature:

> The divine being is nothing else than the human being, or, rather, the human nature purified, freed from the limits of the individual man, made objective – i.e. contemplated and revered as another, a distinct being. All the attributes of the divine nature are, therefore, attributes of the human nature.[8]

God is understood in terms of human qualities of goodness, love or power, but these qualities are considerably amplified: God is perfectly good, all-loving and infinitely powerful. The human qualities projected, in this way, onto an imaginary being are, according to the term which comes to play a significant role in Marx's ideas, 'alienated'. In comparison with a perfect and omnipotent God, humanity sees itself in negative terms as lacking the qualities it has alienated to God. Religion 'can enrich God only by impoverishing man'.[9]

Thus, religion must be reinterpreted as a species of human knowledge, albeit not of the divine or supernatural, but of humanity itself. Religion is distorted human self-knowledge: '[R]eligion is man's earliest and also indirect form of self-knowledge.'[10] It is an indirect or distorted self-knowledge, because, as believers, we are ignorant of the true essence of religion as alienation of human capacities. Ignorance is clearly 'fundamental to the peculiar nature of religion', since as soon as we recognize the true meaning of religious faith, we lose it.[11] The same is true of the main function served by religious belief, namely the consolation it offers us in the face of our dependence on nature and fortune, our vulnerability to accident, sickness, suffering and death. Consolation is based on the illusion of a beneficent deity, who gives meaning to suffering and who will reward us in the end with eternal life. Religion solves the problems of human existence, if only in illusion. In Kamenka's words: 'Religion is a dream, a fantasy-picture which expresses man's situation and at the same time provides a fantasy gratification of man's wish to overcome that situation.'[12] Feuerbach, like Hegel, expresses his position in terms of history. He describes an historical progression from primitive polytheism to more advanced monotheistic religions such as Judaism and Christianity. Protestantism, with its emphasis on the inward experience of faith and the direct relationship between the individual and God, comes closest to recognizing as human what less advanced religions idolatrously worship as divine. Still, Feuerbach believes that it is only by means of a thoroughgoing demystification of all religion that humanity can fully reappropriate its alienated capacities and achieve a real rather than a merely illusory satisfaction of its needs.

In *The Philosophy of the Future* Feuerbach extends the critique of religious mystification to 'speculative philosophy' or, in other words, Hegelian idealism, as the final obstacle to the undistorted self-knowledge of humanity.[13] He accuses speculative philosophy of having 'torn philosophy out of its natural alliance with science' and 'subjected it to the religious impulse'. The Hegelian reconciliation of religion and philosophy is really the transformation of philosophy into theology (albeit the 'true, rational theology'), and theology is neither philosophy nor religion.[14] In fact, theology is by no means preferable to religion. Religion is the 'real essence' or 'content' which contains distorted truths about humanity, whereas theology is the 'false essence' or 'form' of religion and involves an even more intense and self-conscious alienation of human capacities. Philosophy should not imitate theology in its attempt to produce a systematic reconstruction of the universe in ideas, but should, rather, be critical and materialist. Idealism, with its abstract and universal notions, remains too close to religion. Like the empiricists, Feuerbach believes that 'the beginning of philosophy is the finite, the determinate, the actual'.[15]

But Feuerbach also recognizes the one-sidedness of previous empiricism. 'Man' is not just a passive receptacle for impressions, but is actively and productively involved in the constitution of his experience. What is more, this involvement is not just the abstract and disembodied activity of a pure self-consciousness or Kantian transcendental ego. It is the practical activity of the whole person, which therefore involves interests, passions, fears and hopes as well as understanding or intellect. Knowledge belongs to 'man' as a sensual, physical being, not as disembodied ego or mind; nor is knowing the activity of an isolated cognitive subject: it necessarily involves other people. Knowledge requires the intersubjectivity of the 'I–Thou' relationship. As Hegel's philosophy also implied, knowledge is carried by historically situated cultures and societies, rather than by either isolated monadic subjects or the abstract universal subject of Enlightenment epistemology. Knowledge, in sum, is practical – knowledge is social and embodied activity. For Feuerbach, only if humanity successfully overcomes both religion and speculative philosophy can it begin to tackle the problems of its condition in a real rather than an illusory way. In common with other Young Hegelians, this would involve a combination of liberal politics and the application of natural science. Natural science furthers the development of technology and the gradual mastery of the natural world, reducing humanity's vulnerability to sickness, natural disaster and want. Liberal politics would eliminate the remnants of feudal despotism, modernize the institutions of European states and institute a broad programme of democratic reforms.

Both Feuerbach's philosophy and the political liberalism of the Young Hegelian movement provide important starting points for Marx's earlier thought. However, in two of his earliest works, Marx already expresses dissatisfaction with any exclusively political solution to the alienation of humanity manifest in religion and speculative philosophy.[16] In the first place, the constitutional monarchies of his time clearly did not represent such a solution. In his 'Critique of Hegel's Doctrine of the State', Marx is critical of Hegel's apparent satisfaction with the Prussian state despite the fact that he shows considerable insight into the defects of contemporary capitalist society. In *The Philosophy of Right* Hegel portrays 'civil society' as an antagonistic sphere of competitive market relations dominated by individual self-interest. This sphere, which had become increasingly important with the rise of capitalism, could not provide a satisfactory basis for a fully human existence. However, according to Hegel's characteristically dialectical solution, the antagonism and conflict of civil society is transcended by the state, properly understood as the complex totality comprising both civil society and the political sphere. In the modern state, the political sphere represents and mediates the particular sectional interests of civil society. The bureaucracy is a 'universal class' without any selfish interest of its own, which reconciles the otherwise antagonistic atoms of society. However, Marx is far from satisfied with Hegel's solution. It seems obvious to Marx that, far from reconciling the particular interests of civil society, states themselves represent sectional interests. In his later writings, he reinforces this picture of the 'bourgeois' state as vehicle of the interests of the capitalist class.[17]

Again, in his essay 'On the Jewish Question', Marx argues against the sufficiency of any merely political solution. The political emancipation of the Jews would not ensure their full human emancipation, 'because political emancipation is not the complete and consistent form of *human* emancipation'. Even a secular state such as the United States, which guarantees religious toleration, does not resolve the underlying problem. The proliferation there of by no means moderate religious denominations suggests that, despite a liberal constitution, the underlying problem remains and, 'since the existence of religion is the existence of a defect, the source of this defect must be looked for in the nature of the state itself'.[18] Marx, at this stage, seems content to advocate radical democratic reforms as the means of bringing about a real rather than merely illusory transcendence of the opposition between state and civil society. In McLellan's words: '[Marx] expected universal suffrage to inaugurate the reform of civil society by bringing back to it the social essence of man as a communal being that had been stolen from him and transferred to the sphere of constitutions that had no effect on his real life.'[19] Liberal 'rights of man' (including freedom of conscience and the right to property) are inadequate reflections of bourgeois society. They are 'quite simply the rights of the *member of civil society*, i.e. of egoistic man, of man separated from other men and from the community'. On the other hand, Marx explicitly defends the democratic 'rights of the citizen', whose 'content is *participation in the community*'.[20] Electoral reform, however, is advocated not simply for its own sake, but because it will inevitably lead to a more radical resolution of the contradictions of civil society: '*[E]lectoral reform* in the *abstract political state* is the equivalent to a demand for its *dissolution* [*Auflösung*] and this in turn implies the *dissolution of civil society*.'[21]

It is not yet made entirely clear what is involved in the dual dissolution of state and civil society. However, even in these early essays Marx refers to the role of private property. His ultimate diagnosis of the pathology of contemporary society as essentially economic was influenced by his reading, in the early 1840s, of French socialists like Fourier and Proudhon, who were fiercely critical of capitalism. But he was also influenced by 'classical economists' such as Ricardo and Smith. Adam Smith (1723–90) provides an early and largely enthusiastic account of 'commercial society'. A system of 'natural liberty', which allows individuals to pursue private interests in their own way, will, through the 'invisible hand' of the market, lead to the greatest possible expansion of the 'wealth of the nation' and so to the ultimate advantage of all. Though every individual 'intends only his own gain', he is 'led by an invisible hand to promote an end which was no part of his intention'.[22] However, even Smith is aware of some of capitalism's defects. The division of labour is responsible for the immense productivity of commercial society, but it also leads to the stunting of workers, who have to perform only a few simple operations and have less and less say in the organization of the work process. Almost inevitably, too, wealth accrues to the owners of capital, leaving the working class in relative poverty. But the classical economists thought that such defects could be remedied without fundamentally transforming capitalism.

Both Marx and his friend Engels, by contrast, came to accept the socialist aim of abolishing private property and the capitalist system of production altogether.[23] Only in this way would it be possible to overcome the contradiction between the 'perfect idealism of the state' and the 'perfect materialism of civil society' – the unmediated opposition between an only abstractly universal state and an antagonistic realm of individual competition and greed.[24] The socialists revealed that the economic system described by the classical economists is not the only possible one, let alone the most efficient and rational mode of production. There is nothing inevitable about a system which exploits workers and makes capitalists rich. By the same token, once capitalism is defined as the problem, then it is natural to look for the solution in the working class or 'proletariat'. But the working class will overthrow capitalism not only in its own interest, as the exploited class, but in the universal interest of humanity. Not only is the proletariat systematically excluded from the benefits of capitalism, but, through its future role in a socialist revolution, it will liberate humanity from its alienated condition. As Marx says in the

Economic and Philosophical Manuscripts of 1844, the proletariat is
a revolutionary agent, 'not because it is only a question of their
emancipation, but because in their emancipation is contained universal human emancipation'.[25] The proletariat is the universal class
Hegel had mistakenly identified as the bureaucracy. Significantly,
Marx sees capitalism not just as the source of much human suffering
or strictly economic exploitation, but as the root cause of a deeper
and more far-reaching alienation. Under capitalism, 'man' is
estranged or alienated from his true nature, or what Marx calls
'species being'. Human species being is realized through labour
understood as 'the practical creation of an *objective world*, the *fashioning* of inorganic nature'.[26] The labour of the worker under capitalism is alienated in at least four ways. Workers are alienated from
the products of their labour, which accrue to the capitalist; from the
act of production, which they no longer control; from labour, as the
medium for the expression of their species being as creative produc-
ers; and, finally, from other men, as a result of the antagonistic,
atomized relationships of capitalist civil society.[27]

Marx's theory of alienation is, in fact, a direct application of his
materialist critique of Hegelian idealism, which transforms the dialectic of spirit or ideas into a materialist dialectic of labour and class
struggle. Marx saw great value in Hegel's philosophy. He shares
Hegel's disdain for the empiricists, the 'contemplative' materialists of
the Enlightenment, who 'left out the subjective, creative side of man's
interaction with nature'.[28] But he is also clearly inspired by Feuerbach's critique of Hegel, with its emphasis on the intersubjective and
embodied basis of human knowledge. What Marx does is combine
Feuerbach's version of materialism with Hegel's historical account of
the dialectical progression of forms of knowledge. The result transposes the dialectic to an explicitly social and embodied context. In
effect, the universal and eternal categories of the Kantian transcendental subject are reinterpreted in terms of historically unfolding
social forms. Our understanding of reality, what we take to be nature
at a particular stage of our development, reflects the forms of social
organization which prevail at that time:

> [Feuerbach] does not see how the sensuous world around him is, not a
> thing given direct from all eternity, remaining ever the same, but the
> product of industry and of the state of society; and, indeed, in the sense
> that it is an historical product, the result of the activity of a whole succes-
> sion of generations, each standing on the shoulders of the preceding one,
> developing its industry and its intercourse, modifying its social system
> according to the changed needs.[29]

It is not, as Hegel's philosophy had suggested, ideas which represent the essence of a particular epoch. Rather, it is our historically produced 'social being' which determines our ideas or consciousness. The 'human essence' is neither the abstract individual or disembodied subject of the Enlightenment nor the historically unfolding 'spirit' of Hegel, but 'the ensemble of the social relations'.[30] According to his own description, Marx 'puts Hegel back on his feet', replacing the idealist dialectic of spirit with a materialist dialectic of work or labour.

Marx's materialist critique of Hegel thus leads to a materialist conception of history. Labour, as the true essence of humanity, is the activity through which humanity creates its own nature in a series of historical stages, which are the various ways human societies have organized the process of production. The meaning of history is not the coming to self-consciousness of absolute spirit, but the dialectical unfolding of a series of 'modes of production'. Like Rousseau in the 'Discourse on Inequality', Marx proposes a theory of history as driven by the evolving relationship between human beings and nature, by the different modes in which human beings satisfy their material needs: 'life involves before everything else eating and drinking, a habitation, clothing and many other things. The first historical act is thus the production of the means to satisfy these needs, the production of material life itself.'[31] Marx describes the development of 'productive forces' (methods or techniques of production, technology, human resources and so on) and contradictions which result between forces and 'relations of production' (the forms of property ownership which define a particular economic system as feudalism, capitalism, communism etc.). The relations of production within a particular economic system imply a particular division between social classes, essentially between those owning or controlling the means of production and those excluded from ownership and control. Contradictions between forces and relations of production are expressed in the form of class struggle. History as a whole is driven not by the contradictions within particular ideas or worldviews, but by the conflict between social classes. This understanding of class struggle transposes into materialist mode an important motif from Hegel's *The Phenomenology of Mind*, namely the dialectic of 'lordship and bondage'. Hegel sees the struggle by one subject for recognition by another as an essential stage in the development of consciousness. But in seeking recognition, consciousness enters into a dialectical struggle, in which the dominated subject is reduced to the status of object, and so becomes incapable of delivering true recognition (as opposed to the mere obedience of a slave). Hegel's dialectic supposedly culminates in a stage of harmonious mutual recognition and equality, which corresponds to Marx's understanding of the classless society of communism.[32]

In fact, according to this materialist conception of history, the development of all aspects of human life, including ideas, 'all the different theoretical products and forms of consciousness, religion, philosophy, ethics, etc. etc.' are to be explained in terms of the 'real process of production'.[33] Marx's remarks on 'ideology' suggest that the development of ideas is determined by relationships of power deriving from the mode of production rather than the reverse:

> The ideas of the ruling class are in every epoch the ruling ideas, i.e. the class which is the ruling material force of society, is at the same time its ruling intellectual force. The class which has the means of material production at its disposal, has control at the same time over the means of mental production, so that thereby, generally speaking, the ideas of those who lack the means of mental production are subject to it.[34]

The materialist conception of history undermines 'idealist' explanations of historical change in terms of new ideas, great individuals or the 'spirit of the time' (*Zeitgeist*). It follows that, if the true basis of history is materialist, then neither philosophical critique nor moral and political exhortation are likely to bring about the next dialectical stage of history. Marx attacked the position of the Young Hegelians, who sought change through 'mental criticism'. Change will only come about as a result of developments at the level of the mode of production – 'not criticism but revolution is the driving force of history.'[35] Revolution will only come about if the social conditions are already 'pregnant' with the new social order.

Thus, while Marx agreed in broad outline with the political goals of the French and English socialists, both he and Engels were highly critical of what they dubbed 'utopian socialism', which they thought was as little likely to bring about genuine social change as the measures proposed by the likes of Adam Smith. Socialists like Robert Owen (1771–1858), Henri de Saint-Simon (1760–1825) and Charles Fourier (1772–1837) failed to develop clear ideas about the actual means, including potential agents, of social transformation, relying instead on persuasion and small-scale utopian experiments. Although the ideals of the utopian socialists appealed to certain groups of workers, especially the skilled artisans who were being displaced by new machinery and the factory system, these groups were relatively small and declining in number. Their interests were not the same as those of the growing number of unskilled workers in the newly mechanized industries who were taking their place. Marx is also contemptuous of any socialist doctrine that advocates equality as a simple levelling down of available resources, an approach which under conditions existing at the time could only universalize deprivation and need. Communism will only become possible with the help of the enormous productivity of capitalism, which has the power to eliminate material scarcity altogether.

The decisive implication of Marx and Engels's 'scientific socialism' is that communism cannot be achieved by halting or reversing the course of capitalist economic development, but only by bringing that development to completion. Marx's attitude to capitalism and the 'bourgeoisie' is, accordingly, ambivalent or 'dialectical'. He is unstinting in his condemnation of capitalism as an intensification of class conflict, bringing misery and alienation. Capitalism is a system of exploitation, which extracts wealth from workers for the sake of the capitalists. Even the abolition of capitalism will, in the short term, allow only the realization of the socialist principle of economic justice, that each should be rewarded according to his or her contribution to the social product. This principle 'tacitly recognizes unequal individual endowment and thus productive capacity of the worker as natural privileges' and therefore remains '*a right of inequality, in its content, like every right*'.[36] Only the dynamic productivity of capitalist society, the fact that 'the bourgeoisie cannot exist without constantly revolutionizing the instruments of production', offers the prospect of a society in which everyone can have whatever they need.[37] For the first time, goods will be distributed according to the communist principle, 'From each according to his ability, to each according to his needs!'[38] Equally, the dynamic expansionism of the capitalist market promises to draw other nations into an ultimately progressive worldwide transformation: 'The bourgeoisie, by the rapid improvement of all instruments of production, by the immensely facilitated means of communications, draws all, even the most barbarian, nations into civilization . . . it compels them to introduce what it calls civilization into their midst, i.e., to become bourgeois themselves.'[39] Overall, whereas utopian socialists simply oppose capitalism, both Marx and Engels see it, in effect, as a necessary evil. Capitalism's successor can only come about as a result of the complete development of capitalism. The vicissitudes of history, like the stages in the Hegelian dialectic, cannot be avoided simply by means of the good intentions of an enlightened politics.

Marx's later work focuses on the economic and sociological analysis of capitalism.[40] It is designed to uncover tendencies leading to the collapse of capitalism. The industrial revolution had already physically assembled large bodies of workers in huge factories and sprawling industrial cities. The mechanization of production had destroyed the special status of skilled artisans, such as the hand-loom weavers of the Luddite rebellions, and further automation seemed destined to lead to further levelling and homogenization. Trade unions were signs of the stirring self-consciousness and activism of the working class. Marx's economic theory suggests that capitalism will eventually succumb to contradictions of its own making. His 'labour theory of value' analyses capitalist exploitation as the extraction of 'surplus value' from workers. Wages only compensate workers for the value of their labour power (their capacity to labour), which is equivalent to the value of the commodities required to reproduce it – essentially, 'subsistence' or resources sufficient to keep workers alive. The difference between this value and the value of the actual labour workers can be made to perform is the ultimate source of 'surplus value' or profit. This theory implies that workers' wages will always tend to a subsistence level. A further factor, which Marx thinks will tend to reduce wages, is the rising 'organic composition of capital'. The proportion of 'fixed capital' (e.g. plant and machinery) rises, and the proportion of 'variable capital' (or labour) declines, with the seemingly irreversible trend towards greater mechanization and automation. Since labour rather than fixed capital is the source of profit, there must be a tendency for the rate of profit to fall, although this tendency may be counteracted by other tendencies. If the rate of profit falls, capitalists will be driven to increase the rate of exploitation either by intensifying the pace of production or by reducing wages. The resulting 'pauperization of the proletariat' can only encourage a further escalation of class struggle. The self-consciousness and unity of the proletariat as a class is all the more likely to come about as divisions and inequalities between groups of workers disappear. A united, impoverished and self-conscious working class can hardly fail to bring about communist revolution and the end of class society. Marx's undoubted revolutionary optimism would later be misinterpreted as a firm prediction of the inevitability of communist revolution.

Marx's critical appropriation of German idealist philosophy, classical economics and English and French socialism produced an explosive amalgam of abstract intellectual speculation and political engagement. In his famously concise 'Theses on Feuerbach', Marx distinguishes his conception of materialism from that of the Enlightenment, which even Feuerbach does not leave completely behind. Whereas the 'old' materialism is 'the contemplation of single individuals and of civil society', the standpoint of the 'new' materialism is 'human society, or social humanity', which inevitably refers to the future form of social existence: communism. The critique of religion and philosophy leads ineluctably to the commitment to change existing society. In other words, in Marx's hands philosophy is inseparable from political action. Most famously, until now 'The philosophers have only *interpreted* the world, in various ways; the point is to *change* it.'[41] This marrying of 'theory' and 'practice' tied Marx's ideas to historical and political events in a novel way. But partly as a result, the determining factor in the ultimate fate of these ideas would be the fashioning, from Marx's diverse, fertile and not always consistent writings, of Marxism as a systematic doctrine and even dogma – Marxism as orthodoxy. Marx's critical 'surpassing' or 'transcending' of philosophy was taken as its outright rejection, as sufficient prelude to the down-to-earth and ultimately more useful pursuits of politics and science. Marxism was the basis for a scientific politics without metaphysical illusions or moral pretensions, a politics without philosophy.[42]

Two factors played a decisive role in the fate of Marxism as orthodoxy. In the first place, when Marx died in 1883, Engels – his long-time collaborator and financial supporter – was left to edit, interpret and popularize his friend's ideas. A second factor was that Engels's role coincided with the growing political influence of Marx's ideas, which were 'beginning to become the official doctrine of a mass political movement'.[43] Both factors served to divert attention from the complexities and tensions in Marx's own writings, precipitating the more systematic but one-dimensional version of his thought dubbed 'the materialist conception of history' – later, 'historical materialism'. This phrase, as Carver puts it, 'brought Marxism into existence'.[44] Engels's contribution reflected his own scientific and philosophical interests. In particular, Engels had considerable sympathy with the positivist climate of nineteenth-century thought. Positivists such as Comte and Spencer restated the empiricist position in historical terms. Natural science is seen as the most advanced form of human knowledge, supplanting both religion and speculative philosophy.[45] Engels was also greatly influenced by recent developments in the natural sciences, such as Darwin's theory of natural selection, and even offered his own account of '[t]he part played by labour in the transition from ape to man'. He praises Darwin's theory in supposedly Hegelian terms as a 'grandiose' attempt to 'demonstrate historical evolution in Nature', despite its non-dialectical method.[46]

By implication, historical materialism applies a similar method to the evolution of society. In his widely read popularizations of Marx's ideas, Engels exaggerates the similarities between Marxian political economy and explicitly deterministic theories in natural science, stressing its rigorous grasp of the 'laws of motion' of capitalism and its ability to predict the outcome of historical processes of transformation. The Marxian dialectic is seen as the general science of the development of nature, human society and thought. That said, Engels does sometimes also present the materialist conception of history as a critical tool, revealing the inadequacy and one-sidedness of idealistic explanation, rather than as the rigidly mechanistic model of historical change that it would become. Economic determinism is qualified by the admission that material causes assert themselves 'only in the last resort': 'The economic situation is the basis, but the various elements of superstructure also exercise their influence upon the course of the historical struggle and in many cases preponderate in determining their form. There is an interaction of all these elements.'[47] Nevertheless, Engels's overall emphasis prepared the ground for later simplifications of Marx's ideas and their further assimilation to positivist principles. The seal was set on the emergence of Marxism as a systematic but intellectually infertile doctrine by the central role it came to play in the politics of the working class.

From the start, however, the Marxist project was beset with difficulties. These have ranged from the non-occurrence of revolution in the capitalist West and the sustained efforts of Western states to undermine socialist revolutions to the degeneration and now collapse of communist regimes in Eastern Europe and the former Soviet Union. On the one hand, revolution failed to occur in the most economically developed capitalist societies where, on Marxist assumptions, it was most to be expected.[48] Where revolutions were successful, the results have been, to say the least, disappointing. With the events of 1989 and after, it is no longer obvious that Marxism has any contemporary historical significance. With the fall from power of the communist parties of the Soviet Union and Eastern Europe, the break-up of the former 'evil empire' of the Soviet Union and the beleaguered state of the regimes in Cuba and North Korea, communist China is the only significant survivor – and then only by dint of substantial free market reforms. Even the social democratic parties of many Western countries are in ideological retreat, with major elements of their programmes in question. So it is perhaps not surprising that essays abound on the historic defeat of communism, the bankruptcy of social democracy and, on the other side, the apparent triumph of capitalism, liberalism and democracy. In 1992 Francis Fukuyama even enthusiastically, albeit in retrospect prematurely, proclaimed the end of history.[49]

The continuing relevance of the ideologies of communism and social democracy is an issue beyond the scope of this book. But despite the fact that the organized workers' movement has, if anything, shown signs of a deficiency rather than an excess of philosophy, the practical problems and failures of the socialist project have given rise to some considerable contributions to continental philosophy. A number of thinkers have made significant contributions to Marxist theory, including Vladimir Ilich Lenin, Leon Trotsky, Rosa Luxemburg and Antonio Gramsci. Arguably, though, their influence has not been strictly philosophical. A more philosophical renewal of Marxism assumes a variety of forms and has been attempted within what is known as 'Western Marxism'. Louis Althusser's 'structuralist' Marxism was influenced by Spinoza as well as by Lenin. The existentialist Jean-Paul Sartre, who had a complex relationship with the French Communist Party, also left his mark. Sartre and Althusser represent opposing 'humanist' and 'anti-humanist' approaches to Marxism.[50] A particularly influential body of thought has been produced by the Frankfurt School.

The critical theory of the Frankfurt School

For a significant tradition of Western Marxists the practical failures and failed successes of revolutionary Marxism reflect inadequacies in the theory of historical materialism itself. The Frankfurt School consisted of a group of theorists, originally associated with the Frankfurt Institute for Social Research, who sought to rescue the valuable kernel of Marx's theory from a rigid, increasingly hollow and ideological doctrine. In the spirit of the Marxian and Hegelian insight into the historically situated nature of thought, they propose a renewal of Marxism in the light of contemporary conditions and experience. This renewal involves a threefold return – to Hegel, to the earlier and more Hegelian Marx and to philosophy. The return to the more Hegelian ideas of the early Marx was reinforced by the belated publication of *The German Ideology* and, in 1932, of Marx's *Economic and Philosophical Manuscripts* (1844).[51] Where orthodox Marxism understands Marx's materialist turn as the straightforward replacement of philosophy by science and revolutionary practice, theorists like Theodor Adorno (1903–69), Max Horkheimer (1895–1973) and Herbert Marcuse (1898–1979) reclaim a central role for philosophy. Marx's critique of philosophy was not anti-philosophical. On the contrary, as Adorno and Horkheimer remark of their own account of the *Dialectic of Enlightenment*, 'It is a critique of philosophy, and therefore refuses to abandon philosophy.'[52] Central to their account is an awareness of the ambivalent legacy of modernity. They share Hegel's fears about the abstract rationalism of Kant and the Enlightenment. They also echo Marx's materialist retort to Hegel, that the logic of the historical process cannot be a predominantly intellectual or conceptual one. They regard capitalism as an important symptom of the pathology of modernity. However, the Frankfurt School sees the degeneration of Marx's ideas into the historical materialism of orthodox Marxism as another expression of the same pathology. Only a whole-hearted return to philosophical critique promises escape from the fateful dialectic of enlightenment.

The Institute for Social Research was founded in Frankfurt in 1923 under Carl Grünberg, though Max Horkheimer, who was director from 1930, had a more lasting impact on its work.[53] The historical context of the Frankfurt School's formation was also to mark its future theoretical orientation. In Germany the 1930s saw the rise to power of the national socialists under Hitler and the enforced migration of the Frankfurt Institute to Geneva (1933) and then to the United States (1935). Traces of the trauma of these years can be detected in much of the later work that came out of the School. Fascism was a dramatic demonstration that the transition to socialism and communism was far from imminent in the West. The degree of popular support for fascism, which attracted significant elements of the working class, cast doubt on Marx's casting of the proletariat as an agent of universal emancipation. In addition, there was evidence of a structural transformation of capitalism, which had not been anticipated by Marx. This became particularly clear with the gradual recovery from the Great Depression of the 1930s, which had seemed to herald the final collapse of capitalism predicted by Marx. Whether in the 'totalitarian' guise of fascism or in the more democratically accountable form of the New Deal in the USA, a mixture of Keynesian economics and neo-corporatism – what Frankfurt theorists variously termed 'monopoly' or 'state' capitalism – demonstrated an unforeseen ability, by means of more extensive state intervention, to overcome the limitations of nineteenth-century liberal capitalism.[54]

Other developments in the West cast further doubt on Marxist assumptions about the course of capitalist development. After the Second World War, under the relatively benign conditions of the long economic boom, the working classes of the Western capitalist democracies appeared increasingly integrated and pacified. Working-class political activism was mostly channelled into either social democracy or trade unionism. As Horkheimer wrote in 1968: 'The revolutionary thrust of the proletariat has long since become realistic action within the framework of society.'[55] The 'affluent society' contradicted Marx's pessimistic predictions about the falling rate of profit and inevitable impoverishment of the working class. The experience of Soviet Marxism after the Bolshevik revolution, finally, demonstrated the bankruptcy of orthodox Marxism. The Marxist-Leninist revolution did not ensure safe passage to communist utopia. The similarities between bureaucratic state socialism and the almost equally administered monopoly or state capitalism of the West were more striking than the differences.[56]

In their response to these historical developments, the Frankfurt School theorists held on, at times desperately, to the politically engaged role of theory, encapsulated in Marx's famous remark that until now 'philosophers have only *interpreted* the world, in various ways; the point is to *change* it'.[57] Social theorists should do more than simply describe or explain. They should provide a diagnosis of the faults of existing society and, beyond that, take part in the struggle for its transformation in the interest of the oppressed and exploited. At the same time they were dismayed by the actual development of Marxism as orthodoxy and dogma. The central task facing Frankfurt theorists, then, was the liberation of critical thought from the straitjacket of historical materialism. In pursuing this goal, they took their cue from Georg Lukács, who had argued that the commitment to Marx's critical *method* was more important than any of the particular *contents* of Marxism.[58] Marxism should be capable of self-criticism, capable of applying its critical method to itself. The increasing dogmatism of the revolutionary communist movement also belied Marx's own Hegelian insight into the social and historical constitution of thought. Engaged theory must develop and change in response to important social transformations that had occurred since the 1840s.

Many of the specific claims of Marxist orthodoxy had become vulnerable. Predictions about the falling rate of profit, the tendency for the proletariat to become impoverished and the imminence of socialist revolution in the West were no longer plausible.[59] Rather than being reduced to a level of uniform poverty, the industrial proletariat was divided by new hierarchies of status and skill. A 'new middle class' of technically skilled and professional workers had emerged.[60] Reformist social democratic politics and trade unionism looked more like long-term expressions of working-class activism than the first faltering steps of a still infantile revolutionary will, as they had been portrayed by the early Lenin.[61] But it was not the incorrectness of some of historical materialism's central sociological and economic claims (which, in any case, remain the object of considerable debate), but the degeneration of Marx's critical method which was most disturbing. Indeed, it was the dogmatic petrifaction of the method that made the revision of the specific claims so difficult. The movement had inherited the wise words of its founding father rather than his critical intellect and, contrary to the hopes of a genuinely scientific socialism, vehemently expunged all heresy. In fact, of course, a number of Marxist theorists continued to investigate the new historical reality in a critical spirit, including Karl Korsch, Rosa Luxemburg, Antonio Gramsci and Ernst Bloch. For the theorists who have become known as the Frankfurt School, the only possible response to a foreclosing of critical reflection in the name of science is the reinvention of Marx's critical method as 'critical theory'. An important model of this method was, of course, Marx's critique of classical political economy. Economists like Adam Smith and Ricardo described capitalism as if it were a natural system. However, what they described was really 'false nature', because capitalism is a socially and historically contingent mode of production, rather than something timelessly natural and rational, which Western society happened to stumble upon. Describing capitalism as a natural system conceals, even if unintentionally, the possible transition to socialism and communism. Classical political economy is ideological rather than scientific, because, despite its veneer of scientific objectivity, it serves the sectional interests of the bourgeoisie rather than humanity as a whole. It closes off avenues of social development that could emancipate the working class.

Marx's critique of political economy is taken as the model for a more general critique of 'positivism'. This term was first used by Auguste Comte (1798–1857) to refer approvingly to humanity's mature intellectual stage of 'positive or *scientific* understanding, based only on observable facts and the relations between them and the laws discoverable from observing them'.[62] The positive stage, effectively the Enlightenment seen from an empiricist point of view, follows more primitive 'theological' and 'metaphysical' stages of thought. Comte also coined the term 'sociology', and it is more particularly the application of 'positive' scientific methods to the study of human societies that is now usually described as positivism. A century earlier than Comte, Hume had advocated the 'application of experimental philosophy to moral subjects' in order to lay the 'science of man' on the 'solid foundation' of 'experience and observation'.[63] Geuss provides a workable definition of positivism as follows: 'In Frankfurt usage a "positivist" is a person who holds: (a) that an empiricist account of natural science is adequate, and (b) that all cognition must have essentially the same cognitive structure as natural science.'[64] By contrast, Frankfurt theorists emphatically resist the application of scientific method to human subjects as tantamount to the denial of human potentialities and freedom. By using natural scientific method to uncover laws of economy or society, positivist social theory portrays the regularities of oppressive societies as facts, which can only be accepted with resignation. To theorize alterable social relations as 'second nature' is to obscure possible alternatives to present society. In what came to be known as the 'positivism dispute', Adorno and Horkheimer take issue with any social theory which, under cover of scientific objectivity, effectively conspires with the existing order. In so far as contemporary social science is modelled on the methods and assumptions of natural science, it is, in their terms, a species of 'traditional' as opposed to critical theory.[65]

But the critique of positivism is directed, in the first place, against the positivist petrifaction of Marx's ideas. The notion that a deterministic science of society can identify 'iron laws' of capitalism and predict its imminent collapse is identified as an important source of the defects of both Stalinism in the East and the communist parties loyal to Stalinism in the West.[66] The scientific status of historical materialism insulates party intellectuals and leaders from 'uninformed' criticism. By turning moral or political issues into questions of theoretical or technical expertise, it justifies the 'democratic centralism' of the Bolshevik Party. Surely, decisions should be taken by those with a sophisticated knowledge of Marxist theory rather than by ordinary workers and peasants? In this way, positivism paves the way for the bureaucratic authoritarianism of Soviet Marxism.[67] In some quarters, crudely deterministic versions of the primacy of the economic in the explanation of social change led to the 'economistic' belief in the centrality and sufficiency of struggles at the site of production as well as indifference to broader moral and political activism, considered merely utopian. In more 'voluntarist' style, Leninism exploits the scientific authority of the revolutionary activist, in order to underwrite an energetically political, but no less authoritarian, vanguardism. Expedient violations of 'bourgeois morality' can be excused, because there need be no fear that the scientifically certified advance towards communism will ever be diverted from its predetermined goal by the corruption of the revolutionary movement.[68]

From the point of view of Frankfurt theorists, therefore, Marx and Engels's critique of utopian socialism is distinctly ambivalent.[69] Although Marx rightly emphasizes the importance of relating socialist ideals both to current social and historical conditions and to potential revolutionary agents, the outright rejection of utopian thought by subsequent Marxists was a mistake. The exploration of an alternative moral vision and the anticipation or 'prefiguration' of more emancipated social relations in experimental communities were valuable aspects of utopian socialism that were regrettably absent from the revolutionary communist tradition. A genuinely critical theory must identify human potentialities neglected within the existing social order, and so uncover the 'negative' moment of existing reality – that moment, in other words, which promises further dialectical transformation. Needless to say, it is this negative dimension of present society which is invisible to positive science. Critical theory requires more than the limited resources of the one-sided rationality of Enlightenment science. Utopian political thought, on the other hand, is an example of negative or critical thinking, if only in embryonic form, since it is insufficiently practical.

Even 'bourgeois' philosophy and art hold out a utopian promise which, though unfulfilled, preserves the 'general demand for human liberation'.[70] In an alienated society, suppressed human possibilities are expressed, albeit in politically innocent form, in works of art and in idealist philosophy. Beauty is the foretaste of a more harmonious existence. The dreams and fantasies of Romanticism encode, and so protect, latent human aspirations and needs. In Marcuse's terms, the harmony, proportion and beauty of classical art is 'the sensuous appearance of the idea of freedom', and he advocates a 'permanent aesthetic subversion' of the status quo.[71] Art and art theory, in other words, are politically charged. Some of Adorno's most important works are in the area of aesthetics and musicology.[72] In effect, the Frankfurt School's account of art echoes Feuerbach's demystification of religion and speculative philosophy as expressions of a traumatized humanity that nevertheless contain hidden truths. Accordingly, for Marcuse, only a critical theory imbued with fantasy can fulfil its emancipatory potential: 'Without phantasy, all philosophical knowledge remains in the grip of the present or the past and severed from the future, which is the only link between philosophy and the real history of mankind.'[73] Critical theory should decode and so liberate the utopian potential of religion, art and philosophy, rather than seek, in positivist spirit, to certify them as irrational and unscientific.[74]

Both the Frankfurt School's emphasis on fantasy and imagination and its rejection of positivist or 'traditional' theory raise, with some urgency, the question of the epistemological grounding of critical theory itself. Horkheimer admits that critical theory, being directed to the future rather than based on the present and the past, 'appears, to prevailing modes of thought, to be subjective and speculative, one-sided and useless'.[75] This situation is made worse by loss of faith in the proletariat as privileged epistemological subject – 'even the situation of the proletariat is, in this society, no guarantee of correct knowledge'.[76] In their constructive attempts to ground critical theory, members of the Frankfurt School reveal their debt to the Hegelian dialectic but also their substantial departures from it. Horkheimer rejects Hegel's philosophy of history, the claim to understand history as a totality. Not only, as Marx and the Young Hegelians had complained, is the dialectic of history not yet complete, but we cannot regard the dialectic as 'closed' in the sense of having a foreseeable and final outcome.[77] Adorno resists all such attempts to 'represent the totality' as evidence of a 'desire to control the world'. He denies that there can be any final truth or even any assurance of a 'linear path from ignorance to knowledge'.[78] We should seek to avoid all 'hypostasis of mind', caused by speculative and positivist systems of thought.[79] The nineteenth-century German philosopher Friedrich Nietzsche, with his suspicion of all systematic thought, foundationalist epistemology, metaphysical systems and claims to absolute truth, was a significant source of these critical, anti-metaphysical themes.[80] The aphoristic style of many of Adorno's writings, as well as his belief that only such a style could resist recuperation by the system, also betray the influence of Nietzsche. On the other hand, Frankfurt theorists seek to rebut charges of relativism by means of a continuing commitment to the dialectic, albeit one that is not closed and so not knowable in advance as a totality. The outcome of critique is not the blank rejection or 'abstract negation' of a particular position, but rather its 'determinate negation'. Through 'internal' or 'immanent' critique, the rejection of one position leads dialectically to an alternative position that preserves the strengths while eliminating the inadequacies of the one it supersedes. In this way a limited or one-sided perspective is replaced by a more complete one. An important model of immanent critique is Marx's demonstration of the discrepancy between bourgeois ideals of universal liberty and justice and the actual exploitation and injustice of capitalist society. On this interpretation, socialism promises to realize these values concretely rather than merely abstractly. In this sense critical theory retains a residue of faith in the dialectic. The determinate outcome of critique is presumed to be an advance towards a more emancipated society.

The Frankfurt theorists' anti-positivist critical theory, then, is embedded in a more sceptical philosophy of history, one which refrains both from the speculative ambitions of Hegelian philosophy and the predictive optimism of historical materialism. Their own more modest attempt to tell the story of a highly ambivalent *Dialectic of Enlightenment* explores prominent themes and thinkers of the eighteenth-century Enlightenment against the background of a much longer history of rationality, the more protracted process of 'enlightenment'. Their 'primal history of a subjectivity that wrests itself free from the power of mythic forces' is influenced by Nietzsche's critical assessment of both the Enlightenment in particular and the claims of scientific reason more generally.[81] At first sight, the triumph of rationalism represents a simple victory of reason over all superstition and mythological thinking: 'The disenchantment of the world is the extirpation of animism.'[82] In fact, however, myth and enlightenment are interdependent from the beginning. '[M]yth is already enlightenment; and enlightenment reverts to mythology.'[83] On the one hand, myths and magic are already attempts to gain control over a dangerous and capricious natural world. Humanity's instrumental relationship to the natural world is not invented, only elaborated and intensified, with modern natural science. On the other hand, the victory of scientific rationality over superstition and myth is at best partial and is won at a cost. Enlightenment becomes 'engulfed in mythology'.[84] At the same time as it liberates us from the animistic terrors and uncertainties of nature, scientific reason offers only a diminished and one-sided understanding of nature as an object to be manipulated and controlled: 'What men want to learn from nature is how to use it in order wholly to dominate it and other men', and 'Men pay for the increase of their power with alienation from that over which they exercise their power.'[85] Even at the culmination of this process, with the eighteenth-century Enlightenment's ostensibly rational engagement against all forms of prejudice and dogma, positivist reason remains 'engulfed in mythology'. Positivism insists dogmatically that nature must always be understood in terms of quantitative categories – 'the process is always decided from the start. . . . Mathematical procedure became, so to speak, the ritual of thinking.'[86]

In its attitude to society as well, Enlightenment rationalism positivistically treats the existing order as everlasting. And so, to the disenchantment of nature there corresponds a 'sacralization of reality'. The extension of scientific reason to humanity's self-understanding comes at the cost of an 'introversion of sacrifice', a corresponding loss of our own humanity. An instrumental logic, initially applied to a world of objects, is extended to relations between persons, reducing them to the status of things. As a result, human relationships are impoverished and our access to a full, subjective life is impaired. With capitalism, itself a manifestation of instrumental rationality, human beings are subjected to a 'technical apparatus' originally designed to serve them. As Habermas puts it: 'The permanent sign of enlightenment is domination over an objectified external nature and a repressed internal nature.'[87] There is a further dialectical sting to this analysis. Suppressed 'internal nature' is always threatening to erupt destructively into modern life. National socialism, with its unique combination of organizational efficiency and atavistic barbarism, demonstrates with particular ferocity the interdependence of myth and rationality characteristic of modernity. In this light, the Marquis de Sade's celebration of unbridled passion and cruelty is understood not as the product of depravity and perversion, but as an honest presentation of the moral implications of enlightenment. De Sade's fantasies are a clear-sighted anticipation of totalitarian order, which 'gives full rein to calculation and abides by science as such', and whose 'canon is its own brutal efficiency'.[88]

The Frankfurt School's account of modernity and enlightenment is deeply indebted to the sociologist Max Weber (1864–1920). It is influenced, in particular, by his account of the rationalization of society.[89] Weber sees both capitalism and bureaucracy as instances of more general processes of rationalization characteristic of modern civilization. With bureaucracy, the state organizes efficient administrative means for the realization of particular ends, in the same way that capitalism reorganizes productive resources for profit. However, both bureaucracy and capitalism represent only a one-sided, instrumental rationality. They rationalize society only in the sense of 'formal' rationality, which concerns the selection of efficient means for given ends. Rationalization is indifferent to the 'substantive' rationality of ends, which depends on the exercise of reason in the evaluation of the ultimate goals of human activity.[90] So the formal or instrumental rationalization of society is compatible with the occurrence of substantively irrational outcomes. States can be efficiently organized to realize undesirable or even obnoxious ends. Moreover, rationalization dislodges traditional religions and worldviews, offering little in return for a disenchanted world bereft of meaning. The one-sided rationalization of society confines human beings to an alienated and bureaucratically regulated 'iron cage'. But whereas Weber sees the process of rationalization as inevitable, Frankfurt theorists insist on searching for a way out of the iron cage.

In the Frankfurt School's analyses of contemporary society a significant role is also played by the psychoanalytic theories of Sigmund Freud (1856–1939).[91] Freud's psychological explanations of the formation of character and desire promised to fill a gap in Marxism, for example by helping to explain the proletariat's considerable loyalty to an exploitative capitalist society. Freud's ideas, like Weber's, were again given an optimistic twist. Whereas Freud saw the frequent neuroses and occasional psychoses of *fin de siècle* Vienna as symptoms of an inevitable sacrifice of pleasure, or 'eros', for the sake of 'civilization', Frankfurt theorists blame rationalization and hold out the hope of a less repressed society.[92] Thus, Marcuse reckons the costs of modern society in terms of a repression of 'eros' that is now superfluous.[93] Just as the neurotic adult unconsciously repeats patterns of behaviour fixed by childhood trauma, so the members of contemporary society behave in ways more appropriate to the scarcities of the past. Affluent Western societies impose a level of self-denial, a curtailing of the 'polymorphous perversity' of the 'pleasure principle' that is no longer necessary in an era of unprecedented productive potential. The pathological work ethic and equally obsessive and dutiful consumerism of the United States are expressions of a redundant but pathologically fixed 'performance principle'. But in contrast to Freud, Marcuse expects revolutionary release from the 'surplus repression' of an obsolete system. Written in the conformist 1950s in the United States, Marcuse's analysis would be taken up with enthusiasm in the 'permissive' decade of sexual revolution that was to follow.

Perhaps most influential have been the Frankfurt School's studies of the 'culture industry'. In contrast to the high art or 'intellectual culture' of the bourgeoisie, which is potentially if only obliquely critical of the existing order, the culture industry serves to reinforce conformity. Popular or 'material' culture has been transformed by its integration with the capitalist mode of production. Walter Benjamin's (1892–1940) classic essay, 'The Work of Art in the Age of Mechanical Reproduction', sees progressive potential in the spread of mechanization and mass production to the area of culture. Drawing his examples mainly from photography, printing and film, Benjamin claims that the mechanical reproducibility of cultural artefacts destroys the magical, almost sacred 'aura' of works of high culture, detaching them from ritual and tradition: '[T]hat which withers in the age of mechanical reproduction is the aura of the work of art.'[94] Benjamin associates this development with the 'increasing significance of the masses in contemporary life' with their 'sense of the universal equality of things' and sees it as potentially progressive:[95] 'Mechanical reproduction of art changes the reaction of the masses toward art. The reactionary attitude toward a Picasso painting changes into the progressive reaction toward a Chaplin movie.'[96]

Referring to the role of ritual and propaganda in 1930s Germany, Benjamin claims that the insistence on the autonomy of art or 'art for art's sake' is 'consummated' with the 'introduction of aesthetics into political life' by fascism. The 'post-auratic' work of art, on the other hand, can connect with politics in a different way when 'Communism responds by politicizing art.'[97] Art should serve the revolution, though not by faithfully (and tediously) portraying the hardships and heroism of proletarian life or resorting to outright propaganda, as socialist realism and 'agitprop' set out to do.[98]

Other theorists associated with the Institute for Social Research are more pessimistic. They refer to the 'culture industry', not to 'mass culture', because the latter term gives the false impression that the capitalist organization of culture serves the needs of the masses rather than, as in reality, the needs of capital. Although the culture industry 'undeniably speculates on the conscious and unconscious state of the millions towards which it is directed', the masses are really an object of calculation, an appendage of the machinery.[99] Cultural artefacts are subjected more systematically to the logic of the profit motive and capital accumulation. The critical potential of intellectual culture is undermined by the conformist, or 'affirmative', products of the culture industry, which facilitate the individual's adaptation to capitalism. Affirmative culture provides an escape from reality, which requires little effort or concentration from workers demoralized and dulled by an alienating work process. The various techniques used to achieve these ends are also analysed. Adorno describes techniques of 'standardization' (e.g. the standardized plots of Westerns), 'pseudo-individualization' (the introduction of insignificant differences of plot which obscure the 'formula'), and the use of 'response mechanisms' such as canned laughter, which are designed to guarantee the 'correct' response from the audience.[100] Like fascist propaganda, these devices appeal unconsciously to the audience's emotions and discourage critical responses.[101] Even popular astrology has conformist implications. It reinforces fatalism and short-term pragmatism, reconciling people to a social system they can neither understand nor control:

> In as much as the social system is the 'fate' of most individuals independent of their will and interest, it is projected upon the stars in order to thus obtain a higher degree of dignity and justification in which the individuals hope to participate themselves. At the same time, the idea that the stars, if only one reads them correctly, offer some advice mitigates the very same fear of the inexorability of social processes the stargazer himself creates.[102]

Popular music encourages 'compulsiveness' and suggestibility. It can only be listened to in a state of 'deconcentration' or distraction: 'If the standardized products, hopelessly like one another except for conspicuous hit lines, do not permit concentrated listening without becoming unbearable to the listeners, the latter are in any case no longer capable of concentrated listening.'[103] In contrast to this attitude to popular culture, Adorno welcomes the more challenging, formally innovative products of contemporary intellectual culture. The music of Schoenberg and Webern 'gives form to that anxiety, that terror, that insight into the catastrophic situation which others merely evade by regressing'.[104] But Adorno's position is not just elitism. Rather, Adorno objects to the blurring of the boundaries between high and low art to the detriment of both. Popular art loses 'the rebellious resistance inherent within it as long as social control was not yet total'.[105]

The much-vaunted liberties of liberal capitalism are stifled by a parallel series of transformations. According to Marcuse's analysis, the potentially revolutionary class conflict of liberal capitalism has been eliminated from the 'one-dimensional' societies of advanced capitalism, which, as a result of the increasing incorporation of the working class into the structures of welfare state capitalism, now lack genuine opposition. These societies appear to be free because of their free elections, free press, consumer choice and the apparent contrast with totalitarian communism. But the freedom of advanced capitalism is really 'repressive tolerance', which serves – even more effectively than totalitarian censorship – to divert attention from, and so entrench, the manipulation and conformism of an increasingly administered society.[106] The critical public sphere of early bourgeois societies (seen in the rapid expansion of newspaper and book publishing, coffee houses and salons of the late seventeenth and eighteenth centuries) has given way to a 'manipulated publicity'. Public opinion is something to be measured and managed by state and media, a mere reflection of the prevailing order. It is no longer an independent source of criticism or opposition.[107] Marcuse's bleak portrayal suggests a society of uninterrupted manipulation and control with few obvious grounds for hope. With the seamless mediocrity of its mass-produced entertainment, its overfed complacency and positivistically disarmed sociology and philosophy, contemporary Western society either stifles or marginalizes genuine opposition, all but eliminating any possibility of revolution. In fact, Marcuse, as the critical theorist most directly concerned with political practice, looks to those excluded from the system, to 'the substratum of the outcasts and outsiders, the exploited and persecuted of other races and other colours, the unemployed and the unemployable', for potential agents of transformation. But this turn to political practice seems artificial and, in the end, not that distant from Leninism. For these groups will bring about revolution only if they are led by the radical students and youth, who represent 'the most advanced consciousness of humanity'.[108] Although Marcuse's views were heard sympathetically by the New Left and student activists of the 1960s, particularly in the USA and Germany, a critical theory attributing such responsibility to critical intellectuals could not but renew fears of revolutionary vanguardism as well.

From one point of view, then, the Frankfurt School's return to a broader, 'superstructural' agenda of aesthetic, cultural, psychological and sociological studies enriches the Marxist critique of ideology, opening the way to more adequate explanations of fascism, Soviet communism and advanced capitalism. It is less obvious whether their critical theories really help us to escape the oppressive labyrinth of modernity. In the end, the Frankfurt School's exhaustive inventory of the subtlety and all-pervasiveness of mechanisms of power is double-edged. The more the conformity of contemporary society is explained, the more any upsurge of revolutionary enthusiasm seems unlikely. Reinforced by such a range of argument and research, the mood of pessimism haunting the Frankfurt School's account of contemporary society is not coincidental. The tendency to inspire resignation rather than revolt is exacerbated by a relative inattention to potential agents of social transformation. In Paul Connerton's phrase, there are no 'structural gaps within the system of repressive rationality'.[109] Adorno and Horkheimer soon lost faith in the revolutionary potential of the working class. Marcuse's identification of new revolutionary agents is no less problematic. To adapt the phrase Gramsci made famous, pessimism of the intellect threatens optimism of the will.[110] For critical theory, which defines itself in terms of the essential relationship between radical theory and transformative practice, this problem is fundamental.

Habermas and the renewal of critical theory

More recently, the critical theory of the Frankfurt School has been renewed by the wide-ranging, ambitious and influential project of the German social theorist and philosopher Jürgen Habermas (1929–).[111] Habermas combines a philosophically informed and critical sociology with a philosophy grounded in categories of social action. His project involves a protracted critical engagement with the distinct but interrelated ideas of Marx and historical materialism, on the one hand, and the limitations of positivist social science and

Enlightenment rationalism, on the other. In this sense, Habermas can be understood as the most recent representative of the tradition of thought that can be traced from Kant, Hegel and Marx to the Frankfurt School. Habermas's work is also marked by a serious encounter with analytical philosophy, particularly the speech act theory of J. L. Austin and John Searle and the later philosophy of Ludwig Wittgenstein. Habermas reworks the Frankfurt School's critique of positivism on what he sees as more secure epistemological foundations. This involves the explication of a fuller conception of rationality, one that is not reducible to instrumental rationality. He starts out from basically Hegelian and Marxian premises. Knowledge and values are not the timeless accomplishment of a transcendental subject. They can only be understood in the context of the material history of human societies, the biological reproduction and social evolution of the human species.

The basic direction of Habermas's critique and renewal of historical materialism is signalled by an early distinction between two kinds of action, 'labour' or 'work' and 'interaction' – later referred to as 'purposive-rational' and 'strategic' as opposed to 'communicative action'. The concept of work is intended to correspond to Marx's concept of labour which, in the form of historically developing modes of production, is the most basic category of historical materialism. The act of satisfying human needs by means of labour is, for Marx, distinctive of human as opposed to merely animal existence and so is the act that founds human history. Marx's materialist conception of history charts a series of dialectically unfolding modes of production, different ways of organizing labour.[112] Habermas defines labour as a form of 'purposive-rational action', which can largely be explained in the limited terms of instrumental rationality. Purposive-rational action simply 'realizes defined goals under given conditions'. It includes labour, or 'instrumental action', which 'organizes means that are appropriate or inappropriate according to criteria of an effective control of reality'. 'Strategic action' is a related form of action in the social sphere, which manifests a similarly controlling attitude towards other people. Strategic action, which 'depends on the correct evaluation of possible alternative choices, results from calculation supplemented by values and maxims'.[113] The significant point about strategic action is that, although values play a role, the form of rationality involved is still merely calculative, having no bearing on the validity of the values themselves. It is a social variant of the familiar form of instrumental rationality most clearly embodied in natural science and technology. Scientific knowledge and technological development follow 'a logic that corresponds to the structure of purposive-rational action regulated by its own results, which is in fact the structure of work'.[114]

Work is distinguished from interaction or communicative action. Communicative action refers to the pragmatic domain of relations between human subjects. Where purposive-rational action involves an instrumental relationship of control over a realm of objects and people, communicative action depends on mutual understanding between subjects. Where labour applies technical rules in order to control external reality, communicative action depends on moral (or 'practical') norms. It is 'governed by binding *consensual norms*, which define reciprocal expectations about behavior and which must be understood and recognized by at least two acting subjects'.[115] If purposive-rational action is the domain of natural science, technology and bureaucracy, communicative action is the domain of values, norms and the 'life-world' (*Lebenswelt*). Just as purposive-rational action provides a pragmatic context for the explication of instrumental rationality, communicative action provides a pragmatic context for the interpretation and validation of moral norms. This context provides the basis for Habermas's reconstruction of communicative rationality. Corresponding to 'substantive rationality' in Weber's sense or Hegel's 'reason' (*Vernunft*), communicative rationality is designed to correct the Enlightenment's one-eyed account of rationality, supplementing the instrumental assessment of means for the realization of particular ends – merely 'formal rationality' or 'understanding' (*Verstand*) – with the discursive validation of norms governing relations between subjects.

According to Habermas, critical theory must shift its attention to the domain of communicative action in order to reinforce the critique of an oppressive social reality. This is because both the Marxist category of labour and positivist social science provide only a partial and one-sided basis for understanding society. The limitations of the category of labour are reflected in the Marxist account of modernization. In fact, science and technology play a progressive role for Marxism equivalent to the role allotted to scientific rationality by the Enlightenment. The state of development of science and technology is closely related to the level of development of the forces of production, which include the human, natural but also technological resources available for production at a particular time. As the industrial revolution demonstrates, advances in science and technology dramatically increase the productivity of labour. But for Marx and Engels, this development of the *forces* of production ultimately leads to the progressive transformation of society more broadly, through transition to a more advanced *mode* of production and society.[116]

However, Habermas is just as sceptical of guarantees of progress based exclusively on a dialectic of labour as he is of the Enlightenment's more straightforward assumptions about progress. Progressive changes in what Marxism regards as the 'superstructural' spheres of law, politics, philosophy or morality cannot simply be predicated on developments within the scientific or material basis of society. In Habermas's terms, developments within the pragmatic context of work do not lead automatically to progress in the intersubjective context of communicative action. This is confirmed more broadly by the one-sided achievements of Western modernization or development. The 'project of modernity' is radically incomplete, because the dramatic expansion of our (instrumentally rational) ability to control nature has not been accompanied by a corresponding rationalization of our 'life-world'.[117]

Recognition of the distinctive rationality of communicative action is urgent, because of the changed role of science and technology within contemporary society since the Enlightenment. According to Habermas's account in *The Structural Transformation of the Public Sphere* (1962), the Enlightenment was able to expose religious dogma and traditional authority to critical rationality, because rational discourse could occupy the space created by an emerging 'public sphere' between civil society and the state. The public sphere of late seventeenth- and eighteenth-century Europe, with its clubs, salons, novels, newspapers and journals, allowed the formation of an informed and critical public opinion.[118] Although clearly bourgeois in its membership and perspectives, the public sphere provided the institutional infrastructure not only for literary and aesthetic criticism and scientific debate, but also for political opposition and critique. The critical public sphere was, however, short-lived. In industrial capitalist societies it has, since the nineteenth century, been transformed by a series of developments which turned a 'culture-debating' into a 'culture-consuming' public. Public opinion now takes the privatized form of anonymous voting at elections. Public opinion is the object of polling and scientific research designed to make it more readily manipulable. At the same time, in place of bourgeois ideology, which at least still claimed intersubjective validity for certain moral norms, there is an increasingly pervasive 'technocratic' consciousness. Contentious political issues are transformed into technical problems that can be decided by technical experts and expertise. For example, what has been described as 'economic rationalism' converts issues of social justice and distribution, which evidently require moral discussion and political resolution, into supposedly uncontentious questions of economic management subject to the authoritative scientific judgement of economists. In this context, scepticism about the possibility of 'intersubjectively binding' agreement concerning moral values – whether in the form of ethical relativism, subjectivism, 'decisionism', positivism or postmodernism – only serves to reinforce technocratic consciousness by undermining the conditions of moral and political discourse.[119] The combination of all these developments – which earlier Frankfurt School theorists discussed in terms of the rise of positivism and the 'culture industry' – confirm the changed role of scientific rationality from a critical to a conservative one. With what, in an earlier formulation, Habermas describes as 'the expansion of the rational form of science and technology . . . to the proportions of a life form', science and technology have become ideology.[120]

Up to this point, Habermas's argument might be understood as a restatement of the Frankfurt School's core theoretical position. However, his more constructive approach is designed to correct a basic inadequacy in the position of these earlier theorists. It is apparent that Habermas's categories of work, purposive-rational and strategic action correspond to the Frankfurt School's conception of instrumental rationality and to Weber's concept of formal rationalization. However, although these theorists recognize the limitations of instrumental rationality, they fail to provide a convincing account of any more adequate conception of rationality. Weber describes how processes of rationalization dissolve values and traditions and lead to 'disenchantment', but he sees no alternative basis for a substantive rationality of ends – only the arbitrary choices and subjective decisions of private individuals. Analogously, Horkheimer and Adorno show how the unrestricted expansion of instrumental rationality suppresses our 'internal nature', reducing human beings to the status of objects. Marcuse portrays the repression of our instinctual life or 'eros' as the cost extracted by an unfettered productive process detached from real human needs. However, these accounts of the 'dark side' of the dialectic of Enlightenment offer no politically and philosophically convincing alternative to instrumental rationality. There is a need, therefore, for a more persuasive and, above all, a more constructive alternative.

Habermas's first (and still powerful) attempt to flesh out this ambitious project is presented in *Knowledge and Human Interests* (1968), which develops more explicitly and systematically the connection between purposive-rational and communicative action, on the one hand, and distinct categories of knowledge and rationality, on the other. The outcome is a kind of transcendental pragmatism. The achievements of the knowing subject are related to historicized contexts of social action, which provide the categorial framework for particular kinds of experience and knowledge. Natural scientific knowledge (including the application of science in technology) is understood in terms of the pragmatic context of purposive-rational action. The objectivity of the 'empirical-analytic sciences' is grounded in purposive-rational action, and organized in terms of a technical interest in the control of external reality: '[F]acts relevant to the empirical sciences are first constituted through an *a priori* organization of our experience in the behavioural system of instrumental action.'[121] Natural science does not, as realist accounts of science suppose, describe reality as such, but only from the point of view of an underlying 'cognitive interest' in control. This is reflected in the hypothetico-deductive structure of scientific theories, whereby the predictions derived from certain theoretical assumptions are 'confirmed' or 'refuted' by experiments and observations.[122] Habermas's account of natural science also draws on the philosophy of science of the American pragmatist Charles Sanders Peirce (1839–1914). Peirce suggests that 'the task of methodology is not to clarify the logical structure of scientific theories but the logic of the procedure with whose aid we *obtain* scientific theories.'[123] Natural science can then be conceived as a 'self-regulating, cumulative learning process' within the framework of instrumental action.[124] In effect, science self-consciously systematizes and formalizes activities of problem-solving necessary for the reproduction of human societies.

However, Habermas argues *against* Peirce that natural science cannot be understood in this way as a practical activity without breaking more radically with the 'scientistic self-understanding' of positivism. This is because the practice of science depends on a scientific community and so, inevitably, on the achievement of mutual understanding by means of language and communication. In other words, science cannot be understood without reference to the pragmatic context of communicative action as well:

> [T]he communication of investigators requires the use of language that is not confined to the limits of technical control over objectified natural processes. It arises from symbolic interaction between societal subjects who reciprocally know and recognize each other as unmistakable individuals. This *communicative action* is a system of reference that cannot be reduced to the framework of *instrumental action*.[125]

Reflection on science as a social activity implies a different kind of knowledge, which is based on a different cognitive interest and different conditions of objectivity. Here Habermas draws on Dilthey's 'hermeneutic' account of the 'cultural sciences' (or

Geisteswissenschaften), which emphasizes the role of interpretive 'understanding' (or *Verstehen*).[126] What Habermas calls the 'historical-hermeneutic sciences' find the basis of their objectivity in the pragmatic context of communication. History, literary criticism and other disciplines centrally concerned with the interpretation of texts, utterances and meaningful symbols are all included in this category. These disciplines serve a cognitive interest in mutual understanding, providing 'interpretations that make possible the orientation of action within common traditions'.[127] Unlike the empirical-analytic sciences, they do not imply a manipulative or instrumental relationship with objects, but a relationship of mutual understanding between subjects. But just like the control of external reality, communication and mutual understanding are essential to the continuing life of any society. They are necessary both for the social coordination of activities and for the historical accumulation of knowledge through processes of socialization and cultural transmission. Hermeneutics, then, is the 'scientific form of the interpretive activities of everyday life', just as the experimental method of natural science 'refines the everyday pragmatic controls of rules of instrumental action'.[128]

Habermas proceeds to identify a third kind of knowledge, corresponding to the idea of critical theory. In *Knowledge and Human Interests*, the 'critically oriented sciences' are motivated by an 'emancipatory cognitive interest' and grounded in the further pragmatic context of 'self-reflection'. No more than natural science can the hermeneutical sciences provide a full and satisfactory account of human knowledge. Habermas rejects the 'universality claims' of hermeneutics just as, with the critique of positivism and scientism, he dismissed the claim to universal validity of natural scientific method. On the one hand, Habermas does not deny that the methods of natural science have a valid domain of application in the control of nature for the material reproduction of human societies. Even the establishing of 'law-like correlations' between social phenomena has a role in the social sciences. But here, as the critique of positivist social science implies, critical social science must go beyond the identification of law-like correlations 'to determine when theoretical statements grasp invariant regularities of social action as such and when they express ideologically frozen relations of dependence that can in principle be transformed'.[129] The last phrase recalls Marx's critique of bourgeois economics as the prototype of a critical theory which uncovers and helps to dissolve the otherwise 'immutable' regularities of capitalism.

On the other hand, and parallel to this argument for the limited validity of the methods pioneered in the natural sciences, Habermas argues for the insufficiency of hermeneutic knowledge as well. As a consequence of its exclusive concern with the meanings of utterances, texts and symbols, hermeneutic knowledge is not equipped to uncover ideological forms of consciousness. Typically, the hermeneutic stance seeks to reconstruct the meaning of otherwise obscure or misleading human expressions. It is not concerned with the causal context of these expressions and, as a result, is insufficient for a critique of ideology. Ideologies, for both Marxism and critical theory, are systems of thought and value that justify the dominant position of one group (such as the bourgeoisie) at the expense of another (like the proletariat). Crucially, as the 'ruling ideas' of an epoch, ideologies are *imposed* (whether visibly or invisibly) on their victims. But hermeneutics is blind to such forms of false consciousness or 'distorted communication', which bear the imprint of power or domination. There is thus an indispensable role for critical theory, which sets out to uncover the effects of power and so loosen the hold of oppressive ideologies. At this stage, Habermas also takes Freudian psychoanalysis as a methodological model of critical theory in this sense. Mental disorders such as neuroses are recognized as obsolete defence mechanisms, resulting from past traumas, which inhibit the individual's transparent 'internal communication'. Psychoanalysis looks beneath the explicit symptoms of neurosis to uncover the lasting impact of childhood trauma on the unconscious mind. The psychoanalytic interpretation penetrates beneath the surface complex to its underlying causes and so, once it is understood and accepted by the patient, cures the neurosis. In both Marxist and psychoanalytic variants, critically oriented theories serve an interest in emancipation, whether from relations of domination and the ideologies that sustain them or from the inhibiting opacity of a disordered mind.[130]

Although Habermas retains much of the spirit of this account of critical theory, he soon became dissatisfied with his epistemological grounding of critical theory in the 'self-reflection' of what appeared to be a thinly disguised version of Kant's transcendental subject.[131] At the same time, he continues to insist on the need to provide more substantive foundations for normative critique. Previous members of the Frankfurt School advocated an immanent critique, whereby society is transformed by rendering explicit the tensions and contradictions within it. The 'sham universality' of bourgeois justice would provide the basis for its own transcendence. But the Frankfurt School's own analysis of contemporary society suggests that the enterprise of immanent critique is now endangered because universalistic values have given way to technocratic consciousness. Bourgeois consciousness has, in the meantime, become too 'cynical', so that its immanent critique can no longer be expected to lead to emancipatory social transformation.[132] The alternative pursued by Habermas is to ground critique in a theory of communication and communicative rationality, which has the advantage of replacing the 'philosophy of the subject' with an irreducibly intersubjective foundation for critical theory. The clearest picture of the structure of communication is provided by language. However, it is neither the propositional contents nor the syntactic structure of language, but the way we use it, or, in other words, the 'pragmatics' of language that promises to reveal the fundamental values underlying our social interactions. Implicit in language, Habermas claims, are the essential normative foundations of critical theory:

> The human interest in autonomy and responsibility is not mere fancy, for it can be apprehended *a priori*. What raises us out of nature is the only thing whose nature we can know: language. Through its structure, autonomy and responsibility are posited for us. Our first sentence expresses unequivocally the intention of universal and unconstrained consensus.[133]

Since communication between subjects is an unavoidable condition of human society, it is also plausible to suppose that these values will have universal validity. In fact, it is crucial to Habermas's argument that his account is valid in *every* society – he describes it as a theory of *universal* pragmatics – if it is to provide the basis for a universally applicable critical theory. As McCarthy puts it, Habermas's ambitious claim is 'that the goal of critical theory – a form of life free from unnecessary domination in all its forms – is inherent in the notion of truth; it is anticipated in every act of communication'.[134]

The theory of universal pragmatics uncovers basic values implicit in communication. By looking beyond the propositional content of language to the pragmatics of communication, Habermas is able to locate values other than truth. Specifically, according to his account, every act of communication raises three validity claims corresponding to three 'world relations'. These validity claims reflect the relation of communication to a realm of intersubjectivity or society – raising claims of morality or rightness (*Richtigkeit*) – to external reality or nature – raising claims of truth (*Wahrheit*) – and to the 'internal nature' of the speaker's own feelings, beliefs and intentions, which depends on the truthfulness or sincerity (*Wahrhaftigkeit*) of the speaker. In other words:

> The speaker must have the intention of communicating a true [*wahr*] proposition (or a propositional content, the existential presuppositions of which are satisfied) so that the hearer can share the knowledge of the

speaker. The speaker must want to express his intentions truthfully [*wahr-haftig*] so that the hearer can believe the utterance of the speaker (can trust him). Finally, the speaker must choose an utterance that is right [*richtig*] so that the hearer can accept the utterance and speaker and hearer can agree with one another in the utterance with respect to a recognized normative background. Moreover, communicative action can continue undisturbed only as long as participants suppose that the validity claims they reciprocally raise are justified.[135]

It follows that validity claims also correspond to the various kinds of challenge an interlocutor might raise against a particular utterance. The listener can challenge an utterance as factually false (or based on falsehood), as insincere or untruthful, and as normatively inappropriate. It also follows that to the extent that we are able to engage in communication with other subjects we can be assumed to understand these values. Our communicative competence includes 'mastery of these values, the basis of our ideas of truth, freedom and justice'.[136]

Clearly decisive for Habermas's account, if it is to provide the basis for a critical theory of society, is how problematic validity claims are resolved. After all, challenges to particular utterances have in the past been met by appeals to authority (of priests, oracles, sacred or scientific texts), or by the use of force and other inducements (the Inquisition, psychiatric treatment, bribery or threats of imprisonment). In some cultures, and in Western culture before the Enlightenment, these responses have been regarded as perfectly legitimate. But Habermas believes that a more rational response is not only to be preferred but, in some sense, implicitly presupposed whenever people enter into communication. Disagreements regarding truth and moral rightness are to be resolved by engaging in an unconstrained discourse aiming at agreement. It is in this sense that Habermas says: 'Our first sentence expresses unequivocally the intention of universal and unconstrained consensus.'[137] Factual and scientific claims are resolved in 'theoretical' discourse. Claims to rightness are addressed in moral or practical discourse, where the only criterion of validity is the agreement or consensus of all participants. But a consensus does not ensure validity if it depends on inadequate information or if it has been imposed or is the product of coercion. A moral claim is vindicated only when it is the object of a fully rational and unconstrained consensus – when the participants in discourse are subject only to 'the peculiarly unforced force of the better argument'.[138] Discourse is to be measured against the standard of what Habermas sometimes calls an 'ideal speech situation'. An ideal discourse is free from relations of power or domination, and it is undogmatically committed to the consideration of all available evidence and, where necessary, alternative conceptual schemes. This implies, crucially, that consensus is only ever *provisional*, because it is always vulnerable to the appearance of new evidence and novel ideas, and the inclusion of those hitherto excluded from full and equal participation in discourse. Put another way, ideal discourse is what is ruled out whenever distorted communication prevails, whether within society in the form of ideology or within the individual as some form of barrier to 'internal communication'. By the same token, critically oriented theories are designed to uncover previously hidden deviations from ideal discourse.

If successful, the theory of universal pragmatics promises to reconstruct a substantive conception of communicative rationality, which is rich enough to ground societal norms and critical theory. However, Habermas's ambitious and original reconstruction of universal communicative competence has been criticized as a return to the doomed Enlightenment project of finding timelessly rational foundations for moral values. It has been seen as Kantian transcendentalism in a new guise, despite Habermas's pragmatic emphasis on actual discourse taking place between individuals (as opposed to the abstract reflections of a transcendental subject). Certainly, many critics have been sceptical of the universal status accorded to unconstrained discourse as a criterion of moral truth. How can we suppose that members of every culture, whatever its values or worldview, have always implicitly raised precisely the same validity claims, discursively redeemable in the way Habermas describes, as members of any other culture? Some postmodernist critics have even seen Habermas's commitment to universal consensus as constraining and potentially oppressive in its own way – although this is to ignore his repeated insistence that consensus is only ever anticipatory and provisional, always subject to future challenges and revisions.[139] In the light of some of these criticisms, Habermas has significantly qualified the status of his enterprise. In the terms of Hegel's critique of Kant, Habermas now explicitly limits the scope of discourse ethics to the validation of universal norms of 'morality' (*Moralität*), which govern relations between individuals. It is not competent to judge values and forms of 'ethical life' (Hegelian *Sittlichkeit*) that are inseparably linked to the particular identities of groups and individuals and, through these, to concrete cultural traditions. A universalistic morality in the style of Kant is unable to adjudicate between concrete life forms and customs, which are inextricably bound to particular human communities.[140]

Habermas nonetheless claims credit for decisively opting for inter-subjectivity in the face of the exhaustion of all 'philosophies of the subject'. This choice reflects the fact that it is 'only the communicative use of propositionally differentiated language that is proper to our sociocultural form of life and is constitutive for the level of a genuinely social reproduction of life'.[141] Habermas's theory of communicative rationality has inspired a range of normative approaches in 'discourse theory' in addition to his own.[142] His emphasis on discourse and consensus translates readily into a deliberative theory of democracy, which emphasizes that, beyond electoral procedures and party politics, genuine democracy requires popular participation in discourse (or deliberation).[143] Habermas himself provides a subtle and nuanced reformulation of the normative basis of liberal and democratic theory in *Between Facts and Norms*, which deploys the communicative force of discourse to resolve normative tensions between individual liberal rights and democratic will formation – or, in other words, between private and public autonomy. The result is a suggestive reconciliation of liberal and republican traditions of political thought. At the same time, Habermas seeks to resolve the oppositions between legal positivism and natural law, and between considerations of pragmatic effectiveness and ideal validity, tensions which run through liberal and democratic jurisprudence.[144]

The enormous range of Habermas's theoretical concerns and intellectual resources is undoubtedly impressive. He draws on a wide range of thinkers and approaches in continental philosophy as well as the broad tradition of empirical and theoretical social theory, sociology, anthropology and linguistics. In addition, he appropriates many of the characteristic methods and concepts of analytical philosophy. In the process, Habermas has no doubt moved a considerable distance from his originally Marxist and Frankfurt School origins. But his fundamental guiding insight – that individual autonomy depends on discursive interaction with other people within a public sphere – continues to reflect his Hegelian heritage.[145] Also characteristic (albeit less exclusively) of continental philosophy is Habermas's lifelong engagement as a 'public intellectual' in a wide variety of political and ethical debates. These have included the 'historians' dispute' over the interpretation of Germany's National Socialist past and the Holocaust, the eclipse of the nation-state by the 'postnational constellation' of globalization and the moral implications of the genetic engineering of human nature.[146] In the light of the 'self-instrumentalization' implicit in the latter, Habermas has recently advocated (and himself engaged in) an open dialogue with religion. This has involved rethinking his otherwise secular assumptions and approach in order to recognize the continuing contribution of religious communities and traditions.[147] In a related response to the terrorist attacks of 11 September 2001 ('9/11') and the ensuing 'Global War on Terror', he has taken part in a thoughtful exchange with his long-time intellectual adversary, Jacques Derrida.[148] In order to avoid the risk of polarization between an inadequately grounded 'ethos of liberal citizenship' and resurgent religious fundamentalisms, Habermas proposes a renewed dialogue between secular reason and religious traditions, whose fruitfulness depends on the fulfilment of two conditions:

> [T]he religious side must accept the authority of 'natural' reason as the fallible results of the institutionalized sciences and the basic principles of universalistic egalitarianism in law and morality. Conversely, secular reason may not set itself up as the judge concerning truths of faith, even though in the end it can accept as reasonable only what it can translate into its own, in principle universally accessible, discourses.[149]

Alternatives to the Enlightenment's overly hasty dismissal of religious experience are traced to the diverse approaches of Kant, Hegel, Schleiermacher and Kierkegaard.[150] Overall, Habermas's ingenious and still evolving intellectual synthesis remains the most fertile of the series of dialectics of emancipation we have followed from Hegel, Feuerbach, Marx and the Frankfurt School.[151]

Further Reading

Ludwig Feuerbach's classic work is *Essence of Christianity*. Karl Marx's famous 'Theses on Feuerbach' is included, with other important essays, in *Karl Marx: Early Writings* (ed. L. Colletti). Also seminal are some works he wrote with Friedrich Engels, including *The Communist Manifesto* and *The German Ideology*. The key work is, of course, *Capital: A Critique of Political Economy*, especially the first volume. Herbert Marcuse is probably the most accessible thinker associated with the Frankfurt School. His later work, *An Essay on Liberation*, provides a readable introduction to more challenging works like *Eros and Civilization* and *One-Dimensional Man*. Similarly, Theodor Adorno's *The Culture Industry: Selected Essays on Mass Culture* and *Minima Moralia* are preparation for *Negative Dialectics*. Perhaps most influential is the work Adorno wrote with Max Horkheimer, *Dialectic of Enlightenment*. See also Max Horkheimer, *Critical Theory: Selected Essays* and *Eclipse of Reason*. The collection of Walter Benjamin's essays in *Illuminations* is a good introduction to his thinking. Jürgen Habermas's prolific output makes it difficult to select just one or a few works. The most complete account of his mature system is *Theory of Communicative Action* (two volumes). A gentler introduction to some of his ideas is provided in *Autonomy and Solidarity: Interviews with Jürgen Habermas* and some collections of his essays, including *The Future of Human Nature* and *The Postnational Constellation*, and his early, more historical work, *The Structural Transformation of the Public Sphere*.

There are relatively few recent commentaries on Feuerbach, who is usually (and unfairly) considered only in the context of Marx. V. A. Harvey, *Feuerbach and the Interpretation of Religion*, is a good place to start. Works on Marx and Marxism are, by contrast, plentiful, including David McLellan's shorter and longer accounts in *Marx* and *Karl Marx: His Life and Thought*, and Shlomo Avineri, *The Social and Political Thought of Karl Marx*. The most comprehensive history of the Frankfurt School is Rolf Wiggershaus, *The Frankfurt School*. A sympathetic guide to its major ideas and to Habermas is David Held, *Introduction to Critical Theory: Horkheimer to Habermas*. A more analytic approach is followed in *The Idea of a Critical Theory: Habermas and the Frankfurt School* by Raymond Geuss. Useful guides to individual thinkers include J. M. Bernstein, *Adorno: Disenchantment and Ethics*, Simon Jarvis, *Adorno: A Critical Introduction*, Susan Buck-Morss, *The Origin of Negative Dialectics: Theodor W. Adorno, Walter Benjamin and the Frankfurt School*, Peter Stirk, *Max Horkheimer: A New Interpretation* and David Kellner, *Herbert Marcuse and the Crisis of Marxism*. Useful essays on Habermas are collected in R. J. Bernstein, *Habermas and Modernity* and M. P. d'Entrèves, *Habermas and the Unfinished Project of Modernity*. A recently updated guide is William Outhwaite, *Habermas: A Critical Introduction* (2nd edn).

4

Historicism, Hermeneutics and Phenomenology

Outline

Hegel's aim to ground 'Absolute' knowledge in an historical dialectic of ideas could not ultimately be sustained. However, his emphasis on history and historical knowledge encouraged a revival of critical historiography in the nineteenth century. At the same time, there was a reaction – variously inspired by Romanticism, political conservatism and religion – against Hegel's highly intellectual and theoretical approach. This led to a philosophical emphasis on the uniqueness of subjective existence and human 'life'. Responding to these concerns, Wilhelm Dilthey's 'critique of historical reason' matched Kant's critique of 'pure' or scientific reason on the historical and cultural terrain opened up by Hegel. Dilthey's 'hermeneutics' applies rigorous method to the understanding or interpretation of meanings in 'human sciences' such as history, psychology and the study of art and literature. Hermeneutic categories are employed to more traditionally philosophical ends in Edmund Husserl's 'phenomenology' – a term that can, once again, be traced to Hegel and Kant. Martin Heidegger's explorations of 'Being' and Hans-Georg Gadamer's ontological hermeneutics attempt, in related ways, to represent human understanding and the pre-scientific 'life-world' as fundamental and universal grounds of human experience, knowledge and life. Phenomenology and hermeneutics have been predominantly apolitical or, in the hands of Heidegger and Carl Schmitt, tended towards authoritarianism. Phenomenology is given a distinctly republican twist by Hannah Arendt, who develops a thoroughly anti-authoritarian account of political action and experience.

Dilthey, philosophy of life and hermeneutics

A significant array of approaches in continental philosophy emphasize history, understanding, interpretation, meaning and subjectivity as fundamental categories of knowledge in opposition to the dominance of natural scientific reason. This approach emerges most clearly in the context of nineteenth-century German philosophy, which was dominated by two associated products of the decay of Hegelian philosophy, 'historicism' and 'philosophy of life' (*Lebensphilosophie*). A number of related but not always consistent strands of thought, loosely and sometimes confusingly referred to as historicism, reflect the central role played by history in the thought of some of the most influential critics of the Enlightenment.[1] Both Herder and Hegel were sceptical of Enlightenment assumptions of a universal human nature, natural law or morality, stressing instead the 'spirit' of different historical communities and, in Hegel's case, the 'world spirit' (*Weltgeist*) of history as such. For Herder, human beings differ from other animals because their behaviour is not determined by natural instinct but, rather, is historical. Mind and language are related expressions of an historically changing humanity. The languages of different nations are manifestations of the unique temperament or spirit of a people (*Volksgeist*). Again, for Hegel, morality exists, above all, as the expression of the distinctive culture, institutions and practices or 'ethical life' of a concrete community. By implication, any adequate understanding of human life, ideas and societies must be an historical understanding. Mind or spirit, as opposed to physical nature, can only be understood in terms of its genesis through the unfolding stages of development by which less adequate worldviews or forms of life give birth to more adequate ones.[2] Hegel sees the different manifestations of spirit as stages in the dialectical unfolding of a single world spirit towards the ultimate *telos* or goal, the realization of Absolute knowledge. Hegel's philosophy, which seeks to express the truth of this Absolute as fully as possible, is inextricably linked to his philosophy of history, by which human history is accorded meaning and significance as the essential medium for the more complete articulation of reason.

In general, historicist currents of thought regard history as central to the understanding of human life. But in Hegel's speculative philosophy of history, the insight that the present can only be understood historically had, according to some critics, led to an interpretation of the past and of other cultures distorted by the concerns of the present. This was, in part, because Hegel thought history itself could only be properly understood in terms of philosophy, which had reached its culmination in the present. But historicists were sceptical of Hegel's philosophy of history, which made the cultural values of nineteenth-century Europe the ultimate goal of previous human history. Hegel's philosophy attributes an overall purpose to history, which the people who make history, playthings of the 'cunning of reason', necessarily ignore. Individuals 'are the living instruments of what is in substance the deed of the world mind and they are therefore directly at one with that deed though it is concealed from them and is not their aim and object'.[3] To a more sceptical historical consciousness, which ironically Hegel himself had also helped to inspire, other cultures could not be assessed from the perspective, and against the standards, of one's own time and philosophy in this way. This raised philosophical questions about the status and validity of our knowledge of the past. One outcome of the decay of Hegelianism was thus the emergence of what is called 'critical philosophy of history', a tendency which also drew inspiration from Schleiermacher, Savigny and others. Where speculative philosophy of history assigns an overall purpose to human history as a whole, critical philosophy of history investigates the nature of historical knowledge and appropriate methods of historical research. It was associated with the emergence of history as a respectable academic discipline.[4] Many historicists drew the explicitly relativist conclusion, that the values and norms of different cultures are, in their particular social and historical context, equally valid. If moral values can only be understood in terms of the community to which they belong, and it is no longer plausible to locate different human societies within a historical dialectic, then there is no obviously rational way to decide between conflicting values. The validity of values can only be judged for a particular time rather than for all time. In this variant, moral and cultural values are historicized.

For other critics, including the life philosophers, Hegel's grand system was, for all its dialectical sophistication and comprehensive synthesis, the product of an exclusively theoretical or intellectual consciousness. In response, several currents of thought placed value on 'life' or 'existence', as opposed to the theoretical rationality demonstrated no less by Hegel than by more mainstream Enlightenment thinkers. Romantics defended spontaneity, emotion and individuality against the reductive categories of theoretical reason. Poetry rather than science provides the most adequate path to truth, the most adequate understanding of humanity. In this respect, the mature Hegelian system is less adequate than the poetic achievement of the friend of his youth, Friedrich Hölderlin.[5] Again, for Søren Kierkegaard, now often regarded as the first existentialist, even the most impressive and dialectically mediated feats of theoretical reason must inevitably fail to capture the 'subjective truth' of human life or existence, which is essentially religious.[6] For these approaches a more adequate understanding of human life requires a radical break with cognitive or theoretical reason or the 'philosophy of consciousness'. Life philosophy, too, implied that the most important features of human life could not be captured with the abstract categories of theoretical reason. Life in this sense 'referred to the collected inner powers of man, especially the irrational powers of feeling and passion as over against the prevailing power of rational understanding'.[7] For life philosophers, only a less reductive understanding of human life offers some hope of answering basic questions of philosophy and life, such as the nature of happiness or the good life. For these philosophers, both subjective experience and history, as the accumulated experience of humanity, are primary sources of genuine understanding.[8]

In his varied writings on philosophy, history and the human sciences, Wilhelm Dilthey (1833–1911) combines elements of both historicism and life philosophy with respect for the achievements of natural science. Historicism and life philosophy come together in the conviction that history is the key to the understanding of human life. Human individuals and societies can only be understood historically, so the study of history and the methods appropriate to this study must be of central concern. Like the life philosophers, Dilthey thinks that the positivist attempt to apply the methods of the natural sciences to the study and understanding of human life inevitably leaves out or distorts essential features of human existence. But criticisms of the mechanistic and reifying implications of scientific reason, made by the Romantics and the life philosophers, can easily degenerate into merely subjective and ultimately futile protest. The celebration of passion and will may even encourage a potentially dangerous irrationalism. Equally, the 'speculative idealism' of Hegelian reason, though opposed to the reductive rationalism of positivism, is dogmatic and ultimately unsustainable.[9] Even in less rationalistic variants of German idealism, the deification of will may encourage irrationalist tendencies similar to those inspired by Romanticism.[10] Dilthey never underestimates the rationality, objectivity and rigour demonstrated in natural science. Rather, he seeks to do justice to the concerns of historicists, life philosophers and Romantics in an account of history and the 'human sciences' (*Geisteswissenschaften*) capable of reconciling scientific objectivity with an appreciation of the fullness of human life.[11]

As a convinced empiricist, then, Dilthey regards all knowledge as ultimately derived from experience. He is influenced in this by British empiricists such as Locke and Hume, but above all by the critical philosophy of Kant. He accepts the empiricist (or 'epistemological' view) that all knowledge is based on 'inner experience' or 'the facts of consciousness'. But the approach of previous empiricists overemphasizes intellectual or cognitive experience and neglects emotion and will:

> No real blood flows in the veins of the knowing subject constructed by Locke, Hume and Kant; it is only the diluted juice of reason, a mere process of thought. Cognition seems to develop concepts such as the external world, time, substance and cause from perception, imagination and thought. However, my historical and psychological studies of man as a whole led me to explain cognition and its concepts in terms of the powers of man as a willing, feeling and imagining being.[12]

The historical dimension of human experience, its 'historicity', is also a central aspect of what a positivist approach inevitably fails to capture:

> For [Dilthey] the present is not an extended instant but a small, structured, part of the flow in which the immediate experience is always enriched by awareness of the past and anticipation of the future. So every moment of life has a distinctive meaning according to its place in the temporal sequence. . . . This connection between the temporal structure and the categories of life makes man a historical being.[13]

By implication, even intellectual or cognitive experience occurs within a flow of human experience which is irreducibly historical.

Dilthey's more full-blooded account of human experience suggests a resolution of the contradiction between Romanticism, life philosophy and idealism, on the one hand, and positivism, on the other. He hopes to provide a firm epistemological basis for a 'science' of humanity, which can both do justice to the irreducible qualities of mind or life and yet aspire to an objectivity and rigour equal to that of the sciences of nature. In order to secure the human sciences from the distorting influence of positivism, Dilthey clarifies the distinctive methodology and standards of objectivity within such disciplines as history, classical and literary studies, anthropology and psychology.

In order to lay 'a foundation for the study of society and history',[14] it is important to recognize the different grounds of objectivity in the human sciences. Unlike the kind of objects studied by astronomy, mechanics or other physical sciences, human beings have both mental and physical attributes and must therefore be studied in a different way. Since the defining feature of human experience is its historicity, it is historical knowledge which is central to an understanding of the human sciences more generally. Recalling Kant's famous critique of pure or theoretical reason, Dilthey describes his project as a critique of historical reason, which is designed to set the limits and establish the fundamental principles of historical understanding.

Dilthey describes two contrasting approaches to the acquisition of knowledge as 'explanation' (*Erklären*) and 'understanding' (*Verstehen*). Explanation is the primary goal of the natural sciences and involves the formulation of general causal laws: 'By an explanatory science we understand the subsumption of a range of phenomena under a causal nexus by means of a limited number of unambiguously defined elements (i.e. constituents of the nexus).'[15] Explanatory science is obviously the main concern of Kant's critique of pure reason as well as the dominant model of knowledge for positivism. Explanation, however, is not by itself an adequate model for the human sciences, whose 'object' of study is humanity itself. Human beings have a physical existence and, to that extent, can be studied by the methods of explanatory science. But the human sciences are more concerned with the various expressions of mind or spirit. The human sciences deal with actions, utterances, institutions and artefacts which, unlike events in the physical world, have intrinsic meaning and so call for a different cognitive approach: 'We call the process by which we recognize some inner content from signs received by the senses *understanding*. . . . Understanding is the process of recognizing a mental state from a sense-given sign by which it is expressed.'[16] Where understanding forms part of a 'systematic process with a controllable degree of objectivity', Dilthey talks about 'interpretation'.[17] Understanding is concerned with the recovery of meanings rather than the identification of causal regularities. It is not concerned with generalization, but with the description of the individual in its full complexity and particularity: 'We explain nature; man we must understand.'[18]

In our attempts to understand human beings as opposed to physical events, we seem to have the advantage that we already know how our own minds work. Dilthey embraces 'Vico's principle that the mind can understand what the mind has created' and 'uses our immediate awareness of how our minds work as a key to unlock the impersonal world of mind'.[19] Certainly, it seems that we could never understand the emotions of others if we did not have emotions ourselves. But by the same token, our knowledge of ourselves is imperfect, if we cannot compare ourselves to others: '[T]he inner experience in which I become aware of my own states can never by itself make me conscious of my own individuality. It is only in comparing myself with others that I come to experience what is individual in myself.' But our access to the mental life of others is not direct. It is mediated by the various external manifestations of mind: '[T]he existence of others is in the first instance given to us only from without, in facts of sensation, in gestures, sounds, and actions. It is only by reconstructing that which thus falls under the observation of our senses in particular signs that we add this inner reality.'[20] The various 'expressions of life' are only encountered to the extent that they are externalized or objectified as 'objectifications of the mind'. These can take an immense variety of forms, including written documents, financial accounts and official reports, letters, works of literature or art, buildings, archaeological remains, gestures and so on. Together, these form the basis of our knowledge of other human beings.

In order to analyse what is involved in the process of understanding objectifications of the mind, Dilthey builds on the discipline of 'hermeneutics'. In fact, hermeneutics, in the sense of systematic reflection on the practice of interpretation or understanding, has a long history in Western culture. The term derives from the ancient Greek word for interpretation (*hermeneuein*), which is related etymologically to the god Hermes – in Greek mythology, the bringer of messages and inventor of language and writing.[21] In the second century AD Artemidorus wrote a learned treatise on the interpretation of dreams, which were widely regarded as messages from the gods, and even then was able to draw on a considerable range of sources. Artemidorus describes how these often unhelpfully opaque messages from the gods can be deciphered.[22] With the advent of Christianity, problems of biblical exegesis became the major spur to the development of hermeneutic principles. The spread of Protestantism, which encouraged a more critical attitude to the authority of the church, made the interpretation of particular passages from the Bible a matter of widespread concern. Hermeneutic manuals, produced mainly for Protestant pastors, spread throughout Europe during the second half of the seventeenth century.[23] In Germany, Herder's thought itself helped to foster further hermeneutic reflection, particularly in the work of Friedrich Ast (1778–1841) and Friedrich August Wolf (1759–1824).[24]

Dilthey, however, was most directly influenced by the philosopher and theologian, Friedrich Schleiermacher (1768–1834). Initially, hermeneutic techniques were designed to overcome obvious difficulties or failures of understanding, typically when passages from a religious text were found to be obscure or inconsistent. Schleiermacher realized that the fact that we are unconscious of obscurities or inconsistencies in a text is no guarantee that our interpretation of seemingly clear passages is correct. Understanding is always potentially mistaken because we can never assume that familiar words mean what we think they do when they occur in a historical text. As Linge puts it: 'Misunderstanding arises naturally because of the changes in word meanings, world views, and so on that have taken place in the time separating the author from the interpreter. Intervening historical developments are a snare that will inevitably entangle understanding unless their effects are neutralized.'[25] Hermeneutic principles are therefore called upon whenever we seek understanding, not just when we experience difficulties. Like Schleiermacher, too, Dilthey stresses the interdependence of parts and whole in his account of the process of interpretation:

> Here we encounter the general difficulty of all interpretation. The whole of a work must be understood from individual words and their combination but full understanding of an individual part presupposes understanding of the whole. This circle is repeated in the relation of an individual work to the mentality and development of its author, and it recurs again in the relation of such an individual work to its literary genre.[26]

What has become known as the 'hermeneutic circle' is a fundamental and unavoidable feature of interpretation as well as a recurring motif of continental philosophy. Evidently, we cannot achieve an adequate understanding of the individual components of a text (words or phrases) without understanding the text as a whole. The same words, or even sentences, mean different things in different contexts. We only become confident of a particular interpretation when we see how it fits with the rest of the text. But obviously we cannot understand the text as a whole without some understanding of its parts. The interdependence of whole and parts reflects the fact that the elements making up a text cannot be analysed as discrete and independent parts in the way that the physical elements of a mechanical system seemingly can be. Meanings and words behave in significantly holistic ways. By implication, the practice of interpretation is irreducibly circular. As Dilthey's remark also makes plain, the 'wholes' in terms of which meanings must be understood are also various. Individual authors use language in distinctive or even idiosyncratic ways, so knowledge of the author's *oeuvre* is an indispensable aspect of interpretation. Similarly, we must know to which kind of discourse or *genre* the text belongs. The interpretation of a text depends on whether it is considered as philosophical treatise or comic novel, as camouflaged theology or political polemic. Nor can authors be understood in abstraction from their cultural milieu and historical context. For example, the interpretation of political writings may depend critically and in quite complex ways on assumptions about date of publication and relationship to contemporary events and ideological currents.[27]

To the pessimist, the inevitable circularity of hermeneutic practice might be thought to present an almost insuperable barrier to comprehension. The interpreter seems victim to a vicious and inescapable regress, since understanding the whole is impossible without understanding the parts and an understanding of the parts is impossible without an understanding of the whole. Dilthey is more optimistic about the possibility of objectively valid interpretations. He believes that through 'honest subordination' to the text and extensive knowledge of the totality in which it occurs, the interpreter can achieve an ever-improving, if never perfect, understanding. In fact, in principle it is even possible for interpreters to know the author better than he or she knows him- or herself. A rigorous process of interpretation 'will enable the student to recover, re-enact, or even re-experience the original meanings, or at least come very close to this ideal'.[28] Dilthey's faith in the possibility of objectively true or valid interpretations depends on the assumption of a common humanity, underlying the variety of human language, culture and personality. In understanding, 'the personalities of the interpreter and his author do not confront each other as two facts which cannot be compared: both have been formed by a common human nature and this makes common speech and understanding among men possible.'[29] This assumption of a common human nature is not necessarily incompatible with Dilthey's belief in the historical constitution of humanity, since the characteristics he supposes to be universal to humanity are relatively abstract ones. He claims only that 'mind has an innate structure which gives rise to typical connections between mental processes', that 'our mental life is purposive', that we express 'our mental states by physical manifestations' and that we both perceive and evaluate the world around us.[30] According to his earlier, more psychologistic formulations, through a kind of empathy the historian can relive or re-experience the thoughts, intentions or feelings of past individuals.

But this approach is vulnerable to charges of subjectivism. It is difficult to reconcile the apparent vagueness and insubstantiality of empathy with the aspiration to objective validity of interpretation. In later writings, influenced by Husserl's strictures against psychologism, Dilthey places more weight on 'the insight that experience itself is organized by symbolic structures' (such as language).[31] The task of hermeneutics is to decode these symbolic structures. Overall, Dilthey still believes that, although 'the results reached in interpretation can never have demonstrative certitude', it is possible for interpreters to overcome their historical situation and achieve valid interpretations.[32] However, even this qualified optimism would be substantially undermined by the subsequent development of hermeneutic theory and philosophy.

Husserl and phenomenology

Throughout his philosophical career, Edmund Husserl (1859–1938) was, like Dilthey, concerned to resist the imperialist tendencies of natural scientific reason, particularly in the area of moral and cultural value. Thus positivism and other forms of 'naturalism' attempt to derive an evaluative philosophy of the world and of life from the findings and methods of natural science alone. The naturalist makes claims to knowledge in questions of value, which cannot be sustained according to his own assumptions and so falls into contradiction: 'The naturalist teaches, preaches, moralizes, reforms. . . . But he denies what every sermon, every demand, if it is to have a meaning, presupposes.'[33] However, despite his hostility to naturalism, Husserl emphatically appreciates the achievements of the 'theoretical attitude' of the natural sciences, products of the strong 'will for rigorous science' that can be traced from Socrates and Plato to Galileo and modern science. For Husserl, it is not the theoretical attitude itself which is suspect. Rather, what is to be resisted is the exclusive identification of rigorous science with the methods of the natural sciences, as a result of their undoubted successes within their proper sphere. 'Spirit' is not of the same order of 'being' as the objects of the natural world and should not be subjected to the same categories of explanation.

What particularly troubles Husserl about naturalism is the cultural scepticism and relativism which, when properly understood, it implies. Husserl is equally unconvinced by Hegel's attempt to overcome relativism by means of a dialectical philosophy of history. It is in this respect that Husserl departs most clearly from Dilthey, whose relativist 'philosophy of worldviews' (*Weltanschauungphilosophie*) was one of the by-products of the decay of the Hegelian system. Indeed, Dilthey's relativism and historicism are held partly to blame for the prevailing cultural atmosphere. Husserl quotes Dilthey's remark that 'the formation of a historical consciousness destroys more thoroughly than does surveying the disagreement of systems a belief in the universal validity of any of the philosophies that have undertaken to express in a compelling manner the coherence of the world by an ensemble of concepts'.[34] Husserl believes that Dilthey fails, in the end, to provide a sufficiently firm bulwark against the relativist force of historical consciousness, because he remains satisfied with a dualism of understanding and explanation, of human and natural sciences. Instead, Husserl believes that the category of understanding can supply a new basis for a single and complete philosophy of the knowing, feeling and acting subject. His strategy is no longer simply, as it was for Dilthey, to secure an autonomous domain for the human sciences free from the universalizing pretensions and reductive categories of the natural sciences. Attacking naturalism on its own ground, he wishes, as Dews puts it, '[to] constitute a new, rigorously scientific philosophy which will place the empirical sciences themselves on an apodictic basis, while at the same time . . . preventing the "objectivist" impetus of the sciences from leading to a culturally disastrous obliteration of awareness of the constituting role of subjectivity'.[35] A new understanding of the subject of consciousness will allow him to refute the pretensions of both naturalism and historicism without relapsing into either Hegelian idealism or irrationalism.

In this ambitious spirit, Husserl makes no concessions to a narrow, positivist conception of rationality. But he is also equally unwilling to relinquish the high aspirations towards rigorous truth implicit in the critical spirit of rationalism. He seeks an account of truth and rationality capable of delivering a rigorously grounded philosophy and, ultimately, a morality too. He asserts the 'imperishable demand for pure and absolute knowledge (and what is inseparably one with that, its demand for pure and absolute valuing and willing)'.[36] Husserl's strategy involves turning the weapons of the sceptic against scepticism. If cultural scepticism is the main problem with both naturalism and historicism, scepticism also provides the basis for a philosophical response to this problem. The critical and sceptical attitude of Enlightenment rationalism must be radicalized. In other words, Descartes's methical doubt is still the model:

[W]ith the radicalism belonging to the essence of genuine philosophical science we accept nothing given in advance, allow nothing traditional to pass as a beginning, nor ourselves to be dazzled by any names however great, but rather seek to attain the beginnings in a free dedication to the problems themselves and to the demands stemming from them.[37]

A rigorous philosophy must be completely free of all presupposition: it can take nothing for granted. In addition, Husserl also accepts (with Descartes, Hume and Kant) the characteristic starting point of modern epistemology, the assumption that the contents of consciousness represent our only certain knowledge.[38]

But Husserl is dissatisfied with the answers of his philosophical forebears to the problem of knowledge, although their various approaches provide him with some important clues. Descartes's method of radical doubt suggests the correct starting point and the overriding principle of a rigorous science free from presuppositions, but Descartes reifies the 'I think' into a 'thinking thing' (*substantia cogitans*) as a kind of 'tag-end of the world' from which the world's reality can be deduced. He fails to make the further step to recognize 'transcendental subjectivity' and so 'does not pass through the gateway that leads into genuine transcendental philosophy'.[39] Kant's transcendental idealism provides the nearest approach to a correct method. Kant, too, starts out from the epistemological premise that we can only have direct knowledge of a 'phenomenal' world of things as they appear to us, and we cannot know with certainty the nature of things as they are 'in themselves'. His crucial insight is that sensations (or 'intuitions') must be organized or 'synthesized' in a certain way if they are to be possible objects of experience for us. Sensations must conform to certain formal features of the mind or subject of experience. Specifically, experience must be organized in terms of categories (e.g. causality and substance), which constitute the objective world as it appears to us. These features of the subject are transcendental, in that they are what make our experience of an objective world possible and so must be conceived as prior to that experience. Kant believes that we can know that we inhabit a world of causally interrelated objects in space and time, because, as transcendental subjects of experience, we must experience the world in that way.[40]

But Husserl is not satisfied with Kant's solution either. Kant's subject of experience is still no more than an abstract and unknowable 'unity of apperception', the mere basis for the attribution of 'my' experiences to an identifiable subject or 'I'. What Kant derives from this conception of the subject is an argument for the necessity of the structure of the objective world discovered by natural science. Once this 'transcendental deduction' has been achieved, no richer conception of consciousness or experience is pursued. Because he identifies the possibility of objective experience with the possibility of scientific knowledge, Kant remains, according to Husserl, confined within a philosophical 'objectivism', which neglects the full contribution of consciousness and subjectivity. As a result, Kant still ends up offering succour to positivism and naturalism.[41] With Kant's philosophical successors, these tendencies become more obvious. Still, despite these criticisms, Husserl proposes to pursue Kant's transcendental exploration of the constitution of our experience. He is still a transcendental philosopher: throughout his philosophical career Husserl will investigate 'the relationship . . . between the subjectivity of knowing and the objectivity of the content known'.[42] All knowledge is founded on the achievements of an 'object-constituting subjectivity' (*leistende Subjektivität*). Husserl cites St Augustine's dictum: 'The truth is not to be found in the external world; it resides in the interiority of Man.'[43]

In contrast to Kant, though, Husserl focuses much more fixedly, even obsessively, on the subject of experience, providing an elaborate description of the nature of consciousness in order to elucidate the notions of subject, object and the 'intentional' relation of the subject to the object. At first Husserl did not clearly distinguish his own approach from a psychological or, to his critics, 'psychologistic' approach. For the naturalistic temper of late nineteenth-century Europe, experimental psychology provided the obvious route to a scientific solution of philosophical problems. After all, psychology is the scientific study of conscious or psychic phenomena, and Husserl had come to the conclusion that the nature of consciousness was the key to the conundrum of epistemology. Husserl was forced to distinguish his own approach to consciousness from a psychological one, as a result of the response to his early work on the foundations of arithmetic. In his *Philosophy of Arithmetic* (1891) he provides a genetic account of the psychological processes through which the concept of number is acquired. Husserl's work was sharply criticized by Gottlob Frege (1848–1925), a major figure in the development of analytical philosophy, as a form of psychologism. Rather than provide an adequate analysis of the necessary truths of arithmetic, Husserl had psychologistically reduced them to the status of contingent and therefore falsifiable generalizations from experience.[44] It was soon obvious to Husserl that experimental psychology, which simply correlates mental or psychic states with physical or neurological ones, could never resolve the problem of epistemology. Naturalistic psychology presupposes nature as an objective external reality and so cannot, without circularity, support arguments for the existence of an external world: '[E]very psychological judgment involves the existential positing of physical nature, whether expressly or not.' A psychological epistemology can never be more than just another manifestation of naturalism.[45]

On the other hand, while accepting these criticisms of psychologism, Husserl still thought that Frege and others were neglecting the 'noetic conditions' or 'subjective aspect of knowledge'.[46] Husserl's attempt to provide a closer examination of the nature of consciousness without succumbing to psychologism takes advantage of the work of his former teacher Franz Brentano (1838–1917). In *Psychology from an Empirical Standpoint* (1874), Brentano argues that the experimental psychology of his day inevitably fails to capture the specific and distinctive properties of consciousness. He is equally sceptical of 'introspectionist' psychology, which seeks to derive knowledge of consciousness from the psychologist's observation of his own mental states. Introspectionist psychology fails to recognize the essential difference between the observation of physical events and the introspection by the psychologist of her own mental states. With mental phenomena, the act of observing inevitably distorts its object: '[T]he attempt to observe, say, our anger – to concentrate our attention upon it – at once, he says, destroys it.'[47] The reliability of introspection is also something which, by definition, cannot be checked by other observers, as is the case with our knowledge of external reality. As Husserl puts it, psychical phenomena are pure phenomena which have no possibility of 'presenting themselves in experience according to diversely varying "subjective appearances"'.[48] Brentano proposes instead what he calls 'descriptive psychology', which depends on a distinction between the 'perception' and the 'observation' of mental phenomena. The introspectionist psychologist simply observes his or her own mental states. The psychologist's observation amounts to a further mental state, which has the original mental state as its object and which, as we have seen, is intrinsically unreliable. Perception, on the other hand, is something which accompanies or is an element of every mental state and so does not involve this problematic supplement. According to Passmore's helpful explanation, 'each mental act perceives itself directly as its "second object" – not as an "appearance", not as something from which the real character of the mental act has to be inferred, but precisely as that mental act actually is.' Perception provides the psychologist with 'an immediate and direct apprehension of the realities which constitute his subject matter'.[49]

Brentano derives the related (and more graspable) principle of the 'intentionality' of consciousness from the scholastic tradition in which he trained as priest. According to this principle, it is distinctive of mental or psychic phenomena that they are 'directed towards an object', that they 'refer to a content' or 'object':

> Every mental phenomenon includes something as object within itself, although they do not all do so in the same way. In presentation something is presented, in judgement something is affirmed or denied, in love loved, in hate hated, in desire desired and so on . . .
> This intentional in-existence is characteristic exclusively of mental phenomena. No physical phenomenon exhibits anything like it.[50]

I remember my great-aunt, I am afraid of the bull, I decide to write a book – in each case the mental state cannot be described without reference to a particular object or content, indicated by the phrases 'my great-aunt', 'the bull' and 'to write a book'. Significantly, the intentional object is not the same as some physical thing in the world (e.g. the bull). This is obvious in the case of mental states whose objects do not, or even could not, correspond to existing entities: consider thoughts about destroyed buildings, David Copperfield, unicorns or four-sided triangles. Thoughts about numbers, logical relations and abstract entities such as anger, jealousy or inventiveness present similar problems. In order to describe the special status of the objects of mental acts, Brentano speaks of their 'intentional in-existence' or 'immanent objectivity' in consciousness. But he also seeks to avoid any idealist misreading of such phrases, to the effect that even 'physical phenomena' are only thought to exist 'in the mind'.[51] The concern with the existential status of such abstract objects of mental states as numbers, relations, universals and impossible objects provided the impetus for Husserl's work on the foundations of arithmetic and mathematics.[52]

Husserl applies Brentano's conception of descriptive psychology to what he regards as the only feasible approach to the epistemological problem. This is the examination of consciousness itself as the only thing which is indubitable. In order to understand the nature of consciousness as 'object-constituting subjectivity', we need to enter the realm of 'pure' or 'transcendental' consciousness, so that the world can then be described 'in all its essential aspects . . . and without bias'.[53] In Husserl's terms, we must examine consciousness 'phenomenologically' or, in other words, as it appears or as pure phenomenon.[54] At the same time, we must rigorously avoid all assumptions about the existence of physical objects in the world, to which our thoughts are normally taken to refer. This involves the 'bracketing' (*epoché*) of the 'natural attitude': the suspension of all those assumptions about existence, causality and so on, which occur in natural scientific and common-sense explanations of events in the physical world.[55] Phenomenology encourages us to distil what is really given in consciousness from what we normally assume as participants in the natural attitude. It is worth stressing, at this point, that Husserl is not trying to answer the sceptic by identifying indubitable foundations for knowledge, as his Cartesian assumptions and admiration for Descartes might suggest. Rather, he believes that a more adequate understanding of consciousness will not allow the sceptical argument to get going.

Husserl takes Brentano's account of psychology to imply that the phenomenological project is a feasible one. Phenomenology involves perception rather than observation in Brentano's terms. Phenomenology is not another version of introspectionist psychology. The phenomenologist does not observe the individual mental components of an actual stream of consciousness. He 'intuits' the 'essence' or *eidos* of mental phenomena: 'Analyses of perception are then "essential" or "eidetic" analyses.'[56] If this is correct, then there is no intrinsic obstacle to a complete account of the distinctive 'being' of consciousness, because the mental phenomenon as essence is exactly what it appears to be. It does not belong to the order of ordinary physical existence, within which appearance and reality potentially diverge. The mental state as essence is pure phenomenon or appearance. In scholastic terms, mental phenomena have no existence (*existentia*, *Dasein* – lit. 'being there') but only an essence (*essentia* or *Sosein* – lit. 'being thus') which, if it cannot be observed, can at least be intuited: '[I]f phenomena have no nature, they still have an essence, which can be grasped and adequately determined in an immediate seeing. . . . Intuition grasps essence as essential being, and in no way posits being-there.'[57] Consciousness can be intuited as pure phenomenon or 'eidetically'.

The method of 'pure intuition' (or 'essential analysis') of the phenomena of consciousness 'by themselves, in pure immanence' is, in effect, the method of phenomenology. In contrast to 'the psychological point of view in which the glance is directed upon experience as the natural standpoint dictates, upon an experience of joy, for instance, as an *inner state* of feeling of a man or an animal', within the phenomenological point of view 'the glance is directed in reflection upon the absolute pure consciousness, giving us the apperception of an absolute experience in its intimate subjective flow'.[58] Although Husserl's technical terms for the phenomenological method are somewhat arcane, his examples are not always so intimidating. Thus it is pure or unmediated intuition which enables us to distinguish between the essences of sound and colour.[59] Phenomenology is also, as this example suggests, Husserl's solution to the problem of universals. The focus on consciousness as 'object-constituting subjectivity' is the other side of the recognition that 'nominalist' accounts of our ability to use certain concepts – the kind of account favoured by empiricism – are inevitably circular. Nominalist accounts of our ability to use concepts rely on our ability to generalize from experience. Having experienced a number of sensations of, say, objects of a certain colour, we acquire the concept of that colour – the universal 'red'. But, as critics of nominalism have long pointed out, however many experiences we have of red objects, we could not acquire the concept of redness unless we already possessed the ability to classify red objects together or, in other words, knew that all red objects have redness in common. But this presupposes that we already have the concept of redness. Husserl's approach at least has the advantage that it focuses our attention on this fundamental achievement of consciousness.[60]

A more extended description of the phenomenological method renders explicit the relationship Husserl finds between the notion of philosophy without presuppositions, intentionality and the distinctive being of consciousness as pure essence:

> [I]f knowledge theory will nevertheless investigate the problems of the relationship between consciousness and being, it can have before its eyes only beings as the correlate of consciousness, as something 'intended' after the manner of consciousness: as perceived, remembered, expected, represented pictorially, imagined, identified, distinguished, believed, opined, evaluated, etc. It is clear, then, that the investigation must be directed toward a scientific essential knowledge of consciousness, toward that which consciousness itself 'is' according to its essence in all its distinguishable forms. At the same time, however, the investigation must be directed toward what consciousness 'means', as well as toward the different ways in which . . . it intends the objective.[61]

The reference here to what consciousness 'means' recalls Dilthey's use of the hermeneutic method for the understanding of mind or spirit and the meaning of its objectifications. But phenomenology applies concepts reminiscent of hermeneutic ones for more explicitly philosophical purposes. Husserl maintains that our perception and knowledge of the external world, even our most basic logical and mathematical categories, must be grounded phenomenologically in the realm of meanings. The 'contents' of consciousness are to be understood in terms of an order of essences or meanings, rather than, as is more typical within the empiricist tradition, reified as straightforwardly 'thing-like' stand-ins for material objects (as 'copies' or 'effects' of real things, as 'ideas' or 'impressions' or 'sense data' which are 'in the mind'). Hume, in this sense, comes close to the domain of phenomenology but remains within the ban of empiricist psychology – he is 'a psychological philosopher of the school of Locke' who 'almost enters its domain, but his eyes are dazzled'.[62]

Despite its evident rigour and ingenuity, Husserl's programme for philosophy as rigorous science has difficulty in fulfilling its more ambitious aims. Also ironic, perhaps, is the abstraction and abstruseness of Husserl's increasingly refined attempts to grapple directly with 'the things themselves'. The difficulty of realizing the project of pure phenomenology is reflected in some of Husserl's last lectures and writings, collected in *The Crisis of European Sciences and Transcendental Phenomenology*. In a piece written after Hitler's National Socialists had seized power in Germany, Husserl, who was born into a Jewish family but became a Lutheran, returns to themes which preoccupied him throughout his life. As a result of the 'positivistic reduction of the idea of science to mere factual science', science is incapable of grounding human values, explaining human freedom or distinguishing reason from unreason. Scientific reason, in the sense both of the objectivist natural sciences and of the humanistic sciences devoted to value-freedom, 'excludes in principle precisely the questions which man, given over in our unhappy times to the most portentous upheavals, finds the most burning: questions of the meaning or meaninglessness of the whole of this human existence'.[63] However, this loss of meaning is now expressed in the rather different terms of a gulf between the practice of science and a historically unfolding 'life-world'. As Pivčević puts it: '[B]ewilderment about the meaning of science is due to science being divorced from its historical human context.' As a result of this separation, the human world itself is becoming increasingly opaque to us: '[M]odern science, although helping us to understand nature better and to dominate it more successfully, tends to conceal from us the world as our world.'[64]

Husserl's response to the crisis of European sciences is now to focus on the role of the life-world as the basic presupposition of all thought and action. Science and philosophy, in particular, must be understood as practices, which are pursued against 'an unquestioned ground of presuppositions', a background of unreflective assumptions, values and practices, which make up the life-world. In all philosophical and scientific inquiry,

> the everyday surrounding world of life is presupposed as existing – the surrounding world in which all of us (even I who am now philosophizing) consciously have our existence; here are also the sciences as cultural facts in this world, with their scientists and theories. In this world we are objects among objects in the sense of the life-world, namely, as being here and there, in the plain certainty of experience, before anything that is established scientifically, whether in physiology, psychology, or sociology. On the other hand, we are subjects for this world, namely, as the ego-subjects experiencing it, contemplating it, valuing it, related to it purposefully.[65]

Positivism and factual science disrupt these pre-theoretical certainties, in whose terms we have previously led our lives, but without providing us with any more scientifically rigorous basis for life. A more rigorous philosophical understanding of the life-world is not made available to us. It is the task of genuine philosophy to supply such a rigorous understanding, bridging the gulf between science and life-world. Husserl believed he could apply the phenomenological method to this task, providing a phenomenological analysis of the essence 'life-world'. But it is difficult to reconcile the notion of the life-world as an intersubjective and historically situated background to the achievements of the knowing subject with the perspective of transcendental consciousness, which is fundamental to Husserl's earlier formulations of phenomenology. Arguably, in his last works Husserl begins to move beyond the theoretical framework of transcendental phenomenology.[66]

In the end, Husserl's philosophical system, with its ambitious epistemological claims and elaborate technical apparatus, its relentless proliferation of neologistic terms and sometimes abstruse distinctions, has found few followers. It is rather Husserl's idea of going back to the things themselves, of going back to things as they are 'before science and philosophy', which has proved germinal. As Bubner puts it: 'The inheritance of phenomenology has thus consisted for a long time in a certain attitude to the business of philosophizing, not in the completion of Husserl's system.'[67] In the work of Maurice Merleau-Ponty (1908–61), a phenomenological description of the contents of experience and an original critique of experimental psychology provide a suggestive basis for the philosophical discussion of the body, perception, sexuality and gender.[68] In opposition to Husserl's intellectualism, Max Scheler (1874–1928) emphasizes emotions and will, the ethical and the intersubjective. His phenomenological anthropology is based on the interdependence of self and other and a notion of the person as something more than just a knowing subject. Alfred Schütz (1899–1959) adapts the notion of the life-world for a sociological investigation of the common-sense presuppositions of everyday life.[69] But it is above all in the 'ontological hermeneutics' of Heidegger that some of the ideas of Husserl and also Dilthey find their most fertile continuation and development.[70]

Heidegger's phenomenology of being

The writings of Martin Heidegger (1889–1976) represent a significant node within the development of the continental tradition in philosophy.[71] His earlier philosophy left its imprint on existentialism, particularly through the work of Jean-Paul Sartre. Heidegger is also a major point of reference for poststructuralism, deconstruction and postmodernism, but here it is his later work that tends to be most highly regarded. His philosophy affected the Frankfurt School's critique of instrumental reason. Perhaps the most direct lines of descent lead to the philosophical hermeneutics of Gadamer and Derrida's philosophy of deconstruction. Heidegger also brings together a number of important themes from previous philosophy. Like Hegel, he is committed to a view of life and philosophy as essentially historical. For him the practice of philosophy is inseparable from the interpretation of previous philosophical texts. Through the course of his career he wrote major studies of Kant, Nietzsche and Hegel, and his thinking returned continually to the ideas of Socrates, Plato, Aristotle and the pre-Socratics as well as to medieval thinkers such as Duns Scotus. A significant role in Heidegger's philosophy is also played by the history of language. He is not only extremely sensitive to nuances of meaning and association, but he also uses (some would say abuses) words in the light of their etymology (or what he takes their etymology to be).[72] A related dimension of his project is the attempt to recover meanings and insights lost over the course of the Western metaphysical tradition. It is necessary to recover these meanings in order to remedy a basic distortion of that tradition. Heidegger's attempt to overcome Western metaphysical thought is influenced most directly by Husserl, and particularly his diagnosis of the naturalism and scepticism of Western culture. It is also in phenomenology and hermeneutics that Heidegger finds the most useful starting point for an alternative philosophical method.

For Heidegger, the very character of Western metaphysical thought is responsible for the all-pervasive influence of scientific reason and technology, which, in common with Husserl, he regards as an ultimately destructive influence on Western culture. Specifically, Heidegger identifies a pathological distortion in the predominance of what he calls an 'ontotheological' conception of substance as something absolutely unconditional, something which depends on nothing else for its existence.[73] Western metaphysics is governed by the underlying conviction that there must be some being or beings, which are fundamental or 'truly real' in both an explanatory and a justificatory or normative sense. In other words, all other levels or kinds of being are causally dependent on them and all norms and values have their ground or justification in them. The history of Western metaphysics consists of a number of attempts to identify such a fundamental being or beings, from Plato's 'Forms' and Aristotle's 'unmoved mover' to the God of medieval theology and Hegelian 'spirit'. According to Heidegger's account, Western scientific reason sets out from the failure of these attempts. But scientific reason retains the underlying metaphysical conviction that it makes sense to speak, if not of the normative, then at least of the causal foundations of things as absolutely or unconditionally real. The privileging of this scientific 'ontology' – the assumptions of natural science about what really exists – has led to our culture's prejudice in favour of science and scientific method as the only genuine knowledge. In order to challenge the hegemony of scientific reason, then, it is necessary to get down to the most fundamental assumptions of Western metaphysics, where the idea of something as absolutely and unconditionally real first takes root. Heidegger thinks that by taking a different direction at this basic and original level, the level of ontology, it will be possible to exorcize the yearning for absolutes, the longing for ultimate metaphysical foundations.

A central problem with the ontology of scientific reason is the status of the subject. Heidegger believes this has been a problem for ontotheological conceptions of substance since Plato and Aristotle. But it becomes most clearly visible with the philosophers of the modern period and, in particular, with Descartes's dualist metaphysics of mind and matter. Descartes conceives the world as a mechanistic realm of extended material objects, which is mysteriously connected to a spiritual domain of mind or consciousness.[74] The difficulty of explaining how mind and matter can ever interact, already regarded as a major problem by Descartes's contemporaries, is just one consequence of this metaphysics. The inappropriateness of applying natural scientific method to the understanding of an essentially historical mind or spirit was a theme of Dilthey's philosophy of the human sciences. But, as Husserl realized, even human sciences governed by hermeneutic methodology cannot provide a satisfactory basis for values. Historicism is no more able to resist cultural scepticism and nihilism than is scientism. Philosophy, it seems, must provide a radically different account of the subject and subjectivity.

A direct attempt to found value on 'subjective truth' had been made by Søren Kierkegaard, in retrospect often described as the first existentialist.[75] Heidegger's reaction to Kierkegaard's attempt provides a useful introduction to some of his most important ideas. Heidegger acknowledges the importance of both Kierkegaard and life philosophy as responses to the limitations of scientific rationality. But despite their emphasis on the irreducibility of mind, life or existence, they are only 'on the way' to an understanding of life. Kierkegaard's championing of subjective truth, though valuable, is fundamentally limited because he fails to make a sufficiently radical break with Western ontology. In effect, Kierkegaard, like Dilthey, defends the subjective domain of mind or existence from the incursions of scientific reason and its ancestor, ontotheological metaphysical thinking, but he does not fundamentally challenge the ontological basis of science and metaphysics on their own ground. In Heidegger's terms, Kierkegaard does not address the 'question of Being' in all its 'existential' fullness and complexity, because his analysis is merely concerned with the 'existentiell' characteristics of subjective existence:

> In the nineteenth century, Søren Kierkegaard explicitly seized upon the problem of existence as an *existentiell* problem, and thought it through in a penetrating fashion. But the *existential* problematic was so alien to him that, as regards his ontology, he remained completely dominated by Hegel and by ancient philosophy as Hegel saw it.[76]

Heidegger uses the term 'existentiell' to refer to the subjective point of view intrinsic to the existence of conscious beings. An exploration of this perspective does not *ipso facto* illuminate what Heidegger sees as the crucial 'existential' question of 'the ontological structure of existence'.[77] In other words, although Kierkegaard provides important insights into one region of being (subjective existence), he nevertheless fails to pursue the implications of his insights for knowledge, truth and the ontological question of Being (*Sein*) as such.

Heidegger offers a similar diagnosis of Dilthey. He cites approvingly the view of Count Yorck von Wartenburg that Dilthey's investigations of the 'historical' are significant as contributions to a truer philosophical understanding of life, to 'raising up "life" into the kind of scientific understanding that is appropriate to it'. But Dilthey, like other life philosophers, was only 'on his way towards the question of "life"', because he does not mount the required challenge to Western ontology.[78] Any attempt to break the grasp of scientific reason and the category of substance must do more than simply reassert the importance of subjectivity against but, as it were, alongside an objectifying positivism. It is necessary to rethink the fundamental categories of Western thought for the understanding of matter and spirit, body and mind. Within Western metaphysics, scientific rationality's 'objectivist' conception of nature as simply a collection of things is the counterpart of a 'subjectivist' view of mind as disembodied and isolated. In other words, subjectivism and objectivism are contrasting symptoms of the same underlying disorder of Western thinking, what Gadamer has called the ' "objectivistic" subjectivism of the modern age'.[79] It is not enough to reassert the 'subjective' pole of life or existence as a distinct order of being opposed to the 'objective' pole of the being of physical things in space. It is necessary to address the primordial question of Being in general.

In his best-known work, *Being and Time* (1927), Heidegger makes his first determined attempt to 'break away from the traditional domination of western thought by the category of substance (thinghood)'.[80] In effect, he restates Husserl's strategy in his own terms. Where Husserl sought a phenomenological understanding of consciousness as the means to a more adequate understanding of the nature of both 'physical' and 'mental' phenomena, Heidegger similarly attempts to reconcile the 'ontic' and the 'Historical'. To achieve an adequate understanding of life does not involve simply adding to our factual knowledge of the 'ontic' (which includes both everyday, pre-scientific knowledge and the kind of knowledge contributed by natural science). A truer understanding of life can only be achieved 'by bringing both the "ontical" and the "Historical" into a *more primordial unity*, so that they can be compared and distinguished'.[81] In order to realize this goal, Heidegger sets out to determine just what it means for something to be. He calls this the 'question of Being'. This question is so important, because it allows him to connect both 'ontic' and 'Historical' dimensions of inquiry in the appropriate way: 'The idea of Being embraces both the "ontical" and the "Historical". It is *this idea* which must let itself be "generically differentiated".'[82]

In order to address the very abstract question of 'what it means to be', Heidegger believes (at least in his early work) that the question of Being can best be explored by asking what it means to be the kind of being who can ask that question. The question of what it means to be must be asked from the perspective of that 'being for whom Being is a question' or, in other words, from the perspective of human beings. The human being is unique in that he 'not only *is*, but has some understanding of and some responsibility for who he is'.[83] If we are able to pose the question of Being at all, then we must have some implicit understanding of Being already. Heidegger thinks that the content of this understanding is made manifest in human existence. Heidegger's term for human existence – 'This entity which each of us is himself and which includes inquiring as one of the possibilities of its Being' – is '*Dasein*'. Literally 'being there' (but also 'being *here*'), *Dasein* is the German scholastic term for 'existence' as opposed to 'essence' (*Sosein* or 'being thus').[84] It was already apparent to the scholastic philosophy of the Middle Ages that the existence or 'substance' of a thing is fundamentally different from its essence – its qualities or attributes. In the terms used by Kant (and taken up in the predicate calculus of modern symbolic logic), 'existence is not a predicate'.[85] Heidegger's use of the term *Dasein* is, however, much more specific. He builds on the idea, already articulated by Kierkegaard and other thinkers, that human existence is something radically different from the mere subsistence of ordinary things. The term *Dasein* is reserved for distinctively human existence. Thus *Dasein* is to be the key to the meaning of Being in general.

In order to provide a description of *Dasein* as the key to the understanding of Being, Heidegger assumes the phenomenologist's stance of describing the world and reality as they are experienced. But he is concerned to avoid falling into the same traps as previous phenomenologists. In particular, he is determined to avoid any view of consciousness as simply the abstract bearer and organizer of experience. Accordingly, Heidegger describes *Dasein* as irreducibly situated and intersubjective. *Dasein* is from the beginning both 'Being-in-the-world' and 'Being-with-others'. Consciousness is not primarily or originally a detached and abstract bearer and organizer of experience. Rather, it is something which can only be such a bearer of experience against the background of a certain understanding of what it is to be, of the individual subject as person or individual. In other words, Heidegger is describing what Husserl discusses in his last work as the life-world. *Dasein* thus bears no resemblance to the detached and contemplative consciousness or '*theoria*' of the Western philosophical tradition.

The primary relationship of *Dasein* to the world is one of practical, personal involvement or 'care' (*Sorge*) – 'the Being of *Dasein* itself is to be made visible as *care*'.[86] We do not originally encounter the world as detached observers but as involved participants, for whom things in the world are 'ready-to-hand' (*zuhanden*) rather than simply 'present-at-hand' (*vorhanden*). Things exist originally as tools or 'equipment' we can use in particular ways. Equipment always exists in relation to other things in an 'arrangement' corresponding to a range of related practices.[87] The world is originally and, for Heidegger, fundamentally constituted as a practical totality. The objectivity of the world is first conveyed to us through its resistance to desire and will. By contrast, the presence-at-hand of objects is a secondary or derivative mode of being, corresponding to the contemplative attitude of scientific theory – an attitude which is secondary to the originally practical relationship of care. In these terms, the Western metaphysical tradition goes astray by treating what is fundamentally readiness-to-hand as if it were presence-at-hand. Crucially, it is impossible to think of the situated *Dasein* of Heidegger's ontology as a detached observer of the world like the Cartesian ego: 'Being-in-the-world is a structure which is primordially and constantly *whole*.'[88] *Dasein*, as 'being-there', is inseparable from the world, and so it is essentially Being-in-the-world. It is equally important to realize that, by implication, the world is just as inseparable from the idea of conscious existence as *Dasein* is inseparable from the world. Heidegger's radical challenge to the 'objectivistic subjectivism' of Western metaphysics, which treats subjective and objective realms as detached and essentially unrelated dimensions of reality, could not be more apparent.

By the same token, *Dasein* is primordially 'Being-with-others'. If our primary relationship to the world is the practical relationship typified by work, then in our encounters with ready-to-hand tools or products we also encounter the others, for whom these products are made or who supplied the materials we are using.[89] In his discussion of Being-with-others, Heidegger again makes clear that he wishes to avoid the solipsistic predicament. He does not propose to 'start by marking out and isolating the "I" so that one must then seek some way of getting over to the Others from this isolated subject': 'the world is always the one that I share with Others'.[90] Just as the fundamental relationship of *Dasein* to the world is care, so the primordial relationship to others (as *Dasein*) is one of 'solicitude' (*Fürsorge*). But crucially, the relationship of *Dasein* with others also brings with it the possibility of 'inauthenticity'. Although it is possible for *Dasein* to be with others authentically, the relationship with others is also the basis for an inauthentic relationship of conformity to the 'they' (*das Man*).

> We take pleasure and enjoy ourselves as *they* [*man*] take pleasure; we read, see, and judge about literature and art as *they* see and judge; likewise we shrink back from the 'great mass' as *they* shrink back; we find 'shocking' what *they* find shocking. The 'they', which is nothing definite, and which all are, though not as the sum, prescribes the kind of Being of everydayness.[91]

In effect, Heidegger restates in ontological terms criticisms of mass society, which play a significant role in the writings of existentialists such as Kierkegaard and Nietzsche. When *Dasein* is subjected to an impersonalized other, its own authentic selfhood is lost.

The possibility of authentic or inauthentic relationships to others highlights a crucial dimension of *Dasein*, namely its directedness to future possibilities and projects. Unlike other entities, *Dasein* has no determinate essence. Put another way, *Dasein* is distinguished by its freedom to make itself: '*Dasein* always understands itself in terms of its existence – in terms of a possibility of itself: to be itself or not itself . . . *Dasein* is an entity whose Being has the determinate character of existence.'[92] In other words, human beings are free to make or remake themselves. They do not simply fulfil a predetermined 'essence' as, it seems, plants or animals must do. If human beings embrace their freedom, they have the possibility of authentic existence. If they do not, they fall into inauthenticity and are, in Heidegger's terms, 'fallen'. Fallenness is absorption in the everyday, in the present and in the conformity of the 'they'. It involves abdication of that freedom and possibility intrinsic to authentic *Dasein*. It is that kind of Being-in-the-world 'which is completely fascinated by the "world" and by the *Dasein*-with of Others in the "they"'.[93] Free or fallen, authentic or inauthentic, these possibilities of *Dasein* reflect the historicity and temporality of human existence. Human projects are aimed at the future. It is a feature of consciousness that we can formulate projects, that our actions are aimed at goals in the future. Equally, our projects are inevitably limited by the 'facticity' of the situation we inherit from the past. Our freedom is a situated one, in the sense that not all projects are available to us as possibilities.

But why are we constantly tempted to relinquish authentic existence and to abdicate our freedom? The reason is that authentic existence – an existence lived in the full awareness of our freedom to act, to realize our own projects rather than the projects of the 'they'

– is an extremely arduous state. Awareness of freedom is inseparable from anxiety. It is much easier simply to 'go with the flow' and to conform to the everyday. Authentic *Dasein* is possible only with intense awareness of the ever-present possibility of death. In an important sense, 'Care is Being-towards-death.'[94] Like Kierkegaard, Heidegger sees awareness of the prospect of our own death as an important condition of a genuinely authentic existence. Death forces us to confront our evasion of the most important questions, our absorption in the trivia of everyday life. The awareness of death can awaken us from the conformist forgetfulness of the everyday, from our fallen state of 'fleeing in the face of death': 'Death is a possibility-of-Being which *Dasein* itself has to take over in every case. With death, *Dasein* stands before itself in its ownmost potentiality-for-Being. . . . If *Dasein* stands before itself as this possibility, it has been *fully* assigned to its ownmost potentiality-for-Being.'[95] More prosaically, our awareness of death helps us to live more authentically.

Being and Time exerted a profound influence on continental philosophy (at roughly the same time as it became, for the logical positivists, the favourite example of the meaninglessness of metaphysics). Ironically, though, this work was understood at first mainly as a sophisticated statement of existentialism and, as a result, it contributed substantially to the vocabulary of existentialist philosophers such as Jean-Paul Sartre. This reception effectively ignored Heidegger's claim that the main purpose of the exploration of human existence as *Dasein* was the illumination of the deeper question of Being in general. It is a matter of some controversy whether *Being and Time* ultimately fails to fulfil this ambitious goal and relapses into something more like an existentialist exploration of subjective truth (of the 'existentiell' rather than the 'existential').[96] It is a matter of further controversy whether Heidegger's later writings represent the continuation of his earlier philosophy or a radical change of direction and 'turning' (*Kehre*) away from it.[97] Certainly, in the later work what many had taken to be an existentialist preoccupation with individual existence as anxious, caring, authentic or fallen *Dasein* gives way to a more impersonal preoccupation with Being. Heidegger places increasing emphasis on the importance of diverting our 'thinking' from its individualistic concerns, from the concerns of the subject of consciousness, towards a greater 'attentiveness' to Being. Only by transcending the limited perspective of the Cartesian subject, 'who may deign to release the beingness of beings into an all too loudly bruited "objectivity"', can 'thinking' 'realize the proper dignity of man' as 'the shepherd of Being'.[98] The 'subjectivism' exemplified in Enlightenment epistemology is still the counterpart of that 'forgetfulness of Being', for which the world is simply a collection of things present-at-hand.

Accompanying what is at least a significant change of emphasis, there is in Heidegger's later writings an overriding preoccupation with language as 'the house of Being'.[99] With this idea Heidegger comes close to restating the themes of philosophical idealism. The world is inseparable from our conceiving of a world: there is only the indivisible being-in-the-world. But our conception of the world is inextricably tied to our language. This train of thought leads Heidegger to a distinctive account of truth. He suggests an alternative and more literal translation of '*aletheia*', the Greek word normally translated as 'truth', as 'unconcealment'.[100] In these terms language is clearly inseparable from truth, because it is language which 'discloses' Being or 'brings it into the open': '[L]anguage alone brings beings as beings into the open for the first time. Where there is no language, as in the Being of stone, plant, and animal, there is also no openness of beings, and consequently no openness either of nonbeing and of the empty.'[101] Language is the 'clearing' of Being, the possibility of Being's unconcealment. Once again, Heidegger speaks of language rather than consciousness here, in order to avoid falling into the familiar metaphysical pitfalls of subject and object. Language unmistakably transcends the individual subject, transcends individual consciousness and existence. At the same time, Heidegger becomes increasingly preoccupied with poetic and creative uses of language. The true philosopher is the poet who, through a 'projective saying', allows new aspects of Being to reveal themselves: 'The essence of art is poetry. The essence of poetry, in turn, is the founding of truth.'[102] Needless to say, the truth of poetry is not to be confused with the merely factual truths of scientific discourse.

Gadamer and the universality of hermeneutics

Thus there is undoubtedly no understanding that is free of all prejudices, however much the will of our knowledge must be directed toward escaping their thrall. Throughout our investigation it has emerged that the certainty achieved by using scientific methods does not suffice to guarantee truth. This especially applies to the human sciences, but it does not mean that they are less scientific; on the contrary, it justifies the claim to special humane significance that they have always made. The fact that in such knowledge the knower's own being comes into play certainly shows the limits of method, but not of science. Rather, what the tool of method does not achieve must – and really can – be achieved by a discipline of questioning and inquiring, a discipline that guarantees truth.[103]

Gadamer's philosophical hermeneutics grows directly from the philosophy of Heidegger. Like the *later* Heidegger, however, Gadamer is more immediately concerned with language, interpretation and art than with the explicitly ontological question of the meaning of 'being'. On the other hand, although issues concerning the nature and possibility of interpreting or understanding works of art and texts clearly lie at the heart of his philosophy, Gadamer still develops an ontological rather than merely epistemological hermeneutics. In Palmer's words, understanding is 'not conceived as a subjective process of man over and against an object but the way of being of man himself'.[104] That is to say, Gadamer is concerned with hermeneutics not, like Dilthey, as the characteristic method of the human sciences, but as the key to the nature of truth in understanding and interpretation and, related to this, the nature of human, historical existence. In other words, he adopts from Heidegger the idea that understanding and interpretation, as these are practised in the so-called human sciences or *Geisteswissenschaften*, are simply a more explicit form of an activity which we are engaged in all the time. Understanding is the basic way in which self-conscious, historically existing beings relate to the world. Understanding has ontological significance. Thus Gadamer responds to the universalist pretension of natural scientific reason with an ontological hermeneutics whose claims are no less universal. Hermeneutic categories are regarded as fundamental, not merely to specific cognitive enterprises such as history, aesthetic appreciation and legal interpretation, but rather to the very nature of self-consciousness and of the world as our world.

Gadamer shares with the hermeneutic tradition as a whole the belief that understanding, this most fundamental dimension of human existence, cannot be made sense of within the categories of the 'methodical' natural sciences. It is particularly important, in this context, that the conjunction of the terms 'truth' and 'method' in the title of Gadamer's best-known work, *Truth and Method*, is not misunderstood. A method, in Gadamer's terms, is a set of explicit procedures or rules designed to purge knowledge of all distorting or idiosyncratic subjective influences. Bacon and Descartes proposed a method in just this sense as the only reliable means of securing objectivity in the natural sciences. But Gadamer does not seek to formulate an equivalent method for the human sciences in order to secure the objectivity of its interpretations in analogous fashion. This, in effect, was the project of Dilthey. On the contrary, Gadamer's aim is to demonstrate the limits of methodical science. While the idea of method plays a valid role in natural sciences such as physics or chemistry, it cannot account for the practice of interpretation or understanding within the human sciences. These 'non-methodical' sciences can achieve truth only by renouncing all claims to methodical objectivity and relying instead upon the fundamental human capacity for understanding. What is more (and as we shall see in more detail in what follows), according to Gadamer, even the methodical natural sciences ultimately have their foundation in this hermeneutic capacity. As some commentators have suggested, therefore, truth *or* method might have been a less misleading title. In Bubner's words, Gadamer's project is 'a matter of explicating the *reciprocal relations between methodical science* and an *original truth* which transcends the methodical'; as such it is a 'reflection on . . . methodological dogmatism'.[105]

In order to overcome the dogmatism of method, Gadamer, again like Heidegger, seeks to displace the subject from its pivotal position in the Western philosophical tradition. In particular, he denies the subject that radical epistemological autonomy which modern philosophy since Descartes has tended to accord to it. The Cartesian view of the subject, together with the associated conviction that the knowing subject is capable of, and ought to strive for, absolutely certain knowledge, goes hand in hand with the glorification of an objectifying scientific knowledge and a manipulative, instrumental stance towards nature.[106] The characteristically modern celebration of humanity, which is considered capable of a comprehensive and objective scientific knowledge of nature, ultimately involves the 'dominance of the human subject and its calculating techniques and methods over the world considered as a realm of things'.[107] The exaggerated role accorded to the subject ultimately explains modern philosophy's tendency to reify nature as a realm of mere objects. What is worse, the untrammelled expansion of this calculating reason threatens to reduce human beings to the same condition as well.

In fact, of course, Husserl too had recognized the interdependent objectivism and subjectivism of modern thought. But for Gadamer, Husserl remains under the spell of his Cartesian and Kantian heritage. Husserl's starting point within transcendental consciousness condemns him to an endless replaying of dilemmas familiar from foundationalist epistemology. Despite the subtlety of his analyses, he never really escapes the labyrinth. Husserl comes closest to overcoming the standpoint of subjective consciousness with his concept of the life-world. But he still refuses to relinquish the standpoint of transcendental consciousness, insisting instead on a phenomenological account of the essence 'life-world' from the point of view of transcendental consciousness.[108] It is clear to Gadamer, on the other hand, that, properly understood, 'the notion of the "life-world" has a revolutionary power that explodes the framework of Husserl's transcendental thinking'.[109] There can be no transcendental perspective on the life-world because all our thinking inevitably occurs within, and so is necessarily conditioned by, the life-world. Philosophy must follow Heidegger's lead and turn, without either metaphysical preconceptions or transcendental pretensions, to the exploration of the life-world itself as the historical and intersubjective horizon of all human experience.

The recognition of the life-world as the unsurpassable horizon of all human experience and activity has radical implications for hermeneutics as well as for philosophy. According to Gadamer, previous theorists of hermeneutics had, despite their valuable contributions, failed to recognize the universality of its claims. Certainly with Schleiermacher, hermeneutics, which had previously been no more than a collection of disparate techniques for the interpretation of obscure or broken passages in ancient texts, was turned into a more organized procedure for securing the objectivity of interpretations. Schleiermacher recognized that hermeneutics was needed even when we experience no difficulty of understanding. We often merely think that we understand when in fact we do not, because we fail to recognize changes in the meaning of terms that have come to be used in different ways. Dilthey systematically developed this conception of hermeneutics as a methodical procedure for overcoming the subjective limitations of understanding in the historical and human sciences. But for Gadamer, Dilthey remains too close to the dogmatism of method. He remains wedded to the traditional model of method as a reliable instrument capable of generating objective truth, because he fails to recognize the full implications of acknowledging the subjective pole of understanding, still regarding the subjective and historically located point of view of the interpreter as simply an obstacle to be overcome on the path to objective knowledge. Dilthey, on Gadamer's reading, believes that 'scientific knowledge obliges one to sever one's bond with life, to attain distance from one's own history, which alone makes it possible for that history to become an object'.[110]

For Gadamer, by contrast, the subjective and historical foundation of understanding is not something to be eliminated or overcome in this way. Understanding is always inevitably *for* a subject as much as it is *of* some object; and it is inevitable that 'in such knowledge the knower's own being comes into play'.[111] Recognizing this subjective pole of understanding means acknowledging that even mutual understanding *within* a particular cultural horizon can never be taken for granted. Even the *interpretation* of an historical text has itself to be understood by the interpreter's contemporaries. The interpretation is, strictly speaking, no more self-evident than the text whose meaning it claims to capture. Linge elucidates this 'reflexive dimension' of understanding as follows: 'The familiar horizons of the interpreter's world, though perhaps more difficult to grasp thematically, are as integral a part of the event of understanding as are the explicit procedures by which he assimilates the alien object.'[112] The interpreter's subjectivity occurs within a present horizon of meanings and pre-judgements or what Gadamer calls 'prejudices', which is as much a part of history – and as vulnerable to the vicissitudes of misunder-standing – as the historical texts studied by interpreters working within that horizon. In other words, historicity characterizes not just the object but also the subject of acts of understanding. There is no fixed, 'transcendental' pole of subjectivity capable of sustaining the possible objectivity of interpretation in the way that methodical dog-matism requires. Understanding always inevitably occurs within a historically situated, intersubjective life-world which itself depends on the achievement of understanding.

One corollary of this recognition of the essentially historical char-acter of subjectivity is the unattainability of the Enlightenment's conception of science as a reliable method leading to an objective knowledge purified of all presupposition and prejudice. As Gadamer provocatively asserts, 'there is undoubtedly no understanding that is free of all prejudices'.[113] Every interpretation is liable not only to the difficulties of understanding an object obscured by distance and time, but also to the limitations implied by the historical situation of the subject of understanding. The interpreter's point of view is not some-thing which can ever be escaped, however much we must also dili-gently try to do so. We are products of a particular history and tradition just as much as we are interpreters of other historical tradi-tions. History is not simply an object to be known; history is also what has made us into the particular 'subjects' who attempt to under-stand it. Accordingly, there can be no such thing as a hermeneutic method, only what Gadamer describes as 'a discipline of questioning and inquiring'.[114] But by the same token, the fundamental importance of the discipline of interpretation must also be recognized. Even the cognitive activities of natural scientists must occur within the horizon of a particular conceptual structure, a particular conception of knowl-edge, truth and scientific practice. The usefulness of the methods employed by the specialized sciences is not disputed here, only their claim to stand outside a linguistically constituted and hermeneutically grounded intersubjectivity. The specialized sciences presuppose the life-world and the hermeneutic capacities on which it depends. So these sciences cannot, as philosophical naturalism would have it, either ground the hermeneutic categories of the life-world or replace them with scientifically 'purified' categories of their own. On the contrary, we must acknowledge that hermeneutics gives access to truth in its own right, even though, in fact only on condition that, it does not aspire to the status of an objective method.

Gadamer's ontological construal of understanding also corresponds to a revised account of the *practice* of interpretation, albeit an account that is as important for its illumination of human being-in-the-world as for any light cast on our more specifically hermeneutic activities. In the first place, there can be no uniquely true interpretation for any particular text – though there can certainly be better and worse or incorrect interpretations. Because it is always a question of understanding some meaning from the perspective of a particular historically situated interpretive horizon, understanding is irreducibly relational. At best there can be the correct interpretation from that perspective, which can coexist with different interpretations from other perspectives. Hermeneutics is always the link between two horizons rather than, as Schleiermacher and Dilthey thought, something which can in principle restore a forgotten text to the pristine clarity of an original meaning. We can only avoid distorting truth for the sake of such unattainable ideals of scientific objectivity if we recognize that we always seek understanding *from* as well as *of* a particular situation and horizon. Significantly, here, the complementary concepts of situation and horizon are to be understood positively as well as negatively. The possibility of vision, too, is inseparable from the idea of a particular perspective or situation which also limits vision. A situation is 'a standpoint that limits the possibility of vision', but situation also implies a 'range of vision that includes everything that can be seen from a particular vantage point'.[115]

A further aspect of the practice of interpretation derives from the fact that the questions and concerns that we bring to the study of historical texts (and which make up our horizon of understanding) must themselves be seen as, at least in part, the product of the tradition which these texts helped to form. History 'determines in advance both what seems to us worth inquiring about and what will appear as an object of investigation'.[116] If we deny the effect of our history, we risk once again falling into a false objectivism which, like statistics, is such good propaganda because it appears to 'let the "facts" speak' at the same time as it organizes them in terms of a particular set of questions and concerns. Instead, 'we should learn to understand ourselves better and recognize that in all understanding, whether we are expressly aware of it or not, the efficacy of history is at work.'[117] Interpretation serves the interests and concerns of the present as much as it is directed towards the past, but we must also recognize that these concerns have themselves been shaped by the past and by tradition. It is in this sense that Gadamer speaks of the importance of the 'history of effect' (*Wirkungsgeschichte*) of the text, or, in other words, the way the text has taken effect in history and helped to shape the present.[118]

It is also important for Gadamer that this 'history of effect' should be regarded positively. The act of interpretation should not be seen, in the way Dilthey and historicism tended to do, as simply the more or less successful recovery of a meaning lost or obscured by time. Rather, we should 'recognize temporal distance as a positive and productive condition enabling understanding'.[119] Gadamer illustrates this with reference to the understanding of both events and works of art. He points out that it is more difficult to understand the historical significance or the aesthetic value of a contemporary work of art than it is of a work from the past. This is because the temporal distance between a work of art or historical event and its contemporary interpreter is a distance filled by the labours of past interpreters, whose insights (and even mistakes) may help the interpreter in the present to make sense of the work or event in the past. Temporal distance filters out certain misunderstandings which, for contemporaries, are difficult or even impossible to avoid, and 'new sources of understanding are continually emerging that reveal unsuspected elements of meaning'.[120] Through the continuity of a tradition of interpretation, the meaning of events, texts or works of art continues to unfold. Through interpretation, the past continues to be effective in the present, and so interpretation is inseparable from the continuity and productivity of tradition. History is not an inert object which needs to be reconstituted, but something which, through understanding, continues to be active and to have effects in the present.

The productivity which is inseparable from texts and traditions has the further implication that meaning is strictly 'inexhaustible'. A single interpretation can never recover the meaning of a work fully and definitively for all times, for all interpretive horizons. The interpreter can never aspire to a final, unique and timelessly valid interpretation. It is in this sense that the meaning of the work is inexhaustible. On the other hand, this does not mean that all interpretations are equally valid. In fact, Gadamer assumes that every text or work has some definite meaning. Otherwise there would be no constraints on the process of interpretation at all: hermeneutically, everything would be permitted. In that case, too, it would not be obvious why what might be very different interpretations should nevertheless be regarded as interpretations of the same work. Rather, for Gadamer, the meaning of a work is analogous to the 'thing-in-itself' in Kant's philosophy. Though strictly unknowable, the 'thing-in-itself' is what must be presumed to underlie and ultimately account for the orderly succession of appearances or 'phenomena', which makes up our experience of an external world of objects.[121] Similarly, a text's meaning is what both underlies and accounts for the succession of possible interpretations which the work inspires – interpretations which, according to Gadamer, the work can even be said to produce. All valid interpretations must bear some relationship to this meaning. But the meaning of the work, like the Kantian thing-in-itself, is never itself directly encountered in the succession of interpretations. So we can never test the accuracy of an interpretation simply by comparing it directly with the meaning of the work. There can be no correspondence theory of interpretation. All that we can ever do is to investigate the series of different interpretations in the same way as, in our experience of the external or physical world, we never escape from the 'manifold of appearances'.[122]

It is important to realize, though, that Gadamer's conviction that the work has some definite meaning does not support any authorial veto (whether actual or posthumously alleged) over possible interpretations. The author cannot be assumed to have an absolutely privileged relationship to the meaning of the work. The productivity of the work, manifest in the endless proliferation of possible interpretations, is not circumscribed by the supposed intentions of the author. Although we might expect the author's intentions to bear an important relation to contemporary or later interpretations, their authority is far from absolute. On the one hand, since understanding is relational, the text may support as many interpretations as there are historically distinct horizons of interpretation. But equally, the meaning created by the author of a work itself depends on the horizon of meanings within which it was produced. This hermeneutic context is always much richer than the author can ever comprehend. It is this all-encompassing horizon of language and meaning, rather than the author's intentions, which ultimately determines meaning. Language speaks through individual subjects as much as they speak through language. Gadamer is drawn to the image of play which, properly understood, is not reducible to the intentions of the individual players. Those playing the game are absorbed into the activity in such a way that 'play is not to be understood as something a person does. . . . [T]he actual subject of play is obviously not the subjectivity of an individual, who among other activities, also plays but is instead the play itself.'[123] This 'primacy of play over the consciousness of the player' provides a suggestive analogy both for the relationship of the individual speaker to language and for the way the process of interpretation has a life and a direction of its own. Language – and so also interpretation – transcends the intentions of individual subjects.

Gadamer's account of hermeneutics very closely aligns the practice of interpretation with 'application'. Application, in the specific sense that interests Gadamer, is involved whenever a general principle or rule is applied to a particular case. Application has traditionally played an important role in both legal judgement and biblical exegesis. How should some law, always necessarily at least partially abstract, be applied in particular, concrete situations? What is the moral or spiritual lesson for people today of a particular biblical parable or saying? In answering such questions, application, like interpretation, involves mediating between past and present, between what is taken to be the meaning of the text or law and what might be the very different conditions and concerns of the present. The correct application of law, in Gadamer's terms, must be faithful to the 'original meaning' or spirit of the law in question, but it must also 'take account of the change in circumstances and hence define afresh the normative function of the law'.[124] Analogously, interpretation attempts to grasp the original meaning of a text but always from within a present horizon of meanings. Interpretation 'applies' the original text within a tradition which has, in the meantime, moved on. But it is also important to realize that in both application and interpretation it is not a question of first recovering the uniquely true meaning of a sacred or legal text and then applying that meaning in the present. Rather, it is only through the conscientious application of law or interpretation of text that genuine understanding takes place at all: 'Application does not mean first understanding a given universal in itself and then afterward applying it to a concrete case. It is the very understanding of the universal – the text – itself. Understanding proves to be a kind of effect and knows itself as such.'[125] Both application and interpretation, then, are productive activities or, in other words, examples of 'historically effected consciousness'. They do not simply make use of the resources (meanings or judgements) of a particular tradition, they also continually produce and reproduce those resources.

Application is such a significant model of hermeneutics because it entrenches Gadamer's view of understanding as a creative, productive and yet highly disciplined activity. But in what ways can the practices of application and interpretation be described as disciplined? Certainly, the valid application of law in a particular case is never just 'arbitrary revision'.[126] The judges who apply the law do not *make* the law, at least not in the same sense that legislators do. Rather, application is intended to preserve the law's 'normative content' or 'function' in a different context.[127] But clearly, like interpretation, application can be no exact or methodical science either.[128] Rather (and here Gadamer emphasizes the connection between his own account of hermeneutics and an older tradition of European humanism), application is an important instance of that distinct human capacity identified by Aristotle as 'practical knowledge' or *phronesis* – a capacity most directly involved in moral and aesthetic judgement. Unlike theoretical knowledge, exemplified in the methodical natural sciences, which seeks universal truths, practical knowledge is 'directed towards the concrete situation'; it includes (though is not equivalent to) 'the capacity to subsume the individual case under a universal category – what we call "judgment" '.[129] Application thus involves the kind of 'just weighing up of the whole' typified in moral and aesthetic judgement.[130] Like interpretation or understanding, it is unmethodical but certainly not, for that reason, merely arbitrary. It is essential to Gadamer's view, then, that interpretation, like application, can be disciplined without being methodical. Neither practice can be subsumed under the categories of technical or methodical knowledge. Both rely on the less mechanical but, for Gadamer, no less rigorous human capacity of judgement or practical knowledge.

The upshot of Gadamer's account of understanding is an emphasis on the importance of tradition as an ongoing dialogue or 'dialectic' between past and present.[131] Understanding works as a dialectic between the horizon of the present and the horizon of the past. This relationship is genuinely dialectical, because the past is not simply an inert or passive object of the hermeneutic process but more like a partner in dialogue. The interpreter only distorts the past if she or he reduces its works to the status of mere objects. The interpreter who seeks genuine understanding, on the other hand, is engaged in a common pursuit with an interlocutor from the past, approaching the truth through a series of questions and answers. What is more, this dialogue not only serves to improve our understanding of the past and its texts, it may also unsettle some of our own convictions and lead to revisions in our present horizon of meanings. Understanding is always a productive fusion of horizons, through which the past continues to be active and 'effective' or productive in the present.

Gadamer's positive evaluation of the past and of tradition has led some to see his philosophy as essentially conservative. Certainly, he maintains that our understanding is always 'prejudged' by the horizon of meanings within which we act and think: 'Our being-in-the-world conditions us to certain structures of anticipated meanings. We pre-understand, or anticipate meaning in the very process of coming to understand.'[132] And in this sense, 'there is undoubtedly no understanding that is free of all prejudices.'[133] But Gadamer also emphasizes that horizons of meaning are always open to the possibility of critique and revision, including revisions deriving from a more adequate understanding of the past. Our prejudices are only obstacles to critical reason if they are dogmatically insulated from criticism. If anything, alert to the role that prejudices inevitably play, we are in a better position to challenge them. Thus Gadamer does not so much reject the Enlightenment's commitment to critical rationality as question its favoured view of reason as something absolutely other than and opposed to both tradition and authority:

> The Enlightenment's distinction between faith in authority and using one's own reason is, in itself, legitimate. If the prestige of authority displaces one's own judgment, then authority is in fact a source of prejudices. . . . But this is not the essence of authority . . . authority has to do not with obedience but rather with knowledge.[134]

Authority is rational if it is based on superior knowledge or genuine wisdom. Nor is obedience to authority blind if it is based on the free and informed acknowledgement of the knowledge of that authority. On such grounds, we usually accept the authority of doctors, lawyers, nuclear physicists and ecological scientists – though it is obviously critical when, how long and in which areas we accept their authority. It is Gadamer's claim that even the most ambitious rationalism cannot hope to escape from a similar dependence on authority. Reason can never achieve and should not even aspire to the independence from tradition and prejudice claimed on its behalf by Enlightenment philosophers. But Gadamer is equally convinced that a more modest rationalism need not be any less radically critical. Although 'there is undoubtedly no understanding that is free of all prejudices', still, 'the will of our knowledge must be directed toward escaping their thrall'.[135]

Gadamer's philosophical hermeneutics thus holds out the possibility of a distinctive solution to one of the central dilemmas of post-Enlightenment rationalism. He claims to be able to navigate the difficult course between, on the one side, a reductive objectivism, with its universalist pretensions on behalf of calculating, methodical reason, and, on the other, the relativist or historicist abdication of truth implicit in subjectivism. Like Hegel, Husserl and Heidegger, Gadamer regards the various manifestations of both objectivism and subjectivism as antithetical symptoms of the same underlying disorder of the Western philosophical tradition. The disembodied subject of post-Cartesian philosophy is the logical counterpart of a reductive objectivism, for which reality is no more than a mechanical system of matter extended in space. Gadamer rejects the standpoint of a transcendental subject outside both history and life-world and with it both the timeless truths of reason and the universalist claims made on behalf of an all-encompassing methodical science. Ultimately, both truth and subjectivity are founded historically and hermeneutically in the life-world, always dependent on the precarious and always-to-be-recreated achievement of mutual understanding.[136] Both subjectivist and objectivist pathologies derive from a neglect of this foundation.

However, Gadamer's insistence on the universality of hermeneutics has led less sympathetic critics to see his approach as no more than a species of relativism.[137] Gadamer's hermeneutic ontology certainly implies that criticism of one horizon of meanings or prejudices can only come from within some other horizon. We can never escape from our life-world altogether, even if we may come to revise some of its fundamental assumptions. But Gadamer nevertheless rejects accusations of relativism or subjectivism. For him, the fact that understanding always presupposes the standpoint of particular historical contexts or horizons need not imply that genuine critique and mutual understanding between them is impossible. In this sense, Gadamer's position has, at least for his defenders, a clear advantage over the later philosophy of Wittgenstein, which presents a picture of language as comprising disparate 'language games' – in Linge's words, as 'a multitude of hermetically sealed usages and corresponding life forms', a 'monadic isolation of language games'. This picture implicitly denies the 'assimilative power of language as a constant mediation and translation' between horizons or language games.[138] According to Gadamer, we can indeed, through our diligent efforts at understanding, escape the 'monadic isolation' of our particular horizons of understanding, albeit never absolutely or once and for all. The dialogue between cultures and times is productive. It always brings fresh insights. In the end, Gadamer is confident that 'what the tool of method does not achieve must – and really can – be achieved by a discipline of questioning and inquiring, a discipline that guarantees truth.'[139]

The phenomenology of political
action – Hannah Arendt

Original political thought has not figured prominently in the phenomenological and hermeneutic traditions. Emphasis on the meaning of experience, understanding and the life-world has sometimes been associated with a conservative reverence for the 'pre-judgements' (or prejudices) of tradition, as with Gadamer. Brentano, Husserl and Levinas are not noted for their *political* thought, although this is obviously not to comment on their personal commitments and political activities. Jean-Paul Sartre and Maurice Merleau-Ponty were fully engaged Marxist intellectuals, but their political writings owe more to Marxism and existentialism than to phenomenology.[140] Martin Heidegger's intense and troubled involvement with National Socialism is, of course, a much discussed but hardly inspiring example.[141] The thinker who develops the most fruitful and original approach to politics from a phenomenological perspective is Hannah Arendt (1906–75). Heidegger's student in the 1920s, Arendt's influence now spans a broad range of contemporary approaches, both analytical and continental, in political philosophy. Despite her strong personal relationship with Heidegger and considerable respect for his philosophical achievement, Arendt uses his phenomenological insights to very different effect.[142] Her experience of fascism as a Jewish refugee from the Nazi regime and her dismay at the complicity of so many intellectuals precipitated a lifelong concern with politics. It is not 'forgetfulness of Being' (as with Heidegger) but, rather, neglect of the nature of human action that provokes Arendt's thinking. Not only totalitarianism and fascist tyranny, but a more widespread and insidious 'rise of the social' threatens to engulf once common insights into the active essence of human life. We are forced, according to one of her favourite images, like the pearl diver 'to pry loose the rich and the strange, the pearls and the coral in the depths . . . and bring them up into the world of the living' as 'thought fragments . . . perhaps even as everlasting *Urphänomene*'.[143]

In *The Human Condition*, Arendt develops subtle phenomenological descriptions of three essentially different modes of the active life or '*vita activa*': labour, work and action. These descriptions are indebted not only to Aristotle's philosophy but also to her understanding of ancient Greek *polis* life.[144] 'Labour' refers to those forms of human activity that are concerned solely with the maintenance of life – eating, housework and sexual reproduction. The repetitive drudgery of *homo laborans*, therefore, does not distinguish us in any fundamental way from other animals. In ancient Greece, labour was performed by women and slaves.[145] More distinctively human is the 'work' of *homo faber*, which makes use of natural resources in order to fashion all those enduring artefacts which comprise our human world. Work 'fabricates the sheer unending variety of things whose sum total constitutes the human artifice'.[146] Work also distinguishes different groups of people from each other – the tools of work are 'so intensely worldly objects that we can classify whole civilizations using them as criteria'.[147] Work is, of course, the mode of human activity that informs most directly Heidegger's understanding of our practical involvement with the world. It is also significant, as we shall see, that work implies a degree of violence, which is inflicted on the objects it transforms. Neither labour nor work, however, is equivalent to 'action', which is the uniquely human mode of practice. Action alone must be understood in the intersubjective context of human society. Action takes place *between* individuals by dint of acts of speech and self-disclosure. It is also creative and innovative: 'To act, in its most general sense, means to take an initiative, to begin (as the Greek word *archein*, "to begin," "to lead," and eventually "to rule," indicates).'[148]

Hannah Arendt's analysis of the *vita activa* lends depth and richness to her understanding of ancient Greek political life, which she is at pains to distinguish from the *anti-political* prejudices of ancient philosophers whose ideas continue to distort our contemporary understanding of politics. According to Arendt, the trial and execution of Socrates caused Plato and subsequent philosophers to lose faith in action, persuasion and opinion (*doxa*), which were at the heart of *polis* life, and seek solace in the contemplation of eternal truth. Ironically, Socrates himself still held onto a favourable attitude to politics – his dialogues engaged directly (if sometimes perversely) with the untutored opinions of his fellow citizens. The mission of the 'philosopher-kings' of Plato's ideal *Republic*, by contrast, is to subject the active life of politics to the unchallengeable certainty of philosophical truth.[149] At first sight, this anti-political attitude might not seem relevant to modern societies, which have well and truly abandoned the contemplative ideal of 'theory' (*theōria*). But the modern turn from theory to practice has in fact only served to reinforce the neglect of action, because labour and work have been privileged at the expense of action. The reigning categories of both liberal capitalism and Marxist socialism, which nominally opposes it, are production and consumption. As a result, human practice is effectively confined to the level of mere labour – a repetitive if ever expanding process of production and consumption of commodities.

What Arendt describes as the rise of 'the social' threatens to smother rare eruptions of political action. It accounts, for example, for the ultimate failure of the American Revolution, despite its promising restoration of genuine republican politics and its celebration of the virtues of *public* happiness and *public* freedom. These auspicious beginnings were soon displaced, on Arendt's account, by the pursuit of private and apolitical satisfactions in an increasingly consumerist society.[150] The degeneration of the French Revolution which, in contrast to the American Revolution, took place amidst widespread poverty and misery, was, by contrast, both swifter and more brutal, because the 'social question' dominated from the start: 'The result was that necessity invaded the political realm, the only realm where men can be truly free.'[151] The invasion of necessity tipped the balance in favour of partisans of absolute political sovereignty inspired by Jean Bodin's *Six Books of the Commonwealth* (1576) and Thomas Hobbes's *Leviathan* (1651). Politics in the sovereign state is concerned exclusively with *rule* – the imposition by a single authority of decisions and laws on the collective body of the people. Another thinker who shared this view of politics was Jean-Jacques Rousseau, whose ideas also influenced the revolutionaries. Rousseau has been criticized for his idea of the 'general will' and his 'positive', republican conception of freedom as democratic participation. Both seem to imply that we must sometimes be 'forced to be free', compelled to recognize our real interests by the sovereign people.[152] However, according to Arendt, such authoritarian implications follow not from Rousseau's republican idea of freedom, which she endorses, but from his notion of sovereignty. This is because to understand politics exclusively in terms of sovereignty and rule is, once again, to ignore its essential nature as action that takes place *between* people.

Arendt's understanding of politics and political action can usefully be contrasted with that of her (much longer lived) contemporary, the German jurist, legal and political theorist Carl Schmitt (1888–1985). The comparison is illuminating, because both thinkers rely on similar existentialist and Heideggerian premises. An ardent critic of the Weimar Republic in the 1920s, Schmitt was later actively complicit in the Nazi regime. Ironically, despite these fascist associations, his 'agonistic' conception of politics as essentially conflictual has recently become influential for radical and egalitarian thinkers of the left. In the words of Tracy B. Strong, Schmitt 'comes close these days to being the Martin Heidegger of political theory'.[153] In effect, Schmitt develops an existentialist view of politics in a direction diametrically opposed to that taken by Arendt. He famously defines politics as conflict between 'friends' and 'enemies': 'The specific political distinction to which political actions and motives can be reduced is that between friend and enemy.'[154] The aim of politics is always to defeat one's existential enemy and protect the unity and safety of one's friends. According to this formal definition, politics has no essential content or theme. The decisive political issues at any time will vary according to circumstances – they may concern property or economic questions, religion, culture, nationality and so on. Like human life or Heideggerian *Dasein*, politics cannot be defined substantially in advance of its concrete existence.[155] Rather, actual political relations serve to define what passes for the 'essence' of politics at any particular time. To adapt Sartre's famous existentialist slogan, the existence of politics precedes its essence.[156]

Schmitt's definition of politics has two important corollaries. In the first place, just as existentialists see freedom as the only 'essential' feature of human life, Schmitt's 'decisionism' implies that a fundamental decision always lies at the heart of politics. Only decision defines the collective political entity that is the state and, derivatively, serves to identify its friends and enemies. It follows, secondly and more disturbingly, that there is no absolute distinction between politics and war, since both are modalities of the struggle to defeat one's enemy. Hobbes's absolutist theory of the 'Leviathan' is, by the same token, still the best guide to the true nature of the state and sovereignty. Only a state with unfettered sovereign authority can guarantee peace and security – and hence freedom from the 'natural' human condition of perpetual war.[157] Not surprisingly, Schmitt is contemptuous of the constitutional principles and procedures of liberal democracy, an attitude reinforced by his experience of the ineffectual Weimar Republic, which lasted from Germany's defeat in the First World War until Hitler's seizure of power in 1933. Ignoring other possible explanations, Schmitt sees the increasing chaos of Weimar as the inevitable outcome of its commitment to party politics and parliamentary procedure.[158] The weakness of the modern parliamentary state is, for him, the lamentable result of a slow accretion of constitutional limits, individual rights and principles of toleration under the influence of thinkers like John Locke and Immanuel Kant. Schmitt's anti-Semitism leads him to heap particular obloquy on the 'Judeo-Christian tradition' and individual Jews like Spinoza and Moses Mendelssohn.[159] Pluralism and liberalism are fatal to the sovereign state, Hobbes's 'mortal God', because they prevent it from deciding and acting at all times with absolute unity and undivided force.

Arendt provides an effective antidote to Schmitt's authoritarian view of politics, because she shows that it is possible to recognize its agonistic and existential character without being bewitched by sovereignty, which obscures the true nature of politics and disarms us in the face of totalitarian dictatorship. In fact, her first major study was a complex and wide-ranging exploration of the social and ideological roots of anti-Semitism, fascism and totalitarianism. She defines totalitarianism in terms of its absolute opposition to political action properly understood, which depends on plurality: 'Politics is based on the fact of human plurality. . . . Politics deals with the coexistence and association of *different* men.'[160] Totalitarianism eliminates the space between individuals and, therefore, all possibility of genuine relations between them. Its ultimate goal is the total eradication of spontaneity and freedom, 'the permanent domination of each single individual in each and every sphere of life'.[161] Under National Socialism, even stable hierarchies of authority within party and state were eliminated for the sake of the 'fabrication of mankind' according to Nazi racial doctrines and the will of the Führer. All laws and all human plurality were destroyed by the 'iron band of terror'.[162] By the same token, the Nazi concentration camp was not simply an accidental, if extraordinarily brutal, accessory of the state. It was 'the true central institution of totalitarian organizational power', an expression of the logic of totalitarianism at its most 'pure' and absolute.[163]

Although Arendt provides a far less detailed account of Stalinist communism as another variant of totalitarianism, in her later writings she shows how Marxism also loses sight of the crucial importance of political action and thus conspires in the dominance of 'the social'. Historical materialism inscribes socialist and communist revolution within a dialectic defined by the development of humanity's productive forces. It thus shares with liberal ideology the tendency to subordinate politics to economics. Liberals seek to protect the market economy from 'unjust' and 'disruptive' government interference. Marxism demotes the state and politics to the status of dependent variables, elements of the 'superstructure' which is causally determined (at least, 'in the final instance') by developments at the level of the forces of production. Even more directly linked to the totalitarian degeneration of communism is Marx's 'novel idea' of 'making history' as a form of fabrication or, in Arendt's terms, work.[164] Scientific socialism equips communist revolutionaries with the tools they need in order to fashion a classless communist society out of materials supplied by capitalism. Historical materialism thus neglects the indispensable role of *action*, creating the illusion that history is, like artefacts, something that might be completed at some point.[165] Even worse, the violence inseparable from acts of fabrication is imported into the human world: 'In the idea of world history, the multiplicity of men is melted into one human individual, which is then also called humanity. This is the source of the monstrous and inhuman aspect of history, which first accomplishes its full and brutal end in politics.'[166] The totalitarian degeneration of Marxism is thus, for Arendt, no more coincidental than that of National Socialism.

In order to recognize the centrality of action for genuinely human existence, a very different conception of history is required. In *The Human Condition*, history is understood in broadly hermeneutic terms as a meaningful narrative of human actions – a narrative which helps to motivate the public lives of citizens and, in the ancient world, statesmen and heroes: '[Action] "produces" stories with or without intention as naturally as fabrication produces tangible things.' In fact, history is the most reliable witness to the lives we lead, because it has the undeniable benefit of hindsight: 'Action reveals itself fully only to the storyteller, that is, to the backward glance of the historian, who indeed always knows better what it was all about than the participants.'[167] Arendt struggles in later works to understand how action can 'initiate' new events and, in revolutionary insurrections, create novel and sometimes lasting political institutions. She finds some inspiration in Walter Benjamin's dense and elusive 'Theses on History'.[168] Benjamin also rejects any view of history as an inevitable process – a view, he believes, which 'corrupted the German working class' and undermined opposition to fascism, because it persuaded them that all opposition was futile. To escape such consequences requires a conception of time as something other than a homogeneous and empty continuum filled by historical processes: 'A historical materialist cannot do without the notion of a present which is not a transition, but in which time stands still and has come to a stop.' Innovative political action – and Benjamin's principal examples are the French and socialist revolutions – 'explode' the 'continuum of history'.[169] We live, we only truly *act*, then, when we experience the present as inserted in the space 'between past and future'. Indeed, only action keeps open this vital gap:

> Seen from the viewpoint of man, who always lives in the interval between past and future, time is not a continuum, a flow of uninterrupted succession; it is broken in the middle, at the point where 'he' stands; and 'his' standpoint is not the present as we usually understand it but rather a gap

in time which 'his' constant fighting, 'his' making a stand against past and future, keeps in existence.[170]

Arendt's political philosophy may seem too dramatic and demanding to be relevant to our current situation. She has even been accused of nostalgia for the slave-owning, misogynist and bellicose public life of ancient Athens – accusations which, at times, she seems to provoke.[171] But for all its tensions and incompleteness, Arendt's political vision at least offers a powerful antidote to the complacent assumptions of liberal democracy. It helps us to recognize that, unlike human artefacts – the relatively enduring products of *homo faber* – political institutions remain forever dependent on human intervention and will:

> Political institutions, no matter how well or how badly designed, depend for continued existence upon acting men; their conservation is achieved by the same means that brought them into being. Independent existence marks the work of art as a product of making; utter dependence upon further acts to keep it in existence marks the state as a product of action.[172]

The familiar but often grubby and dispiriting realities of everyday politics inevitably but invisibly rely on that unpredictable and elusive resource, the easily 'lost treasure' of political action.

Further Reading

Wilhelm Dilthey's *Selected Writings* (ed. H. P. Rickman) is a useful preparation for his *Introduction to the Human Sciences*. *Cartesian Meditations* is a later work of Husserl, which provides a good introduction to his philosophy. Heidegger's key work is undoubtedly *Being and Time*, but some of the essays collected in *Basic Writings* are essential reading as well, including the 'Letter on Humanism', 'The Origins of the Work of Art' and 'The Question Concerning Technology'. Gadamer's *magnum opus* is *Truth and Method*, but, again, some of the essays in *Philosophical Hermeneutics* provide helpful bridges to the more systematic work. Hannah Arendt's writings range from her philosophical treatise on *The Human Condition*, through the fascinating but dense essays of *Between Past and Future: Six Exercises in Political Thought* to the shorter and lighter *Essays in Understanding: 1930–54*.

Dermot Moran's *Introduction to Phenomenology* provides a reliable overview of the tradition as a whole. Dilthey's thought is explored in Jos de Mul, *The Tragedy of Finitude: Dilthey's Hermeneutics of Life* and Rudolf A. Makkreel, *Dilthey: Philosopher of the Human Studies*. John Macquarrie's *Martin Heidegger* is a clear guide to a challenging philosopher. For Gadamer, consult Jean Grondin, *The Philosophy of Gadamer* and Georgia Warnke, *Gadamer: Hermeneutics, Tradition and Reason*. Margaret Canovan provides a readable and comprehensive guide in *Hannah Arendt: A Reinterpretation of Her Political Thought*. In *Arendt and Heidegger: The Fate of the Political*, Dana Villa provides an authoritative explanation of the complex relationship between Arendt and Heidegger. Some helpful guides to (otherwise challenging) individual works include A. D. Smith, *Husserl and the 'Cartesian Meditations'*, S. Critchley and R. Schürmann, *On Heidegger's 'Being and Time'* and H. L. Dreyfus, *Being-in-the-World: A Commentary on Heidegger's 'Being and Time', Division I*.

5

Beyond Theory: Kierkegaard, Nietzsche, Existentialism

Outline

The philosophical attempt to capture the distinctive significance of human life finds alternative expression in Søren Kierkegaard's commitment to 'subjective truth'. Kierkegaard maintains the futility of all systematic or theoretical attempts, including Hegel's, to resolve the 'problem of existence'. His approach is also determinedly anti-historical, looking for the significance of life in neither our historical origins nor some anticipated future state of humanity. Kierkegaard's anti-theoretical philosophy, which is often seen as the source of twentieth-century 'existentialism', is expressed through a variety of discursive forms – including extended essays and letters, music criticism, sermons and collections of aphorisms, often attributed to invented characters representing contrasting attitudes to life. Systematic philosophical discourse is also avoided by Friedrich Nietzsche, whose trenchant aphorisms and essays are overwhelmingly critical and sceptical. Nietzsche's discussion of the 'death of God' and the problem of moral nihilism, and his hostility to both humanism and Christian 'slave morality', continue to exert a broad and diverse influence on contemporary thought. Although there are some affinities between Nietzsche and existentialism, his influence and concerns are much more diverse. The self-conscious existentialism of Jean-Paul Sartre, Simone de Beauvoir and Albert Camus owes much to the writings of Kierkegaard, Nietzsche and also Heidegger. Prominent themes, including the radical nature of human freedom and the absurdity of existence, are explored in novels, plays and autobiography, as well as more systematic philosophical works.

Søren Kierkegaard

The Enlightenment espoused a conception of knowledge and rationality closely modelled on the natural sciences. Enlightenment rationalism was correspondingly corrosive of what many took to be the truths of traditional morality and religion. In these terms, Hegel's philosophy has been understood as an attempt to save these truths from an overhasty critique and place them on more secure philosophical foundations. His dialectical system is designed to express moral and religious truths in a more fully rational form. The limited insights of both scientific reason and dogmatic religion are transcended within the higher synthesis of Absolute knowledge. The antagonistic relationship between reason and faith can be overcome with the help of a more adequate understanding of them both. Hegel still believed, in Rohde's words, that 'it was possible to unite faith and thought and create an all-comprehending synthesis in which all oppositions could be reconciled'.[1] On this interpretation, Hegel is close to the tradition of humanist theology, which seeks to harmonize human reason and faith by making faith acceptable to reason. If faith does not survive in its original form, then this is the price that dogmatic religion has to pay for its rescue from a sceptical rationalism. Hegel was, of course, criticized by protagonists of Enlightenment rationalism, who saw his philosophy as a straightforward relapse into mysticism. Others, like Marx, though sympathetic towards his dialectical and historical method, were still inclined to reject Hegel's philosophy as simply religion in another guise. In their different ways, these thinkers criticize Hegel from the point of view of rationalism and humanism, whether simple or more sophisticated.[2]

By contrast, Søren Kierkegaard (1813–55) proposes a radical defence of religious faith which, far from attempting to reconcile reason with faith, emphasizes the gulf between them. In effect, he renews the theological tradition of 'fideism', for which religious faith is diminished rather than strengthened by its reduction to merely human reason.[3] In retrospect, Kierkegaard has, for reasons which will become clear, been identified as the first 'existentialist'. For the fideist tradition, which includes such thinkers as St Augustine, Meister Eckhart, Pascal and Luther, faith surpasses human understanding. Human reason is the limited capacity of an imperfect and sinful being, who is, not surprisingly, unable to comprehend an omnipotent, omniscient and perfectly benevolent God. The high point of reason in these terms is the recognition of its own limits. In the words of Pascal: 'Reason's last step is the recognition that there are an infinite number of things which are beyond it.'[4] The attempt to formulate a rational religion is really an expression of arrogance, which can never hope to do justice to the spiritual meaning of faith. This claim makes obvious sense in relation to the lifeless abstraction of Enlightenment deism, which, though it preserved a metaphysical role for God as creator or 'first cause' of the universe, evidently failed to satisfy the specifically religious needs of humanity. For Kierkegaard, what is more, even the baroque edifice of Hegelian idealism concedes too much to humanism and rationalism and, as a result, neglects or distorts the meaning of faith.[5] In response, Kierkegaard develops a radical version of the fideist position, maintaining that religious faith not only does not require the support of reason but is essentially at odds with it. Religion has no particular significance, if it simply expresses in different terms truths which can be stated without it. The significance of religion is inseparable from its violation of merely human rationality and even morality. In Tertullian's phrase, *credo quia impossibile* – I believe *because* it is impossible to believe. It is as if Kierkegaard takes seriously the ironic taunt of David Hume who, after demolishing to his own satisfaction all rational grounds for belief in miracles as evidence of the truth of religion, remarks that anyone who still has faith 'is conscious of a continued miracle in his own person, which subverts all the principles of his understanding, and gives him a determination to believe what is most contrary to custom and experience'.[6]

A crucial part of Kierkegaard's strategy is to reject the rationalist conception of objective knowledge or contemplative theory, which plays a central role in the Western philosophical tradition. The idea of theory (*theōria*) as the disinterested and essentially unpractical contemplation of the world or cosmos is first clearly expounded in classical Greek philosophy. Aristotle describes theoretical knowledge as contemplation of the eternal and unchanging: '[T]he object of scientific knowledge necessarily exists. Consequently it is also eternal; for things that are of necessity in the unqualified sense are eternal; and things that are eternal are ungenerated and imperishable.'[7] With the Enlightenment this conception of theory is transformed into an understanding of scientific knowledge as fundamentally instrumental. Scientific knowledge is inseparable from the 'technological' capacity to manipulate and control the external world.[8] Still, objectivity remains an essential characteristic of theory, surviving from the originally contemplative ideal. Theory must avoid all subjective bias, it must transcend all purely subjective points of view, in order to attain an intersubjective and eternal truth. Much of the Western tradition of epistemology sees its task as establishing with certainty that this goal has been or can be achieved. Truth, on this view, is only attained when theory has expunged all connection with the merely subjective life of knowing subjects.

But according to Kierkegaard, this ideal of objective knowledge, which was championed by the Enlightenment and then deployed against it with such ingenuity and persistence by Hegel, is constitutionally blind to the inner life or subjective existence of the human individual. Objective theoretical knowledge makes no useful contribution to understanding human life. We are mistakenly inclined to think that it does, because the intellectual approach to life (the attempt to understand life in theoretical terms) gives a deceptive impression of completeness. It seems that it can tell us something about everything when it does not even begin to tell us that we need to know in order to live. In fact, we can understand life intellectually without really existing at all. Thus Kierkegaard can say of someone (a character he has invented in order to present a view he rejects) that 'he has thought everything possible, and yet he has not existed at all'.[9] As a result, any attempt to weave the truths of religion into a theoretical account of the world, however sophisticated or dialectical, inevitably distorts or falsifies them. The truths of religion belong to the sphere of subjective existence and cannot be grasped by the abstract categories of theoretical knowledge. Existence can only be known or understood subjectively or from within. The problem of existence must, in Rohde's words, be thought 'not dispassionately and objectively, but with the whole of our personality'.[10]

The fundamental move from objective theory to 'subjective truth' is reflected in a number of aspects of Kierkegaard's work.[11] In the first place, he adopts a method radically different from the theoretical approach of mainstream Western philosophy. Subjective truth cannot be expressed with the categories of abstract reason or a detached and impersonal philosophical discourse. Rather, it must be expressed through 'indirect communication'. Like the Zen master, philosophy can only express the truth indirectly. It can only be the catalyst for an active process of subjective understanding, which must be performed by individuals for themselves. In this spirit, Kierkegaard accords an important role to the concept of irony as an important means of indirect communication. In his doctoral thesis he claims that 'the concept of irony makes its entry into the world through Socrates'.[12] The Socratic dialogue represents the ideal method for the philosophical exploration of human existence. Socrates leads his interlocutors to revise their limited, common-sense conceptions of justice or truth through irony and humour as much as through demonstrative argument. Irony can provoke subjective insights beyond the grasp of theoretical reason, leading to genuine understanding rather than merely intellectual knowledge. It can achieve what Hollander aptly describes as the 'negative liberation of subjectivity'.[13]

In pursuit of indirect communication, Kierkegaard has recourse to an impressive array of discursive styles and registers in addition to more conventional philosophical discourse. More dramatist than theorist, Kierkegaard often presents ideas which are not his own. His writings as a whole, mostly written at a frenetic pace between 1841 and 1849, explore a variety of subjective perspectives and, to this end, employ a number of pseudonyms and complex framing devices in order to place more or less distance between himself and the particular attitude to life under consideration. For example, one of Kierkegaard's best-known works is ostensibly a miscellaneous collection of essays, aphorisms, a diary, letters and a sermon, written by two unknown authors and accidentally discovered and published by a somewhat mysterious scholar, one Victor Eremita.[14] Kierkegaard also wrote a series of 'edifying discourses', which are more akin to religious sermons. A related aspect of Kierkegaard's approach is the autobiographical reference of much of his work.[15] His writings reflect important periods or decisive events in his life. Their pessimism recalls the stern atmosphere of his early childhood, his father's severe religiosity and the guilty secret of his father's illegitimate child. Kierkegaard's youthful life as a rich dandy, whose outward wit and bohemian excess concealed profound inner melancholy, is rehearsed in the despairing hedonism of the 'aesthetic' existence. His prolonged and ultimately abortive engagement with Regine Olsen, apparently broken off because of his feelings of inadequacy and sexual disgust, provoked the emotional crisis which sparked Kierkegaard's most productive creative period and also figures indirectly in the discussion of the ethical significance of marriage in the second volume of *Either/Or*. In the last few years of his life, most of his energies were absorbed in a bitter quarrel with Bishop Mynster and the state church in Denmark, and, as a result, he wrote very little.

A further consequence of Kierkegaard's concentration on subjective truth is a direct challenge to the central element of Enlightenment accounts of theoretical knowledge, the demand for certainty – the demand classically pursued by Descartes through his method of radical doubt.[16] Subjective truth does not aspire to the certainty of objective theoretical knowledge based on indubitable foundations and logical argument. Kierkegaard shares with the sceptic the belief that there can be no rationally certified moral system or religion. There are no irrefutable rational arguments within either ethics or theology in favour of living life in a particular way. In any case, theoretical certainty about moral or religious truth would abolish freedom at the same time as it relieved us of uncertainty. Again, even if rational argument could assure us intellectually that we were living correctly, it could never convince us subjectively or actually put us in a position to live in that way. For Kierkegaard, then, uncertainty is not so much a defect of subjective truth as its essence. Uncertainty is a consequence of what is most essential to human life, namely our freedom to choose or decide.[17]

At the same time, freedom implies responsibility. Even if we cannot aspire to theoretical or intellectual certainty, we nevertheless have a responsibility to strive for truth. We have no choice but to choose, because we must live life in one way or another, and live with the consequences of that choice. And, of course, not to choose is also to make a choice of a certain kind, albeit a less conscious one.[18] It is an important principle for Kierkegaard (and it will become axiomatic for later existentialists) that we are responsible even when we appear to be unaware of our freedom. Ambivalence about human freedom is thus at the heart of Kierkegaard's philosophy and is part of his legacy to the subsequent existentialist tradition. Human beings are uniquely free in their ability to choose, uniquely burdened by the necessity to choose. Our responsibility to choose and to strive for subjective truth means that freedom is something which human beings endure as well as enjoy. Freedom is inextricably associated with a state of 'anxiety' or 'dread', which shares the ambivalence of freedom. Dread is both attractive and repulsive to 'man': 'He cannot flee from dread, for he loves it; really he does not love it, for he flees from it.'[19] Dread is often described in terms which convey this ambivalence: 'One speaks of a sweet dread, a sweet feeling of apprehension, one speaks of a strange dread, a shrinking dread.'[20] Anxiety is experienced as 'a feeling of fear which does not apply to anything definite and which both frightens and fascinates at the same time'; it is the counterpart of the enormous weight of responsibility carried by each individual. But it is also 'the state of mind which precedes the act of freedom'; it points 'towards the possibility of freedom and spiritual realization'.[21]

The ambivalence of Kierkegaard's interrelated concepts of freedom and dread reflects his dualist metaphysics. Human beings are understood as an uneasy mixture of the material and the spiritual, the animal and the divine: 'A human being is a synthesis of the infinite and the finite, of the temporal and the eternal, of freedom and necessity.'[22] This opposition has a long history in Western and Christian thought. It is prominent in both the philosophy of Plato and St Paul's account of Christianity, in which spirit or soul and the possibility of salvation is opposed to the body, nature and perdition. The rational will of Kant's moral philosophy depends on the existence of a 'noumenal' self transcending the causally determined order of nature. For Kierkegaard, too, the possibility of freedom depends on our spiritual nature. But human beings are also animals. As pure souls, human beings would, like angels, experience freedom as an unalloyed good, but the human individual straddles two mutually antagonistic realms. Still imprisoned in the body, still subject to the causal nexus of physical nature, the individual is weighed down by more earthly inclinations and drives. So freedom is experienced as conflict and dread. 'Dread is the point of intersection between two worlds inside man, that of spirit and that of nature, that of God and that of animal.'[23]

The most basic choice faced by human beings is whether to acknowledge their freedom or attempt to evade it. The evasion of freedom is something Kierkegaard strongly associates with nineteenth-century mass society. As Hannay puts it: 'Kierkegaard detects in contemporary life-styles, in the kinds of goals people set for themselves, in their ideals of fulfilment, a fundamental fear of conscious selfhood. He calls it "despair".'[24] People conform to conventional standards of behaviour. They are satisfied with the mediocre or the average. Rather than face up to the inevitability of death, they seek distraction in transient pleasures. Kierkegaard castigates 'petty bourgeois vulgarity' with as much vehemence as Marx:

> Devoid of imagination, as the petty bourgeois always is, he lives within a certain orbit of trivial experience as to how things come about, what is possible, what usually happens, no matter whether he is a tapster or a prime minister. This is the way in which the petty bourgeois has lost himself and God.[25]

Despair 'is exactly man's unconsciousness of being characterized as spirit'.[26] Consequently, despair is at its most extreme when it is not even recognized as such: 'In his ignorance of his own despair a person is furthest from being conscious of himself as spirit.'[27] The sickness that characterizes the human condition in the absence of God is therefore a sickness which gets better only by getting worse.

Kierkegaard's chosen mission is to make the individual aware of its despair and so bring it to recognize itself as free spirit. In *The Sickness Unto Death* Kierkegaard describes the various ways in which human beings can either passively ignore or actively deny their selfhood. Only the self which comes to a self-conscious decision to accept God overcomes despair. The progression of selfhood through a series of ascending stages culminates in the 'infinite self', which stands directly before God: '[T]he self is intensified in proportion to the standard by which the self measures itself, and infinitely so when God is the standard. . . . Only when a self, as this particular individual, is conscious of being before God, only then is it the infinite self; and that self then sins before God.'[28] As the last remark implies, despair is exchanged for a condition which is no less arduous and painful. Full self-awareness before God presents the individual with the clearest possible choice between sin and faith, for 'the opposite of sin is faith'.[29] Significantly, *The Sickness Unto Death* was published under one of Kierkegaard's pseudonyms, the convinced Christian Anti-Climacus, and is subtitled 'A Christian Psychological Exposition for Edification and Awakening'. But why should the agnostic be persuaded by Anti-Climacus' vigorous assertion of the Christian faith? Kierkegaard is adamant that even if choice is free, it is certainly not arbitrary. The fully self-conscious individual can only choose between faith and sin.

But what can persuade the sceptic or agnostic to come to the same conclusion if there can be no intellectually irresistible proofs in questions of religion and morality? Kierkegaard's response is to elucidate a series of distinct 'spheres of existence' or 'stages on life's way'. Our most important decision can be informed by a subjective understanding of the alternative approaches to life from which we must choose. In the first place, he describes what is essentially a life lived in the absence of resolute decision. The 'aesthetic existence' is empty and drifting, a life of disconnected and ultimately meaningless pleasures and moods. The aesthetic individual is prey to 'the soul's momentary passion' and his ultimate fate is melancholy and boredom:[30]

> My soul is so heavy that thought can no more sustain it, no wingbeat lift it up into the ether. If it moves, it sweeps along the ground like the low flight of birds when a thunderstorm is approaching. Over my inmost being there broods a depression, an anxiety, that presages an earthquake.[31]

In what has sometimes been taken to be a description of Kierkegaard's own rather dissipated youth, the anonymous author of the first part of *Either/Or* dwells somewhat tediously (and so, perhaps, all the more effectively) on the ultimate futility of his existence.

The second volume of *Either/Or* gives expression to a different sphere of 'ethical' existence where, in contrast to the shifting and aimless drifting of the aesthetic sphere, 'The thinker gives himself stable ethical reality by forming and renewing himself in critical decisions which are a total inward commitment (decisions, for example, as to vocation, marriage, faith).'[32] The first part of the second volume consists of a long letter on the 'aesthetic validity of marriage', supposedly written by a certain Judge William to the wayward author of the aesthetic reflections of the first volume. The romantic love celebrated from the aesthetic point of view is merely transient. Its claim to be eternal is deception, since 'the eternity it claims' is 'built upon the temporal'.[33] Only Christian marriage can unite love with duty and so render love both reflective and eternal. Although the aesthete regards duty as 'the enemy of love', it is in fact love's friend. Marriage embeds love in a context of social responsibility, giving it permanence. Less attractively, perhaps, dutiful love also involves a degree of resignation, a relinquishing of the endless possibilities of passion and desire.[34] But if the ethical life, as exemplified by the commitment of marriage, ultimately appears unappealing, this is because it only represents a transitional stage on the way to a fully adequate, religious existence. The ethical sphere corresponds to the merely social dimension of life, which harbours dangers of mere conformity to social convention and the 'despairing' abdication of freedom associated with that.

Only religion offers the possibility of a fully satisfactory existence, though the choice of faith is once again emphatically not an easy one. Only religion answers to the fully self-conscious individuality of authentic existence. Here it is crucial for Kierkegaard's account that the religious sphere is not simply an alternative manifestation of the ethical. In fact, the demands of religion may even be incompatible with the demands of morality. God's will may go against not only our strongest human feelings, but also our deepest moral convictions. Kierkegaard makes this point in terms of an extended discussion of God's command to Abraham, that he should kill his son Isaac. Issued without apparent justification or reason, this command goes against both the natural emotional ties of parental love and the basic moral principles of any conceivable human society. In its absoluteness and unconditionality, God's command marks the strict separation of the religious from the ethical sphere. Abraham has faith and acts to obey God's will, but in the end he is not required to sacrifice his son:

> All along he had faith, he believed that God would not demand Isaac of him, while still he was willing to offer him if that was indeed what was demanded. He believed on the strength of the absurd, for there could be no question of human calculation, and it was indeed absurd that God who

demanded this of him should in the next instant withdraw the demand. He climbed the mountain, even in that moment when the knife gleamed he believed – that God would not demand Isaac.[35]

The story of Abraham reveals faith as 'monstrous paradox', 'a paradox capable of making a murder into a holy act well pleasing to God, a paradox which gives Isaac back to Abraham, which no thought can grasp because faith begins precisely where thinking leaves off'.[36]

For Kierkegaard, then, we must believe even though, or perhaps even because, faith violates human rationality, nature and morality. A faith which was humanly reasonable, a faith conforming to human moral intuition, would have no distinctive significance. It is the absurdity of religion which proves its unique value, its irreducibility. But why, then, should human beings believe in what they must find irrational, unnatural and immoral? Kierkegaard's fideist reading of Christianity presents the transition to faith as an ungroundable 'leap of faith' or *saltus mortale*.[37] He supposes that once the fundamental choice in favour of faith has been made, then the overwhelming value of the religious life will be apparent. His varied and ingenious writings can be seen as heroic attempts to give both the non-believer and the merely conventional Christian some idea of what that life involves. He hopes to awaken his contemporaries to the urgency of self-conscious and authentic decision, to counteract the soporific effect of a conformist society. At the same time Kierkegaard presents a powerful and passionate case for the essential inwardness of religious life and the emptiness of merely external observances within the established church. What he calls 'objective Christianity', which includes the historical evidence, the established church and practising Christians, is totally inadequate. It obscures the full and severe demands of true Christianity. The Christian should admit that these demands are unfulfillable but nevertheless resolve to fulfil them and be prepared to live in a state of permanent tension. Like the revivalist preacher, Kierkegaard calls for inward renewal, a return to the original purity and ferocity of Christianity. In that sense Kierkegaard is certainly an important figure in the development of Protestantism.

However, Kierkegaard is also important for philosophy more generally. In his attempts to illuminate the nature of faith, he also sheds light on the subjective or, in later terms, 'existential' truth of the human condition. If his *solution* to the problem of existence does not convince everyone, his *diagnosis* of the problem is nonetheless compelling. In his intense preoccupation with the choice between faith and unbelief he uncovers the significance of freedom and responsibility. He leaves us in little doubt that the theoretical reason of the Enlightenment cannot help much with either. The emphasis on individual existence and decision is complemented by a critique of the inauthenticity of modern, urban life, of the worldly superficiality of careerism and materialism. Kierkegaard's central concepts of anxiety or dread, despair, freedom and authenticity, which illuminate his exploration of the basic dimensions of human existence, can be seen as precursors of existentialism. But it is crucial to this later tradition, that Kierkegaard's explorations are not intended simply as descriptions of contingent psychological states to which particular individuals may be more or less susceptible, let alone as the autobiographical reflections of someone who was, by all accounts, a fairly eccentric individual. Rather, they must be seen as a powerful attempt to chart the distinctive space of human subjectivity, whether or not Kierkegaard's advocacy of religion is ultimately accepted.[38]

Friedrich Nietzsche

Friedrich Nietzsche (1844–1900) did not come across Kierkegaard's writings until about 1888, shortly before he became insane, and at first sight seems to have little in common with him.[39] Nietzsche was suspicious of religion and is notorious for his announcement of the 'death of God', his absolute conviction that religious faith is no longer tenable and that this has fateful implications for Western culture and civilization. At times his suspicion of religion turns into outright hostility. He describes the faith of Pascal and the early Christians, similar in many ways to Kierkegaard's, as a 'protracted suicide of reason', which involves 'sacrifice of all freedom, all pride, all self-confidence of the spirit, at the same time enslavement and self-mockery, self-mutilation'.[40] Nevertheless, there are significant affinities between them. Like Kierkegaard, Nietzsche is as contemptuous of the thin-blooded abstractions of Enlightenment deism as he is of attempts to ground religious belief on rational principles.[41] He also sees little value in secular moral philosophies, such as utilitarianism, which gained ground in the nineteenth century as religious values gradually lost their appeal. He sees both religious and secular versions as complacent and half-hearted attempts to avoid the nihilistic implications of Enlightenment rationalism, as unprincipled compromises with conventional bourgeois morality. Nietzsche is equally hostile to the historical dialectic of Hegel.[42] Nietzsche shares Kierkegaard's scepticism that any systematic philosophy can fill the moral vacuum within Enlightenment thought and, like him, values the individual and the present moment rather than either historical process or collective social agents. On the other hand, Nietzsche does not believe that nihilism can be outwitted by sophisticated manoeuvres of a Kierkegaardian kind either. He is determined to avoid the characteristic weakness of systematic philosophers and 'metaphysicians' of all kinds, who wish 'to solve all with one stroke, with one word' and so become 'unriddlers of the universe'.[43] Kierkegaard falls victim to a parallel temptation, albeit practical rather than intellectual, when he founds everything on the single decision to accept God. Nietzsche's response is very different. Rather than evade the logic of Enlightenment rationalism, he sets out to apply the critical force of reason with even greater ruthlessness.

Thus, although Nietzsche shares his hostility to religion with many Enlightenment free thinkers, he is much more acutely aware of the drastic implications of the widespread loss of faith associated with modernity. Recognition of these implications was, in effect, delayed by the intervention of humanism, which at its most extreme simply replaces belief in God with something akin to worship of humanity. After all, scientists had demonstrated the ability of unaided human reason to discover the laws of the natural universe. The Renaissance expressed a similarly self-confident celebration of the beauty of the human form and of human accomplishments, in its art and architecture, its poetry and philosophy. Humanist theology interpreted religious beliefs in ways that conformed to human conceptions of value and reason. More radically still, some arrived at the conclusion that humanity need no longer subject itself to divine law at all. Feuerbach argued that alienated human capacities, magnified and projected self-abasingly onto a non-existent God, should be reappropriated. Morality should be based directly on the value of human life and its achievements.[44] But the rush of self-confidence that came with the thought that there is no greater being than 'man' had delayed the consequent realization that, without God, humanity's claim to metaphysical primacy no longer has any absolute basis. The self-abasement of humanity before God had always harboured the less modest presumption of a special relationship with the Creator. With the 'death of God', then, humanism finds itself in the precarious position of the cartoon character poised over the precipice, suspended only by its ignorance of the drop. A philosophy still permeated by essentially religious conceptions fails to realize the devastating blow inflicted upon it by the demise of religion. Humanism, like metaphysics, remains a species of faith.[45] Related scientific developments had implications for the status of humanity. Copernican astronomy implied that the earth, and with it humanity, was not at the centre of the universe as had been assumed. The earth moves and its inhabitants are little more than specks of dust upon its surface: 'Since Copernicus man has been rolling from the centre toward "x".'[46] In the nineteenth century, Darwin's theory of evolution confirmed our familial ties with the beasts and brutes. Human beings are simply animals with a number of distinctive attributes, which have evolved by a process of natural selection.[47]

An early inspiration for Nietzsche's uncompromisingly anti-metaphysical and anti-humanist approach was the philosophy of Arthur Schopenhauer (1788–1860), which is set out most fully and systematically in the two volumes of *The World as Will and Representation*. Schopenhauer offers an original response to Kant's ultimately unconvincing dichotomy between the 'phenomenal' world of appearances and the 'noumenal' world of things-in-themselves. For Kant, the noumenal can never be the object of direct knowledge even though it must be presupposed as the precondition of the self's rationality, freedom and morality.[48] In contrast to Kant, Schopenhauer believes that we can indeed know the real nature of both the self and the ultimate reality underpinning the superficial phenomena of our experience. Partly inspired by his explorations of Hinduism and Buddhism, he claims that the ultimate metaphysical reality is blind, purposeless, impersonal 'Will' (*Wille*). This cosmic force manifests itself throughout the natural world as 'vital force' or 'will-to-life', which we experience subjectively through our own fundamental nature as willing beings. In fact, will is manifest in the life-force of all animals, akin to what Spinoza referred to as the universal 'striving' (*conatus*) of all natural entities to 'persist in their own being'. Although Schopenhauer claims, in this way, to have absolute metaphysical knowledge of reality, the outcome of his philosophy is equivalent to a radical form of naturalism.[49] Unlike most 'first philosophies', in Schopenhauer's case metaphysical truth does not reveal the deeper meaning of natural phenomena. On the contrary, it tends to undermine any such meaning. A striking example of this is his demystifying explanation of romantic love. Romantic writers and philosophers had emphasized the centrality of passionate love to human life, its immense power and often devastating consequences of frustration and unhappiness, social disorder and even death. Schopenhauer fully recognizes the 'existential' significance of love, but then proceeds to unmask it as no more than a self-deluding expression of the sex instinct, which is itself just the subjective manifestation of 'the will-to-live as a precisely determined individual'.[50] More generally, whatever our intentions or desires, our actions are really always in the service of the impersonal life-force of the cosmos. Not surprisingly, the outcome for individual human beings is – in the end and on balance – always one of disappointment, suffering and death. Schopenhauer's radical pessimism leads him to an ethical stance of radical asceticism, the determined renunciation of all will and desire in order to minimize the extent and depth of our inevitable suffering. A life of contemplation and artistic beauty is our only consolation.[51]

Schopenhauer's penetrating demystification of human pretensions made a seminal contribution to Nietzsche's anti-humanism. Nietzsche's own systematic demolition of humanism can be approached through his attitude to the ideals of truth, reason, beauty and goodness. For humanism, it is our access to these ideals which confirms the almost godlike status of humanity, our transcendence of merely animal existence. As a philologist and classicist, Nietzsche's demystification of these ideals first emerges in his discussion of the origins, in ancient Greece, of tragedy as a distinctive art form. For humanism, the artistic achievements of ancient Greece were the inspiring embodiment of the ideals of beauty, harmony and perfection. But in his first book, Nietzsche accounts for the origins of Greek tragedy in terms quite unsettling to the humanist consciousness. Thus, art owes its continuous development to the interaction of two fundamentally opposed forces, the Apolline and the Dionysiac. The god Apollo is associated with the order and harmony of Greek poetry, sculpture and visual art, and the 'principle of individuation' (*principium individuationis*), which sustains the identity of 'the individual man' 'in the midst of a world full of suffering'.[52] As Kaufmann explains:

> Apollo represents the aspect of the classical Greek genius extolled by Winckelmann and Goethe: the power to create harmonious and measured beauty; the strength to shape one's own character no less than works of art; the 'principle of individuation'; the form-giving force, which reached its consummation in Greek sculpture.[53]

But for Nietzsche, still impressed by Schopenhauer, the world of orderly appearances and secure individuality is an illusion. Apollo is also associated with dreams, with the 'beautiful illusion of the inner fantasy world', through which 'life is made both possible and worth living'.[54]

The Apolline is constantly struggling against the underlying chaos and oneness of reality, the impersonal 'will' of Schopenhauer's metaphysics, which is expressed in the Dionysiac.[55] Dionysus was the Greek god of music, intoxication and the collective oneness of Bacchanalian revelry and dance. Intoxication induces 'complete forgetting of the self' and access to a deeper wisdom, an overcoming of the illusory bonds which separate us from other men and from nature.[56] As Kaufmann puts it: 'Dionysus . . . is the symbol of that drunken frenzy which threatens to destroy all forms and codes; the ceaseless striving which apparently defies all limitations; the ultimate abandonment we sometimes sense in music.'[57] Nietzsche's account implies that the serenity and harmony of Greek culture is not so much the expression of serene and harmonious minds in contact with an eternal world of Platonic Forms as the product of a hard-won victory over the creative but disruptive forces of the Dionysiac. Art is valuable, therefore, not as the reflection of a harmonious cosmos but as the productive overcoming of disorder.[58] The sublime in classical art is 'the artistic conquest of the horrible'.[59] The tragedies of Aeschylus and Sophocles, in particular, represent the ideal fusion of the two conflicting principles. However, at this formative moment of Western culture the precarious balance of Apolline and Dionysiac is squandered under the combined influence of Euripides and 'aesthetic Socratism'. It is Socrates who imposes an extraneous moral purpose on art, seeing morality in the exclusively Apolline terms of intelligibility, consciousness and individuality. The result is the 'excision of the primitive and powerful Dionysiac element from tragedy, and the rebuilding of tragedy on non-Dionysiac art, morality and philosophy'.[60] Evidently, Nietzsche's account is a significant challenge to the humanist conception of art and beauty. Far from being proof of the near-divine abilities of human beings, art can only be understood as a modified expression of the chaotic, frenzied and destructive force of the Dionysiac. This does not mean that Nietzsche sees art as anything less than essential. On the contrary, he inherits from Schopenhauer the conviction that art can give meaning to existence. Art alone can turn 'thoughts of repulsion at the horror and absurdity of existence into ideas compatible with life'.[61]

The humanist conception of truth fares even worse at Nietzsche's hands than the ideal of beauty. Socrates' subjection of art and the aesthetic to moral and intellectual goals is linked to a further illusion: 'The unshakeable belief that rational thought, guided by causality, can penetrate to the depths of beings, and that it is capable not only of knowing but even of *correcting* being. This sublime metaphysical illusion is an instinctual accompaniment to science.' Nietzsche sees the Western metaphysical tradition, at least since Socrates, as engaged in a sophisticated but futile attempt to distort reality. Metaphysics is 'the science that treats of the fundamental errors of mankind – but does so as though they were fundamental truths'.[62] ' "Reason" is the cause of our falsification of the evidence of the senses; . . . [i]t is what we *make* of their evidence that first introduces a lie into it, for example the lie of unity, the lie of materiality, of substance, of duration.' In what seems like a direct reply to Kant, giving a quite different emphasis to Kant's basic view of experience, Nietzsche claims that the phenomenal world of appearances is 'the only one: the "real" world has only been *lyingly added*'.[63] What Kant sees as the constitution of objective experience by the transcendental self, Nietzsche calls lie and deception. There is still truth, but only in the chaotic flux of subjective appearances, the evidence of the senses.[64] Nietzsche's radicalization of the Enlightenment's critical reason thus brings him to a position close to Humean empiricism. Nietzsche responds sceptically to Kant's Copernican revolution in philosophy:

> [I]t is high time to replace the Kantian question 'how are synthetic judgements *a priori* possible?' with another question: 'why is belief in such judgements *necessary*?' – that is to say, it is time to grasp that, for the purpose of preserving beings such as ourselves, such judgements must be *believed* to be true.[65]

Rather than engage in the futile task of supplying our beliefs with metaphysical foundations, we should look for the actual origins of our beliefs, their reasons for existing. Hume had found such origins in mental habits induced by the 'constant conjunction' of events.[66] Once we pursue this 'genealogical' approach, we will come to recognize that these origins are much more lowly than humanists suppose. We will discover the origins of truth in error, deception and even the covetousness behind the 'pure radiant gaze' of the sage. It is just another prejudice of the philosophers to insist that 'the higher must not be *allowed* to grow out of the lower, must not be *allowed* to have grown at all'.[67]

Nietzsche applies his genealogical method to the demystification of other areas of human experience. Morality is a particular object of concern. When Enlightenment thinkers had doubted the religious basis of morality, they tended to substitute a corresponding faith in the natural dispositions of 'man'. Rid of the corrupting effects of civilization (with Rousseau) or the state (with Godwin), man is naturally good or at least capable of improvement.[68] Even a hard-headed sceptic like Hume supposes that: '[W]here interest or revenge or envy perverts not our disposition, we are always inclined, from our natural philanthropy, to give the preference to the happiness of society, and consequently to virtue above its opposite.'[69] Nietzsche's genealogy of morals is far less reassuring. He sets out to trace the contingent and highly questionable origins of our 'moral prejudices' in Christianity. The result is not simply a challenge to the truth of Christian belief, which after all was a common object of Enlightenment scepticism, but rather a challenge to Christian *values* themselves, values that even most atheists had wished to preserve more or less intact.[70] According to Nietzsche, these values represent the historic and highly regrettable victory of the mediocre masses over an earlier aristocratic morality. Pity, humility and self-sacrifice are values which serve the interests of envious slaves, seeking to abolish the superior position of their betters. This 'slave morality' of good and *evil* is contrasted with the more aristocratic opposition of good and *bad*. Values such as courage, generosity and magnanimity or greatness of spirit reflect the strength and vitality of 'the noble, powerful, high-stationed and high-minded, who felt and established themselves and their actions as good, that is, of the first rank, in contradistinction to all the low, low-minded, common and plebeian'.[71] Nietzsche's genealogy raises a disturbing possibility: 'What if a symptom of regression were inherent in the "good", likewise a danger, a seduction, a poison, a narcotic, through which the present was possibly living at the expense of the future? Perhaps more comfortably, less dangerously, but at the same time in a meaner style, more basely?'[72] To the extent that conventional secular morality embodies Christian values, it may be not so much the highest expression of human civilization as an obstacle to man's 'highest power and splendour'.

Nietzsche's genealogy of morality is reinforced by a series of acute psychological analyses, which foreshadow the psychoanalytic theories of Sigmund Freud.[73] Nietzsche's observations are in the tradition of satirists such as Dean Swift and French '*moralistes*' like La Rochefoucauld, whose concise maxims uncover the selfish motivation at the root of apparently moral or altruistic behaviour. Selfishness outwits even the best intentions: 'Selfishness is cleverer than the cleverest man.'[74] In a similar way, the moral and psychological analyses of *Human, All Too Human* point to the real motivations behind conventionally lauded human emotions and attitudes. Nietzsche refers to La Rochefoucauld in his well-known discussion of pity, which he sees as the characteristic virtue of Christianity. Live among 'invalids and the mentally afflicted', he suggests,

and ask yourself whether their eloquent moaning and complaining, their displaying of misfortune, does not fundamentally have the objective of *hurting* those who are with them: the pity which these then express is a consolation for the weak and suffering, inasmuch as it shows them that, all their weakness notwithstanding, they possess at any rate *one power*: the *power to hurt*.[75]

The strategies of weak or 'reactive' individuals underlie the valuations of slave morality. Aristocratic values, on the other hand, are treated more approvingly as manifestations of strength or power. Thus gratitude is an expression of the strong or 'active' individual who demonstrates his power:

It is a milder form of revenge. If he did not have the compensation of gratitude, the man of power would have appeared weak and thenceforth counted as such. That is why every community of the good, that is to say originally the powerful, places gratitude among its first duties.[76]

Justice is not so much a selfless expression of natural benevolence as 'requital and exchange under the presupposition of an approximately equal power position', when 'a contest would result in mutual injury producing no decisive outcome'.[77] Evil acts are 'motivated by the drive to preservation or, more exactly, by the individual's intention of procuring pleasure and avoiding displeasure'. They only become evil when the individual is subjugated by a more powerful individual or collective.[78] In general, values are judged in terms of their source in the perspective of either 'active' or 'reactive', strong or weak individuals, and approved or disapproved of accordingly. Values are the varied manifestations of an underlying and universal 'will to power':

What is good? – All that heightens the feeling of power, the will to power, power itself in man.
What is bad? – All that proceeds from weakness.[79]

In this sense Nietzsche is really closer to Spinoza than to the French *moralistes*. Indeed on his first encounter with Spinoza's philosophy, Nietzsche remarked, 'my lonesomeness [*Einsamkeit*] . . . is now at least a twosomeness [*Zweisamkeit*]'.[80] The difference lies in the fact that for La Rochefoucauld the detection of egoism immediately implies moral condemnation: in Pascal's words, 'the self is detestable'.[81] Altruism is desirable even if unattainable. La Rochefoucauld's stance is still recognizably Christian in its disapproval of the devious stratagems of the 'hateful self' from a vantage point which, by his own analysis, no human can ever attain. Spinoza, on the other hand, who is similarly sceptical of claims to act altruistically, sees self-interest as the legitimate basis for our evaluations. Ethics is based on the *conatus* or 'will', the desire to 'persist in its own being', which constitutes the essence of every individual. He condemns hypocrisy and self-delusion rather than self-interest which, if adequately understood, is the proper basis of ethics. Spinoza also distinguishes 'active' from 'passive' emotions, active emotions corresponding to the increased perfection and pleasure of the organism. In a parallel way, Nietzsche's moral and psychological studies ultimately led him to posit a universal will to power, which both explains existing varieties of reactive morality and provides the basis for a 'transvaluation of all values', the discovery of more active values 'beyond good and evil'.[82]

The notion of will to power has often been misunderstood as implying a universal will to dominate or subjugate others. But for Nietzsche, the will to power is not equivalent to the desire for worldly power. On the contrary, Nietzsche's psychological investigations are designed to show that it is the weak who need to hurt others in their frustrated lust for power. The powerful have no need to do so. The powerful individual is quite the opposite of the petty tyrant or the scheming neurotic. His actions and virtues are manifestations of independence and strength rather than a desire to dominate. Thus, although a worldly ruler like Julius Caesar is one of Nietzsche's examples of a powerful individual, more often artists or philosophers such as Goethe and Schopenhauer are held up as models. In fact, power is expressed most clearly in all forms of 'self-overcoming'. It is even manifest in the apparent self-denial of asceticism, because 'ascetic self-torture is the source of the greatest possible feeling of power'.[83] Self-control, the disciplining of inclinations and ruthless self-criticism may all be motivated by the will to power if they lead to the greater power and perfection of the individual.[84]

In this respect, too, there is ambivalence in Nietzsche's attitude both to religion generally and to Christianity in particular. He has considerable respect both for Jesus Christ as a historical individual and for 'Christianness', in the sense of that which the founder of Christianity 'did and desired'. Christ is praised as a rare individual, who was willing to accept the evil done to him by others.[85] On the other hand, faith in Christ is an evasion of responsibility and the expression of a reactive or weak will. Particularly in its Lutheran form, faith is the resort of the individual who feels otherwise incapable of doing what is right. Nor is self-overcoming equivalent to the elimination of animal instinct or selfish inclination. That is the practice of the church, which 'combats the passions with excision in every sense of the word: its practice, its "cure" is *castration*'. Rather, power is evident in the continuing tension of an always fragile mastery of passion, the attempt to 'spiritualize, beautify, deify a desire', just as the highest art involves a difficult balance between the Apolline and the Dionysiac, between order and chaos.[86] Finally, for Nietzsche as for Spinoza, the powerful individual is also the rational individual. One of his most frequent charges against Christianity is its hostility to reason, its 'sacrifice of the intellect': 'Christianity also stands in opposition to all *intellectual* well-constitutedness – it *can* use only the morbid mind as the Christian mind, it takes the side of everything idiotic.'[87] According to Kaufmann's plausible interpretation, Nietzsche takes rationality to be the mark of great power: 'Rationality . . . gives man mastery over himself; and as the will to power is essentially the "instinct of freedom", it can find fulfilment only through rationality.' Power is measured in terms of 'man's willingness to subject even his most cherished beliefs to the rigour of rationality'.[88] The will to power is the opposite of the sacrifice of the intellect perpetrated by Pascal or Kierkegaard.

However, religion is not the only way in which the rigorous demands of the will to power are evaded. Nietzsche is equally vehemently opposed to any faith in the process and ultimate meaning of history. Hegel's ambitious dialectical system is seen as little more than the pursuit of religion by other means, the substitution of history for divine providence.[89] The problem of life is deferred rather than resolved by a philosophy of history which values present existence only as a stage on the way to the foreordained reconciliation of Absolute spirit. Marx's materialist theory of history is similarly eschatological in structure. The sufferings undergone during the pre-history of class struggle have meaning only in so far as they are necessary for the attainment of communism. Nietzsche is radically opposed to philosophy of history in either sense. Against the prevailing historicism of nineteenth-century thought, he maintains that there is no inevitability of progress, however dialectically mediated. By the same token, he resists the absorption of individual existence by the collective agencies of the world-historical process. It is not the historical fate of the collective which is significant or valuable, but individuals, particularly exceptional individuals: 'No, the *goal of humanity* cannot lie in its end but only *in its highest exemplars.*'[90] Whether history is understood in terms of Hegelian spirit or the social classes of Marxism, the meaning of individual existence is lost rather than confirmed by any philosophy of history.

If the meaning of existence cannot be found in the final stage or ultimate goal of history, then it must be sought in the intensity of the present moment. The point of existence lies in the immediacy of present experience: 'Enough of becoming, let me be.'[91] Nietzsche is drawn to the ideal of the 'supra-historical man', 'who does not envisage salvation in the process but for whom the world is finished in every single moment and its end attained'.[92] His famous doctrine of 'eternal recurrence' (or 'eternal return'), 'this highest formula of affirmation that is at all attainable', is an affirmation of the value of present existence in this sense.[93] The meaning of eternity here lies not in the infinite expanse of time but in the intensive quality of the moment. The joy of the powerful, life-affirming individual is expressed in that 'love of fate' (*amor fati*) which is willing to affirm the eternal recurrence of the present moment: 'All joy wants the eternity of all things.'[94] For this reason Nietzsche also values 'supra-historical' powers, which 'lead the eye away from becoming towards that which bestows upon existence the character of the eternal and stable, towards art and religion'.[95] In other words, ultimate value lies in the cultural, intellectual or personal achievements of exceptional individuals, in whatever time they exist. Socrates or Plato, Christ or Julius Caesar, Goethe or Spinoza were individuals who might never, probably would never, be surpassed.

Nietzsche's emphasis on individual life and the present moment also implies a relatively distanced relationship to conventional politics. As Kaufmann puts it, Nietzsche develops 'the theme of the antipolitical individual who seeks self-perfection far from the modern world'.[96] Certainly, only an overhasty reading could blame Nietzsche for the rise of fascism, even though some of his favourite terms, such as 'master race' and 'will to power', would later be adopted by Nazi ideologues.[97] There is little justification for seeing him as an anti-Semitic racist or nationalist. He was openly hostile to both nationalism and the nation-state, which he saw as one of the principal forces of mediocrity and conformity. He was particularly contemptuous of German nationalism and the new Reich. Nietzsche advocates race mixture as a stimulus to the development of culture and conceives the 'master race' as (in Kaufmann's words) 'a future, internationally mixed race of philosophers and artists who cultivate iron self-control' – not exactly the self-indulgent gangsters of the National Socialist leadership.[98] Partly responsible for this misreading of Nietzsche was his eventual collapse into insanity, which left him for the last decade of his life under the control of his sister, Elisabeth Förster-Nietzsche. She was a self-confessed anti-Semite and German nationalist who spent several years in Paraguay, attempting to set up an Aryan colony of pure race. During her brother's insanity and after his death she used her control of his papers and manuscripts to further her own ideological beliefs. For their part, the Nazis had a pressing need for intellectual credentials and these were willingly provided by Förster-Nietzsche. Misunderstanding is all the easier, since Nietzsche's style is aphoristic, deliberately unsystematic and often ironic. His sense of humour, which is not always easily distinguished from later episodes of megalomania, further adds to difficulties of interpretation. On the other hand, it is difficult to deny that Nietzsche was elitist, anti-democratic and anti-liberal. He was convinced that the value of humanity resided in its outstanding individuals rather than in the ordinary masses of nineteenth-century European society.[99]

In effect, then, Nietzsche reacts to the loss of religious faith and the hollowness of humanism as devastating but also liberating blows to the values underpinning nineteenth-century morality and society. Once the supernatural aura of Christian morality has disappeared, we should recognize it for what it really is, a slave morality incompatible with the full development of human powers. Nietzsche is contemptuous of the hypocritical other-worldliness of Christianity and of conventional bourgeois morality. He self-consciously confronts the stark possibility of nihilism. Can human life have value in a world without God? In the words of a character of Dostoyevsky, he considers the possibility that, 'were mankind's belief in its immortality to be destroyed ... nothing would be immoral any longer, everything would be permitted'.[100] Nietzsche's vivisection of conventional morality is designed to lay bare a kind of thinking capable of resisting the descent into nihilism. And following at least one line of intellectual descent, his emphasis on the individual, creativity and the present moment is echoed in the 'existentialism' of Jaspers, Marcel, Sartre and Camus. Authenticity and the individual's unconditional responsibility for his or her life become pre-eminent (if not always unambiguous) values.

More recent waves of interpretation, particularly in France, put more emphasis on Nietzsche's anti-humanism and less on his apparent celebration of heroic individuals and authentic existence. On this view (one substantially inspired by Heidegger) Nietzsche proclaims an even more radical break with the Western philosophical tradition and its metaphysical or 'ontotheological' quest for truth.[101] This Nietzsche is a practitioner of what Gilles Deleuze calls 'counter-philosophy' or 'nomad thought', whose 'statements can be conceived as the products of a mobile war machine and not the utterances of a rational, administrative machinery, whose philosophers would be bureaucrats of pure reason'.[102] This discourse does not aim for any kind of ultimate truth or knowledge of reality. No univocal meaning is intended, for '[t]he "signifier" is really the last philosophical metamorphosis of the despot'.[103] Meanings are allowed to proliferate, freed from the proprietorial grasp of either author or reader. From this perspective, the ambiguities of Nietzsche's aphoristic, metaphorical and playful style, his humour and irony are far more than merely formal features of his writing. Rather, they reflect the elusive essence of a philosophical discourse subversive of all codes and conventions.

Jean-Paul Sartre and French existentialism

Jean-Paul Sartre (1905–80) is perhaps the best-known philosopher of existentialism and a complex and intriguing figure. His philosophical preoccupations were at first mainly metaphysical. An important point of departure, in common with much modern philosophy and most French philosophy, is the methodical doubt and *cogito* of Descartes. But it is from the phenomenological method of Husserl and Heidegger that Sartre adapts his philosophical method. Still, Sartre's main influence has been as an existentialist philosopher of freedom, a politically engaged intellectual and, later in his life, theorist of Marxism. As an existentialist philosopher, he reiterates themes already encountered with Kierkegaard and Nietzsche – themes which also figure, albeit in more ontological guise, in Heidegger's earlier philosophy. His works contain nuanced explorations of a variety of human situations and emotional states. Like Kierkegaard, too, he exploits a range of discursive forms from short stories, plays and philosophical novels to political essays and biography as well as more conventional philosophical exposition. Sartre differs from both Kierkegaard and Nietzsche, however, in the privileged status he accords to social existence as opposed to the religious or aesthetic and cultural experience of the individual. In contrast to most earlier existentialists, Sartre is concerned from the beginning with embodiment, sexuality and intersubjectivity. His more social and embodied approach is complemented by a strong emphasis on political experience and action and the 'engagement' of the intellectual.

Sartre's major philosophical work, *Being and Nothingness* (1943), develops Heidegger's ontological-hermeneutic analysis of the meaning of 'being' from the perspective of human existence or 'being-in-the-world'. From the beginning, though, Sartre's philosophical interests are different. According to Heidegger, this leads Sartre to misunderstand *Being and Time* as an existentialist tract.[104] Sartre's ontological odyssey can be understood as an attempt to respond to the problem, clearly formulated but less convincingly resolved by Kant, of how to account for freedom and responsibility in a world which we experience as a causally determined order of things. Sartre steers a difficult path between realism and idealism, rethinking the relationship between mind or consciousness and the world in order to preserve the possibility of freedom without falling into the trap of idealism. It is evident to Sartre that idealism cannot tell us anything about the world in its brute materiality and contingency – about the 'being' or existence of the world as opposed to its formal or essential or ideal structure.[105] At the heart of idealism is a deceptive view of consciousness as a kind of receptacle which contains sensations (impressions or ideas) within itself. Sartre absolutely rejects this 'alimentary' view of consciousness, though he admits that it exerts a certain attraction: '[W]e have all believed that the spider-mind attracted things into its web, covered them with a white foam and slowly digested them, reduced them to its own substance. What is a table, a rock, a house? A certain assemblage of "contents of consciousness", an order to these contents.'[106] He finds the clue to overcoming this view of consciousness in phenomenology and, in particular, the insight that the distinguishing feature of mind or consciousness is its 'intentionality' or 'directedness toward an object'. Sartre takes the intentionality of consciousness to imply a radical break with any reifying view of consciousness – any way of conceiving either the mind or its 'contents' as things or thing-like. In characteristically flamboyant style, Sartre describes consciousness as an active 'explosion' towards objects in the world. Aronson's explanation here is helpful:

[C]onsciousness was 'a connected series of explosions which tear us away from ourselves, which do not even allow a "myself" the leisure to form behind them.' This totally active consciousness was totally spontaneous, and such a consciousness was nothing at all. It existed only as it moved out of itself, towards objects.[107]

And of course, a consciousness which is not a thing is nothing (the point alluded to in the title of *Being and Nothingness*).

Sartre's resistance to any kind of reification of consciousness leads him to criticize Husserl for reverting to the epistemological project of Kant. Both Kant and Husserl describe experience in terms of a transcendental ego, something supposedly 'behind' consciousness. But once the self is conceived as a thing in this way (whether as a Cartesian self or soul or as that transcendental agency which makes experience of a world possible), any explanation of the relationship between self and world becomes highly problematic. Having misunderstood the implications of his own insight, Husserl, according to

Sartre, falls victim to those perennial traps of Western philosophy, solipsism and idealism. Sartre's attempt to make a radical break with the assumptions of modern epistemology owes a great deal to Heidegger's revival of fundamental ontology. Heidegger too criticized Husserl for relapsing into transcendentalism and overemphasizing the subject at the expense of the world. For Heidegger, the fundamental ontological entity is the unanalysable unity 'being-in-the-world': conscious existence or '*Dasein*' and the objective world are aspects of an inseparable unity. Sartre proceeds to explore the being-in-the-world of consciousness, though his path diverges from Heidegger's in its greater preoccupation with the body, emotions and relations with other people. Sartre also arrives at an unashamedly existentialist position.

Sartre nevertheless attempts to define consciousness, albeit in a non-reifying way, independently of its situation in the world and so, in effect, he analyses the unanalysable unity of 'being-in-the-world' after all.[108] Even in his early Husserlian works on the 'image' and 'imagination', Sartre identifies the distinctive nature of consciousness as a kind of nothingness.[109] In this respect, perception is not the best guide to the nature of consciousness, because it is essentially passive or receptive and contains, as it were, too much of what is not pure consciousness. An exclusive focus on perception encourages a view of consciousness as the merely passive receptacle for external sensations. The phenomenological analysis of imagination, where no such element of receptivity is involved, is more likely to cast light on the creative spontaneity of mind. According to Sartre's analysis, imagination is both more certain and less rich than perception. An object which is perceived has an infinity of potential aspects or 'profiles' (*Abschattungen*), corresponding to the infinity of possible perspectives we can adopt in relation to it. Perception is, in that sense, inexhaustible. The relative poverty of the image stems from the fact that there is no more to it than we are aware of. The existence of an image is simply its being 'perceived' by consciousness (its *esse est percipi*). As a result, imagination is also more certain. It does not involve any surprises. The image 'teaches nothing, never produces an impression of novelty, and never reveals any new aspect of the subject. It delivers it in a lump. No risk, no anticipation: only a certainty.'[110] There is also a clear phenomenological difference – a difference for consciousness – between the mental contents involved in imagining and perceiving. The image presents itself to consciousness as *only* an image and, in this sense, is more 'negative' than a perception: 'The image presented its object as *absent*, and itself, therefore, as *only* an image. At the heart of the experience of imagining was negativity, known and accepted as such from the outset.'[111] For Sartre, imagination and consciousness are essentially negative in character and at their most pure when they are most negative. Already in these early works the dualism of Sartre's basic ontology is apparent in outline:

> Never could my consciousness be a thing, because its way of being in itself is precisely to be *for* itself; for consciousness, to exist is to be conscious of its existence. It appears as a pure spontaneity, confronting a world of things which is sheer inertness. From the start, therefore, we may posit two types of existence. For it is indeed just insofar as things are inert that they escape the sway of consciousness; their inertness is their safeguard, the preserver of their autonomy.[112]

The negative spontaneity of consciousness is set against an inert and positive realm of existence.

In *Being and Nothingness* these two orders of existence are presented more explicitly and extensively as 'being-in-itself' (*l'être-en-soi*) and 'being-for-itself' (*l'être-pour-soi*). The being of the 'for-itself' is presented in terms of a critique of Descartes for his neglect of the intentionality or 'positionality' of consciousness, a neglect which ultimately leads to the positing of a substantial soul. Sartre hopes to avoid the problems associated with such a reifying view of consciousness by insisting on a rigorously ontological definition of consciousness as 'positional consciousness':

> The first procedure of a philosophy ought to be to expel things from consciousness and to reestablish its true connection with the world, to know that consciousness is a positional consciousness of the world. All consciousness is positional in that it transcends itself in order to reach an object, and it exhausts itself in this same positing.[113]

The essence of consciousness is its intentional relation to the objects of an objective world. The corollary of this view is rejection of Descartes's epistemological or cognitive reading of consciousness as a 'reflective' or knowing consciousness. Reflective consciousness always involves self-consciousness, in the sense that 'To know is to know that one knows.' On the Cartesian view, consciousness must be accompanied by self-consciousness for it to be genuinely consciousness. It is only on this assumption that Descartes's 'I think therefore I am' is actually valid, or, in other words, that the existence of a thought implies knowledge of the existence of a thinker of that thought. But if my consciousness of some object must involve knowing that I am conscious of it, then *self*-consciousness must involve my knowing that I am conscious of myself. Thus, by introducing the epistemological dualism of subject and object into our understanding of consciousness, the Cartesian view inevitably leads to an infinite regress. Self-consciousness, understood as knowledge of consciousness, is only possible if we have knowledge of that knowledge of consciousness, and so on *ad infinitum*.[114]

It follows, according to Sartre, that we must understand consciousness ontologically rather than epistemologically as an 'immediate, non-cognitive relation of the self to itself', as 'non-reflective consciousness':

> Thus reflection has no kind of primacy over the consciousness reflected-on. It is not reflection which reveals the consciousness reflected-on to itself. Quite the contrary, it is the non-reflective consciousness which renders the reflection possible; there is a pre-reflective cogito which is the condition of the Cartesian cogito.[115]

Reflection, understood as a kind of knowledge of self, is secondary to non- or pre-reflective consciousness. Consciousness is always accompanied by an awareness which makes self-reflection possible, but consciousness does not depend on self-reflection in a way which would require it to be the intentional or positional object of another consciousness. To regard consciousness in this way leads, as we saw in the previous paragraph, to an infinite regress.[116] Sartre's notion of pre-reflective consciousness can avoid the regress, because consciousness is no longer regarded as an object standing in a particular relationship to other objects. Pre-reflective consciousness is a 'consciousness (of) objects', where the 'of' is parenthesized in order to make the point that no duality of subject and object is involved. Descartes's cognitive or 'reflective' cogito is thus preceded by a more fundamental 'pre-reflective cogito', which is therefore ontological rather than epistemological.

Because consciousness does not presuppose the existence of a substantial ego or 'I' which sustains or carries particular mental states, there is nothing to the existence of consciousness other than its occurrence – the '*esse*' or existence of consciousness is its '*percipi*' or 'being perceived'. This contrasts with the case of real objects in the world, whose 'being perceived' does not exhaust what it is for them to exist – except for idealists such as Bishop Berkeley.[117] Being perceived is a sufficient but not a necessary condition for the existence of material objects: if we genuinely perceive an object then it exists, but we also suppose that objects continue to exist when they are not being perceived. By contrast, it is of the essence of consciousness that it is a sufficient condition of its own existence: 'The existence of consciousness comes from consciousness itself.'[118] More strongly, Sartre claims that existence is the *only* essence that consciousness has. He illustrates this with the point that pleasure and the consciousness of pleasure are inseparable. Not only can there be no such thing as an unconscious pleasure, but there cannot be a conscious pleasure which is not a pleasure and, to that extent, consciousness is also infallible:

> There is an indivisible, indissoluble being – definitely not a substance supporting its qualities like particles of being, but a being which is existence through and through. Pleasure is the being of self-consciousness and this self-consciousness is the law of being of pleasure. This is what Heidegger expressed very well when he wrote (though speaking of *Dasein*, not of consciousness): 'The "how" (*essentia*) of this being, so far as it is possible to speak of it generally, must be conceived in terms of its existence (*existentia*).'[119]

Consciousness can have no other essence, because that would require it to have substance as well: 'Consciousness has nothing substantial, it is pure "appearance" in the sense that it exists only to the degree to which it appears.'[120] And, of course, consciousness can only appear to itself. Consciousness is being 'for-itself' rather than being 'in-itself'. More provocatively put, consciousness is not a thing in the world, it is nothing.

Sartre's account of being 'in-itself' is equally economical in ontological terms. He rejects the positing of any Kantian 'noumenon' or thing-in-itself behind appearances, '[f]or the being of an existent is exactly what it appears'.[121] On the other hand, as we have seen, there is more to the being of real things in the world than their appearing to consciousness or being perceived. The objective existence of a world outside consciousness is implied by the intentionality of consciousness: 'Consciousness is consciousness of something. This means that transcendence is the constitutive structure of consciousness; that is, that consciousness is born *supported* by a being which is not itself.'[122] Sartre accepts here something very close to the phenomenological account of the constitution of the objective world. The reality of an object is to be sought, not in some underlying substance, which would inevitably be inaccessible and unknowable, but in the 'inexhaustibility' or 'infinity' of the series of appearances. The difference between images and sense perceptions is that the latter occur in a particular order, which is not dependent on consciousness. As we move around an object, for example, we experience a series of perceptions, corresponding to the different perspectives we assume in relation to the object. Although, as embodied beings, we can choose the series of perspectives – by moving around the object in a clockwise or anti-clockwise direction, for example – we cannot choose the resulting series of perceptions. Equally, it is a characteristic of real existents, that there is an inexhaustible infinity of possible perceptions: we can never see something from every possible perspective. The essence of 'existents' in the world, then, is the principle of this series of perceptions: 'The essence of an existent is no longer a property sunk in the cavity of this existent; it is the manifest law which presides over the succession of its appearances, it is the principle of the series.'[123]

If the essence of existents is defined in terms of the series of appearances, then prior to the 'negating' activity of consciousness, on which depends the conceptual differentiation of these appearances, the in-itself must be conceived as undifferentiated and featureless positivity, as brute existence. It is timeless and therefore changeless; it is 'neither passivity nor activity'; it is neither necessary nor possible but simply is, it is pure contingency; it is 'equally beyond negation as beyond affirmation'. All that can be said is that 'being is what it is'.[124] Roquentin, the hero of Sartre's philosophical novel *Nausea*, has a disturbing experience of the absurdity of brute, nameless existence while sitting in the park looking at the root of a tree:

> And then, all of a sudden, there it was, as clear as day: existence had suddenly unveiled itself. It had lost its harmless appearance as an abstract category: it was the very stuff of things, that root was steeped in existence. Or rather the root, the park gates, the bench, the sparse grass on the lawn, all that had vanished; the diversity of things, their individuality, was only an appearance, a veneer. This veneer had melted, leaving soft, monstrous masses, in disorder – naked, with a frightening, obscene nakedness.[125]

The familiar world of differentiated existents in space and time, on the other hand, depends on the negating activity or 'nihilation' of consciousness: '[N]othingness is given as that by which the world receives its outlines as the world.'[126] Sartre, like Heidegger, takes the stance of someone posing a question about being as the basis for his account of consciousness as nihilation. Because any question may be answered by either 'yes' or 'no', either affirmatively or negatively, Sartre can say that, with the first question, being is supplemented by non-being or negation: '[A] glance cast on the question itself has revealed to us suddenly that we are encompassed with nothingness.'[127] The in-itself can only be ascribed specific properties in relation to the negating activity or nihilation of consciousness. To characterize being in a particular way is to negate it, in the sense that to ascribe a particular property or quality to being is to exclude a range of other properties.[128] The world as differentiated, objective reality depends on the particular projections of consciousness: '[N]on-being always appears within the limits of a human expectation. . . . The world does not disclose its non-beings to one who has not first posited them as possibilities.'[129] In other words, the conceptual structure, in terms of which our experiences are organized, is a projection of consciousness. Different conceptual schemes are conceivable. Beyond that, consciousness itself is not anything, it remains nothing.[130]

The nothingness which comes into the world with human existence also goes by another name – 'it is *freedom*'. With consciousness and negation comes the possibility of human freedom, the possibility of escaping the circuit of being – the determinism of the world of things – whereas, by itself, '[b]eing can generate only being'.[131] The negativity of consciousness is, for Sartre, the essential foundation of the possibility of human freedom. It is only because we can imagine alternative futures, conceive of possibilities that we may or may not ultimately realize, and project those possibilities onto the world, that human reality can be detached from the world and we can be free. In fact, freedom is equivalent to consciousness and defines the human essence: 'What we call freedom is impossible to distinguish from the *being* of "human reality". Man does not exist *first* in order to be free *subsequently*; there is no difference between the being of man and his *being-free*.'[132] Rather, the fundamental existentialist principle that for human beings 'existence comes before essence' implies the absolute freedom of individuals from any pre-given essence and consequently their absolute responsibility for their own lives. Our existence defines our essence, in the sense that we are free to create our own lives and values. To allow oneself to be constrained by custom, ideas of human nature or divine will, or any other notion of human essence, is to deny one's freedom and to live inauthentically or in 'bad faith'. Bad faith is the equivalent of despair in Kierkegaard's account of the 'sickness unto death'. As with Kierkegaard, too, freedom is something to be endured rather than enjoyed: we are 'condemned to liberty'. We experience our freedom as anxiety – the 'reflective consciousness of freedom' is anxiety.[133] Because the practice of freedom is exceedingly difficult, we are always tempted to claim that our actions were caused rather than freely chosen, and so disclaim responsibility. Sartre sees the unconscious mind postulated by Freudian psychoanalysis as little more than a useful accomplice in our bad

faith, allowing us to attribute our actions and emotions to unconscious impulses and complexes acquired in early childhood that are
beyond our control.[134]

Sartre provides a number of illuminating examples of the self-
deception involved in bad faith: 'a woman who has consented to go
out with a particular man for the first time' who denies to herself
that she 'knows very well the intentions' which he 'cherishes regarding her'; a waiter who is acting as if he were a waiter and nothing
more; being sad as a deliberate 'conduct' which we are really free to
abandon.[135] Perhaps most interesting is the example of a homosexual,
who denies that he is essentially or 'by nature' a 'paederast', a denial
that Sartre commends as the recognition of his freedom. But the same
homosexual falls into bad faith when he claims that he is essentially
not a paederast 'in the sense in which this table *is not* an inkwell'.[136]
Significantly, the 'sympathetic' friend who insists on a sincere admission from the homosexual of his homosexual nature is equally in bad
faith. Sincerity is just another stratagem of bad faith, since the sincere
man 'constitutes himself as a thing' by claiming to be essentially what
he in fact has freely chosen to be.[137] Even worse, he seeks further
advantage by distancing himself from the evil, thing-like self he guilt-
ily confesses himself to be:

> He derives a *merit* from his sincerity, and the deserving man is not the evil
> man as he is evil but as he is beyond his evilness. At the same time the evil
> is disarmed since it is nothing, save on the plane of determinism, and since
> in confessing it, I posit my freedom in respect of it; my future is virgin;
> everything is allowed to me.[138]

Not only, however, is freedom an extremely arduous responsibility,
always likely to be evaded, it is also inevitably unrewarding. Sartre
describes the condition of 'human reality' as a 'useless passion'
(*passion inutile*). The for-itself of consciousness is constantly striving
to realize its projects, to actually become whatever it posits as a goal
for itself, and so become a for-itself-in-itself. But it can never achieve
this state of fulfilment without ceasing to be what it is as negativity
or 'nothingness' – as the projection of further unrealized possibilities.
As Aronson explains:

> Consciousness can exist only as it sees the world as lacking, only as it
> rejects and surpasses it in order to give it meaning, only as it projects its
> possibilities as goals to be realized. Hence, consciousness is doomed to
> frustration. By nature consciousness is that which detaches itself from the
> world because the world is not enough; by its very nature the world is that
> which lacks.[139]

In effect, Sartre incorporates something very like the pessimism of the Schopenhauerian worldview. Human beings are doomed to the frustration of ceaseless striving because, once a particular goal has been achieved, their consciousness must posit further goals or else cease to be genuinely for-itself. Fulfilment exists either as future promise or as fond memory, but never as present and lived reality. Once consciousness has achieved a particular goal, it ceases to have value for it, and consciousness ceases to experience satisfaction: 'But pleasure is the death and the failure of desire. It is the death of desire because it is not only its fulfilment but its limit and its end.'[140]

The inevitable frustration of human existence is particularly evident in sexual love for another person, which aims at the possession of the other as free selfhood through his or her body, but which can succeed only in possessing the body:

> It is certain that I want to *possess* the Other's body, but I want to possess it in so far as it is itself a 'possessed', that is, in so far as the Other's consciousness is identified with his body. Such is the impossible ideal of desire: to possess the Other's transcendence as pure transcendence and at the same time as *body*, to reduce the Other to his simple *facticity* because he is then in the midst of my world but to bring it about that this facticity is a perpetual appresentation of his nihilating transcendence.[141]

For Schopenhauer, the obvious implication is that human fulfilment can only be fully and finally realized in death, an idea which finds expression in the famous '*Liebestod*' (or 'attainment of love in death') of Wagner's *Tristan and Isolde*. There are also resonances here with Freud's notion of the 'death wish' as an essential counterpart of 'eros', or the pleasure principle. For Sartre, the futility of human striving is an immediate reflection of the ontological commitment of consciousness to become a for-itself-in-itself. In fact, it reflects humanity's wish to be God, the only entity that could correspond to the concept of a for-itself-in-itself. This idea is perhaps best understood in terms of the Feuerbachian claim that the idea of God is really a projection of human aspirations.

It would be wrong, though, to give the impression that Sartre understands human existence as abstract and disembodied consciousness. He also provides an acute phenomenological description of the human situation as both embodied and essentially related to the 'Other'. We must also recognize the 'facticity' of consciousness, the fact that 'the for-itself *is*' both 'in so far as it appears in a condition which it has not chosen' and 'in so far as it is thrown into a world and abandoned in a "situation" ': 'It *is* in so far as there is in it something of which it is not the foundation – its *presence to the world*.'[142] An important aspect of the facticity of the for-itself is its embodiment. With his account of embodiment Sartre seeks, above all, to escape the 'reef of solipsism', which is implicit in any dualist account of body and mind as separate entities – entities which must somehow, mysteriously, be brought into relation with each other. The for-itself must not be conceived as simply located within a body or connected to a body: 'Being-for-itself must be wholly body and it must be wholly consciousness; it can not be *united* with a body.'[143] The body as 'being-for-itself' is 'a point of view and a point of departure': it is the perspective from which the world as an 'instrumental complex' unfolds and the centre from which consciousness projects its possibilities.[144]

The essentially embodied state of consciousness also implies and is implied by a 'primary relation between my consciousness and the Other's'. The Other appears to the for-itself as embodied also. The perception of another person creates an absence or 'hole' at the heart of my world, which follows from the recognition of a different 'point of view and point of departure' from my own. The perception of the Other 'unfolds a spatiality which is not my spatiality'. The situation is dramatically transformed, once again, with the 'look'. When the Other looks at me, I come to recognize myself as object and, reciprocally, the Other as subject: 'It is in and through the revelation of my being-as-object for the Other that I must be able to apprehend the presence of his being-as-subject.'[145] Subjected to the gaze of the Other, I become an object for his freedom. I live 'my being as it is written in and by the Other's freedom' and apprehend myself as nature.[146] Relationships with others are, as a result, characterized by the inevitability of conflict, which follows from the reciprocal interdependence of subject and object, freedom and thinghood, for-itself and in-itself. Subjects are condemned to an ultimately futile struggle for mutual recognition. It follows that sadism and masochism are not so much extreme pathologies as fundamental modalities of human relationship.[147]

Of course, Sartre's claim that we are always free to act or to feel in any way whatsoever, that it is never true to say that we 'had no choice', has been regarded as highly implausible. A concern more internal to Sartre's philosophical interests – and one to which he directs considerable attention – is the difficulty of deriving a concrete morality or ethics from his philosophical position. The freedom of consciousness implies its absolute ability to project any values whatever. Sartre attacks any view which assumes the objective existence of values independently of human choice as a symptom of the 'spirit of seriousness' (*l'esprit de sérieux*) typical of bourgeois morality.[148] The archetypal expression of human freedom is the apparently unmotivated 'arbitrary act' (*acte gratuit*). It even seems as if the more meaningless or irrational the act is, the more safely we can regard it as free. This impression is supported by an example from one of Sartre's novels, when, for no apparent reason, the hero Mathieu stabs his own hand with a knife.[149] Subsequently Sartre attempted to derive a more concrete moral position from his philosophy. In the popular essay, *Existentialism and Humanism*, he defends existentialism from the reproach that it represents no more than a morbid and individualistic celebration of despair and anxiety, leading inevitably either to political quietism or to nihilism.[150] He maintains there that our choices have social and political implications as well. Individuals must regard their free decisions as proposals for the adoption of corresponding values by humanity in general. However, this existentialist reformulation of Kant's categorical imperative faces similar problems to the original.[151] It is unclear, in particular, why or how the seemingly arbitrary choices of an individual, unconstrained by convention or pre-existing moral norms, carry such universal moral weight. How does the individual distinguish between an evil action and one which might be recommended to humanity? It is not obvious, in other words, how it is possible to avoid bad faith without complete arbitrariness.

In fact, Sartre draws quite radical ethical and political conclusions from his philosophy, whether or not he is strictly entitled to do so. Throughout his life he argued for the political and social responsibility of both the artist and the intellectual. In *What is Literature?* (1948), he argues that literature can help to dissolve bad faith by encouraging us to act more reflectively, with greater self-awareness. His Japanese lectures in the 1960s are less confident of the role of the artist, but still confront intellectuals with activist political demands.[152] Sartre himself was involved with the French resistance to the German occupation during the Second World War. After the war he embarked on a long and tortuous relationship with Marxism and the French Communist Party. In 1948 there was a short-lived attempt, with Merleau-Ponty and others, to set up an alternative and more democratically revolutionary party of the left, the Revolutionary People's Assembly. He was a prominent figure in the opposition both to American 'imperialism and genocide' in Vietnam and to France's rearguard colonialism in Algeria; this culminated in 1961 with a terrorist attack on his apartment.[153] Sartre's political commitments were also expressed through a long-standing involvement, starting in 1945, with the political review *Les Temps Modernes*. He wrote a large number of political articles, pamphlets and tracts. On the other hand, as the autobiographical sketch *Words* makes clear, he always stood in a close relationship with the 'unreal' (*irréel*) world of art and literature. Even in his philosophical works he sometimes represents art as the only reliable context for the expression of freedom. In fact, much of Sartre's literary output is also political. In a series of novels and plays he explores various aspects of political practice and experience, from the complex existential and political concerns of *The Roads to Freedom* to the moral dilemmas of the political terrorist in *Les Mains sales* and a portrayal of the formation of a fascist sympathizer in the short story, 'Childhood of a Leader'.[154] This politically engaged literature supplements the more metaphysical concerns of his earlier novel, *Nausea* (1938).[155]

In later theoretical works Sartre attempts to combine the insights of existentialism and Marxism, but at the level of social action rather than individual engagement. His suggestive but problematic *Critique of Dialectical Reason* theorizes human society and history according to the principle that human beings make history under conditions of scarcity.[156] He describes a series of social forms mediating between individual and society, including the group, the organization and class. Here, in contrast to his earlier ontological pessimism, he holds out the optimistic promise that, in Poster's words, 'human beings can attain freedom through the recognition of freedom in the other and in the consequent action of solidary groups pursuing this freedom'.[157] Particularly interesting is his analysis of different kinds of collective or 'ensemble': the alienated, 'serial' interaction between individuals relating to one another as things, as for example in a bus queue; the 'indirect gathering' of the passive and isolated listeners to the radio broadcast; and the 'impotent bond' of individuals buying and selling in a free market.[158] This analysis is designed to pose the problem of genuinely collective action in a novel way. How can we explain the occasional and often unexpected eruption of solidary action in the 'fused group', that sudden 'upsurge of mutual recognition in the context of daily life' which is now seen as the precondition of emancipation?[159] Much of the *Critique* goes on to describe how revolutionary collective action, once achieved, rapidly degenerates as revolutionary spontaneity is subjected to the constraints of formal organization and centralized leadership. By what is presented as an almost unavoidable dialectical logic of social forms, revolutionary organizations either suppress or purge internal differences and opposition and then proceed to impose a new order, which is not necessarily less oppressive than the order it replaces. The second, unfinished volume of the *Critique* applies the analytical categories of the first volume to an exhaustive description of the experience of the Soviet Union under communism and Stalinism.

In another significant contribution to existentialism, Simone de Beauvoir (1908–86), beginning from the assumptions of Sartrean existentialism, in particular his conception of freedom, addresses the question of woman as the 'perpetual Other' of man – woman as 'second sex'. The peculiar situation of woman is that:

> [S]he – a free and autonomous being like all human creatures – nevertheless finds herself living in a world where men compel her to assume the status of Other. They propose to stabilize her as object and to doom her to immanence since her transcendence is to be overshadowed and for ever transcended by another ego [*conscience*] which is essential and sovereign.[160]

She emphasizes throughout that the factors distinguishing women from men, even biological differences, do not necessitate the oppression of women: 'Woman is the victim of no mysterious fatality; the peculiarities that identify her as specifically a woman get their importance from the significance placed upon them.'[161] In fact, her account of woman's 'situation and character' represents quite a radical departure from the tenets of Sartrean existentialism. In particular, it implies that the freedom of the individual can indeed be limited by social conditions, that it is not necessarily an instance of bad faith for woman's consciousness to be affected by these conditions. Woman's oppression denies her access to the consciousness of freedom (as expressed in existentialist philosophy) required to overcome her genuinely involuntary servitude. In effect, Beauvoir attempts to mediate between the radical freedom and individualism of Sartre's existentialism on the one hand and the evidently social and psychological oppression of women on the other.[162] An analogous intellectual role is played by Frantz Fanon's analysis of racism, which applies Sartrean philosophy to the condition of the colonized.[163] On the other hand, it is not clear that Sartre's existentialism can be consistently socialized and politicized in this way. If the individual's actions are constrained by a sociocultural complex such as patriarchy, what other causal complexes are to be admitted as factors mitigating prima facie instances of bad faith? It is difficult to draw the boundary between unconditioned ontological freedom and a social condition of oppression. Still, Beauvoir's reworking of existentialism exerted a significant impact on feminism. It also helped to inspire the later, more political writings of Sartre as well as his biography of Jean Genet.[164]

However, Beauvoir's feminism has also been criticized for being unduly influenced by Sartre's misogynist view of femininity and the female body. In *Being and Nothingness* Sartre associates woman with the 'sliminess' of the in-itself, the self reduced to the status of a thing, with its tendency to engulf the transcendent subjectivity and untrammelled freedom of the for-itself: 'Slime is the revenge of the in-itself. A sickly-sweet, feminine revenge . . . a soft yielding action, a moist and feminine sucking.'[165] Femininity threatens to reduce a presumably masculine for-itself to the inertness and passivity of 'sticky existence'. What is worse, Beauvoir 'shares this view of femininity as "the Other" that threatens the free consciousness with its cloying and "appealing" nature'. Women are biologically weaker than men, they suffer 'instability', 'lack of control' and are 'fragile'; they are condemned by their biology to motherhood and by their socialization to an emotionally dependent and narcissistic femininity.[166] Accordingly, women's fuller participation in social and intellectual life is thought to require the sacrifice of their feminine otherness or difference as women – in order to be free, women must become more like men. In Moira Gatens's words: '[W]omen's participation in this fraternity is predicated on her repudiation of the female body and femininity. A symmetrical repudiation of the male body and masculinity is not in evidence in the case of men's participation.'[167] If this interpretation is correct, then clearly Beauvoir's feminism contrasts with more recent (including postmodernist) feminisms, which value woman and femininity as unconditional and irreducible 'difference'.[168] It is not, as Beauvoir implies, that women are oppressed by being made feminine, as the slave is oppressed by being made servile. Rather, patriarchal oppression devalues and disempowers female biology and feminine qualities.

Albert Camus (1913–60) gives a quite different account of the philosophy and politics of existentialism.[169] He differs most strikingly from Sartre in his conception of the absurd. For Sartre, absurdity belongs to the world prior to the conceptual projections or nihilating activity of consciousness. Camus's idea of the absurd is more self-consciously located within the existentialist tradition of Kierkegaard and Nietzsche. The absurd is a direct consequence of the absence of God. Without religion the discrepancy between human aspirations and the world is acute. The human condition is characterized by the probability of suffering and the certainty of death, a fate which human reason cannot accept as reasonable. In the face of this absurdity the 'universal reason, practical or ethical' of the Enlightenment has nothing to say: 'At this point of his effort man stands face to face with the irrational. He feels within him his longing for happiness and for reason. The absurd is born of this confrontation between the human need and the unreasonable silence of the world.'[170] In his novel *The Plague* (1947) this confrontation is epitomized in the painful death of a young and unquestionably innocent child from an unexplained outbreak of pestilence. The arbitrariness of the plague parallels the absurdity of existence. At the end of the novel one of the characters remarks: 'But what does it mean, the plague? It's life and that's all.'[171] The absurdity of existence raises the question of suicide and the meaning of life as 'the one truly serious philosophical problem'.[172] The myth of Sisyphus gives Camus a potent image of the futility of existence. Sisyphus is condemned to roll a heavy stone up a great hill, only to see the stone roll down again and face the prospect of repeating the same task over and over again for all eternity. Camus's response is that only the 'lucid' recognition of the absurdity of existence liberates us from belief in another life and permits us to live for the instant, for beauty, pleasure and the 'implacable grandeur' of existence. Lucidity is that clarity and courage of mind which refuses all comforting illusions and self-deception. Lucidity, in other words, is the counterpart of the notion, common to both Kierkegaard and Sartre, of anguish as the self-conscious and unflinching apprehension of freedom. But in the end Camus is more positive than either Kierkegaard or Sartre. Though living with absurdity is 'a confrontation and a struggle without rest', Camus concludes his account of the mythical Sisyphus with defiance: 'One must imagine Sisyphus happy.'[173]

Camus draws a political moral from the absurdity of existence in *The Rebel* (1951), a series of essays on a variety of topics from the French and Russian Revolutions, de Sade, Marx, Nietzsche and nihilism to anarchism. In a move similar to Sartre's existential modulation of the categorical imperative, Camus makes a dramatic, and for French philosophers seemingly obligatory, allusion to Descartes. Camus attempts to derive collective solidarity from individual defiance or 'revolt' in the face of the absurdity of existence: 'I rebel – therefore we exist.'[174] His ethic of uncompromising honesty and lucid revolt against absurdity encounters its most obvious enemies in the stifling atmosphere of conventional bourgeois morality and, more horrifyingly, in the concentration camp and totalitarianism of both fascist and Stalinist varieties. Though briefly a member of the Communist Party in his youth, Camus is openly hostile to communism. Above all, he rejects both the idea that the ends can justify the means and the arrogance of philosophies of history, which claim to know the end of history in advance. Both ideas were, of course, resorted to in defence of revolutionary expediency and even the Stalinist terror. Camus was attacked by Sartre for keeping clean hands at the expense of political engagement on the side of the exploited. Camus's political reputation also suffered when he supported his former compatriots, the French colonists, in the Algerian war of independence.[175]

The ultimate contribution of French existentialism is complex and sometimes paradoxical. Camus has been more influential as a novelist and stylist than for either his philosophy of the absurd or his more overtly political writings. Sartre increasingly distanced himself from existentialism to work on Marxist social theory. If *Being and Nothingness* is undoubtedly an impressive contribution to philosophy, it must be admitted that it bequeaths a problematic legacy. At the heart of this legacy is Sartre's concept of freedom. This has been criticized most vehemently for its detachment from social and political conditions, for example by theorists associated with the Frankfurt School. Because freedom is grounded in a basic ontological lack, a tendency to frustration is intrinsic to consciousness rather than something socially or politically conditioned. The uselessness of existence is unavoidable and so, from a political point of view, irrelevant. Marcuse sees existentialism as an apolitical and ultimately futile attempt to resolve, by philosophical means, problems of 'concrete existence' which demand a political solution, a critical theory of society. Like the Stoic, who withdraws to a subjective world beyond the reach of social and political realities, the underlying tendency of Sartrean existentialism seems conservative or, at best, apolitical.[176] Although Beauvoir and Fanon develop existentialism in a social and political direction, it is not clear that their reconciliation of radical freedom and social oppression can ultimately be sustained. On the other hand, there are a number of similarities between Sartre's Marxism and that of the Frankfurt School. Both include a 'humanist' commitment to the freedom of the individual subject, both reject the determinism of orthodox historical materialism and both envisage an important role for art and creativity in the transcendence of existing social conditions. Not surprisingly, then, both are prime targets for the proponents of a further distinctive constellation of ideas within continental philosophy. Both the philosophy of Nietzsche and the later writings of Heidegger play a significant role in the 'anti-humanist critique of the subject'. This critique is inseparable from the interrelated intellectual tendencies of structuralism and poststructuralism.

Further Reading

Kierkegaard's complex and paradoxical thought is best approached through *Fear and Trembling*, *The Concept of Dread* and *Either/Or* (two volumes). Nietzsche's similarly disparate oeuvre is well represented by the essays and aphorisms of *Untimely Meditations*, *On the Genealogy of Morals*, *Human, All Too Human* and *Beyond Good and Evil*. Sartre's popular essay *Existentialism and Humanism* is a gentle introduction to some of the ideas of *Being and Nothingness*. Simone de Beauvoir's most influential book is *The Second Sex*, but *The Ethics of Ambiguity* is philosophically interesting as well. Albert Camus's best-known philosophical works are *The Myth of Sisyphus* and *The Rebel: An Essay on Man in Revolt*. Distinctive of Sartre, Beauvoir and Camus are their numerous works of philosophical fiction and drama, notably Sartre's *Nausea* and the three completed volumes of *Roads to Freedom*, Beauvoir's *The Mandarins* and Camus's *The Stranger* and *The Plague*.

Some of the philosophers discussed in this chapter are commonly identified (if not always by themselves) as existentialists. A clear guide to this school of philosophy is John Macquarrie, *Existentialism*. Individual thinkers are helpfully explained by Alastair Hannay, *Kierkegaard*, Ronald Aronson, *Jean-Paul Sartre: Philosophy in the World*, E. Fullbrook and K. Fullbrook, *Simone de Beauvoir: A Critical Introduction* and S. E. Bronner, *Camus: Portrait of a Moralist*. The *Cambridge Companion* series provides useful collections of essays on Kierkegaard (ed. Hannay and Marino), Sartre (ed. Howells) and Camus (ed. Hughes). Both Walter Kaufmann's *Nietzsche: Philosopher, Psychologist, Antichrist* and R. J. Hollingdale's *Nietzsche* helped to free Nietzsche from unjustified associations with anti-Semitism and National Socialism. But their emphasis on existentialist themes is challenged by commentators focusing on Nietzsche's relationship to science, such as those collected in G. Moore and T. H. Brobjer, *Nietzsche and Science*. Nietzsche's affinities with poststructuralism and postmodernism are explored (controversially for some) in D. B. Allison, ed., *The New Nietzsche: Contemporary Styles of Interpretation* and Gilles Deleuze, *Nietzsche and Philosophy* – and compare the more extensive discussion of these philosophical approaches in chapters 6 and 7 (below). Richard Schacht, *Nietzsche*, attempts a balanced interpretation of his more philosophical works that takes account of both analytical and continental preoccupations.

6

Beyond the Subject: Structuralism and Poststructuralism

Outline

A number of strands of post-Enlightenment thought serve to qualify the epistemological, moral and political authority accorded to the 'subject' by modern philosophy from Descartes and Kant to existentialism and phenomenology. Hegel's historical idealism, Marxist materialism, 'depth' hermeneutics and Freudian psychoanalysis all, in their different ways, undermine the 'humanist' subject's certainty about its knowledge, moral convictions and political beliefs. Even the subject's meanings and desires can no longer be taken for granted. At the same time, these theories offer a variety of remedies for the deficiencies they uncover, from further development of either philosophy or society to a rigorous, 'in-depth' analysis of what subjects say and want. By contrast, both structuralism and poststructuralism are encouraged by the 'anti-humanism' of Nietzsche and Heidegger to dispense altogether with the subject's privileged status. Whether as knowing or judging consciousness, or as the author of actions, texts and meanings, the subject must be replaced – whether by an impersonal system of linguistic 'signs' (with Ferdinand de Saussure) or the cultural codes of Claude Lévi-Strauss, by Michel Foucault's 'subjectifying' discourses and disciplinary practices of 'power-knowledge' or the unstable and endlessly 'disseminating' field of '*différance*' which, according to Jacques Derrida, is inseparable from any attempt to think, speak or act.

Decentring the subject

Structuralism and poststructuralism can be understood as the culmination of a number of more sceptical strains of post-Enlightenment thought. These philosophical positions emerge clearly in the twentieth century, as a reaction to Hegelianism and Marxism on the one hand and Sartrean existentialism and phenomenology on the other. The associated critiques of humanism and the 'subject' develop tendencies apparent for some time both in philosophy and in the human and social sciences.[1] In this development, Nietzsche, the later writings of Heidegger and the linguistics of Saussure play an important role. The major outcome of these changes is a radical questioning of the privileged philosophical and political status of the subject within humanism and rationalism. Both what we have termed the dominant tradition of Enlightenment thought and some of its most influential continental critics rely on views of the philosophical subject which, according to structuralists and poststructuralists, cannot be sustained. But in what sense does Enlightenment rationalism tend to accord a privileged status to the subject?

In effect, the philosophical rationalism of the modern period holds human reason, or subjectivity, responsible for the validity of its own beliefs, values and decisions. Human reason is regarded as the sole and sufficient arbiter of truth, goodness and justice. Rationalism also challenges the authority of inherited tradition, whether in the form of the received wisdom of classical antiquity or the supernatural claims of religion and the church. Knowledge, values and even political power are to be placed on new and more secure, because more rational, foundations. In support of these ambitious claims for the power of human reason, rationalist philosophers make certain assumptions about both the cognitive and the practical subject – that is, the subject both as site of knowledge and as source of values. Both epistemology, or the theory of knowledge, and the attempt to provide rational foundations for morality become central preoccupations. Descartes's founding of knowledge on the certainty of self-consciousness is an influential instance. Kant transposes epistemological inquiry to a transcendental level, depersonalizing the subject or ego in the process. The subject of knowledge becomes abstract mind or reason, a reconstruction of the cognitive capacities of human or rational beings in general, or in other words capacities which every sane individual can be presumed to possess. The cognitive subject in this sense remains central to much subsequent philosophy in both continental and analytical traditions.

Emerging alongside philosophical rationalism was a variety of forms of moral and political individualism. From the sixteenth century, the Protestant Reformation expressed this tendency within the religious sphere, pointing to individual conscience rather than the authority of priests as the criterion of right action and salvation. Taking this tendency to its extreme, in the nineteenth century Kierkegaard would assert the 'subjective truth' of existence against the institutionalized Protestant Church.[2] The ultimate moral authority of the individual is also implicit in such philosophical doctrines as utilitarianism, intuitionism and subjectivism, which account for morality in terms of the pleasure or pain (happiness or unhappiness), the considered moral intuitions or the attitudes and emotions of individuals respectively. Liberalism asserts the right of the individual to a 'private sphere' free from all external interference. The ideal of democracy affirms the political right of individuals – at first, of course, only men – to take part in or to determine the actions of their own government.[3] The bounds of legitimate political agency are extended beyond the restricted sphere of monarchs or rulers to include 'responsible' citizens or 'men of property' and their parties and factions. Rulers are expected to justify their actions in the face of a largely bourgeois public opinion. Politics in the modern sense, as opposed to mere rule, begins to assume a historically novel importance. Overall, a similar position of authority is claimed for the subject in the practical sphere as epistemology implies in the theory of knowledge.

However, both in philosophy and in the human or social sciences a series of developments soon began to threaten the newly acquired status of the subject. The intellectual 'decentring' of the subject can be traced even to Kant's transcendental philosophy, despite the fact that he promotes the subject to a position of the highest epistemological and moral importance. The subject is made responsible both for the essential structure of reality and, as self-legislating rational will, for the moral law as well. Kant claims to identify the necessary and eternal or 'transcendental' features of any subject of knowledge or action. But precisely the transcendental status of his conclusions – the necessity of exactly those structural characteristics of the subject he identifies – proved difficult to sustain. Unconvinced by Kant's transcendental deduction, Hegel historicizes and collectivizes the philosophical subject. The bearer of knowledge and ethical life becomes a particular, concrete manifestation of 'mind' or 'spirit' (*Geist*), embodied in the life of a particular historical community. Ultimate truth, or the 'Absolute', is only guaranteed in the historical culmination of a dialectically unfolding series of forms of life and worldviews. By implication, the site of rational assessment is no longer located within the sphere of competence of ordinary historical individuals. The dialectic takes place behind the backs of individual subjects. History manifests the 'cunning of reason', which realizes the aims of the world spirit as the unintended by-product of the actions of individual agents. The site of rational assessment is removed to the final stage of the dialectic (whether already achieved or yet to be realized) or, perhaps, the authority of Hegel himself as self-proclaimed herald and philosophical guarantor of the Absolute.[4]

With Marx, a parallel narrative of humanity's historical self-constitution materializes the already historicized subject of Hegelian idealism. The dialectical development of the subject is explained in terms of the relationship between humanity and nature through work or production. The historical process is driven by contradictions within the mode of production rather than by intellectual or conceptual oppositions within worldviews.[5] The Marxist theory of ideology makes plain the implications of this view for the subject. Consciousness, whether as knowledge or as will, depends on the achievements and limitations of a collective subject which, in turn, corresponds to society's level of social and economic development. More pointedly, consciousness depends on class. Our beliefs and attitudes, even our most deeply held moral convictions, reflect our position in society rather than any absolute truth.[6] The characteristically Enlightenment commitment to universal values of liberty, fraternity and equality is merely a reflection of bourgeois conscience and, what is worse, self-interest. These values are no more than projections of the interests of the capitalist class, ideological weapons that could be used to undermine feudalism without hindering capitalist exploitation.

The Marxist theory of ideology represents a further blow to the self-confidence of the cognitive and practical subject. Individual subjects can no longer be presumed to have reliable access to rational criteria of theoretical or moral truth. But as with Hegelian idealism, Marxism does not so much abolish as displace the privileges of the individual subject. These privileges are transferred to a collective historical subject, namely the proletariat which, in virtue of its position within the capitalist mode of production, is destined to overthrow capitalism and achieve true consciousness. Individuals can only achieve true consciousness, as it were vicariously, by subordinating their alienated self to the collective will of the class. In the Leninist tradition, the centre of cognitive and practical privilege is further removed to the leadership and policies of the revolutionary party. With the abolition of capitalism and the arrival of communism, the ideological distortions of class society will come to an end. Social relations will become transparent and individuals will attain their true 'species being', the full and undistorted flowering of all their human capacities.

A further major decentring of the subject, this time more psychological than sociological, occurs with the 'psychoanalysis' of Sigmund Freud (1856–1939). Nineteenth-century psychology took a variety of forms, but two of its most influential currents correspond to the predominant mind–body dualism of post-Cartesian metaphysics. Experimental psychologists investigated the physiology of the brain and nervous system as the causally explanatory reality underlying the mind. Introspectionist psychologists described the distinctive character of mental or psychic states 'from within' or, in other words, through their own subjective experience. In the main, studies of mental disorder or 'pathology' were restricted to the exhaustive description and classification of the sometimes startling phenomena of nervous disease, dementia, hysteria and sexual 'perversion'.[7] Much more unsettling to the assumptions of nineteenth-century thought were Freud's theories of the unconscious mind. Freudian psychoanalysis challenges the status of the conscious subject of experience, because it suggests that individual consciousness and behaviour can only be understood in terms of the less than rational and transparent workings of the unconscious mind. But again, like Marx, psychoanalysis does not so much cancel as transfer the privileges of the subject.

Freud's distinctive approach can be traced to his early work with Breuer and Charcot on the causes of 'hysteria'. Freud originally qualified as a physiologist and, in fact, throughout his career retained a preference for mechanistic models of explanation and neurophysiological hypotheses. Like Charcot, then, he was struck by the curious physical symptoms involved in cases of hysteria, a nervous disorder suffered mainly by women and traditionally blamed on the erratic behaviour of the womb.[8] These symptoms often made little sense in physiological terms. For example, in the case of a patient complaining of paralysis of the hand, the region of paralysis would correspond to the patient's common-sense ideas about physiology rather than the actual workings of the body, which do not allow such limited dysfunction.[9] There also seemed to be a relationship between hysterical symptoms and hypnosis. Symptoms could be induced by suggestion, when someone was in a hypnoid state. Later, Freud used hypnosis in both diagnosis and cure. These and other observations led Freud to postulate an 'ideogenic' – psychological or mental – rather than physiological aetiology for hysteria. On the other hand,

Freud was convinced that the symptoms of the hysteric were not simply voluntary or consciously faked. At least some patients genuinely suffered from an extremely unpleasant mental disorder, which made anything like an ordinary life impossible. If such disorders were involuntary, but nevertheless caused by mental rather than physiological factors, then only *unconscious* mental states could provide an explanation.

Freud went on to elaborate a series of related concepts describing the relationship between the conscious and the unconscious mind. Concepts such as trauma, repression, resistance, ego, id and superego have become part of our everyday vocabulary. He also developed a number of techniques for gaining access to the unconscious mind. Most famously, word association and the analysis of dreams are two significant tools in what he began to call 'psychoanalysis'. In his case studies Freud claimed a number of impressive cures with the help of these techniques.[10] But the implications of his theories extend far beyond the realm of mental pathology. In fact, Freud is concerned with a much wider range of mental phenomena. The impact of the unconscious mind can be recognized in a wide range of apparently normal behaviour. Jokes and slips of the tongue, the forgetting of names or appointments, dreams and fantasies, religion and culture – all can only be properly understood in terms of the unconscious mind.[11]

Freud's concept of the unconscious mind has far-reaching implications.[12] It implies that consciousness never gives us more than a partial and distorted view of our mental life, so the Cartesian principle that the mind or subject is simply equivalent to a fully transparent consciousness is undermined. For Freud, the reasons we give for our actions may be no more than rationalizations, obscuring the real origin of our behaviour in the trauma or unresolved emotional conflicts of early childhood. The conscious mind, even when it enjoys 'healthy' or 'normal' functioning, is ultimately the plaything of the unconscious, the creature of its whims and fancies – subject, in the final instance, to its repressive veto.[13] In this sense, clearly, Freudian psychoanalysis betokens a further decentring of the subject. The individual subject has no guarantee of 'knowing its own mind'. We may be dupes of our unconscious, just as, for Marx, we are, for the most part, dupes of history and class. On the other hand, and again with parallels to Marx, psychoanalysis holds out for the conscious self at least some prospect of recovering its sovereignty. A protracted dialogue between analyst and patient promises eventual relief from neurotic and even psychotic symptoms – what has been described as a 'talking cure'.[14] The self can, in principle at least, come to understand the unconscious springs of its conscious states and impulses. In the terms of Lorenzer and Habermas, analysis can help to remove the barriers to the free 'internal communication' of a potentially transparent subjectivity.[15] Through the 'depth hermeneutics' of psychoanalysis, individuals can hope to approach, if perhaps never to attain – analysis may turn out to be 'interminable', repression and neurosis may be the unavoidable accompaniments of 'civilization' – something like the ideal of transparent selfhood held out by the Cartesian tradition.[16] The subject, as site of cognitive and practical rationality, is dethroned only provisionally.[17]

The break with humanism

Hegelian idealism, Marxism and Freudian psychoanalysis displace the subject from its privileged position, yet they do not break irrevocably with humanism. Each of these theoretical approaches retains a qualified or conditional role for the subject and so remains within the pale of humanist assumptions. A more decisive break with humanism occurs with further developments in two areas of intellectual activity, namely hermeneutics and linguistics. Both areas are closely concerned with language and, as a result, are of obvious significance for both philosophy and the human sciences. In fact, traditional hermeneutics involves only a provisional decentring of the subject analogous to the decentring of the subject implicit in Marxism and psychoanalysis. The development of the hermeneutic approach within the human sciences, which are concerned in a major way with the interpretation or criticism of texts and the historical reconstruction of past events, reflects increased awareness of the difficulties of mutual understanding. Hermeneutic principles are called upon, not only where texts present obvious difficulties of interpretation, but all the time, since mutual understanding between subjects can never be taken for granted. To understand any text or utterance involves knowledge of the social and linguistic context in which it was produced – understanding of the part depends upon understanding of the whole. This realization further undermines the position of the subject of discourse, since meaning can no longer be regarded as being completely under the control of the individual speaker or writer, who cannot take account of every aspect of his or her linguistic context. However, traditional hermeneutics regards this dependency as remediable. Thus, for Dilthey, the recovery of the original intentions or meaning of the author can be achieved through knowledge of the broader cultural and linguistic context. The practice of hermeneutics promises an always improving, though in some versions never perfect, interpretation of meaning – an always improving degree of mutual understanding between subjects.[18]

From this point of view, the radical hermeneutics of both Heidegger and Gadamer represents a more decisive break with humanist assumptions. Although it is particularly in his later writings that Heidegger explicitly distances himself from humanism, his abandonment of epistemology for ontology directly implies a rejection of the exaggerated role accorded to the subject in modern Western philosophy. The overemphasis of the subject within epistemology corresponds to a reductive 'objectification' of the world by metaphysics associated with the destructive reign of instrumental thinking and technology. The fundamental starting point of his philosophy is thus the indivisible unity of 'being-in-the-world' (in effect, the unity of subject and object). Heidegger's position is evident in his reaction to Sartre. Although Sartre claims to follow Heidegger in rejecting the assumptions of modern metaphysics and epistemology, he still falls into subjectivism. In his 'Letter on Humanism' (1947) Heidegger explicitly responds to Sartre's claim that existentialism is also a humanism, taking issue in particular with the Cartesian assumption that 'one must take subjectivity as his point of departure'.[19] Sartre's *Being and Nothingness* applies Heidegger's 'hermeneutic of Being' in an explicitly existentialist direction and so misunderstands its basic point. Heidegger's anti-humanist critique of the subject–object dichotomy of Western thought leads instead to advocacy of 'thinking' as the 'letting-be' of a transcendent Being. Thinking is to be understood not as the directed activity of a conscious subject but, rather, as an impersonal openness or receptiveness to the world. Heidegger advocates something close to a religious attitude of humility, a deferential attentiveness to Being. Indeed, the almost mystical status accorded to Being has led some to see it as a cipher for God, despite the fact that, according to Heidegger, this attitude 'can be theistic as little as atheistic'.[20] Still, it can hardly be denied that 'thinking' takes us a long way from the humanist assumptions of Enlightenment rationalism.

Of course, anti-humanism in Heidegger's sense is not equivalent to the assertion of the worthlessness of human life. There is a clear distinction between anti-humanism and the 'affirmation of inhumanity'.[21] Rather, anti-humanism is opposed to any philosophy of 'values', which reduces the worth of things to their status as 'valued by some subject'. There are thus clearly affinities with Nietzsche, who provides an incisive diagnosis of humanism's arrogant premise:

The whole attitude of 'man *versus* the world,' man as world-denying principle, man as the standard of the value of things, as judge of the world, who in the end puts existence itself on his scales and finds it too light – the monstrous impertinence of this attitude has dawned upon us as such, and has disgusted us – we now laugh when we find 'Man *and* World' placed beside one another, separated by the sublime presumption of the little word 'and'![22]

Indeed, humanism is held responsible for many of the characteristic vices of modern society, including its not infrequent inhumanity. For the technological attitude, which is one significant expression of humanism, all beings, whether human or non-human, are manipulable objects available for exploitation. Nature too is 'set-upon' as a mere object, as nothing more than a 'standing-reserve' or resource for human use. Even with what would now be called ecological tourism, nature is treated as 'an object on call for inspection by a tour group ordered there by the vacation industry'. Even 'man', as the supposed subject of this instrumental relationship with nature, is reduced to an object in the same way: 'If man is challenged, ordered, to do this, then does not man himself belong even more originally than nature within the standing-reserve?'[23] Indeed, the historical guilt of humanist philosophy may extend even further than this. Humanist arrogance is held responsible for colonialism, genocide and even the Holocaust. The technological and bureaucratic sophistication of the Nazi genocide is a striking instance of modernity and, for some, also humanism, despite its evident inhumanity.

Certainly, then, although Heidegger's philosophical anti-humanism may explain his less than robust commitment to Enlightenment values such as equality and liberty, it cannot be blamed for his association with Hitler's National Socialism or his subsequent tardiness in disowning this involvement.[24] The injunction to be 'attentive to Being', like the call to obey the will of God, is in principle compatible with almost any political stance. On the other hand, the evident difficulty of 'thinking' in its full Heideggerian sense, with the suggestion that only the philosophically adept are capable of achieving the appropriate relationship with Being, provides a possible foothold for authoritarian claims. It *may* be true that when Heidegger spoke in 1935 of 'the internal truth and the greatness of the movement', he was not speaking of the Nazis. As Lyotard interprets it, Heidegger's position was that,

[T]hose people [who] were far too limited in their thinking . . . could only mask and mislead the authentic anxiety that Heidegger thinks he recognises in the desperate search (the 1930s) which, at that time, projects the

Volk towards a decision, a resolution that may be in accord with what is 'peculiar' to it. The movement that derives from the unbearable anxiety of being thrown before nothingness, Heidegger believes, needs 'knowledge' in order to guide and resolve itself to a decision.[25]

But a philosophy shelving so steeply into obscurity and mysticism is surely that much more vulnerable to the blandishments of a charismatic despot.

Gadamer's ontological hermeneutics represents a less questionable development of Heidegger's anti-humanist approach. In a clear departure from Cartesian assumptions, which ground the existence of both an objective world and other minds on a self-founding and transparent consciousness, for Gadamer it is the subject which is ontologically derivative. The subject exists only within the irreducibly intersubjective medium of understanding and language. Understanding is not only and not primarily one dimension of the knowledge of a subject, as it was for Dilthey, but, rather, the medium in which the subject has its existence. In other words, Gadamer repeats Heidegger's move from epistemology to ontology. Understanding is conceived not 'as a subjective process of man over and against an object but the way of being of man himself'.[26] Accordingly, hermeneutics is not simply the characteristic method of the human sciences, but the key to truth in general. By the same token, the close relationship between understanding and historicity, already identified by Dilthey, characterizes not just the objects but also the subjects of acts of interpretation. It is not only the historical text which is inseparable from a concrete historical, cultural and linguistic context. The subject is situated not only, as it were, horizontally in the dimension of language or understanding, but also vertically in the dimension of history and tradition. Understanding always as much derives from a particular perspective as it is directed towards a specific historical context. A corollary of this view of the subject is that the author of a historical text can no longer be regarded as the ultimate authority on its meaning. The work is understood not solely or, perhaps, even principally as the product of an individual subject. From the perspective of Gadamer's hermeneutics, the subject – whether as author or as interpreter – is much less important than the surrounding medium of understanding or language itself.

An even more radical challenge to the subject is evident in the thought of Emmanuel Levinas (1906–95), who blames the humanist focus on identity, sameness and the subject for a deep-seated neglect of the 'other' in Western thought – a neglect which finds its most horrifying expression in the death camps and killing fields of the twentieth century. Levinas's 'genetic phenomenology' is clearly influenced by Hegel, Husserl and Heidegger, but diverges from them in crucial respects. Unlike Hegel, Levinas's dialectic leads not to the comprehensive totality of the 'absolute', but towards 'alterity' or otherness. To this end, Levinas also dissociates phenomenology from any remaining Husserlian infatuation with the transcendental subject. Even Heidegger's ontological overcoming of subjective consciousness for the sake of a greater 'attentiveness to Being' is left behind. It is Western philosophy's very insistence on the primacy of epistemology and ontology, on 'knowledge and understanding' or on 'being and truth', which must be abandoned in the face of the fundamental primacy of the ethical. In Richard Cohen's words: '[A]lterity must be acknowledged in terms of what *surpasses* understanding absolutely, what is *superior* to the horizons of being and the truth of being, what exceeds or precedes the beginning of philosophy: the *surplus* or *excellence* of ethical command and the infinite responsibilities it calls forth.'[27]

In the process, the 'existent' or subject must be radically decentred: '[T]he *I* is *first* for-the-other *before* the very firstness of its being for-itself.'[28] The 'radical passivity' of the good will is referred to a 'Desire' which 'has its center outside of itself'.[29] The subject only comes into existence as always already responsible to otherness. As Bauman puts it: 'I become responsible while I constitute myself into a subject. Becoming responsible *is* the constitution of me as a subject.'[30] Levinas also draws deeply on religious texts, particularly those of Judaism, in order to develop his views. In a phrase derived from the Old Testament – and in obvious contrast to Descartes's privileging of consciousness with his 'I think, therefore I am' – the 'Here I am!' founds the self as '*subjectum*, subjectivity as substitution and expiation for the other'.[31] The active, heroic will favoured by existentialism and even the earlier Heidegger is replaced by a passive will, which declares its availability for the ethical demands of the other. Although, like both Heidegger and Gadamer, Levinas's later work attends increasingly to the nature of language, it is the ambiguous, open expression of the 'saying' rather than the 'coherent language' and 'contaminated' logic of the 'said' that is celebrated.[32] Saying speaks 'the hyperbolic passivity of giving, which is prior to all willing and thematization'.[33] It allows a responsibility for the other, which is lost once the 'logocentric' certainties of the 'said' take over: 'Saying opens me to the other before saying what is said, before the said uttered in this sincerity forms a screen between me and the other.'[34]

Language, albeit in a very different sense, is at the heart of another important source of anti-humanist thought. The 'structural linguistics' of Ferdinand de Saussure (1857–1913) has been the main inspiration for the approach known as structuralism.[35] Like Gadamer, Saussure focuses on language rather than the speaking or interpreting subject. The challenge to the conventional view of the relationship between subject and language is already evident in Saussure's primary distinction between 'language' (*langue*) and 'speech' (*parole*). It seems obvious to Saussure that language exists as a system of signs (words and meanings) independently of the particular 'speech acts' of individual speaking subjects. The latter are instances of *parole* in the sense of the 'actual speech, the speech acts which are made possible by the language'.[36] Speakers can only say or mean something with the help of a language, which already exists before they speak. By implication, the meaning of language cannot be accounted for in the subjective terms of either phenomenology or psychology. Meaning cannot depend on the subject's conscious acts of intending or meaning, as phenomenology suggests, any more than it can be understood as the product of some kind of psychological or mental association between sign and meaning.

A second important step towards structuralism results from Saussure's argument for a 'synchronic' rather than a 'diachronic' approach to language.[37] The study of language must break radically with diachronic approaches, which study the changes undergone by language over time. Thus classical philology traces the meaning and phonetic character of words in contemporary languages to their roots in earlier ones. But diachronic accounts can never really explain how a language works. After all, even if the etymological roots of a word can be traced, nothing guarantees that the word has not radically changed meaning in the meantime. In any case, we need to establish the meaning of the root word itself, and we cannot refer this to *its* etymology without falling into a vicious regress. However interesting may be the findings of philology, language must ultimately be explained synchronically. In other words, the meaning and functioning of language depend on facts about an existing system of signs and meanings rather than on any genetic or developmental story about the origins of this system.

But if meanings are neither inherited from the past nor the creation of intending subjects, how are they to be explained? In Saussure's terms, an explanation of the meaning of a sign must provide an account of the relationship between the 'signifier' – the word or sign considered as a particular sound or set of written characters – and its 'signified' – the meaning or concept the signifier represents. Crucially for Saussure, this relationship does not reflect any intrinsic or essential quality of the signifier, as if meaning were the property of an underlying linguistic substance. The mere existence of different languages proves that the relationship between signifier and signified must be an arbitrary one. Only onomatopoeic words such as 'splash' or 'quack', which sound like the thing to which they refer, are not clearly arbitrary in this way.[38] According to Saussure, what gives particular words their meaning is the language as a whole, considered as a structured system of elements. Meaning depends on the differential relations or contrasts between elements, which in the case of language are signs: 'Since the sign has no necessary core which must persist, it must be defined as a relational entity, in its relations to other signs.'[39] The meaning of a term like 'blue', for example, depends on the particular colour contrasts that the language allows: blue is whatever is *not* green or red or yellow, and so on. Significantly, different languages embody different conceptual distinctions, which may involve more or less refined gradations of meaning and may even draw conceptual boundaries in different places.

One obvious result of this account is that translation between languages is always imperfect, as there can be no guarantee of a one-to-one correlation between their elements. It also implies that the acquisition of language involves, above all, mastery of the particular system of distinctions and contrasts that it comprises. A child first learns to speak *not* by learning the meanings of more and more words as discrete entities, but rather by making basic distinctions between words for mother and father, self and other, good and bad, proceeding to ever more refined distinctions. From this structuralist perspective, the only essential property of any language or code (the only thing that is not arbitrary from the point of view of the linguist) is the fact that it consists of a number of distinguishable and differentially related elements. In principle, there is no difference or priority between spoken and written languages or between these and the 'signed' languages used mainly by deaf people. A structuralist account of meaning also helps to explain how an apparently abstract medium such as music can have meaning, since music can also be understood as a system of differentially related elements. Overall, the structural analysis of meaning reinforces the anti-humanist implications of Saussurean linguistics, because meaning can no longer be attributed to individual speaking subjects. Speakers are only able to mean something with their words thanks to the pre-existing system of linguistic and semantic oppositions embodied in language.

Structuralism is, in effect, the result of extending Saussure's structural method and the associated critique of the subject and humanism to the entire field of the human sciences. With his project of a general semiotics or theory of the sign, Saussure had himself anticipated an extension of that kind. Developments in mathematics, logic, biology and psychology – associated with the group of mathematicians known as Bourbaki, Claude Bernard and Waddington in biology and *Gestalt* psychologists – lent support to structuralism.[40] By the 1960s an array of approaches in the social and human sciences argued that social and cultural phenomena should be treated neither as the intentional products of human subjects nor as the unintentional by-products of history, but rather as structured systems of elements with specific and irreducible rules of combination and transformation. By abstracting from everything subjective (from the conscious self and its intentions or acts of meaning), structuralists also hoped to demonstrate the strictly scientific nature of their enterprise. As Dreyfus and Rabinow put it: 'Structuralists attempt to treat human activity scientifically by finding basic elements (concepts, actions, classes of words) and the rules or laws by which they are combined.'[41] On the other hand, structuralists distanced themselves from the reductively atomistic, analytical approach of the dominant tradition of science, emphasizing instead the distinctive properties of systems as wholes, which are more than the sum of their parts. Structuralism is also a species of holism.[42]

Perhaps most famously, the structural anthropology of Claude Lévi-Strauss (1908–2009), probably the most persistent, austere and unashamed advocate of structuralism, influenced a generation of social scientists. Lévi-Strauss certainly acknowledged his debt to Saussure as well as to Roman Jakobson.[43] Lévi-Strauss also suggests a link with Freud, when he claims that 'anthropology draws its originality from the unconscious nature of collective phenomena'.[44] Like the rules of a language, patterns of social organization are typically reproduced from one generation to another without being either consciously understood or deliberately chosen. Accordingly, society, like language, cannot be understood by simply examining the intentions or actions of individual social agents. Again like Saussure, Lévi-Strauss's approach is synchronic rather than diachronic. Social and cultural forms are not explained in terms of their origin or genesis, a method which only pushes the problem of explanation one step further back. Rather, each element is explained in terms of its position within the overall system of society as it exists at any one time. The various dimensions of social life (including kinship systems, mythology and rituals) are understood as structured systems of elements with their own distinctive and irreducible rules of combination and transformation. Lévi-Strauss adapts Jakobson's phonological model of binary oppositions between discrete sounds or 'phonemes', analysing mythology as a structured system of 'mythemes'. Similarly, totemism is understood as a sophisticated set of isomorphisms between the structures of the natural and the human world, whereby classifications of animal or plant life correspond to a parallel ordering of human kinship relations.[45] More dubiously, Lévi-Strauss combines his structuralist methodology with the universalist claim that there is a 'fundamental unity of all cultures'. In other words, he supposes that the diversity of structures found in human societies and cultures can be shown to derive from a single underlying structure (or structure of structures) common to humanity as a whole. Implicitly, such an underlying structure must depend on a conception of shared human nature, albeit a nature that determines how rather than what people think.[46]

Another influential example of structuralist and anti-humanist theory was the Marxism of Louis Althusser (1918–90).[47] Structuralist Marxism was exciting to many, because it promised to apply the apparently ahistorical, synchronic categories of structuralism, which has often been accused of eliding the dimension of history altogether, to an explicitly and irreducibly historical body of theory. It also seemed to offer a more scientific alternative to historicism and idealism, which had dominated French intellectual life since the revival of interest in Hegel from the 1930s.[48] Certainly, contemporary capitalist society was readily susceptible to structuralist analysis. After all, Marxism was always an explicitly holistic theoretical approach. Society cannot be understood in the reductive atomistic terms of bourgeois social science, but only according to the dialectical categories of historical materialism, for which society is, in Lukács's terms, a 'totality'.[49] Althusser's account of the structural relations between relatively autonomous state and non-state 'apparatuses', therefore, is compatible with the spirit of Marx's original theory (though some would claim that it does not add very much either). More radically, Althusser argues that the historical dimension of Marx's theory can be subjected to a similarly structuralist analysis. All that is required are 'diachronic' rules of transformation to supplement the 'synchronic' rules of combination that govern the structural elements of society at any one time. Once applied, these rules of transformation reveal history as a series of 'ruptures' or discontinuous transformations from one structured whole to the next. In similar terms he provides an account of Marx's own intellectual development, identifying a fundamental break between his earlier 'pre-scientific' writings, which are still infected with essentialism and humanism, and the mature and fully scientific achievement of *Capital*.

Although his immediate adversaries were uncritical followers of the French Communist Party's line, Althusser's interpretation of Marx is also directed against Sartre's attempt to combine the insights of existentialism and Marxism. Equally clearly, it is diametrically opposed to the Marxism of the Frankfurt School too. For those unashamed 'humanists', it is precisely the scientific pretensions of the later economic writings that prepare the ground for the positivist and Stalinist degeneration of Marxism. By contrast, Althusser sees Stalinism as a kind of humanism. He describes socialist humanism as an ideological formation that reflects problems unresolved during the Stalinist period in the Soviet Union, just as eighteenth-century bourgeois humanism 'was the visible counterpart to a shadowy inhumanity' or, in other words, to capitalism.[50] On the other hand, Althusser's anti-humanist Marxism raises a problem often attributed to structuralist analyses, namely how to account for political practice without resorting to some notion of the subject. Revolutionary political practice apparently depends on the deliberate choices of actual historical agents. But an account of history as the rule-governed transformation of impersonal social structures seems hostile to, or at least uninformative about, deliberate human practice of that kind. As a result, it is not clear in the end whether structuralism leaves much room for politics.[51] The problem is even more pressing when the strictly structural transformations of the capitalist system no longer point in the direction of communism. The problem of accounting for political agency will recur in later incarnations of structuralism and poststructuralism.

Foucault's genealogy of the subject

Michel Foucault (1926–84) is responsible for one of the most provocative recent contributions to the anti-humanist critique of the subject.[52] Such has been his influence in the areas of social and political theory and philosophy that it has even been suggested that we are living in the century of Foucault.[53] His critique of the subject is particularly radical for a number of reasons. In the first place, he accepts the critical implications of the decentring of the subject effected by both the Marxist theory of ideology and Freudian psychoanalysis, which unmask the subject as the formed and deformed product of social and psychological conditions. But secondly, like theorists of both radical hermeneutics and structuralism, Foucault does not entertain any hopes of eventually recovering the lost transparency of the subject at a higher level or a later stage, in the way that both psychoanalysis and Marxism appear to do. It is necessary to break irrevocably with the humanist conception of the subject. Furthermore, Foucault's anti-humanism – like that of Althusser, one of

Foucault's teachers at the École normale supérieure in Paris – is explicitly political. According to one of his many programmatic statements, the objective of his work 'has been to create a history of the different modes by which, in our culture, human beings are made subjects'.[54] The play on the ambiguity of 'subject' here reflects his concern, influenced by Althusser's Marxist critique of the bourgeois subject of humanism, to explore, on the one hand, the links between the philosophical subject of modern epistemology and political individualism and, on the other, 'subjection' to authority or power. Humanist faith in the subject is no longer merely a sign of philosophical credulity or epistemological laxity, but, rather, a politically suspect manifestation of modernity. Finally, though, as Foucault's statement also implies, he proposes not so much to dispense altogether with the subject as to provide an historical account of its emergence. His antihumanist critique denies the subject its privileged moral and epistemological status only to place it near the centre of his thought – even if it is sometimes an absent centre. The subject is no longer a premise but still a prime object of analysis.

Foucault regards the subject as a kind of umbilical cord, entangling modern philosophy and the human sciences from their inception. In *The Order of Things* (1966) he discusses the problematic relationship of modern epistemology and the human sciences after Descartes. He is particularly interested in the intellectual transformation that sets the scene for their subsequent symbiotic development. It is most clearly expressed in Kant's transcendental philosophy which, in order to secure the subject as the absolute condition of all knowledge and action, extracts it from the contingencies of nature and history. The failure of this ruse, the recognition that the subject is a finite historical entity, leaves epistemology with a seemingly insoluble problem. If knowledge is based on a finite or contingent subject, then the conditions of knowledge are neither timeless nor universal, and anything like absolute truth is unattainable. This predicament, an aspect of what he calls the 'analytic of finitude', also has serious implications for the 'human sciences', which are implicated in the epistemological conundrum of modern philosophy from the beginning. To ground knowledge in humanity, as the subject of knowledge, makes 'man' both subject and object of his own knowledge. In Dreyfus and Rabinow's words:

> Man, who was once himself a being among others, now is a subject among objects. But Man is not only a subject among objects, he soon realizes that what he is seeking to understand is not only the objects of the world but himself. Man becomes the subject and the object of his own understanding.[55]

Foucault describes the contorted responses of modern philosophy to this problem (some of which should by now be familiar, albeit in slightly different terms). The reductive naturalism of positivism brazenly refuses to be troubled by the fact that knowledge is founded on a contingent being, and simply adds the empirical study of 'man' to its agenda. For the historical eschatologies of Hegel and Marx, absolute truth eventually arrives with the closure of the dialectic or the arrival of communism. But Foucault is dissatisfied with all of these solutions.

Foucault was, however, variously attracted to structuralism, hermeneutics and phenomenology as promising attempts to evade the interrelated problems of the modern philosophy of the subject and the human sciences. But he soon rejects both phenomenology and structuralism as unwitting accomplices in the subjection of the modern subject. We have already touched upon the basic ambiguity in the notion of subject. Foucault identifies both senses with subjugation and power: 'There are two meanings of the word subject: subject to someone else by control and dependence, and ties to his own identity by a conscience or self-knowledge. Both meanings suggest a form of power which subjugates and makes subject to.'[56] The two meanings of subject correspond to complementary processes of 'objectification' and 'subjectification'. In the end, structuralism, like positivism, avoids the Kantian dilemma only by treating human beings as mere objects; it is a symptom of the objectifying tendencies of rationalism and modernity which have constructed modern individuals as objects amenable to power and authority. But hermeneutic practices are implicated in the construction of the modern subject in a complementary way. Both the Catholic confessional and Freudian psychoanalysis are significant examples of the role played by practices of interpretation in the emergence of contemporary subjects prepared to take responsibility for their own subjection to authority and order.[57] Where structuralism is involved in the constitution of the subject as object, phenomenology and hermeneutics are involved in its constitution as subject.

Foucault's eventual 'overcoming' of both phenomenology and structuralism only becomes clear with his return to something like a political perspective on modern society and, with it, the centrality of the concept of power. After brief membership of the French Communist Party in the 1950s, Foucault's work had, after *History of Madness (Folie et déraison)* and *The Birth of the Clinic (Naissance de la clinique)*, seemed almost idealist in its exclusive concern with discourse and in the virtual absence of any concept of power.[58] When he returns to a more 'materialist' approach, it is, however, in terms of Nietzsche rather than Marx. In fact, Marxist philosophies of history become one of the main targets. Foucault is Nietzschean above all in his conviction that power and knowledge are really two sides of the same coin. '[P]ower and knowledge directly imply one another' and, as a result, he sometimes even speaks of 'power/knowledge' as an indivisible amalgam.[59] On the one hand, as with Nietzsche, the will to truth is just one manifestation of an underlying will to power. Our claims to objective knowledge or absolute truth are at best illusions. Knowledge is always the relative and questionable expression of a particular constellation of relations of power or force. On the other hand, 'the exercise of power is accompanied or paralleled by the production of apparatuses of knowledge'.[60] The exercise of power requires knowledge. In Smart's words: '[K]nowledge is not neutral or objective but rather is a product of power relations. In other words knowledge is political in the sense that its conditions of existence or possibility include power relations.'[61] The symbiotic relationship between power and knowledge is, as we shall see, at the heart of Foucault's account of the parallel emergence in modern societies of the human sciences as 'disciplines' with scientific pretensions and what he calls 'disciplinary power'.

The challenge to the Enlightenment's faith in the emancipatory potential of reason, regarded as a reliable instrument for the attainment of universally valid and useful knowledge, is reinforced by a similarly sceptical understanding of history. Foucault is inspired by Nietzsche's project of 'genealogy', which renounces the credulous faith in history as progress and traces specific institutions and forms of discourse to 'naked struggles of power' instead. History should not be understood teleologically as humanity's progress towards some foreordained goal, whether this is conceived as freedom and happiness or the classless society. Genealogy is also hostile to any attribution of historical continuity, an attitude that helps to explain Foucault's early attraction to structuralism. Already in the *Archaeology of Knowledge* Foucault conceives history according to 'categories of discontinuity and difference, the notions of threshold, rupture and transformation, the description of series and limits' as against notions of continuity, tradition, influence, development or evolution.[62] Genealogical history should 'record the singularity of events outside of any monotonous finality'; it must 'maintain passing events in their proper dispersion'.[63] It is Nietzschean will to power rather than any ultimate purpose which lies behind the confusion of historical change. This confusion is not to be wished away or outwitted by a philosophy of history.

With Foucault's return to Nietzsche, the concept of power is placed at the centre of his analysis, and it is important for him to avoid any misunderstanding of its nature. He contests a number of common assumptions that, in his view, tend to blind us to the multifarious manifestations and devious stratagems of power. In the first place, we should not be limited by a 'juridical' view, which sees power only in the negative, prohibitive functions of a repressive state apparatus, law and the police. This view is rendered obsolete by the increasingly positive and productive deployment of power in modern society. Other aspects of the juridical view obscure the nature of this deployment. Power is seen as something that is possessed and consciously exercised by an agent or group of agents over others in order to further its own interests. But power is not a thing that can be possessed or owned in the way such models require. Foucault is unwilling to reify power in this way, preferring to speak of 'power relation' rather than 'power' in order to emphasize that power is not a thing but a mode of interaction: 'Power exists only when it is put into action.'[64] Nor can power relations be traced to a single underlying mechanism or source such as capitalism or the ruling class. Power constitutes a much broader and more diffuse field than such theories imply. Nor, finally, is it correct to assume that power always involves straightforwardly 'binary' or 'top-down' relations. Power is not 'a property located at the summit of the social order employed in a descending direction over and throughout the entire social domain'.[65] Relationships of domination exercised by one group over another (for example, by the bourgeoisie over the proletariat or by men over women) are predicated on more finely grained and multidirectional relations of power and resistance at the 'micro-level' of society. Accordingly, social explanation should give priority to this micro-level. In Alan Sheridan's words: 'It is a matter of examining how the techniques and procedures of power operating routinely at the level of everyday life have been appropriated or engaged by more general power or economic interests rather than the converse.'[66]

Foucault's more constructive remarks about the emergence of novel forms of power in Western societies illuminate these rather abstract critical points. He is particularly interested in what he calls the 'threshold of modernity': the transition from the 'classical age' of the seventeenth century to the 'modern world' inaugurated with the French Revolution of 1789.[67] Characteristic of this period is a double operation of power, by which the 'repressive hypothesis' implicit in the juridical conception of power as exclusively prohibitive diverts attention from power's more productive activities. This is significant, because to the extent that we are unaware of these activities, we are less able to resist them: 'Power as a pure limit set on freedom, is, at least in our society, the general form of its acceptability.'[68] The repressive hypothesis is increasingly functional to the operations of power, as the more exclusively repressive, 'classical' mode of government, symbolized in the sovereign's 'power of life and death' over the subject, is gradually replaced by the productive management of individuals and peoples, which Foucault calls 'bio-power'. Regimes become 'managers of life and survival, of bodies and the race': '[W]hat might be called a society's "threshold of modernity" has been reached when the life of the species is wagered on its own political strategies.'[69] The rise of bio-power is also associated with the spread of racist theories in the nineteenth century.[70]

The deployment of bio-power involves a series of transformations in the nature of what Foucault calls 'governmentality'. This term refers to an increasingly autonomous 'governmental rationality', developed since the Renaissance alongside the narrower *raison d'état* first clearly expressed in Machiavelli's *The Prince*.[71] An important contribution to the emergence of distinctively modern forms of governmentality is made by a number of discourses on the 'science of police' or 'policy', written from the seventeenth century onwards. Although 'police' and 'policing' are now words normally associated with the straightforwardly repressive functions of the state, Foucault reminds us of their originally much broader meaning. Early discussions of policing concerned a lot more than law and order in the contemporary sense. They dealt with nothing less than the welfare of the population as a whole, and so helped to formulate a distinctively 'pastoral' conception of power. The centralizing and bureaucratizing tendencies of modern societies have often been highlighted, for example by Weber and theorists associated with the Frankfurt School. However, for Foucault what is particularly novel about pastoral power is its attention not just to the state of the community as a whole, but to each individual in particular and in detail throughout the course of his or her life.[72] Pastoral power's 'individualizing' attention is inspired by the example of the Catholic Church, which, through the confessional and other techniques, develops 'a knowledge of the conscience and an ability to direct it'.[73] Adapting such techniques, modern states apply a similarly pastoral, and similarly intrusive, attention to the health, wealth and welfare of their populations.[74]

As Foucault's conception of 'power/knowledge' would lead us to expect, the rise of pastoral power fosters a new knowledge of 'man'. It is no surprise, then, that the threshold of modernity also sees the emergence of a number of new disciplines within the humanities and social sciences. These 'human sciences' are essentially of two kinds, corresponding to the dual focus of the pastoral state on the population as a whole and on the individuals who make it up. They involve 'the development of knowledge of man around two poles: one globalizing and quantitative, concerning the population; the other analytical, concerning the individual'.[75] In the first place, there are the globalizing, statistical disciplines of economics, demography, epidemiology and eventually sociology.[76] Typically, these describe general laws governing the normal behaviour of the population as a whole; in fact, they give rise to the notions of population and normality as we understand them. These disciplines enhance the state's ability to control and care for the health of its population, to ensure adequate human resources for its military activities, to promote economic growth and so on. But pastoral power also requires detailed and systematic knowledge of individuals and, consequently, a radical break with the Aristotelian view of knowledge as exclusively concerned with the generalities of *genus* and *species*. The more individualizing disciplines of medicine, psychiatry, psychoanalysis and education study individuals in all their potential eccentricity. Thus, in *Discipline and Punish*, Foucault describes how, with the emergence of the modern prison, 'a specific mode of subjection was able to give birth to man as an object of knowledge for a discourse with a "scientific" status'.[77] Similarly, the clinic and the asylum were sites for the development of modern medicine and psychiatry.[78]

As these examples suggest, though, pastoral power is not purely a matter of knowledge but involves, in addition, a range of unmistakably material practices and interventions. These take two principal forms: the global 'regulatory controls' of a 'bio-politics of the population' and an individualizing 'discipline' or 'anatomo-politics of the body'. It is the latter modality of pastoral power that is most interesting and distinctively modern. Alongside the emergence of the human sciences there is an unprecedented expansion of disciplinary practices, deployed by both state and non-state institutions (in some cases initiated variously by 'do-gooders', reformers, helpful doctors or concerned aristocrats). Disciplinary power is directed primarily at the body; it is designed to produce 'subjected and practised bodies, "docile" bodies'.[79] But at the same time it aims for psychological effects. In Smart's words: '[D]iscipline is a power which infiltrates the very body and psyche of the individual, which . . . transforms the life and time of the individual into labour-power, that property essential to the capitalist mode of production.'[80] A variety of techniques are developed to this end, including detailed schedules and timetables, exercises and training, examinations, report-keeping, isolation of inmates and so on. Emblematic of such practices is Bentham's 'pan-opticon', which Foucault describes as an 'architectural figure' of disciplinary power. Jeremy Bentham (1748–1832) designed a prison building with individual cells radiating from a central observation point, ensuring the permanent visibility of the inmates to the warder but their complete invisibility to one another. In Foucault's words, the panopticon is a way of 'arranging spatial unities' in order 'to induce in the inmate a state of conscious and permanent visibility that assures the automatic functioning of power'.[81] As this example also makes clear, in the modern period there is a 'reversal of visibility' between sovereign and subject. The focus of attention is no longer the sovereign but the humble individual, who is the object of an ever intensifying surveillance. Similar disciplinary techniques are developed in a range of 'carceral' institutions modelled on the prison (in schools, hospitals, asylums, factories and barracks), all concerned with 'increasing the utility of individuals'.[82] These characteristically modern institutions are not so much humane products of a more enlightened and rational age as more efficient and more intrusive instruments of an expansive power.

The constitution of the subject as an object of disciplinary practices and objectifying disciplines is, however, only half the story. Of equal significance for the genealogy of modern subjectivity is a parallel series of processes, constituting the individual subject *as subject*. Thus Foucault's history of sexuality traces the emergence of a series of discourses and practices that are designed to make the subject more reliably and extensively responsible for itself. The explosion of discourses on sexuality in the nineteenth century, with their minute attention to the details of 'perverse' sexual variations from the norm, is related to the emergent bio-politics of population, but it also contributes to the more intimate constitution of the subject as subject. Important episodes in this story are the Catholic confessional, Freudian psychoanalysis and the promotion of 'sexuality' from a relatively unimportant fact about bodies to something decisive for the individual's sense of identity.[83] Foucault's analysis implies a critique of the 'depth hermeneutics' practised in different ways in both psychoanalysis and the confession. The deep truths about the mind or the soul which these practices of patient interrogation are supposed to uncover really function as instances of power. Far from uncovering some hidden meaning or truth, they inscribe in the subject 'truths' they themselves produce. In the process, the subject is enticed into assuming responsibility for more and more regions of its life.

Foucault's account of power has radical implications for political theory and practice. In particular, it undermines any 'totalizing theory' which, like Marxism, seeks to unify the diversity of social and historical events within a single explanatory framework. To theorize the complex field of relations of power as an organized totality is a strategy which, even in the hands of critical intellectuals or socialist militants, inevitably contributes to the reproduction of domination. As the experience of bureaucratic state socialism demonstrates, rulers rely on totalizing theories in order to legitimate their authority and exercise power more effectively. Foucault, in conversation with his colleague and friend Gilles Deleuze (1925–95), intimates a less authoritarian role for theory.[84] Just as relations of power are complex and dispersed, so resistance should be multicentred and diverse. The multiplicity of power relations requires an equally multifarious resistance to instances of power, which can nonetheless be conceived as interconnected or as a network. In Sheridan's words:

> Because 'power' is multiple and ubiquitous, the struggle against it must be localized. Equally, however, because it is a network and not a collection of isolated points, each localized struggle induces effects on the entire network. Struggle cannot be totalized – a single, centralized, hierarchized organization setting out to seize a single, centralized, hierarchized power; but it can be *serial*, that is, in terms of *horizontal* links between one point of struggle and another.[85]

Similarly, social and political theory should be a 'local and regional practice'. Rather than a single 'master' theory, there should be a plurality of theories engaging with power at different points and to different ends. The proper stance of the intellectual is also revised:

> The intellectual's role is no longer to place himself 'somewhat ahead and to the side' in order to express the stifled truth of the collectivity; rather it is to struggle against the forms of power that transform him into its object and instrument in the sphere of 'knowledge', 'truth', 'consciousness', and 'discourse'.[86]

Intellectuals should not put themselves forward as representatives of the people or vanguard of the proletariat. They should avoid 'the indignity of speaking for others'.[87] Foucault's recasting of the relationship between theory and practice finds considerable resonance in the politics of contemporary (or sometimes 'new') social movements, with their emphasis on difference, diversity and autonomous organization.[88]

In fact, Foucault's account of the emergence of modern forms of power and governmental rationality has analogies both with

Weber's account of the irreversible rationalization of society and with the Frankfurt School's pessimistic narrative of the fateful 'dialectic of Enlightenment'. Although Foucault has acknowledged these similarities, his overriding aim is not so much to invoke 'the progress of rationalization in general' as 'to analyze such a process in several fields'.[89] His concentration on the actual mechanisms and techniques of power, his emphasis on the individualizing manifestations of pastoral power and suspicion of hermeneutics as complicit in the constitution of subjugated subjects *as* subjects are all distinctive features of his analysis. His Nietzschean anti-humanism also makes him much more consistently sceptical of the value of rationality than second-generation Frankfurt School theorist Jürgen Habermas, who accuses Foucault of promoting a disabling moral relativism and even nihilism.[90] His account of power has been taken to imply 'the equivalence of power with sociality itself', a view that would render resistance to power impossible and, since no alternative to power is imaginable, unnecessary.[91] On the other hand, Foucault also appeals to the normative force of something close to Habermas's model of idealized dialogue. The distinction between dialogue and polemic, for example, is one on which 'a whole morality is at stake, the morality that concerns the search for the truth and the relation to the other'. In dialogue 'the rights of each person are in some sense immanent in the discussion'. The polemicist, by contrast, 'proceeds encased in privileges that he possesses in advance and will never agree to question'.[92] Certainly, Foucault's Nietzschean suspicion of transcendental guarantees for morality and truth does not mean that he regards all values as redundant or simply equivalent. Undoubtedly, both in theory and in life, Foucault was politically engaged; he was not without moral convictions. Whether Foucault's sceptical assumptions entitled him to those convictions remains controversial.

Derrida's deconstruction of Western metaphysics

And philosophy is perhaps the reassurance given against the anguish of being mad at the point of greatest proximity to madness.[93]

Jacques Derrida (1930–2004), following the structuralist path from meaning to sign, from the subject of speech to the anonymous system of language and beyond, carries anti-humanism to the heart of philosophy and metaphysics. His considerable influence on the philosophical scene dates from the publication of three of his major works in 1967.[94] His thought is more exclusively philosophical than Foucault's, although ironically he has had most influence in the field of literary studies, and of all contemporary continental philosophers he is the most reviled within the analytical tradition. This reception is ironic for the further reason that Derrida's deconstruction of Western metaphysics is far from being an easy or flippant dismissal. He is unhappy with the humanism of the Western philosophical tradition but sees no easy escape from this unhappy condition either.[95] Derrida can be described as 'poststructuralist' in the sense that 'Post-Structuralism is a critique of Structuralism conducted from within'.[96] In effect, Derrida draws out the philosophical implications of a structuralist account of language and meaning, overturning the framework of structuralist assumptions in the process. Where Saussure still regards language and meaning as a relatively stable system of oppositions, Derrida believes that Saussure's account of meaning as a differential system of contrasts fatally undermines any account of representation as simple 'presence' and, as a result, removes all fixity and stability from both language and thought. In other words, the contrast between structuralism and poststructuralism is not one of outright opposition or antagonism.[97] Poststructuralism develops the implications of structuralist premises about meaning in order to develop a position which, though recognizably distinct, does not discard those premises altogether.

Derrida's position can be approached initially in terms of his reaction to Husserl. Although he approves of Husserl's philosophical response to the universal pretensions of positivism, he believes that the phenomenological search for essences is mired in the 'logocentrism' of the Western philosophical tradition. Logocentrism is the pervasive tendency of Western thought to associate truth with the voice or 'the word' (*logos*), which is conceived as the immediate expression of the self-presence of consciousness. In Grosz's words: '[Logocentrism] seeks beyond signs and representation, the real and the true, the presence of being, of knowing and reality, to the mind – an access to concepts and things in their pure, unmediated form.'[98] Logocentrism thus also involves a prejudice in favour of 'presence', or what Derrida calls the 'metaphysics of presence'. Husserl's logocentrism is evident in his insistence on the independence of experience, of meanings and the contents of consciousness, from their expression in language. Language is seen simply as a medium for the expression or communication of meanings that are ultimately to be explained in terms of the meaning-giving acts of a subject of consciousness. In other words, pure meanings or 'essences', which correspond to the 'signified' in Saussure's terms, are primary; the sign as 'signifier', as sound or as written inscription, is secondary, the merely derivative and contingent vehicle of thought. Husserl's logo-centrism also leads him to privilege the immediacy and presence of the voice or speech as opposed to writing. In other words, it leads him to reproduce another deep prejudice of Western thought, which Derrida terms 'phonocentrism'. Phonocentrism regards speech as a more transparent medium of thought or meaning than writing. The voice is closer to the immediacy and self-presence of consciousness. As Habermas puts it, the 'fleeting transparency of the voice promotes the assimilation of the word to the expressed meaning'.[99] In speech we are not as aware of the gap between the word-as-sound and its meaning, between signifier and signified.

Husserl falls victim to the metaphysics of presence because he ignores the fundamental and ineliminable role of the signifier in thought. By the same token, Derrida's recognition of the 'quasi-transcendental' role of the signifier is at the heart of his critique and radicalization of Saussure. Derrida's position involves a significant shift in the understanding of the concept of difference, which plays such a central role in Saussure's account of language as a differential system of oppositions. This shift is encapsulated in one of Derrida's best-known neologisms, *différance*, a term subtly but significantly unlike *différence*, the normal French word for difference. In accordance with Derrida's stress on writing as opposed to speech, it is also appropriate that, though the two words are written differently, they are pronounced identically in French. The notion of *différance* is specifically designed to disrupt the metaphysics of presence. It does so by reminding us that the recognition of sameness and difference involved in all acts of representation cannot itself be temporally present. Representation is never sheer presence or immediacy, since it always involves both the recognition of 'difference' and a temporal 'deferral'. Here Derrida relies on the fact that in French '*différer*' means both 'to differ' and 'to defer'. On this point at least, Habermas's reading is helpful:

> The experience that is present 'at the moment' is indebted to an act of representation, perception is indebted to a reproducing recognition, such that the difference of a temporal interval and thus also an element of otherness is inherent in the spontaneity of the living moment . . .
> . . . at the very source of this apparently absolute presence, a temporal difference and otherness looms on the horizon, which Derrida characterizes both as a *passive difference* and as a *deferral that produces difference*.[100]

Derrida's argument here is a direct consequence of the structuralist account of meaning as difference. As Sturrock puts it, 'Every sign contains . . . a "trace" of signs other than itself', and this implies that 'there can be no escape from time in the process of signification'.[101]

The difference and deferral of *différance* is fundamental to all thought and representation and, in that sense, has a 'quasi-transcendental' role, since it 'refers' to the condition of conceptual thought as such. *Différance* produces the differences, without which neither thought nor language would be conceivable. Still, Derrida is at pains to deny *différance* any substantial existence as metaphysical 'origin':

> What is written as *différance*, then, will be the playing movement that 'produces' – by means of something that is not simply an activity – these differences, these effects of difference. This does not mean that the *différance* that produces differences is somehow before them, in a simply and unmodified – in-different – present. *Différance* is the non-full, non-simple, structured and differentiating origin of differences. Thus, the name 'origin' no longer suits it.[102]

In contrast to Saussure's apparently static system of differential oppositions, *différance* is therefore intrinsically temporal and dynamic. This feature of *différance* reflects a more general contrast between the dynamic categories of Derrida's poststructuralism and the static oppositions of structuralism: 'Post-Structuralism differs from Structuralism in being a philosophy of Becoming rather than of Being: it is endlessly dynamic, allowing us no escape or apparent respite from the shifting play of meanings.'[103] His account of representation also helps to show more clearly what is wrong with the metaphysics of presence. Sturrock's explanation here is worth quoting at some length:

> The 'metaphysics of presence' presumes that whatever is present to us is wholly and immediately so, grasped in an act of pure intuition which has no recourse to signs. Presence precedes signification. If this were the case, however, it is hard to see how we could be conscious of it, since consciousness *does* have recourse to signs. Presence, according to Derrida, can never be immediate therefore, only mediated by language. We are conscious of what is present to us as *being* present; and the concept of presence, like all concepts, is not a self-enclosed unity, but one inhabited by its contrary. There can be no meaning to asserting that something is 'present' if there is no possibility of its being 'not-present': the concept of presence entails that of non-presence or absence, for such is the fundamentally differential nature of language.[104]

In other words, Derrida insists on 'the indissoluble interweave of the intelligible with the sign-substrate of its expression', the 'transcendental primacy of the sign as against the meaning'.[105] It follows that writing rather than speech is the best model for an understanding of language and meaning. In contrast to phonocentrism, which privileges the voice and the spoken word, writing makes it obvious that meaning need not, indeed cannot, be guaranteed by the 'living presence' of the subject. Writing makes manifest the fact that meaning is only generated by *différance* or, in other words, the temporally extended system of oppositions between signifiers. This is because, in comparison with the deceptive immediacy of speech, 'the written form detaches any given text from the context in which it arose'.[106] We are not tempted to attribute meaning to presence, because in the case of writing the author is normally absent. The exemplary status that Derrida assigns to writing as opposed to speech also reinforces the contrast between his own approach and that of Saussure. Derrida locates the symptom of Saussure's failure to recognize the implications of his own theories in his tendency, despite his structuralist account of meaning as a differential system of signs, to lapse into the phonocentric prejudice of Western metaphysics. Saussure still assumes that there is a 'natural bond', 'the only true bond', between sound and sense, and refers to writing as a secondary and potentially dangerous activity.[107] The evidence that Saussure's phonocentric prejudices represent a lapse from the logic of his own argument is provided by the fact that he nevertheless frequently resorts to metaphors of writing in order to explain his views of language.

Once we recognize that the meaning of written texts has a life of its own in this way, we are more likely to realize that the same applies to meaning and language as such. Derrida makes this point by describing every use of language, including speech, as an instance of 'writing' in his own more general sense. Significantly, Derrida does not advocate a reverse prioritizing of writing over speech, but rather a revised account of both as the basis for a more adequate account of language, meaning and representation. Language must be understood as a form of 'writing'. In this spirit Derrida assigns transcendental significance to an originary writing or 'arche-writing' (*arché-écriture*): '[W]riting is not only an auxiliary means in the service of science – and possibly its object – but first . . . the condition of the possibility of ideal objects and therefore of scientific objectivity.'[108] 'Grammatology' is Derrida's term for a general theory of writing in this special sense. He believes such a theory can provide a less misleading basis for both philosophy and the human sciences.

Grammatology is thus Derrida's equivalent for what Saussure envisioned as a general theory of the sign or 'semiology'.[109]

In a further series of excursions into the history of philosophy Derrida grapples with a number of earlier incarnations of the logocentric and phonocentric prejudices of the Western philosophical tradition. Plato, not surprisingly, is identified as a major source of the 'idea of a pure self-authenticating knowledge'.[110] In Platonic terms knowledge is conceived as something ideal and eternal, something radically opposed to the changeable, corrupted world of everyday reality. Ordinary human experience of the world represents at best a confused reflection of underlying 'Forms' or 'essences' – in effect, the concepts instantiated in particular experiences. Platonic Forms are eternal, unchanging and ideal. Our nearest approach to pure and absolute truth is through our knowledge of the deductive truths of logic and mathematics. These are truths which, once we have been led to 'remember' them, are self-evident to consciousness and patently independent of the corruptible evidence of the senses. The privileged path to genuine philosophical knowledge is the Socratic dialogue. Only through the 'dialectical' exploration of questions about the nature of justice, truth or beauty, only through the to-and-fro of question and answer which Plato learned from Socrates and set down in his dialogues, can we come to know the ideal Form of these concepts and so make appropriate judgements about the truth, justice or beauty of things.

According to Derrida, this association of truth with the ideal, with mind or consciousness rather than the body and the 'material', pervades Western philosophical and religious traditions.[111] That Plato's philosophy is an example of the metaphysics of presence becomes clear if we consider more closely his conception of the Socratic dialogue. For Plato, significantly, only those who actually attend the Socratic debates are assured of the appropriate relationship to truth. This is because the power of reason and the word, the power of *logos*, must be relived by each in turn, by each for herself. The dialogue can only point towards truth; it works as a kind of intellectual midwifery or 'maieutic'.[112] There is no evidence for the truth superior to the conviction and certainty of one's own immediate consciousness, and anything less than the immediate self-presence of truth represents a falling away from its purity and certainty. Thus even the memory of a recent proof or demonstration is potentially unreliable. For the same reason, Plato is suspicious of writing. In the *Phaedrus*, writing is condemned because it removes the need for the 'active reanimation of knowledge . . . its reproduction in the present' and so encourages loss of memory.[113] It only appears to be good for memory: '[W]riting is only apparently good for memory, seemingly able to help it from within, through its own motion, to know what is true. But in truth, writing is essentially bad, external to memory, productive not of science but of belief, not of truth but of appearances.'[114] Writing is the surrogate science of the sophist. As such, writing threatens the legitimate authority of the teacher, who is the only one qualified to reanimate the truth in the appropriate way. There is thus a parallelism between the relationships of 'father to son, speech to writing'.[115] As Norris puts it, 'It is through writing that the *logos* is deflected from its proper, truth-seeking aim and abandoned to a state of hazardous dependence on the vagaries of *unauthorized* transmission.'[116] For Plato, writing is a less secure means for the transmission of knowledge because it releases the truth from the control and supervision of the teacher and so permits misunderstanding and distortion.

But as Derrida's exegesis makes clear, Plato is caught in a seemingly inescapable paradox. Although he denounces writing as a source of error, writing is nevertheless an essential means for the transmission not only of truth in general but even of his own particular claims about the dangers of writing. After all, it was Plato who preserved the dialogues of Socrates in written form. And like Saussure, Plato's arguments for the superiority of speech constantly appeal to metaphors drawn from writing. As Norris puts it:

> So speech is represented, not only as the opposite of writing, but as a 'good' kind of writing that is inscribed in the soul by revealed or self-authorized truth. Living memory is that which avoids the bad detour through writing (mere marks on a page), but which is still very often defined by metaphors of engraving, deciphering, inscription and other such textual figures.[117]

Plato's philosophical discourse (and, Derrida suggests, Western philosophical discourse generally) is forced to affirm, albeit indirectly and metaphorically, the indispensability of writing at the same time as it overtly accords to it a merely secondary, derivative status. For Derrida, this paradox is epitomized in the ambiguity of the Greek word '*pharmakon*', which can mean either 'poison' or 'cure'. The word captures perfectly philosophy's ambiguous relationship to writing, which it is forced to see both as poison and as cure.

Derrida's reading of Plato is one of the clearest examples of what he calls 'deconstruction'. The critical practice of deconstruction relates to the notion of *différance* and is also partly modelled on Heidegger's projected 'destruction' (*Destruktion*) of Western metaphysics. A deconstructive reading of a philosophical text is designed to bring into the open the tensions between its logical and rhetorical construction, tensions which reflect the problematic relationship between philosophy and writing. Derrida pays particular attention to the unregarded 'margins' of texts, their images and metaphors, the rhetorical resources they find themselves compelled to exploit – even words that are only 'present in their absence'. Thus although the word '*pharmakos*' (wizard, magician, poisoner), a cognate of *pharmakon*, never actually appears in the dialogue of Plato we have been discussing (and for many, of course, this might be thought a significant objection), for Derrida this word belongs to a 'chain of significations' which 'for all its hiddenness, for all that it might escape Plato's notice, is nevertheless something that passes through certain discoverable *points of presence* that can be seen in the text'.[118] The word is present in the sense that its absence is felt. Norris's description of deconstruction is helpful at this point:

> [D]econstruction is the vigilant seeking-out of those 'aporias', blindspots or moments of self-contradiction where a text involuntarily betrays the tension between rhetoric and logic, between what it manifestly *means to say* and what it is nonetheless *constrained to mean*. To 'deconstruct' a piece of writing is therefore to operate a kind of strategic reversal, seizing on precisely those unregarded details (casual metaphors, footnotes, incidental turns of argument) which are always, and necessarily, passed over by interpreters of more orthodox persuasion.[119]

It is also important to emphasize that deconstruction is nothing so fixed or predictable as a method. '[Deconstruction] in its technical sense refers to a series of tactics and devices rather than a method: strategies to reveal the unarticulated presuppositions on which metaphysical and logocentric texts are based.'[120] Its overriding aim is to disrupt the metaphysics of presence. It is 'a means of carrying out this going beyond being, beyond being as presence, at least'.[121]

The practice of deconstruction also reflects Derrida's distinctive hermeneutic. His poststructuralist account of the nature of representation and meaning implies that writing (in all its forms) cannot be referred to the intentions of an author. In fact, texts cannot be tied to any single or univocal source of meaning of any kind. The interpretation of texts depends on a potentially infinite array of possible contexts and interpreters, and so leads to what Derrida describes as 'dissemination', an endless dispersion and multiplication of meanings. Dissemination 'marks an irreducible and *generative* multiplicity'.[122] It undermines all fixities of interpretation, proliferates rather than reduces instances of ambiguity. As McCarthy puts it: '[O]ur meaning always escapes any unitary conscious grasp we may have of it, for language, as "writing", inevitably harbors the possibility of an endless "dissemination" of sense, an indefinite multiplicity of recontextualizations and reinterpretations.'[123] Or as Rorty says, Derrida maintains 'that meaning is a function of context, and that there is no theoretical barrier to an endless sequence of recontextualizations'.[124]

However, as Norris is at pains to point out, and despite what some of the literary theorists influenced by Derrida have thought (and despite, too, it must be said, some of his own less careful statements), this view of meaning does not imply complete interpretive licence. His own deconstructive readings of philosophical and literary texts might at times be thought wilfully obscure or even perverse, but they also demonstrate considerable rigour and a minute attention to detail. Furthermore, in contrast to those like Foucault and Barthes who have enthusiastically proclaimed the 'death of the author', a deconstructive reading aims to go beyond the author's intentions without leaving them behind altogether. As Derrida remarks of Rousseau: 'His declared intention is not annulled by this but rather inscribed within a system which it no longer dominates.'[125] Deconstruction cannot simply ignore the apparent meaning of a text: 'When one attempts . . . to pass from an obvious to a latent language, one must first be rigorously sure of the obvious meaning.'[126]

The difficult practice of deconstruction exemplifies Derrida's refusal to accept any easy solution. He refuses to deny what he sees as the ineradicable tensions inherent in the basic conceptual oppositions of Western thought, which are invariably 'violent hierarchies'. Typical are the oppositions between mind and body, masculine and feminine, reason and emotion, sameness and difference, self and other, where in each case the first of the pair dominates or is thought superior to the second. Deconstruction targets these hierarchies, but without assuming that the tensions they embody can easily be resolved or the hierarchies easily reversed. There can be no absolute break with the fundamental dichotomies of Western metaphysics. This explains Derrida's hostility to the Hegelian dialectic, which makes the futile attempt to absorb and neutralize these contradictions in a stable synthesis. In these terms, the interrelated concepts of deconstruction and *différance* embody Derrida's distance from Hegel: 'If there were a definition of *différance*, it would be precisely the limit, the interruption, the destruction of the Hegelian *relève* wherever it operates.'[127] Instead, deconstruction must embark on an 'interminable analysis' if it is 'to avoid both simply *neutralizing* the binary oppositions of metaphysics and simply *residing* within the closed field of those oppositions, thereby confirming it'.[128] It is also Derrida's insistence on the irresolvable tension of deconstruction that distinguishes his position most clearly from the more Hegelian hermeneutics of Gadamer. Where Gadamer describes a fruitful productivity of interpretation through dialogue, Derrida proposes something more like the unhappy lot of Sisyphus. We are condemned to an endless labour of conceptual disruption without guarantees of success.[129]

Derrida also associates his projected disruption of the violent hierarchies of Western metaphysics with a distinctive political stance. In the end, the refusal of the 'longing for an impossible truth' is politically radical.[130] Violent conceptual hierarchies correspond to oppressive social relations, and to challenge the former is inevitably to undermine the latter. In McCarthy's words:

> [D]econstruction counteracts the 'politics of language' which conceals practices of exclusion, repression, marginalisation, and assimilation behind the apparent neutrality of 'purely theoretical' discourses. Its effects, however, are not confined to language, but 'touch all the social institutions'.

Deconstruction bears witness 'to the other of western rationalism'. It counteracts the associated 'repression of the other in nature, in ourselves, in other persons and other peoples . . . [It] speaks on behalf of what does not fit into our schemes and patiently advocates letting the other be in its otherness.'[131] Certainly, Derrida has espoused a number of radical political causes. He has been involved in the reform of the teaching of philosophy in France. He has written admiringly of Nelson Mandela's role in resisting apartheid. He makes plain both his opposition to neo-colonialism and his support for feminism.[132]

Again, Derrida's approach has influenced a wide range of other theorists. Michael Ryan has recruited the critical resources of deconstruction for an anti-authoritarian socialism, which is 'worked out, as a texture and not as a punctual instance of power', and for which socialist unity need not imply an organized and potentially authoritarian movement but 'the articulation of a diverse, differentiated plurality'.[133] But Derrida himself does little to develop a constructive political stance. Indeed, it is difficult to see how he could do so without abandoning his entrenched resistance to systematic theorizing. His bold claim, that 'all of our political codes and terminologies still remain fundamentally metaphysical', seems to leave little space for anything but the most abstractly intellectual political engagement, or alternatively, political commitments without intellectual motivation.[134] Even his overtly political comments tend to be undercut by irony. On McCarthy's analysis at least, Derrida prefers to avoid the perspective of the participant in social life, who is forced to adopt a position and assume certain values, ending up instead with a stance that is ultimately conservative.[135]

Overall, Derrida does not abandon the Enlightenment project altogether (something he regards as impossible anyway), but rather seeks to occupy a critical and, by all accounts, difficult position within and against it:

> Derrida . . . insists that there is no opting out of that post-Kantian enlightenment tradition, and certainly no question of our now having emerged into a post-modern era where its concepts and categories lack all critical force. On the contrary: it is only by working persistently *within* that tradition, but *against* some of its ruling ideas, that thought can muster the resistance required for an effective critique of existing institutions.[136]

In fact, Derrida's nuanced relationship to Western metaphysics and rationality was signalled in an early reaction to Foucault's *History of Madness*, whose attempt to express a truth beyond a divisive and exclusionary Western reason he sees as precisely the 'maddest aspect' of his project. In Norris's words: '[T]hought is self-deluded if it tries to achieve a standpoint "outside" or "above" the very discourse of philosophical reason.'[137] This view of Derrida, as at heart a 'transcendental philosopher' with an unhappy conscience, is consistent both with his explicitly philosophical interests and the strong influence of Nietzsche and the later Heidegger.[138] Certainly, if Derrida retains a commitment to Western rationality, it is by no means an easy or complacent one, involving endless critical labour, an interminable work of deconstructive analysis. In the end, the difficulty of his position reflects his view of philosophy as a series of impossible attempts to say the unsayable. Philosophers grapple with a truth that cannot be expressed within the received order of reason, only to fall back into forgetfulness and complacency, as they develop a newly authoritative truth, itself destined to become the focus of subsequent philosophical revolt. For 'philosophy is perhaps the reassurance given against the anguish of being mad at the point of greatest proximity to madness.'[139]

Further Reading

For works of and about Hegel, Marx, hermeneutics and Nietzsche, see suggestions for further reading in previous chapters. Freud's most important single work is probably *The Interpretation of Dreams*, but *The*

Psychopathology of Everyday Life is a less daunting exploration of the everyday impact of the unconscious. 'Civilization and its Discontents' (in *Civilization, Society and Religion*) draws political implications from psychoanalysis. Influential works of other major thinkers responsible for the 'decentring of the subject' are Heidegger's 'Letter on Humanism' (in *Basic Writings*) and works collected in Levinas, *The Levinas Reader*. Michel Foucault's essay 'Nietzsche, Genealogy, History' is a concise introduction to more extended studies such as *Discipline and Punish*, *History of Sexuality* (esp. vol. 1) and *History of Madness*. Gilles Deleuze's inventive but difficult philosophy is best approached through his studies of other thinkers – for example, *Nietzsche and Philosophy* and *Spinoza: Practical Philosophy*. Derrida's writings are rigorously anti-systematic, but essays collected in *Writing and Difference* and *Margins of Philosophy* offer helpful samples of his thinking.

Good introductions to the critique of the subject and 'anti-humanism' are Kate Soper, *Humanism and Anti-humanism* and John Sturrock, *Structuralism*. Some useful guides to individual thinkers are J. Culler, *Saussure*, Boris Wiseman, *Lévi-Strauss, Anthropology, and Aesthetics*, Richard Wollheim, *Freud*, D. T. Awerkamp, *Emmanuel Levinas: Ethics and Politics* and essays collected in R. Bernasconi and S. Critchley, *Re-reading Levinas*. Paul Patton offers a lucid guide in *Deleuze and the Political*. Of the manifold works on Foucault, Lois McNay's *Foucault: A Critical Introduction* is a helpful start. Christopher Norris's *Derrida* provides a readable introduction to deconstructionism. On the other hand, Rodolphe Gasché's *Inventions of Difference: On Jacques Derrida* challenges deconstructionist readings and aligns Derrida with Hegel instead.

7

Postmodernism

Outline

Postmodernism refers to a variety of sceptical, 'anti-essentialist' and 'anti-humanist' positions across a range of disciplinary contexts from art, architecture and literature to social theory, psychoanalysis and philosophy. Hostility to the West's 'modernist' assumptions and chauvinism is driven by a series of historical events and developments. Both the twentieth-century horrors of world war, totalitarianism, concentration camps and genocide, and a gradual but relentless intellectual disillusionment with Marxism – each understood as characteristic symptoms of 'modernity' – are important sources of the postmodern 'mood'. The exhaustion of artistic modernism provided a further and more literal impetus. Under the combined impact of these factors, Jean-François Lyotard and Jean Baudrillard take their leave from all 'grand metanarratives' of history, all universal claims to truth and morality and any remaining faith in the Enlightenment's project of rationalizing every aspect of life. Paradoxically, this *philosophical* postmodernism shades almost imperceptibly into a sociologically and historically grounded account of postmodern thought and culture as expressions of the present state of Western society. In both philosophical and sociological variants, however, postmodernism's rejection of 'totalizing' theories with universal pretensions is complemented by positive celebration of diversity or 'difference' and emphasis on the ethically indispensable but always elusive demands of 'the other'.

Varieties of postmodernism

With postmodernism, it is as if we pass through the looking-glass of Western reason. As we do so, apparently reliable conceptual distinctions are inverted or abolished altogether, and what was previously most solid 'melts into air'.[1] Postmodernism attempts a radical break with all of the major strands of post-Enlightenment thought. For postmodernists, both the orthodox Enlightenment 'metanarrative' of progress and emancipation and the 'speculative' narrative of Hegel and Marx have lost their spell.[2] Phenomenology and existentialism are condemned as varieties of humanism or nostalgic philosophies of the subject. Even Derrida's acrobatic manoeuvres on the margins of metaphysics fail to convince. Perhaps not surprisingly, then, it is impossible to provide a straightforward definition of postmodernism. Not only are there conflicting views about what postmodernism is, but postmodernist positions are also adopted within a variety of disciplinary settings. There is a wide range of contexts for what are nevertheless related discourses of modernity and postmodernity. These include history and sociology, philosophy, art and art theory as well as literature and literary criticism. As a result, too, 'postmodern', 'postmodernity' and 'postmodernism' are not always straightforwardly cognate terms either. They have different connotations, depending whether a historical period, a form of society, a philosophical stance or an artistic movement is in question. In other words, postmodernism cannot be regarded as a purely philosophical development. It is just as much a response to the calamitous history of the West.

The genealogy of postmodernist thought involves at least four distinct but interrelated contexts of formation. In the first place, postmodernism draws radical conclusions from a number of developments in philosophy. Certainly, postmodernism reiterates themes that have frequently been explored within the previous continental tradition. Postmodernists are critical of all the most characteristic assumptions of the orthodox Enlightenment. They reject the universal pretensions of natural science and the 'instrumental', 'objectifying' or 'reductive' (sometimes also 'male' or 'masculinist') rationality it embodies. They also reject universal claims made on behalf of moralities founded on pure reason or an essential human nature. Again like some earlier critics, they speak up for traditions, cultures, values and peoples who fared badly at the hands of the 'civilizing mission' of Enlightenment rationalism. Many of these critics, however, continued to acknowledge the role of rationality, albeit a rationality differently constituted and articulated, in the advance and emancipation of humanity. In that sense, they were still committed to a version of the 'Enlightenment project' as a key factor in the momentum of Western modernity. This is clearest in the case of Hegel and Marx, whose dialectical accounts of the advance of reason through history pre-supposed the advanced state of European culture and society. Both retained a clear commitment to modernity, if only as the neces-sary precursor to a more thoroughgoing social and intellectual revolution.

By contrast, postmodernism defines itself, on one level at least, by its rejection of any commitment to modernity or Enlightenment, including the more nuanced commitments of Hegel and Marx. It is here that anti-humanism and the critique of the subject, from Nietzsche and Heidegger to structuralism and poststructuralism, play a decisive role in preparing the ground for a more radical break with the Enlightenment project. In its most radical form, the anti-humanist critique of the subject problematizes all the fundamental categories of modern Western philosophy. Not only the universalist rationalism of the Enlightenment, but also Hegelian and Marxist narratives of the dialectical self-constitution of humanity are challenged. Even more recent phenomenological and existentialist inheritors of the project of modern philosophy are undermined. Foucault's Nietzs-chean genealogy traces knowledge, truth and the modern subject to constellations of power that are seemingly beyond the reach of reason. Derrida's deconstruction of the 'metaphysics of presence' applies a similarly corrosive scepticism to the most basic conceptual opposi-tions of Western thought. But these poststructuralists remain unwill-ing to make the final break with the Enlightenment project. Thus, at the same time as Derrida demonstrates the impossibility of inhabiting the conceptual framework of Western metaphysics, he also asserts the impossibility of simply leaving it behind. For him, to adapt Samuel Beckett's phrase, Western philosophy 'can't go on, must go on'.[3] Foucault too refuses to describe himself as a postmodernist. But equally clearly, the ideas of both thinkers prepare the ground for postmodernism. It is a relatively small step from the uncomfortably sceptical positions they both adopt to a more whole-hearted rejection of modernity and Enlightenment. Though not postmodernists them-selves, Derrida and Foucault provide the most immediate point of entry into that mode of thought.

A second important context for the formation of postmodernist thought is provided by the history of Europe and the West (and the world in so far as it has been a victim of that history) in the twentieth century. This history includes two unprecedentedly destructive world wars, the rise of fascism in Germany, Italy and Spain and a protracted 'Cold War', maintained by the balanced nuclear terror of 'mutually assured destruction'. In the meantime, the colonial mission of modern and 'enlightened' European nations to civilize their 'barbarian' neighbours has lost conviction. Former colonies have been relinquished to movements of national liberation and the atrocities of former colonial regimes widely recognized. Most horrifying, the Nazi genocide of more than six million Jews, communists, homosexuals, gypsies and disabled people (and many others) dealt a fatal blow to any complacent reading of Western history as the privileged site of civilization. The Holocaust refuted in the starkest possible way that combination of ethnocentrism and optimism which had allowed the West to see itself as the embodiment of progress and the very antithesis of barbarism. In Germany, one of Europe's most economically developed, artistically cultured and philosophically creative nations, there had emerged a regime of systematic and relentless brutality. But the Holocaust is shocking not, or not simply, as an atavistic lapse from the path of progress and Enlightenment, but rather as a demonstration of dangers intrinsic to modernity itself. The Holocaust was a very modern affair. The genocide of six million people was carefully planned, administered with bureaucratic thoroughness and carried out with considerable technological inventiveness. In Bauman's words: 'The Holocaust was a unique encounter between the old tensions which modernity ignored, slighted or failed to resolve – and the powerful instruments of rational and effective action that modern development itself brought into being.'[4] The combined effect of these catastrophic events of recent European history, from imperialist slaughter to Nazi genocide, is thus a dual challenge to the West's self-conscious modernity. Is modernity a secure achievement of the West? Is modernity really an achievement at all?

Another important episode from this history provides a third context for the formation of postmodernism, but one this time that is both historical and intellectual in nature. This is the fate of Marxism. It is also in the twentieth century, after all, that Marxism completed its evolution from theory to practice, becoming the official ideology of a number of 'actually existing' socialist regimes.[5] It is, of course, possible to argue that these self-styled Marxist or Marxist-Leninist regimes have been anything but faithful to the more attractive ideals of Marx and Engels or even Lenin. Still, the bureaucratization of the socialist idea and, even more starkly, the Stalinization of both the Soviet Union and major cohorts of the communist movement could hardly fail to have a profound impact on the fate of Marxist theory and philosophy.[6] Less dramatic, but in the long run equally corrosive, has been the stubborn failure of revolution to occur in the more developed capitalist societies of the West. The arrival of relatively widespread affluence and a working class apparently loyal to social democracy has offered scant basis for revolutionary optimism.

Against this discouraging background, a series of traumatic historical events has triggered repeated waves of intellectual exile from communist parties, from Marxism and ultimately from any remaining faith in socialist revolution. These events have ranged from revelations about party purges, 'show-trials', massacres and the 'gulag' of prison camps under Stalin, to the Soviet invasions of Hungary in 1956 and Czechoslovakia in 1968. The French Communist Party's failure to anticipate, and its subsequent attempts to manipulate and co-opt, the Paris 'May Events' of 1968 brought further disillusionment. In the mid-1970s came further revelations, this time concerning the excesses of China's 'cultural revolution' under Mao Tse-tung, with the implication that all was far from well under the Maoist model of socialism as well. Nor, finally, have the fortunes of Marxism and communism improved notably in recent years. Chinese communism survives only by dint of a combination of market reforms and repression. The collapse of communist regimes in the Soviet Union and Eastern Europe since 1989 has eroded any remaining confidence in the Marxist project.

The historical fate of Marxism has had considerable intellectual repercussions. 'Western Marxism', which includes the work of the Frankfurt School and Habermas but also such figures as Gramsci and Althusser, has responded to the double disappointment of the non-occurrence and failure of revolution with theoretical innovations of considerable ingenuity. Despite the recalcitrance of the 'problem of practice', these remain for many fertile currents of thought.[7] But the same historical fate has produced a number of more radical departures. For a variety of reasons, intellectual disillusionment has been particularly marked in France. In post-war France, Marxism was not only a powerful political force, it also dominated the intellectual scene in a way unparalleled in most other Western countries.[8] Althusser's structuralist Marxism exerted considerable influence for a number of years. Even within existentialism and phenomenology, Marxist theory was influential. Merleau-Ponty, Sartre and de Beauvoir were aligned with the revolutionary left for much of their careers. They were all, at various times, members of the French Communist Party. Their socialist commitment was expressed not only in extensive journalistic activities and political articles, but also in much of their philosophical work, including Merleau-Ponty's writings on history and communism and Sartre's lengthy *Critique of Dialectical Reason*.

Even many of those now associated with poststructuralism and post-modernism were previously Marxists. Lyotard and Baudrillard belonged to a variety of Marxist groupings. Foucault was a member of the French Communist Party, albeit only for a short time.

This background is important, because Marxism is arguably the most frequent, if not always the explicit, target of postmodernist critics of modernism. Warnings about the dangers of 'totalizing' theory as well as scepticism about the unfounded pretensions of the philosophy of history are most plausibly read as references to Marxism. Attacks on the totalitarian tendencies of modernism make more sense in relation to the Stalinist degeneration of communism than they do when applied to liberal or pluralist strands of post-Enlightenment thought. And for intellectuals who regarded Marxism as the best available response to this more liberal Enlightenment, it is not surprising that Marxism's apparent failure is taken as final proof of the bankruptcy of the Enlightenment project and modernism. From this perspective, then, it is not just the prevailing forms of power and rationality, the capitalist rationalization of production and the bureaucratic rationalization of the state, which exemplify the baneful condition of modernity. Marxism too is a part of the problem. East and West are the two faces of modernity. By the same token, only an even more radical intellectual critique promises release from a plainly bankrupt Enlightenment project. Only by enthusiastically embracing the 'other' of Western reason can we avoid forever reliving the totalitarian nightmares of modernism.

Developments in art and art theory provide a further context for the formation of postmodernist thought, one which, in terminological terms at least, proves decisive. 'Modern' and its cognates have been used to describe Western society and philosophy at least since the Renaissance quarrel of 'ancients and moderns'. In historical periodizations, the 'modern period' and 'modernity' usually refer to the period of European history from the high Renaissance or about 1500 onwards.[9] However, the term 'modernism' has been restricted to a number of more specialized contexts and, until recently, was largely associated with artistic and literary modernism.[10] Modernism in this sense refers to the deliberate pursuit of formal innovation and the consequent overturning of convention by a self-conscious 'avant-garde'. Although artistic modernism has clear roots in the nineteenth century, it was at its height in the early years of the twentieth. In Gaggi's words, 'modernism' is used 'to apply to those major movements and techniques in the various arts that developed early in the century: Cubism, Fauvism, Futurism, Expressionism, Surrealism, Functionalism, atonality, serialization, and stream-of-consciousness'.[11]

Modernism is thus associated with figures such as Marcel Proust and James Joyce in literature, Arnold Schoenberg and Alban Berg in music and Le Corbusier and the Bauhaus School in architecture and design. Among these movements, Gaggi also usefully distinguishes between a modernism of 'classicist order', for example with Corbusier and Mondrian, and the 'romantic assertion of the self' in primitivism, expressionism, fauvism and cubism.

In theory at least, artistic modernism might seem a potentially limitless project, renewable as each successive avant-garde rebels against the conventions established by a previous generation of innovators. However, by around the middle of the twentieth century it was betraying clear signs of mortality. In the first place, the pursuit of formal innovation for its own sake seemed more and more futile, resulting in novelty without genuine artistic or creative significance. By this time, too, the political hopes associated with aesthetic innovation had dissipated. The revolutionary ambitions of Dadaists and surrealists remained unfulfilled; the futurists were discredited by their association with fascism.[12] Modern artworks belonged increasingly to the establishment, adorning the corporate temples of capitalism and the private collections of millionaires. As David Harvey puts it, modernism was more readily associated with the worship of 'corporate bureaucratic power and rationality' than with any kind of political radicalism.[13] The emancipatory role that Frankfurt School theorists such as Adorno and Horkheimer, in their different ways, assigned to modern art could no longer be sustained either.[14] By the late 1950s more and more artists and critics regarded modernism as aesthetically barren and politically compromised, a prestigious and profitable branch of the artistic establishment it had originally set out to shock.

The point of emergence of postmodernism as an artistic movement in reaction to modernism is usually located in the 1960s (though Barry Smart mentions the use, in the 1930s, by Federico de Onis of *postmodernismo* to refer to a 'kind of exhausted and mildly conservative modernism').[15] Architecture was the first medium to exhibit clear postmodernist tendencies. These include eclecticism, ambiguity, wit and a playful allusion to earlier styles in the form of pastiche. As Jameson explains, pastiche is devoid of the serious ulterior motivation of parody; it does not deviate in order to assert a norm. Rather, it is 'a neutral practice of such mimicry, without any of parody's ulterior motives, amputated of the satiric impulse, devoid of laughter and of any conviction that alongside the abnormal tongue you have momentarily borrowed, some healthy linguistic normality still exists. Pastiche is thus blank parody, a statue with blind eyeballs.'[16] What are more sympathetically described as the playful aspects of postmodernism reflect one of its most important characteristics, namely its challenge to the privileged status of 'high' art and culture. In contrast to artistic modernism, which affirms the quasi-religious significance of art, postmodernism rejects any absolute distinction between high and low culture, between art and entertainment. Walter Benjamin's germinal essay on 'The Work of Art in the Age of Mechanical Reproduction' is thus an important clue to the understanding of artistic postmodernity. Benjamin discusses the disruption of the 'aura' of the great work of art as a result of the easy availability of copies, produced by techniques of mechanical reproduction such as printing, photography and sound recording.[17] Artistic postmodernism can be seen as the outcome of this levelling and demystifying tendency (even though Benjamin foresaw a different outcome), which has since been reinforced by the extensive role of communications and information technology in contemporary societies.

Gaggi also identifies 'self-referentiality' and 'epistemological scepticism' as key features of artistic postmodernism, along with a corresponding 'interest in great works from the past that turn in on themselves or otherwise make art itself the subject of art'.[18] Self-referentiality is also apparent in postmodernist art's playful mixing of previous styles in pastiche. There are clear connections between this interest in self-referentiality and poststructuralist critical theory, which diverts attention from the author and the figurative or representational role of the work of art, focusing instead on language or the work itself as the subject of artistic production.[19] Style and form are the message as well as the medium of art. There is in this context also an interesting interaction between artistic and scientific developments. Einstein's relativity theory and quantum mechanics, notably in the form of Heisenberg's 'uncertainty principle', undermine both notions of absolute space and time and deterministic interpretations of causality. At the same time, realist interpretations of science have come under attack even from analytical philosophers of science such as Kuhn and Feyerabend.[20] In art, chance and uncertainty are the basis of 'aleatoric music', whose completion depends on the unscripted, random choices of the performer, as well as of some aspects of Dadaism. Artistic and scientific tendencies contribute to both the mood of uncertainty and flux and the greater openness to non-Western cultures and worldviews, which are characteristic of postmodernism.

At roughly the same time as the emergence of artistic postmodernism, historical and sociological uses of the term were being canvassed.

Smart refers to Toynbee's discussion in 1954 of a 'postmodern age', associated with the decline of the middle classes from around the turn of the century after their long period of hegemony. At about the same time, Wright Mills identified a 'post-modern period', characterized by loss of faith in both of the major ideologies of modernity, liberalism and socialism. There is also 'an increasingly pervasive sense that modern assumptions about the intrinsic relation of reason and freedom can no longer be sustained'.[21] However, it is not until after 1968 that postmodernism emerges clearly, first as a recognizable intellectual current linking a broader range of philosophical and cultural themes, then as a self-conscious and distinct philosophical position. The events of 1968 represent an important threshold. The last years of the 1960s saw the defeat of the New Left, accelerating disillusionment with Marxism and the frustration, or perhaps diversion, of the utopian aspirations of a generation. These events were also the prelude to the emergence of the multicentred politics of so-called new social movements. This political context, finally, helps to explain a basic ambivalence running through postmodernism. There is a disjunction between 'a postmodernism of resistance and a postmodernism of reaction', a postmodernism of revolutionary disappointment and one of defiant radicalism.[22] The critical evaluation of postmodernism is correspondingly ambivalent, judging it either as the last resort of critical intelligence or thinly disguised neo-conservatism.

In the further development of postmodernism along both of these paths, two separate regions must be distinguished (discussed in the following two sections). In the first place, there is a radically sceptical, philosophical critique of the intellectual universe of modernism. This tendency targets both the Enlightenment project and some of its most influential critics. Postmodernism in this guise rejects all philosophies of history and provides a radical challenge to the most basic categories of Western philosophy and metaphysics. But secondly, and of course not unrelated to this, a number of theorists make a connection between postmodern tendencies in art and culture and the state of contemporary, sometimes 'postindustrial', sometimes 'late' or 'advanced capitalist', sometimes 'postmodern' societies. This is primarily a postmodernism of social and cultural theory, identifying postmodernity as a stage of Western society. Evidently, there are significant tensions between these approaches. Philosophical postmodernism denies what postmodern social and cultural thought presupposes – a philosophy or, at least, an overall account of history.

Philosophical critique of Enlightenment and modernity

The philosophical critique of modernism and the Enlightenment project has emerged most clearly in France in the aftermath of structuralism and poststructuralism. It is largely the product of a number of intellectuals who, while rejecting or at least significantly distancing themselves from Marxism, do not follow the simple return to liberalism of some 'new philosophers' (*nouveaux philosophes*) in the early 1970s.[23] One of the clearest expositions of the philosophical critique of modernity is provided by Jean-François Lyotard (1924–98) in his 'report on knowledge', entitled *The Postmodern Condition*. During his career, Lyotard occupied a variety of political positions ranging from Marxism and 'spontaneist' anarchism to his later identification with the 'mood' of postmodernity. In fact, despite its espousal of postmodernist themes his position retains a tangential allegiance to Marxism in the sense that capitalism remains a problem.

Lyotard describes postmodernity as a 'condition' or 'mood' that corresponds to the present stage of 'postindustrial' society. Postmodernity is, therefore, a sign of the obsolescence of modernity. Lyotard defines modernity in terms of the role played in Western societies since the Enlightenment by 'metanarratives' for the legitimation of both science and the state. A metanarrative in Lyotard's sense is equivalent to a philosophy of history. The contingent events of history are understood in terms of an all-inclusive narrative, which is supposed to encapsulate 'the' meaning of history. The reliance on legitimating metanarratives is intrinsic to 'the choice called the Occident'.[24] Lyotard proceeds to list a number of forms which metanarratives can take, for example 'the dialectics of Spirit, the hermeneutics of meaning, the emancipation of the rational or working subject, or the creation of wealth'.[25] Clearly these narratives correspond to some of the major currents of post-Enlightenment thought considered so far, including Hegelian idealism, hermeneutics, Marxism and theories of economic progress and modernization. But Lyotard isolates two major types, representing what he sees as the two dominant strands of post-Enlightenment thought. These are what we have identified as the mainstream of the Enlightenment and its most influential critique: first, the 'narrative of emancipation' demonstrated both in modern science and in the politics of the French Revolution and, second, the 'speculative narrative' of Hegelianism and Marxism.[26] Both narratives imply that progress is guaranteed, either through the application of reason to production, politics and morality, or as a result of the motor force of the dialectic. Both narratives have played an important role not only in modern philosophy but also in the West's self-consciousness as the embodiment of modernity.

The onset of a postmodern mood or condition, then, is marked by a gradual erosion of faith in meta-metanarratives, provoked by far-reaching developments in both society and culture. Lyotard refers to the onset of 'postindustrial society', a notion associated in France mainly with the work of Alain Touraine.[27] Postindustrial society depends on a mode of production in which, by contrast with earlier forms of society, knowledge and information technology play the central role. In particular, they are involved in 'the technological production of symbolic goods which shape or transform our representation of human nature and of the external world'.[28] Technical knowledge is applied to the production of new commodities, fostering new needs and even cultural values. According to Lyotard, postindustrial society is dominated by the 'spirit of performativity', the attempt to reduce society to an efficient system, which guarantees 'the best possible input/output equation'.[29] The cultural and intellectual counterpart of this social form is a postmodern culture characterized by 'incredulity toward metanarratives'.[30] There is scepticism about all philosophies of history, all claims to foresee the inevitable goal of history and all political ideologies which promise to lead us to that goal. There is even scepticism about the universal validity of the values that define a particular historical future as good or bad. The 'death of God' announced by Nietzsche is closely followed by the death of history and progress. There is even a loss of faith in anything other than the instrumental effectiveness of Western rationality. Paradoxically, this loss of faith is the ultimate outcome of the Enlightenment's own historically novel demand for the rational justification of every claim to truth, rightness and authority. In other words, the Enlightenment project has fallen victim to its own sceptical onslaught against religious dogma, tradition and authority.

If the mood of postmodernity is defined in terms of incredulity towards metanarratives, the politics of postmodernity is radically anti-authoritarian. The sceptical mood of postmodernity is also intolerant of grand projects and ambitious political programmes, which are a prominent feature of modern states and ideologies. Attempts to unify society artificially according to some grand 'totalizing' theory or ideology are no longer convincing. Even more clearly, the consequences of such attempts have often been disastrous.[31] The twentieth century has witnessed unlimited global wars, bureaucratically organized genocide and fascist and Stalinist totalitarianism. Totalitarianism, for Lyotard and other postmodernists, is perhaps the quintessential expression of the modernist search for unity and order. Instead, society should be recognized as a 'heterogeneity of language games' or 'institutions in patches'. Far from being susceptible to theorizing in the unifying style of Newtonian mechanics, society consists of 'clouds of sociality' more amenable to a 'pragmatics of language particles'.[32] With the demise of totalizing theories of society, the value or even viability of centralized state politics is also brought in doubt. As Hoy puts it, Lyotard questions 'the idea of holding state power rationally accountable for a complex modern society'.[33] The state cannot deal with the irreducible complexity of contemporary society except by resorting to the totalitarian imposition of unity and order.

Lyotard's enthusiasm for diversity even makes him suspect Habermas's 'discourse ethics' of potentially authoritarian implications. Habermas's consensus theory of truth ignores the diversity of language games and seeks to reduce heterogeneity to an oppressive unity. For the mood of postmodernity, '[c]onsensus has become an outmoded and suspect value'.[34] Only the diversity and heterogeneity of social and cultural forms can resist the invasive modernist spirit of performativity. It follows that only temporary and local consensus is desirable, only provisional contracts should be sought. The price to be paid for any residue of nostalgia for totalizing theory is 'terror', which is 'the efficiency gained by eliminating, or threatening to eliminate, a player from the language game one shares with him'.[35] *Artistic* modernism, on the other hand, is an ally in Lyotard's 'war on totality', but only if it is understood as a constantly renewed challenge to the rules of image and narration, even those rules instituted by earlier modernisms: 'Postmodernism thus understood is not modernism at its end but in the nascent state, and this state is constant.'[36] The challenge facing each new avant-garde is how to express through the medium of art something previously inexpressible. At the heart of this conception of art is the notion of the sublime as something beyond representation, something 'unpresentable'. Although, by definition, it cannot represent the unpresentable, modern art can at least 'present the fact that the unpresentable exists'.[37] In this way, art should constantly remind us of the limitations of both representational language and calculating reason.

Despite the radical scepticism of these arguments, Lyotard does not endorse ethical or political nihilism. He claims that 'justice as a value is neither outmoded nor suspect'.[38] Far from undermining the value of democracy or justice, which are, after all, central values of modernity, Lyotard's postmodernism is, on John Keane's reading, a 'vigorous agent of the renewal and deepening of modernity's democratic potential', 'a dialectical intensification of its democratic impulses'.[39] The emphasis on the irreducible plurality of language games reinforces the commitment to a diversity of viewpoints and their right to a voice. At the same time, it discourages 'ideological' language games, or, in other words, 'those which demand their general adoption' and the suppression of all rivals. The sceptical mood of postmodernity makes it more difficult to launch totalizing projects on the basis of claims to universal moral or theoretical truths. Postmodernist principles provide strong arguments for democratic institutions, including 'mechanisms capable of preventing absolute state power' and 'civil associations' beyond the state.[40] Nor can Lyotard be convicted of producing a universalizing ideology of his own – a universal veto against universalist ideologies – because democracy is founded on the denial of universal reason in a spirit that welcomes 'indeterminacy, controversy and uncertainty'.[41]

Not everyone, though, is so sympathetic to the mood of postmodernity. Habermas, for his part, has attacked postmodernism as a new form of conservatism, which has prematurely abandoned the uncompleted project of the Enlightenment. In common with other theorists associated with the Frankfurt School, Habermas is well aware of the problematic legacy of the Enlightenment project, but he is unwilling to give up its commitment to bring about human emancipation through the application of reason. Postmodernists, like Nietzsche, too easily bid 'farewell to the dialectic of enlightenment', resorting instead to a Messianism of art, poetry and myth beyond reason.[42] They respond to the one-sided, 'subject-centred' reason of the Enlightenment with an equally one-sided and reductive irrationalism, 'reason's absolute other'.[43] Again, Heidegger, like Nietzsche an important source of the postmodernist stance, gestures towards 'a thinking more rigorous than the conceptual', but his views are easily reconciled with conservatism and prejudice; '[Heidegger's] propositionally contentless speech about Being has, nevertheless, the illocutionary sense of demanding resignation to fate.'[44] Habermas deals with poststructuralist sources of postmodernism just as harshly. Derrida's deconstructionism falsely universalizes the 'poetic use of language specialized in world-disclosure' and so aestheticizes both language and philosophy.[45] Foucault's political stance is the 'arbitrary *partisanship* of a criticism that cannot account for its normative foundations'. The critical practice of genealogy is no more than 'the vertical projection of its position' and is similarly ungrounded.[46]

Habermas proposes instead his own universal pragmatics and discourse ethics as a way of pursuing the Enlightenment project without falling into the problems of the 'philosophy of the subject'. In effect, he thinks that the anti-humanist critique of the philosophy of the subject implies only the abandonment of its 'monological' or individualistic versions. Where a subject-centred reason is based on the monological perspective of the observer, it implies, in Rasmussen's words, 'the concept of a completely isolated subject whose relationship to the world can be only instrumentally conceived and not intersubjectively established'.[47] It is this perspective which underlies both the instrumental, calculating reason of the orthodox Enlightenment and the unattractive face of modernity. By developing the *inter*subjective 'paradigm of mutual understanding' through the theory of communication, Habermas hopes to avoid the impasse of the 'philosophy of consciousness'. It will then be possible to advance further the incomplete project of modernity without falling into the relativist, apolitical and, at least by default, conservative morass of postmodernism.[48] He is also unconvinced that Lyotard's fears about anything beyond local and provisional consensus are really justified. For Habermas, truth is the outcome of an idealized discourse free from the distortions of power but, as he acknowledges, we can never be certain that the ideal has been fully realized. *Genuine* consensus is a state that can only ever be anticipated. *Actual* consensus is always provisional and subject to challenge and revision. What is more, without a concept of truth it is not clear how we can challenge an imposed or 'ideological' consensus as something less than truth, and so provoke a renewal of discussion and inquiry.[49]

Jean Baudrillard (1929–2007), like Lyotard a former Marxist, has also moved increasingly in the direction of postmodernism in his attempts to provide an account of Western society. Emphasizing not only novel features of contemporary culture but, more particularly, the transformed role of the cultural sphere in society, his position has analogies both with the Frankfurt School's analyses of the culture industry and the 'situationist' diagnosis of the 'society of the spectacle'.[50] The transformed state of capitalist society still provides the spur for his theoretical approach, though he sees the result as a society no longer amenable to Marxist categories.[51] For Baudrillard, the unprecedented saturation of both economy and society by the 'image' is definitive of contemporary society. In his earlier (still Marxist) works, Baudrillard identifies an important shift in the role of commodities in 'consumer society', which he sees not simply as a superstructural outgrowth of capitalism but as 'a fundamental mutation in the ecology of the human species'.[52] In this new form of society, individuals are indoctrinated into consumption, where previously they were merely made to work: 'Modern man spends less and less of life in production, and more and more in the continuous production and creation of personal needs and of personal well-being. He must constantly be ready to actualize all of his potential, all of his capacity for consumption.'[53] To earn pleasure through consumption rather than work is the pre-eminent duty according to the 'fun morality' of consumer society. Advertising, market research, television and other media of communication are designed to produce willing and pliable consumers.

But a fundamental shift in the meaning of consumption is also involved. Within liberal capitalism, the production of objects was already determined by monetary profit rather than human need. In Marx's terms, production was determined by the 'exchange value' rather than the 'use value' of things. But in consumer society the object is even more radically detached from use or need, even more radically alienated. The consumption of objects is now determined by their position within a differential system of meanings or 'signs', corresponding to gradations of social status and so on, which are expressed in and reinforced by advertising. According to Baudrillard's evidently structuralist account: '[C]ommodities and objects, like words and once like women, constitute a global, arbitrary, and coherent system of signs, a *cultural* system which substitutes a social order of values and classifications for a contingent world of needs and pleasures, the natural and biological order.'[54] Marxian political economy is no longer appropriate for the new socioeconomic formation, which must henceforth be understood in terms of a 'political economy of the sign'. Because of the interpenetration of meaningful commodities and the capitalist system of production, culture and economy must henceforth be understood as an indivisible amalgam. In Connor's words, 'it is no longer possible to separate the economic or productive realm from the realms of ideology or culture, since cultural artefacts, images, representation, even feelings and psychic structures have become part of the world of the economic'.[55]

In Baudrillard's later, more apocalyptic writings the image or sign displaces reality altogether. In effect, the arguments of poststructuralism are taken up to (and perhaps beyond) their logical conclusion. If, as he takes poststructuralism to imply, there is nothing outside the text, any duality of image and reality, sign and referent must be superseded. Images can no longer be tied to an external referent or reality. The map, to take Baudrillard's example, no longer corresponds to some real territory but rather precedes and even engenders it:

> Simulation is no longer that of a territory, a referential being of a sub-stance. It is the generation by models of a real without origin or reality: a hyperreal. The territory no longer precedes the map, nor survives it. Henceforth, it is the map that precedes the territory . . . it is the map that engenders the territory.[56]

In Baudrillard's somewhat hyperbolic terms, there is no longer any truth or reality, only universal and inescapable simulations. Soap operas and theme parks are the only reality. Disneyland embodies the 'truth' of America and the American way.[57] By implication ideology too has become a thing of the past, because ideology is defined as something falling short of undistorted truth, and no such standard is available in hyperreality. The only remaining ideology is the belief in reality or truth itself, the belief that the social spectacle is more than mere performance: 'It is no longer a question of a false representation of reality (ideology), but of concealing the fact that the real is no longer real.'[58]

In 'The Ecstasy of Communication' Baudrillard provides an evocative, if somewhat impressionistic, account of the contemporary world of simulation. It is a world of information and communication, where 'screen and network' are the only ontological essentials and culture is just 'the smooth operational surface of communication'. Television is 'the ultimate and perfect object' for an era in which everything is invaded by advertising.[59] We have already seen the essential role played by consumption in this world. But the regime of mass media and isolated consumption does not leave the rest of society unchanged. The very sociality of social life is threatened, to the extent that it depends on meeting and talking with other people:

> [W]e have come to live in less proximity to other human beings, in their presence and discourse, and more under the silent gaze of deceptive and obedient objects which continuously repeat the same discourse, that of our stupefied [*médusée*] power, of our potential affluence and of our absence from one another.[60]

And not only do we lose access to a genuine public sphere, there is no longer any secrecy either. The distinction between public and private spheres collapses under the weight of information and communication. Because communication makes 'public' what was once secret, it is obscene: '[W]e live in the ecstasy of communication. And this ecstasy is obscene. . . . All secrets, spaces and scenes abolished in a single dimension of information. That's obscenity.'[61] There is henceforth only the 'promiscuity' of unrestricted connections. Drawing on

Deleuze and Guattari's *Anti-Oedipus*, Baudrillard identifies the characteristic pathology of this universe as schizophrenia. Lost amidst 'the immanent promiscuity of all these networks, with their continual connections', the 'schizo' is 'bereft of every scene, open to everything in spite of himself, living in the greatest confusion', dominated by 'the feeling of no defence, no retreat', 'a pure screen, a switching centre for all networks of influence'.[62]

Nor, in this 'cold universe', is there much space for either the 'theatre of the social' or the 'theatre of politics'.[63] Society and politics, those two children of modernity, are both either dead or dying. Both society, as the object of conventional sociology, and the collective class agents of socialist ideology are disappearing and, along with them, the relevance of existing models of social analysis and political action. But what are we left with after society, after politics, after the individual? Baudrillard announces the arrival of the 'masses' as counterparts to a world of mass media, isolated consumption and public opinion. This is an 'ensemble', to use Sartre's term, which is collective only in the statistical sense. The masses are the apotheosis of 'seriality'. Like listeners to a radio broadcast or television viewers, the masses no longer meet or discuss but simply coexist as a dispersed, passive and otherwise unconnected audience.[64] In a postmodern world dominated by information and communications media, they cannot generate the self-conscious, organized groups required for collective action. In contrast to the militant collective struggle traditionally expected of the proletariat by Marxism, the resistance of the masses assumes the form of passivity, a stubborn refusal of all incitements to speak, to act or to participate: '[T]he present argument of the system is to maximize speech, to maximize the production of meaning, of participation. And so the strategic resistance is that of the refusal of meaning and the refusal of speech.'[65] On Bauman's sceptical reading, '[w]e are now being told that the bovine immobility of the masses is the best form of activity we have, and that their doing nothing is the most excellent form of resistance'.[66] More sympathetically, Baudrillard's position can be seen as symptomatic of a society in which, as Foucault's writings suggest, human beings are the product of relations of power constituting them not only as objects but also as subjects.[67] This diagnosis similarly casts doubt on those characteristic ideologies of modernity, liberalism and socialism, which demand 'the liberating rights of the subject'.[68] Do such demands simply play into the hands of power? Nor, to be fair, does Baudrillard rule out altogether the more active resistance advocated by modern political ideologies. In the end, though, his prognosis for traditional politics is scarcely encouraging.

Postmodernity as a stage of Western society

Marxism is the dark matter of the postmodernist universe. It exerts greater and more complex effects on postmodernist thought and discourse than are at first apparent. The exit from Marxism by French intellectuals, especially after 1968, was one of the major contributing factors in the emergence of postmodernism, and postmodernists typically see Marxism as a significant manifestation of modernism. Lyotard and Baudrillard both belong to a growing diaspora of formerly Marxist intellectuals in exile from their previous theoretical convictions. However, a number of other theorists attempt to accommodate what they see as the insights of postmodernism within a still recognizably Marxist or, at least, materialist framework. In effect, for theorists like Jameson, Laclau, Mouffe, Lash and Urry, postmodern culture and social relations correspond to contemporary capitalism, just as bourgeois ideology and values were the 'ruling ideas' of nineteenth-century liberal capitalism.[69] For these theorists, postmodernity is an inescapable feature of contemporary society, which any relevant social theory must deal with. In effect, they are revisionists who agree with other Western Marxists that a substantial rewriting of Marxist theory is necessary. And in fact, although they emphasize different aspects of the transformation of capitalist society, and a number of other important theoretical shifts occur, there are significant analogies with the approach of the Frankfurt School.[70]

For a variety of revisionist perspectives, then, capitalism has been fundamentally transformed on a number of dimensions since the nineteenth century. In the first place, the working class is a less homogeneous, less united and seemingly less willing bearer, at least in any foreseeable future, of the revolutionary task allotted to it by orthodox Marxism. Reformist social democracy and trade unionism have remained the favoured avenues of working-class activism and can no longer be dismissed as the 'infantile disorders' of an immature class consciousness. The proletariat's retreat from its allotted role reflects a number of other changes to the capitalist economy. The manufacturing industry has declined relative to the more dispersed and less unionized service sector. Finance and production are increasingly globalized, removing power from national labour movements and even national governments. Ownership has been dispersed through joint stock companies. The 'managerial revolution' has led to a growing gap between ownership and control of the production process. A further set of changes has resulted from technological innovations made possible by earlier stages of capitalism. Perhaps most important are the rise of mechanized and electronic mass media and the information and communications revolutions brought about by computerization. These changes have had a profound impact in a number of areas. The work process has been transformed, demanding new kinds of technical expertise from the workforce while deskilling many traditional occupations. Leisure and consumption have been progressively revolutionized by newspapers, film, television, sound reproduction, computers, communications technology, internet and the World Wide Web.[71]

The rapid development of electronic technologies of information processing and communications is inseparable from other important cultural shifts. The expansion of electronic mass media has allowed an unprecedented saturation of everyday life with the imagery of advertising. This, in conjunction with the development of more flexible, post-Fordist processes of production, has encouraged new patterns of consumption.[72] Consumption is increasingly an opportunity to assert difference rather than the equality of social status offered by Fordism. Consumers purchase a 'lifestyle', 'image' and 'identity', which are conceived by product designers, promoted by advertising consultants and supplied by a flexible production process. The fragmentation of production, class membership and consumption is confirmed in the area of politics. In contrast to the monolithic collective agents and norms of solidarity characteristic of socialist politics, there has emerged a multiplicity of struggles, regions of conflict, issues and modes of political action. A plurality of new social movements and corresponding 'subject positions' contribute to an irreducibly pluralist politics of resistance.[73] The movements in question include women, peace activists, environmentalists and 'greens', lesbians and gays, anti-racists, ethnic minorities and indigenous peoples, urban civil rights and citizenship campaigns.

Marxist theorists have discussed these social and cultural transformations in terms of theories of 'advanced' or 'late' capitalism.[74] Alain Touraine (1925–) interprets basically similar features of contemporary society as signs of a transition from 'industrial' to 'postindustrial' society. By choosing this terminology, Touraine both signals his distance from Marxism, as appropriate only to the industrial stage of capitalism, and points to what he regards as the substantial similarities between capitalism and communism as variants of industrial society.[75] Fredric Jameson (1934–) is closer to the first group of theorists. Although he takes very seriously the various ways in which Western society has been transformed, he continues to understand it as a variant of capitalism and so maintains his allegiance to Marxism. Postmodernism is 'the cultural logic of late capitalism':

'[P]ostmodernism is not the cultural dominant of a wholly new social order (the rumor about which, under the name of "postindustrial society", ran through the media a few years ago), but only the reflex and the concomitant of yet another systemic modification of capitalism itself.'[76] Jameson adapts Ernest Mandel's three-stage model of capitalist development, which relates each stage of capitalism to the dominance of a particular technology. Market capitalism (analysed by Marx) is the stage of steam-driven mechanization and, in the cultural realm, artistic realism. Monopoly or imperialist capitalism (described by Lenin and Luxemburg) is the stage of electrical power, the internal combustion engine and artistic modernism. Finally comes the gradual emergence, from the 1950s in the area of technology and from the 1960s in the area of culture, of 'consumer', 'late' or 'multinational capitalism'. The dominant technologies of this stage are electronics and nuclear power. But this stage of capitalism also has its own 'dominant cultural logic', reflected in the prominence of both cultural and intellectual currents of postmodernism.[77]

The cultural logic of late capitalism has two aspects. In the first place, the cultural forms corresponding to this stage of society have familiar postmodern features. Postmodernism in the artistic sphere involves the 'effacement . . . of the older (essentially high-modernist) frontier between high culture and the so-called mass or commercial culture' and the integration of 'aesthetic production' into commodity production.[78] Jameson also notes a declining ability to think historically and 'the disappearance of master narratives'.[79] We are increasingly isolated from our own histories, 'condemned to seek History by way of our own pop images and simulacra of that history, which itself remains forever out of reach'.[80] We experience history through theme parks and TV 'mini-series' rather than the historic projects of political movements or ideologies. But the distinctiveness of the contemporary phase of capitalism does not consist only in the prevalence of postmodern cultural themes. A second aspect of the cultural logic of late capitalism is a new relationship between culture and the rest of the social totality. Postmodernism is not just a new cultural form but a 'cultural dominant', which stands in a novel relationship to the economic system. Culture is both less separate and more pervasive. Postmodern culture invades society. Not only is consumption increasingly defined in cultural terms, but culture itself has also been commodified to an unprecedented extent. In the age of mechanical reproduction, works of art are more and more subject to market forces. At the same time, commodities in general are advertised as works of art. The consumer is encouraged to fashion for himself a unique identity through individualized acts of consumption, placed

on the same level as the creative activity of the artist. The interpenetration of society and culture means both the 'dissolution of an
autonomous sphere of culture' and the 'prodigious expansion of
culture throughout the social realm'.[81]

An important consequence of the distinctive cultural logic of late
capitalism is the impossibility of maintaining an effective 'critical
distance' from its institutions and values. In effect, here, Jameson
incorporates the sceptical conclusions of poststructuralist and postmodernist philosophy, which disqualify Enlightenment attempts to
provide objective rational foundations for moral and political values.
The universal validity once claimed by such moralizing discourses as
Marxism and liberalism is no longer sustainable. Jameson wishes to
defend Marxist theory as a critical discourse without pretensions to
absolute truth. Marxism remains a 'master discourse', but on terms
that remove its absolute status. Marxism is a 'single great collective
story' and 'untranscendable horizon', which subsumes other
approaches; but its 'imperative to totalize' may not be feasible.
Marxism is not the 'affirmation of some place of truth' but 'a perspective and a method whereby the "false" and the ideological can
be unmasked and made visible'.[82] The role of the Marxist literary
critic is 'to engage in a symptomatic analysis that reveals and dis-
mantles the covert ideological content of literary texts'.[83] However,
Jameson is less clear about the practical politics of such a project. He
is sceptical of an unmediated pluralism of social movements or subject
positions which, he claims, reflects not the disappearance of classes
but merely the illusion thereof.[84] We still need a 'genuine' or 'totalizing' politics that takes in the economic or systemic level, and
Jameson is still prepared to name multinational capital and its agents
as 'enemy'. But his more constructive remarks are unfortunately
vague. Possible strategies would involve 'turning the image against
itself' and a 'cognitive mapping' of the space of contemporary capitalism, revealing the need for a 'multilevel strategy'.[85]

Somewhat closer to the anti- or post-Marxist assumptions of
philosophical postmodernism are a number of sociologists who see
postmodernity as an identifiable stage of society that either has, or
is, destined to succeed modernity, but who see no particular connection between postmodernity and Marx's vision of communism. The
sociological critique of modernity and modernization is closer to the
philosophical critique of the Enlightenment project than it is to
Marxism. According to Zygmunt Bauman (1925–), Marxism and
communism are modernity in its purest form. Communism takes
even further the limited conception of rationality manifest in the
modernization of the West. In comparison to capitalism (for Weber

already the 'rationally calculated pursuit of profit'), communism promises to abolish disruptive economic cycles of boom and recession. It promises to replace the chaos of market forces and ruthless competition with planning, to replace politics and class conflict with routine administration in the interests of the needs of the whole community. As Bauman puts it: 'Communism was modernity in its most determined mood and most decisive posture; modernity streamlined, purified of the last shred of the chaotic, the irrational, the spontaneous, the unpredictable.'[86] The Soviet Union, China, Cuba and other communist countries were initially successful in their 'modernizing' programmes of primary industrialization, electrification, education and health care.[87]

By contrast, Bauman describes an emergent *postmodernity* in positive terms, as a 'fully-fledged comprehensive and viable type of social system' in which consumer satisfaction plays a particularly important role.[88] Anthony Giddens too regards postmodernity less as a condition to be endured than as a political ideal. Giddens's perspective has affinities with other theories influenced by the Frankfurt School tradition of social theory. Like John Keane and Claus Offe, for example, he identifies basic contradictions at the heart of the systems of rationality which structure contemporary societies. These contradictions are the by-product of what Barry Smart calls 'the modern quest for order': 'The idea of order as a task, as a practice, as a condition to be reflected upon, preserved and nurtured is intrinsic to modernity.' But, paradoxically, 'ordering interventions seem to promote disorders'.[89] The attempt to impose order on society inevitably generates resistance and, at the extreme, the irruption of disorder. Giddens emphasizes the close interdependence between the ordering impulse of modernity and academic sociology. Sociology emerges as a distinct discipline alongside the characteristic institutions of modern society. It contributes to the self-knowledge or 'reflexivity' of society and hence furthers its potential for self-control and transformation.[90]

Logically, then, the crisis of modernity implies both a potential crisis for 'modern' sociology and the possibility of a postmodern approach to the study of society. Giddens argues for a number of changes. For example, as a result of the globalization of finance, production and consumption, communications and culture, social movements and civil society and so on, the nation-state is no longer an adequate focus for research. Both global and 'micro-social' levels of analysis have been unduly neglected. Sociology and theories of development have traditionally been based on the Eurocentric assumption that Western society is the most advanced or modern and that other societies must gradually evolve along the same path. This assumption must also be rethought. From a similar perspective, Smart argues for a less exclusionary and more imaginative sociology. The perspectives of a diversity of cultures, including those of traditional and religious societies, should be incorporated into a sociology based less on 'modern reason' and more on '*post*modern imagination'.[91] In other words, the disruption of the philosophical assumptions of modernity implies, if not (as with Baudrillard) the complete abandonment of both sociology and 'society', then at least a fundamental recasting of its social scientific self-image.

Politics of difference and ethics of the other

Postmodernism, then, involves a number of divergent currents of thought and a number of disciplinary regions. Its political and intellectual postures range from defiant radicalism to an ironic and, some would say, complacent detachment. Postmodernists provide a number of provocative (if occasionally hyperbolic) descriptions of contemporary Western culture and society, which serve to undermine conventional styles of political action. They are most frequently criticized for their relentless negativism and scepticism, their refusal to offer more positive moral and political recommendations. However, even at the level of scepticism, the value of the postmodernist critique should not be underestimated. The suspicion that this critique touches sensitive spots is confirmed, in the aftermath of the Cold War, by postmodernism's substitution for communism as the 'other' of Western rationality and freedom, the target of ritualized and unthinking abuse as often as serious engagement. At the very least, the postmodern diagnosis is a salutary reminder of the darker episodes of Western history. Twentieth-century totalitarianism is just one example of the dangers inherent in modernity. The postmodern mood also reflects a pervasive anxiety, a sense of 'ontological insecurity' (in Giddens's phrase), and widespread dissatisfaction with bureaucratized capitalist society, even if bureaucratic socialism is not regarded as an alternative either. The aftershocks of colonialism and decolonization and the resurgence of powerful religious fundamentalisms tug at the philosophical roots of Western self-assurance as well. Postmodernity may be a useful concept for an understanding of contemporary society and culture, even if the radical scepticism of the associated philosophical position is rejected.

In fact, the negative, sceptical stance of postmodernism is most frequently taken to have anti-authoritarian implications. Postmodernists disrupt all forms of discourse (and, of course, not only political discourse) which, however secretly, promote the terroristic suppression of diversity or difference. Derridean deconstruction challenges the 'violent hierarchies' of Western reason, and postmodernists, too, oppose any denial of the 'other', any reduction of difference to a devalued otherness for the sake of the security of our own identity. Far from producing some new and grandly unifying theory or inciting organized struggle against the 'system', postmodernists seek to entrench the multiplicity of discourses, knowledges, cultures, struggles and voices. They challenge the claims of all leaders, particularly leaders who claim to be experts or intellectuals, even those who claim to be experts in Marxist revolution or the politics of resistance. They even impugn an intellectual like Habermas, who claims authority regarding the conditions of 'undistorted communication' and democratic will formation. In this respect postmodernists are closer to Adorno, an earlier member of the Frankfurt School, whose 'negative dialectics' resists tenaciously every temptation of positive thinking.

The critical impetus of postmodernist ideas has found particular resonance in a number of discourses and perspectives previously marginalized within (albeit, of course, not *only* within) Western thought. Especially productive has been an interaction between postmodernism and feminism, in which the writings of Lacan and Derrida have probably been most influential. The deconstructive challenge to all 'hierarchized dichotomies' is applied to the opposition between woman and man, masculine and feminine. Where Simone de Beauvoir remains at least partially under the spell of this dichotomy, retaining traces of a negative view of woman as 'lack' and as the 'other' of man, postmodern feminism celebrates unreservedly her specificity and difference. But the challenge is even more radical than that. Postmodernist doubts about the status of philosophy as an autonomous, self-contained and rigorously rational enterprise provide an opening for feminist critique at the most fundamental level. A number of postmodernist feminists suggest that the 'malestream' of Western philosophy depends on an originary exclusion of woman or the feminine. Crucially, then, it is not only the status of women that is in question. The feminist concern with the position of women interacts with a philosophical critique which, if it can be sustained, demands a far-reaching recasting of Western reason.

Grosz expresses the radical nature of the postmodern feminist challenge with some force: 'Destabilising existing forms of writing and knowing is a precondition for the positive assertion of femininity. Without the fissuring of existing intellectual categories and textual norms, there is simply no conceptual space available for women's positive self-representations.'[92] Grosz discusses three French feminists who, in their different ways, contribute to the destabilizing of existing discursive categories and norms. Perhaps most approachably, Michèle Le Doeuff (1948–) deconstructs the 'imaginary' of Western philosophy.[93] Although this imaginary turns out to be male or masculine in significant ways, Le Doeuff's interests are wide-ranging. In particular, she points to the way that the institutionalization of philosophy has always involved a certain relationship between power and knowledge. The actual dependence of philosophical argument on officially excluded subjects and forms of discourse is shown in its reliance on metaphors, images or literary figures drawn from these marginalized domains. These elements of a philosophical imaginary 'both reveal and conceal philosophy's conditions of production and self-justification'.[94] Decisively for the deconstructive case, the philosophical text's imaginary is not just an incidental accompaniment or temporary lapse from a more rigorous train of argument. Rather, the philosophical imaginary is inseparable from the discursive strategies officially recognized within the tradition. In terms of feminist strategy, 'Le Doeuff affirms the position of images, models and metaphors of femininity in masculinist philosophies, seeing them as points of tension and contradiction, points which can illuminate what is at stake in various philosophical positions'.[95] A persuasive example of this strategy is her discussion of Bacon's early formulation of the project of modern science in terms of the relationship between a masterful science and womanly nature.[96]

More exclusively feminist in their concerns, Julia Kristeva (1941–) and Luce Irigaray (1930–) pursue a parallel deconstruction of knowledges and discourses revealed to be covertly male or masculinist in their deepest assumptions and constitution. Both theorists attempt to understand women in their irreducible difference. They theorize woman from a woman's point of view in order to discover a 'feminine feminine', and so overcome a long tradition of regarding woman as lack, as the deficient and subordinate other of man.[97] Although Kristeva's early work was influenced by Althusser, the influence of Derrida is apparent in her deconstructive reading of texts. These readings seek to uncover the repressed desires of the 'maternal', to recover the repressed sex of woman: 'She asserts the play of sexual differentiation running within and between all texts, and overflowing their intentions, which always leaves ineradicable, traceable residues in texts which make these texts amenable to different readings and to the play of sexual pleasures they contain.'[98] In terms derived from Lacan's reading of Freud, Kristeva explores the interplay between the 'pre-symbolic' or 'semiotic' disorder of the unconscious and the 'symbolic' realm of order, which is aligned with consciousness and explicit meaning. The symbolic order incorporates the law of the father, male power and phallocentrism and is 'founded on the repression of the imaginary'.[99] On the other hand, the semiotic realm, which is repressed when the subject enters the order of language at the Oedipal stage, is associated with the mother and woman as well as with the chaotic psychic pleasures and energies of the pre-Oedipal child.

The subject is normally constituted within the dynamic of a repressive hierarchy of symbolic and semiotic, male order and systematically repressed female imaginary. By contrast: '[A] liberated person is someone able to acknowledge "the play of semiotic and Symbolic" – the continual vacillation between disorder and order.'[100] This interplay reflects the actual but denied interdependence of symbolic and semiotic: 'The symbolic provides the semiotic with its only possibilities of expression; in turn, the semiotic provides the symbolic with its raw materials and its energetic impetus.' The semiotic is creatively disruptive when it 'erupts and overflows its symbolic boundaries in certain "privileged" moments of "rupture, renovation and revolution"', which Kristeva associates with 'madness, holiness and poetry'.[101] In parallel terms, Hélène Cixous (1937–) contrasts masculine 'literature' with a feminine 'writing' of movement, subversion and transformation. Feminine writing is more closely aligned with desire than with reason, and 'desire, not reason, is the means to escape the limiting concepts of traditional western thought'.[102]

As a psychoanalyst and philosopher who seeks to liberate 'the feminine from male philosophical thought', Irigaray is critical of the ways in which psychoanalysis and philosophy universalize an essentially male representation of humanity.[103] Because language, society and culture are all constituted on the basis of this false universalization of male perspectives, interests and desires, women can only gain full representation by means of thoroughgoing social reconstruction. In Grosz's words:

> The feminine has thus far functioned in muted, suppressed or unheard ways, obscured by the domination and pseudo-representation of the masculine. . . . For women to be accorded autonomy as women, the entire social fabric requires major reorganisation: only *half* the possibilities, the alternatives, world-views, interests (at best) gain social expression or recognition.[104]

In particular, society and culture must recognize their debt to the 'mother'. Like the child who forgets what it owes to its mother, language and society have repressed the feminine in their original constitution as an essentially masculine order. Important strategies for Irigaray's contestation of this order are interrelated explorations of language and the specific and plural sexualities of women.[105] Woman should be understood not in Freud's negative terms of 'penis envy' or the absence of the phallus, but more positively as the presence of the 'two lips' of the vulva. The suppression of woman as an irreducibly distinct sex has meant that sexual relationships have existed not as the 'meeting of sexually different subjects', but as the insipid encounter between a male subject and his reflection in woman. The recognition of genuine sexual difference, by contrast, would inaugurate a completely different kind of sexual relationship: 'When each sex acknowledges the radical otherness of the other, then mutually rewarding exchanges between them become possible.'[106] Similarly productive exchanges would become possible in other non-sexual forms of sociality, for example in intellectual and ethical relationships.

Other currents of contemporary political thought address identifiably postmodern themes. Iris Marion Young challenges the ideal of community in socialist and some feminist thought. The communitarian desire for 'mutual identification in social relations' is a desire she connects with sectarianism, chauvinism and even racism. The desire for unity, wholeness and identity, here as elsewhere in the postmodernist universe, 'generates borders, dichotomies, and exclusions'.[107] The celebration of otherness and difference, on the other hand, is a potential antidote to these effects of closure and, indeed, an important theme for many contemporary feminists.[108] In analogous terms, Edward Said (1935–2003) describes how 'Orientalism' devalues and distorts colonized cultures as inferior reflections of Western civilization. Subordinated and marginalized groups and cultures can be represented within the discursive regime of colonialism only in relation to Western norms. Discourses of resistance against this regime must appeal to a common 'ethico-discursive principle', namely 'the right of formerly un- or misrepresented human groups to speak for and represent themselves in domains defined, politically and intellectually, as normally excluding them, usurping their signifying and representing functions, over-riding their historical reality'.[109]

Taking the deconstructionist strategy one step further, postcolonial theorists Gayatri Spivak and Homi Bhabha question even the characteristically postmodern opposition between excluding subject or identity and marginalized other. They argue 'the need for the careful deconstruction of the very structures of dominant and marginal', in the belief that 'such oppositional models themselves may derive from and reproduce colonial structures of thought – so that to proclaim oneself as a marginalized or silenced people is implicitly to accept and to internalize the condition of marginality'.[110] In fact, Said too aims to focus 'not on the exterior, countervailing strength of a marginal position, but on the internal contradictions within dominant western forms of knowledge'.[111] Resistance to a particular order of power and discourse struggles, possibly in vain, to avoid defining itself in terms which derive from and so perhaps reinforce that order. Movements of homosexuals (gays or lesbians), indigenous and black people all struggle on the basis of identities originating in the discourse of an oppressor. The work of Kristeva and Irigaray confirms the similar position of women. By implication, we should be suspicious of any 'politics of identity' which seeks to contain the 'flux' or 'flight' of resistance within a fixed and almost certainly compromised identity.[112]

For some critics, though, postmodernism is too inclined to identify with the pure intention rather than the unavoidably compromised reality of resistance. Like anarchism, postmodernism is accused of celebrating the pure moment of rebellion or critique at the expense of the necessarily untidy task of constructing a new political order – an order which, perhaps inevitably, will institute an exclusionary regime of its own. This accusation is reinforced by the fact that the positive political agenda of postmodernism remains unclear. How can postmodernists provide a convincing account of justice without violating their own austere critical principles? In the absence of some such account, we are left with few options. We may be politically engaged on behalf of our friends, but then we forget our commitment to the 'other', to what is not friendly or familiar or like us. In any case, the postmodernist critique seems to depend on an unarticulated normative framework of its own. As Connor remarks: '[W]hen inspected closely, it becomes apparent that the postmodern critique of unjust and oppressive systems of universality implicitly depends for its force upon the assumption of the universal right of all not to be treated unjustly and oppressively.'[113] If some equivalent assumption is not made, then how can universalism or, for that matter, the exclusion and domination of others be condemned? In the absence of some such principle, obvious difficulties face an unqualified politics of difference. A viable politics cannot be deduced from the simple denial of universality or an unqualified respect for difference.[114] Not all cultures, religions and worldviews can be respected simultaneously when they make absolute and incompatible demands of their own. It is not only Enlightenment universalism that devalues other perspectives. Religious, national and ethnic identities may be just as, or even more, exclusive and oppressive. Surely fundamentalists (of whatever variety) have more in common with one another than with postmodern advocates of plurality and difference, who are not as far from liberal pluralists as some postmodernists suggest. Richard Rorty, for one, is happy to admit the connection.[115]

Gaggi even sees dangers in the rigorously negative stance of postmodernism – what Allan Megill calls its 'perpetual holding operation'.[116] On the one hand, 'the fact that it can *only* be subversive and provides no grounds for arguing in favor of any ethical, social, or political system, progressive, reactionary, or otherwise, is a severe limitation on its potential for aiding in social change.'[117] Postmodernism bars itself from systematic and constructive involvement in emancipatory politics and so, in effect, helps to disarm opponents of existing regimes of power. This supports Eagleton's view that postmodernism and poststructuralism encourage an escape from politics and amount to 'conservatism by default'.[118] To see no good reason for active political engagement leads to acceptance of the status quo. After all, the self-styled (though by no means conventional) conservative Michael Oakeshott also directs his attack on 'rationalism in politics' against both of the main parties of modernity. He berates not only 'doctrinaire liberal' advocates of universal human rights and liberties, but also 'left Hegelian' Marxist protagonists of the 'upstart' classes.[119] Even worse, Gaggi suggests, postmodernist scepticism effectively erases the distinction between power and justice and so offers intellectual solace to fascism. Mussolini was aware of the connection: 'From the fact that all ideologies are of equal value, that all ideologies are merely fictions, the modern relativist infers that everybody has the right to create for himself his own ideology and to attempt to enforce it with all the energy of which he is capable.'[120]

Connor, too, is inclined to question the motives behind the postmodernist stance, seeing it as a last-ditch effort by intellectuals to hold on to their positions of privilege in the face of the sceptical onslaught of poststructuralism. The postmodernist bar on explicit criteria of normative critique is just one last desperate ploy by predominantly male critical intellectuals who, in the face of the increasing influence of feminist, anti-racist, anti-homophobic and other forms of critique, seek to retain their traditional monopoly on intellectual opposition. As Hebdige puts it:

> Rather than surrender mastery of the field, the critics who promulgate the line that we are living at the end of everything (and are *all* these critics men?) make one last leap and resolve to take it all – judgement, history, politics, aesthetics, value – out of the window with them. . . . The implication seems to be that if they cannot sit at the top of Plato's pyramid, then there shall be no pyramid at all.[121]

Postmodernism is part of 'an intellectual-discursive process which simultaneously multiplies critical options and binds them into recognizable and disseminable forms'.[122] Connor's hostile reading is supported by an intellectual sociology of postmodernist culture. Why has postmodernism recently become so popular among intellectuals and academics and why particularly in certain fields? On this view, postmodernism's recognition of difference and the sublime in fact belongs to a strategy of recuperation, which names the unnameable only to bring it more effectively under control.

Said's discussion of the relationship between postmodernism and interdisciplinarity intimates a more sympathetic intellectual sociology of postmodernism. He argues that the present academic organization of disciplinary specializations has deeply conservative implications. Postmodernism can be understood as a new way of conceiving the relationship between intellectual disciplines, challenging conventional academic boundaries, for example between literature and philosophy. Postmodernism has certainly become a topic of discussion within a number of different disciplines: in art, art theory and criticism, cultural studies, communication theory, philosophy, history, sociology, anthropology and geography among others. What Habermas sees as regression behind modernity's necessary differentiation of scientific, moral and aesthetic judgement is evaluated more positively by Said. By reproblematizing the divisions between faculties of judgement, postmodernism reintegrates the aesthetic dimension into life and, perhaps, fulfils Schiller's hopes, after Kant, for a playfully creative resolution of the conflict and alienation characteristic of modern subjectivity.[123]

Evidently, postmodernism is now one protagonist in an intellectual scene dominated by radically opposed positions, which do not always pay close attention to the arguments of the other side. In a different spirit, Stephen K. White has proposed a suggestive synthesis of postmodernism with something more like a continuation of the Enlightenment project. He seeks to reconcile central ideas of Heidegger, who is an important source of postmodernist themes, with those of Habermas, who is the most influential continental proponent of the 'incomplete project' of modernity. An adequate political response to the postmodern problematic requires both an ethic of 'responsibility to act' and an ethic of 'responsibility to otherness'. Responsibility to act relates to pragmatic concerns of practical and political effectiveness. It has been the predominant concern of Western reason. But, as a number of critics of Enlightenment and modernity, from Nietzsche and Heidegger to Horkheimer and Adorno, emphasize: 'This modern orientation toward a reason aimed at enhancing human will and control has no limits.'[124] Although it delivers great power over nature and has permitted a dramatic increase in the complexity of human societies, it is vitiated by its systematic inability to recognize and respect otherness. By contrast, both poststructuralism and postmodernism point stubbornly to what is suppressed or neglected as a result of modern reason's 'will to mastery'. Foucault's genealogies 'incite the experience of discord or discrepancy between the social construction of self, truth and rationality and that which does not fit neatly within their folds'. Postmodernist strategies 'bear witness' to the dissonance at the heart of Western reason and so show 'responsibility to otherness'.[125]

Heidegger is the thinker who shows greatest insight into responsibility to otherness and the 'world-disclosing' as opposed to 'action-coordinating' dimension of language to which it corresponds.[126] He understands that genuine community depends on a 'radical willingness to hear and experience the difference of the other'. Above all, his concept of 'nearness' (*Nähe*) embodies recognition of the other in its otherness.[127] Nearness involves a 'playing back and forth in relation to the other', which brings it closer at the same time as it lets it be in its otherness: 'Attentive concern for otherness means that the gesture of nearing, bringing into one's presence, into one's world, must always be complemented by a letting go, an allowance of distance, a letting be in absence, thus bearing witness to our own limits, our own finitude.'[128] Our creative 'bringing into presence' or 'disclosure' of the world through language must not displace that sense of otherness or absence, from which presence emerges and to which it must finally be allowed to return.[129] However, though Heidegger illuminates a strong sense of responsibility to otherness, his sense of 'responsibility to act' is sadly undeveloped. He is unable to conceptualize 'the normative tension and interconnection between actors in social and political life'.[130] He is contemptuous of the everyday conflicts and compromises of politics. His critique of modernity is 'totalistic', because it provides no guidelines for its transcendence, only a vague and potentially authoritarian longing for what is to come (*das Kommende*). Postmodernism's understanding of responsibility to act remains undeveloped because of a prevailing mood of 'impertinence', a deep-seated tendency to prefer deconstructive critique to constructive engagement. According to White's diagnosis: '[A]n *over*emphasis on disruption and impertinence creates for postmodern thinking a momentum that threatens to enervate the sense of responsibility to otherness, subtly substituting for it an implicit celebration of the impertinent subject who shows his or her virtuosity in deconstructing whatever unity comes along.'[131]

White's proposed synthesis in effect combines Habermas's discourse ethics with a suitably refreshed Heideggerianism. Discourse ethics provides a persuasive account of our responsibility to act. But Habermas is still too complacent about our responsibility to otherness, persisting 'in the belief that the problem of otherness can be adequately settled' within his own theoretical framework.[132] White garners from a variety of poststructuralist and postmodernist thinkers a number of clues for the required reconstruction of moral and political thought. Derrida usefully distinguishes a responsibility 'to' the particular other from the more generalized responsibility 'before' others, which is conventionally embodied in law and morality. Close to Heidegger's conception of 'closeness' or 'nearness' (*Nähe*) is the importance Derrida accords to friendship, conceived in Kantian terms as an 'unstable equilibrium' of love and respect, attraction and repulsion.[133] Lyotard's 'sublime of everyday life' and Foucault and Rorty's approval of a non-controlling 'curiosity' point similarly to an attitude of unpossessive care towards others. Feminism, finally, is an important source of insights. Carol Gilligan's discussion of a feminine 'ethic of care', Sara Ruddick's notion of a non-possessive attitude of 'holding' rather than 'grasping' and Seyla Benhabib's emphasis on the 'concrete' rather than 'generalised other' all provide clues.[134] In sum, we should positively delight in difference without tolerating those who would suppress otherness. The state should actively foster a diversity of communities and associations without succumbing to paternalism. The norms required for contemporary society can be derived from a Habermasian discourse ethic reinforced by more whole-hearted commitment to otherness.

Whatever might be thought of this attempt to reconcile Habermas's nuanced version of Enlightenment rationalism with postmodern sensibility, responsibility to act with responsibility to otherness, it serves to highlight the point that postmodernism can be understood only as an episode within the post-Enlightenment tradition of Western philosophy that it is so eager to criticize and deconstruct. The debate between Habermasian critical theory and postmodernism is no doubt an important episode within this tradition. But to hope for an eventual reconciliation of the critical insights of postmodernism with this major alternative current of post-Enlightenment thought would be to conceive the quarrel of modernity and postmodernity in terms closer to Habermas's 'incomplete project' of Enlightenment than to postmodernism's radical scepticism. Postmodernism surely presents a serious challenge to any remaining faith that some combination of reason and politics can be welded into a reliable instrument for the mastery of history in the interest of humanity. The benefits of this kind of politics have been too meagre, its disasters too calamitous. We are left not with a satisfying synthesis, but with an uncomfortable dilemma. It is hard to deny that there is a continuing need for effective principles of political engagement and critique, if only for the sake of those who have scarcely begun to benefit from the achievements of modernity. On the other hand, this is to assume that modernity's gains are not outweighed by a greater loss. Political engagement is unavoidable, its value remains inevitably in doubt.

Further Reading

Many of the primary texts of postmodernism are also founding contributions to the 'critique of the subject', structuralism and poststructuralism (see previous chapter). Also key are writings of Jean-François Lyotard, including *The Postmodern Condition: A Report on Knowledge* and those collected in *The Lyotard Reader*. The evolution of Baudrillard's thought is well represented in *Jean Baudrillard: Selected Writings*. For some commentaries see, on Lyotard, *Judging Lyotard* (ed. A. Benjamin) or Simon Malpas, *Jean-François Lyotard* and, on Baudrillard, Douglas Kellner, *Jean Baudrillard: From Marxism to Postmodernism and Beyond*. Postmodernism in its various dimensions is explored influentially in the works of Zygmunt Bauman, including *Modernity and the Holocaust* and *Intimations of Postmodernity*, and Marshall Berman, *All that is Solid Melts into Air*. Other useful discussions from a variety of perspectives are David Harvey, *The Condition of Postmodernity*, Silvio Gaggi, *Modern/Postmodern: A Study in Twentieth-Century Arts and Ideas*, and the essays collected in Hal Foster, *Postmodern Culture*. An important account from a Marxist perspective is Fredric Jameson, *Postmodernism, or, The Cultural Logic of Late Capitalism*. Habermas criticizes postmodern approaches in *Philosophical Discourse of Modernity* as does Alex Callinicos in *Against Postmodernism: A Marxist Critique*.

8

Radical Departures

Outline

Towards the end of the twentieth century, the fall of communism encouraged the complacent view that Western democracies, as the embodiment of Enlightenment and modernity, had achieved a final victory over their rivals at the 'end of history'. Never plausible, this view was decisively contradicted by the eruption of conflict in the 'Global War on Terror', economic crisis and the looming threat of ecological collapse. These events have encouraged both a turn to 'the political' as well as greater sympathy for religious themes and motifs in philosophy. Attention has been drawn, as a result, to thinkers like Giorgio Agamben, Philippe Lacoue-Labarthe and Jean-Luc Nancy, who explore the nature of community and politics in a philosophical spirit still close to Heidegger and postmodernism. By contrast, Slavoj Žižek, affecting a quite different style (humorous, playful and sometimes wilfully self-contradictory), applies Lacanian psychoanalysis to an understanding of the subject and ideology that is self-consciously opposed to postmodernism. Alain Badiou, though a veteran of the political conflicts and Maoist groupings of the 1960s, proclaims an even more radical break from all previous philosophy in both analytical and continental traditions. The austere axioms of mathematics and set theory, more familiar from analytical philosophy and symbolic logic, are recruited to a seemingly existentialist model of the 'act' and the 'event' which is, paradoxically, supposed to provide rigorous foundations for 'truth' in art, love, politics and even science. Both Žižek and Badiou hold out the possibility of a radical political alternative to the West's favoured model of liberal, capitalist and now multicultural democracy. It is less clear whether these thinkers fulfil their bold claims to philosophical originality and political inspiration.

The resumption of history

Postmodernism sought to define a space for philosophical thinking apart from the assumptions of Western modernity, in order to think and live without the assurances of any 'grand historical metanarrative' of progress or dialectical advance. It is somewhat ironic, then, that the vogue for postmodernism has itself turned out to be vulnerable to historical events. As a result, the controversy about postmodernism canvassed at the end of the previous chapter is no longer the most prominent debate within continental philosophy. Postmodernism's anti-historical animus, it turns out, coincided with a brief historical phase of unprecedented self-confidence and even complacency in the West. The collapse of Soviet and East European communism and the end of the Cold War in the years following 1989 left the West and, in particular, the USA in a position of unprecedented global hegemony – a unipolar 'new world order' without rival superpowers. In philosophy, commitments characteristic of the Enlightenment and Western rationalism – to scientific method, value-free social science and liberal democratic institutions – were similarly ascendant. More radical currents of post-Enlightenment philosophy, such as Marxism and critical theory, found little to inspire hopes of radical social transformation. In Francis Fukuyama's triumphalist view, capitalist liberal democracies should set aside self-doubt and recognize themselves as the best possible social and political model and so as the final goal or *telos* of history.[1] Henceforth, at the 'end of history' progress would take the form of gradual or piecemeal changes rather than any kind of systemic or revolutionary transformation. The Enlightenment project of rationalizing society had supposedly reached its destination. At a time when such triumphalist views could still be taken seriously, postmodernism was, in effect, the guilty conscience of 'actually existing' liberal democracy – the self-critical, self-doubting intellectual counterpart of its world-historical ascendancy and complacency. Postmodern hostility to Western modernity was the philosophical supplement to a societal model that countenanced no alternative. The sceptical assumptions of postmodernism ruled out the possibility of any theoretically compelling basis for revolutionary change. There was now no alternative – not, at least, in the terms of Western Marxism's 'modernist' project. Of course, thinkers associated with poststructuralism and postmodernism, like Derrida, Deleuze, Lyotard and Foucault, were decidedly political and, indeed, often activists themselves. Avoiding modernist political assumptions, they espoused instead a self-consciously *plural* and *diverse* radicalism, a radicalism of 'resistance' and 'transgression', of 'difference' and the multiplicity of 'subject positions'.

Reports of the end of history soon proved, however, to be exaggerated. The twenty-first century presents a quite different historical prospect, and for at least two reasons. In the first place, the shocking destruction of the twin towers of the World Trade Center in New York on 11 September 2001 signalled the end of the short-lived *Pax Americana*. The events of 9/11 shattered any illusion that a globalizing world would adopt the defining principles of Western modernity – secular, liberal democratic, capitalist and rationalist – without dissent or contention. The perpetrators of terrorist attacks employed evidently modern technologies (jet-propelled aircraft and the internet) in pursuit of their 'jihad' or 'holy war' – the latter justified by a decidedly anti-Western but in other ways unmistakably modern ideology concocted from Islam. As a result, far from the 'uninteresting times' of eternal peace at the end of history, we face the prospect of a War on Terror and, perhaps, a 'clash of civilizations' with no foreseeable end.[2] A second factor accounting for the present historical prospect is the arrival, long predicted but now imminent, of environmental limits to the expansion of industrial civilization. At the onset of the new century, the ecological burden of incremental material 'progress' – encompassing technological advances, rising affluence and a rapidly expanding world population – threatens to exceed the carrying capacity of the earth. By implication, the problem with the Enlightenment's vision of rationality and progress is no longer (as it was for some earlier critics) just its limited scope and exclusion of other values and perspectives. Progress, even in the Enlightenment's own limited terms, is rapidly approaching its limit. Ecological collapse is, in Paul Virilio's provocative terms, the 'Great Accident' that has been 'invented' by 'the positivist ideology of Progress'.[3]

The evaporation of premature illusions about the end of history has encouraged greater attention to the nature of 'the political'. No longer derivative or secondary to other preoccupations, the nature of politics and political action have become central and indispensable themes of philosophical reflection. At the same time, speculative philosophies of history in the style of Hegel and Marx – not to mention the Enlightenment's less nuanced faith in the inevitability of social progress – remain unappealing.[4] Political events and social change are (as recent events confirm) stubbornly resistant to prediction and prophecy, whether philosophically or religiously inspired. More to the point, historical teleologies, which imply that the future is inevitable and knowable in advance, make no useful contribution to the decisions and motivation of political actors. Political action is only worthwhile on the assumption that it can conceivably make a difference. If the future is inevitable, then political action is always futile – either superfluous or doomed to failure. A different path is explored, therefore, by those recent thinkers who have attempted to 'rethink the political'. Amongst a variety of sources, the ideas of Heidegger, Nietzsche, Marx, Freud and Lacan figure in their attempts. But the work of Hannah Arendt, Carl Schmitt and Walter Benjamin and, in particular, their distinctive conceptions of history, action and politics resonate strongly.[5] For all their differences, Arendt, Schmitt and Benjamin share a view of the centrality of politics and the openness of history to political intervention. What remains to be considered is whether any of the more recent thinkers considered below really succeed in surpassing them.

The return of the political in Agamben, Nancy and Lacoue-Labarthe

A series of attempts to 'rethink the political' at the turn of the twenty-first century have been made by thinkers who develop the implications of Heideggerian philosophy while seeking to avoid the dubious political direction taken by Heidegger himself. These thinkers aim to rescue Heidegger's philosophy (rather than Heidegger himself) from the taint of fascism and anti-Semitism by 'thinking politically' and, indeed, sometimes radically while starting from a still recognizably Heideggerian approach.[6] Not surprisingly, this project has also helped to revive interest in the thought of Hannah Arendt, who derived an anti-authoritarian political philosophy from Heideggerian phenomenology after the Second World War. More surprisingly, even the ideas of her intellectual opponent, Carl Schmitt, have become prominent again, despite the fact that he was avowedly authoritarian, explicitly anti-Semitic and, for a time, a party-ideologue of National Socialism.[7] Unlike Heidegger, however, Schmitt's ruthless realism and overwhelmingly political (rather than abstractly philosophical) concerns nevertheless help to illuminate the nature of 'the political', albeit at the cost of some of his most cherished prejudices.

Heideggerian themes and influences are developed in the work of Giorgio Agamben (1942–) in ways that have struck a popular chord in the current historical situation (sketched in the previous section). His earlier writings are Heideggerian explorations of language, metaphysics and aesthetics, which also draw on the thought of Georges Bataille.[8] Agamben's current popularity, however, owes more to a series of ethical and political works written from the 1990s, which offer a dark and, at times, apocalyptic vision of the political core of Western modernity. His radical challenge to the complacent self-image of Western states is particularly salient in the aftermath of the West's response to the terrorist attacks of 11 September 2001. In effect, Agamben gives a radical twist to Carl Schmitt's notions of sovereignty and the state, but more in the spirit of Walter Benjamin (1892–1940) who, like the latter's close friend Hannah Arendt, was an intellectual opponent of Schmitt.[9] Agamben accepts the basic elements of Schmitt's analysis but employs them to a completely different end. In effect, Schmitt's authoritarian *ideal* of the sovereign state is taken to represent the unattractive *reality* of the liberal democratic state. Schmitt's Hobbesian portrayal of the state as a 'mortal God' is taken to represent not some lost 'golden age' – or indeed hoped-for authoritarian revival – of the state in its unalloyed majesty, but rather the underlying and ever-present *reality* of the modern state. One way this is manifested is through the persistent and increasing tendency of liberal democracies to rely on the 'state of emergency' or 'state of exception' (*stato di eccezione*).[10] During a state of emergency, for example as a result of war or terrorism, established legal rights and constitutional procedures are overridden by the executive, usually according to emergency provisions contained in the constitution itself. The state of exception thus amounts to a Schmittian moment of arbitrary, sovereign decision at the heart of what are officially pluralist, parliamentary and constitutional democracies.

In fact, as Agamben documents in considerable detail, the legal and political doctrine of the 'state of exception' has a long history in European states. Under the Roman Republic, the constitutional government of the 'senate and people of Rome' (*Senatus Populusque Romanus*) could be suspended, in times of war or internal strife, and replaced by the constitutionally unlimited rule of a 'dictator' (*dictator*). Similar provisions persist in the written and unwritten constitutions governing today's liberal constitutional states, which always include some provision for their suspension.[11] The rule of law and constitutional procedure, in other words, are always conditional on the assumption that 'normal' conditions prevail, that the state currently faces no existential threat or emergency. In effect, the regular application of the rule of law continues only at the pleasure of the absolute sovereign lurking at the dark heart of the constitutional order. The indecisive parliamentary state, lambasted by Schmitt, is little more than a mask worn by the Leviathan during 'normal' times. What is more, the 'state of exception' is more than an abstract theoretical flaw hidden in the deep structure of the constitutional state. Agamben describes how recourse to emergency rule by modern states has become ever more widespread and enduring – the exception is, in effect, becoming the rule. Notoriously, the Nazi regime, which took power in 1933, never actually abolished the Weimar Constitution but, rather, set it aside by declaring and repeatedly renewing a state of emergency until its final collapse in 1945. Even Britain and France, the Allied States that opposed Germany in both world wars in the name of liberty and democracy, also significantly expanded their use of states of emergency.[12] More recently, the response of Western states and, in particular, the USA, Britain and Australia, to the events of 9/11 lends plausibility to Agamben's general point. States have passed laws curtailing rights and liberties and increasing surveillance of both citizens and non-citizens alike. Legal procedures and international conventions governing interrogation, arrest and imprisonment have been overridden or evaded by executive fiat. A 'state of exception' has been invoked, in fact if not in name. What is more, these measures have been taken in response to a 'terrorist threat' and a 'War on Terror' of seemingly indefinite duration. If war is permanent, then the constitutional order should indeed be regarded as the exception rather than the rule.

Some of Agamben's earlier political writings (written before 9/11) argue, in addition, that the 'state of exception' manifests itself not only as a *temporal interruption* but also as a *spatial excision* from the law-governed territory of the state.[13] The War on Terror again provides striking examples in the form of extra-constitutional prisons such as Abu Ghraib and Guantanamo Bay. In these camps, the legal rights of prisoners were either set aside or ignored on the authority of the US President. 'Inmates' were neither recognized as prisoners-of-war under the Geneva Conventions nor even accorded the rights of criminals under US federal law. A similar spatial exception is involved in 'extraordinary rendition', which refers to the involuntary transfer of prisoners to jurisdictions where torture and other violations of international law are routinely practised. In Agamben's terms, these examples belong with the extensive history of concentration camps, which were used long before the Nazi death camps during the Holocaust: by the United States for the confinement of native Americans in the 1830s and by Britain during the second

Anglo-Boer War of 1899–1902.[14] Agamben's account of the camp as a space of exception explicitly draws on Arendt's analysis of this characteristic site of the totalitarian regime where 'everything is possible'. The camp confirms, in the starkest possible way, the emptiness of supposedly natural and universal human rights when they are guaranteed only by international conventions and not entrenched in the laws and practice of an existing state. As Arendt pointed out in her analysis of totalitarianism, such conventions conspicuously failed to protect Jews and other 'stateless' and 'denaturalized' minorities, who were oppressed without restraint and eventually killed without compunction.[15]

Discussion of the state of exception and the camp is pertinent to the specific historical condition of Western states in the aftermath of 9/11. It is ironic, then, that Agamben shares Heidegger's ontologizing tendency to treat contingent and historical features of the political order as 'originary' and epochal properties, which seemingly defy any concrete political project. The authoritarian possibilities of the state of exception are ultimately traced to the very inception of the sovereign nation-state. The deep instability within the constitutional state, which means that it inevitably depends on an ineradicable moment of arbitrary decision and to that extent also on violence rather than legitimate force, corresponds to the always ambivalent status of the state's subjects. Agamben finds the key to this ambivalence in Roman Law's paradoxical notion of '*homo sacer*', literally the 'sacred man' who, because he was condemned by the people for some crime, could be killed with impunity but could never be sacrificed.[16] This seemingly strange and obscure category is, according to Agamben, the key to understanding the sovereign state as such. The state removes human life from the sphere of divine law and punishment but, since the state is ultimately founded on arbitrary decision and violence, this means that even those citizens included within its protection are simultaneously and permanently exposed as 'bare life': 'The sovereign sphere is the sphere in which it is permitted to kill without committing homicide and without celebrating a sacrifice, and sacred life – that is, life that may be killed but not sacrificed – is the life that has been captured in this sphere.' In that sense, 'the production of bare life is the originary activity of sovereignty'.[17] This implies that 'bio-politics', which Foucault associates with such characteristically *modern* pathologies as the proliferation of disciplinary technologies and programmes of surveillance as well as racism and genocide, should rather be understood as the 'unconcealment' of something that was there all along. According to Agamben: '[B]iopolitics is at least as old as the sovereign exception. Placing biological life at the center of its calculations, the modern State therefore does nothing other than bring to light the secret tie uniting power and bare life.'[18]

Heidegger's epochal-ontological pessimism is recalled once again by Agamben's eschatological prophecies of the approaching end of the sovereign state, even though Agamben's utopian musings are anti-capitalist and anarchist rather than authoritarian in spirit. He suggests that the relentless expansion of global capitalism is preparing for what he calls the 'coming community'. An important factor leading to this transformation is the intensification of what Guy Debord dubbed the 'society of the spectacle'.[19] This is a society where reality plays an ever-diminishing role, as images and media messages come to define what passes for the real world. These tendencies are manifest in both advertising and pornography as well as in what Agamben cryptically describes as the 'alienation of the linguistic nature of human beings'.[20] With echoes of Hegelian and Marxist dialectics, he suggests that the alienation of contemporary society presents an opportunity for an emancipatory transformation of both individuals and community towards 'a singularity without identity, a common and absolutely exposed singularity' or a 'whatever singularity'. We are offered the tantalizing but unfortunately obscure prospect of entering into 'a community without presuppositions and without subjects, into a communication without the incommunicable'.[21] Somehow associated with this coming community is Agamben's similarly cryptic advocacy of a 'gestural' politics of 'pure mediality', a politics 'of means without ends'. Relying on a distinction akin to Arendt's contrast between 'work' and 'action', he claims that politics is dangerous when it is assimilated to the instrumental 'means–ends' logic involved in 'making' history and 'fashioning' an alternative society.[22]

Agamben's cryptic remarks on the coming community explicitly allude to the work of long-term collaborators Jean-Luc Nancy (1940–) and Philippe Lacoue-Labarthe (1940–2007).[23] Starting from similarly Heideggerian assumptions, Nancy strives for a notion of community less vulnerable to authoritarian tendencies than 'organic' conceptions, which are associated with chauvinism and exclusive nationalism. The potentially dangerous longing for organic community is also self-deceiving, since it seeks to resurrect an organic togetherness that we never really possessed. By contrast, Nancy's alternative notion explicitly refers to a form of community that has not yet existed – hence Agamben's references to a 'coming community': 'So that community, far from being what society has crushed or lost, is *what happens to us* – question, waiting, event, imperative – *in the wake of* society.'[24] But if we need to understand community as a future possibility, then it remains crucial that we do not direct our actions towards the wrong idea of community as a closed or essential whole or substance. Such an orientation is incompatible with the plurality of genuine politics:

> But I start out from the idea that such a thinking – the thinking of community as essence – is in effect the closure of the political. Such a thinking constitutes closure because it assigns to community a *common being*, whereas community is a matter of something quite different, namely, of existence inasmuch as it is *in* common, but without letting itself be absorbed into a common substance.[25]

Politics is inseparable from genuine social plurality. We must break free from the lure of any 'profane eschatology' promising 'a utopia of the homogenisation of the "social body"'.[26] As Arendt's account of the distinctive nature of political action also implies, community cannot be understood as a 'work' or a product of 'work'. Community must be understood, in the terms Nancy derives from Bataille, as 'inoperative' (*désoeuvrée*), since to see the community as a common work is, once again, to reduce it to a utilitarian and anti-political unity.[27]

Nancy's more detailed rethinking of community foregrounds Heidegger's notion of 'being-with' (*Mitsein*) as its irreducibly plural foundation. A community founded on the relation of 'being-with' should entrench rather than abolish the plurality of its members. The rethinking of community also requires an alternative conception of the individual subject, since the conventional understanding of the 'individual' is a correlate of organic community. Nancy looks for a more helpful notion of the 'singular' in the writings of Bataille.[28] In particular, he draws on Bataille's account of 'the modern experience of community as neither a work to be produced, nor a lost communion, but rather as space itself, and the spacing of the experience of the outside, of the outside-of-self'.[29] The encounter between people in this space is, for Bataille, of a passionate and even sacred nature. Love and passion exist, indeed, can only exist, 'in the space' between people. The singular being thus stands 'ecstatically' in relation – or in 'exposition' – to the other.[30] Community in this sense is what makes possible (and is the correlate of) our separate or singular (but not individual) existence. At the same time, Nancy objects to Bataille's ultimately anti-political tendency to regard the community of lovers as 'a refuge or substitute for lost community'.[31] In the end, it is not clear that either Agamben or Nancy fully escape the ontological weight of their Heideggerian heritage. Nancy's complex and subtle thinking of the 'inoperative community' is most at home within the sphere of language, art and literature. Liberation is sought mainly through the poetic and transformative discourse of what he calls 'literary communism', which is somehow able to break free from the restrictive confines of conventional language.[32] Agamben's bleakly ontological vision of state sovereignty and modern existence similarly fails to make any plausible and sustained connection to worldly political action. On the contrary, the defects of the nation-state are so deep as to be practically unavoidable. His hieratic invocations of a 'coming community' are unlikely to inspire a concrete and genuinely emancipatory politics.

Slavoj Žižek – the fractious subject of ideology

An explicitly political and, indeed, often highly polemical stance is adopted by Slavoj Žižek (1949–) who nevertheless risks, as we shall see, reducing politics to the eternal and presumably unalterable categories of ontology and the subject. Certainly, in contrast to the thinkers of the previous section, Žižek announces a radical break from all varieties of deconstructionist and sceptical post-Nietzschean and post-Heideggerian philosophies. He rejects postmodernism and poststructuralism, particularly in their more ethical concerns, as implicitly religious or (in Badiou's terms) 'anti-philosophical'.[33] Like critical theorists in the tradition of the Frankfurt School, Žižek is preoccupied with capitalism, revolutionary politics and psychoanalysis.[34] It would be misleading, though, to exaggerate his closeness to that intellectual tradition. His often difficult language and indirect, non-discursive style of argument has more in common with Adorno than with Habermas, whom he dismisses as just another postmodernist (albeit one who disguises his scepticism in modernist clothing).[35] It is less obvious whether Žižek makes anything like the same level of philosophical contribution as Adorno. Sharply at odds with Adorno, in addition, are Žižek's conviction that popular culture is a genuine source of insights and his irreverent style, often bawdy humour and flamboyant public appearances. Overall Žižek combines the intellectual pretensions of high theory with the manner and media presence of a rock star. His complex and prolific output contains all the ingredients of radical chic (helping to explain his considerable popularity) at the same time as it places formidable obstacles in the path of any thoroughgoing, let alone definitive, critique. Perhaps least attractive (and reminiscent of sectarian Marxism) is his readiness to dismiss rival theorists as unwitting stooges of the dominant order.

Žižek's opposition to poststructuralist and postmodernist political positions, which typically combine scepticism about what they regard as modernist political projects like Marxism with an ethical emphasis on the recognition of difference and respect for otherness, is most readily approached through his critique of multiculturalism. Some poststructuralist and postmodernist thinkers have actively and, in effect, conservatively celebrated the anti-authoritarian playfulness and endless choices of 'post-Fordist' consumer capitalism. More radical thinkers typically align themselves with the plurality of oppositional social movements, the so-called 'new social movements' that have achieved prominence in Western societies in the decades after 1968. Ethical support for difference then translates into sympathy for the range of novel 'voices' and 'subject positions' of identity politics, which are organized (sometimes self-consciously) on the assumption that no single progressive movement (such as revolutionary socialism or social democracy) could ever eliminate all forms of subordination or oppression on the basis of gender, sexuality, 'race', ethnic discrimination, religious bigotry and so on. Sometimes this support is even extended to movements and belief-systems that are unaffected by, and often hostile to, 'modern' notions of rights, equality and freedom, for example forms of religious fundamentalism, which are seen as victims of the West's universalizing rationalism. Even the fixity and contours of particular cultural identities are further relativized by means of a critical assault on the residual 'essentialism' of identity politics. In other words, the political challenge to Western modernity is affirmed in the form of a 'multiculturalism' which, like a fractal image, reveals on nearer inspection ever more finely grained levels of differentiation.[36]

In a typically brazen move, Žižek blames multiculturalism for precisely those problems it is designed to address. The West's persistent hostility to 'difference' and, since 9/11, its increasingly frequent outbursts of nationalism, xenophobia, racism and religious intolerance, are neither atavistic remnants of premodern prejudice nor products of modernist chauvinism in the face of premodern 'otherness'. Rather, these manifestations of 'organicist populism' should be understood as the predictable expressions of multiculturalism itself.[37] The explanation for this counterintuitive claim is that although multiculturalism officially recognizes a plurality of cultures and communities and so appears to be 'above' such petty expressions of cultural chauvinism on behalf of 'our' community, it is no less communitarian for that. Its fundamental stance derives from the principle that the essential contexts of human life are organic cultural communities, which are irreducibly particular and incommensurable – hence their immunity to the universalist principles and values of modernism and rationalism. So multiculturalism, in Žižek's pithy terms, is really just 'racism with distance'.[38] Even worse, multiculturalism is no less guilty of chauvinism than universalist modern ideologies. The postmodern multiculturalist, according to Žižek, condescendingly recognizes the validity of diverse cultural contexts and communities but does not expect the members of those communities to demonstrate the same postmodern distance and tolerance themselves.

This diagnosis of contemporary politics ultimately depends on Žižek's psychoanalytic account of ideology, which in turn relies extensively on Jacques Lacan's reading of Freud.[39] At the heart of Žižek's account is a challenge to the preoccupation of both modernists and postmodernists with the truth or falsity of ideology. In conventional Marxist (or 'modernist') terms, ideologies are complexes of *false* beliefs and *partial* moral principles, which are designed to secure working-class loyalty to the capitalist system that exploits them. Postmodernists, on the other hand, reject the modernist assumption that there is an objective truth or underlying reality, against which ideological claims can be judged to be false. According to Žižek, however, both approaches fail to recognize the actual mode of functioning of ideology as a 'symptom'. Ideologies have more in common with the psychological pathologies (neuroses and psychoses) investigated by Freud. Žižek maintains that, like psychopathological symptoms, ideologies have such a firm hold upon us, because they are implicated in the deep and problematic relationship between the subject and its unrealizable desires. The typically Žižekian twist is that ideological beliefs may be *true* and yet serve their delusory function all the better for that. Conversely, there may be 'elements within an existing social order which – in the guise of "fiction", that is, of "utopian" narratives of possible but failed alternative histories – point towards the system's antagonistic character and thus "estrange" us to the self-evidence of its established identity.'[40] Put more simply, even false beliefs may play an emancipatory role.

Žižek's reading of psychoanalysis is filtered through (though not entirely clarified by) Lacan's three fundamental categories of 'imaginary', 'symbolic' and 'Real', which Žižek deploys in his own complex and paradoxical ways. In effect, the social order's sustaining ideologies are the imaginary supplement and compensation for the lack and disjointedness of the 'subject' which, once inserted into the symbolic order of society, has an inevitably problematic relationship to the 'Real' of its suppressed 'enjoyment' (or *jouissance*, a word which in

French has sexual connotations). Ideologies function by interpreting society as the solution to this 'castrated' subject's impossible desire: 'The function of ideology is not to offer us a point of escape from our reality but to offer us the social reality itself as an escape from some traumatic, real kernel.'[41] The essential deficiency of the subject is related to what Freud calls the 'death drive'. In Žižek's hands, this refers to the endlessly regenerated mismatch between desire and satisfaction, which results from the (unavoidable) insertion of human beings (in contrast to other animals) into the symbolic order of language and society: '"[D]eath drive" is not a biological fact but a notion indicating that the human psychic apparatus is subordinated to a blind automatism of repetition beyond pleasure-seeking, self-preservation, accordance between man and his milieu.'[42] Put somewhat more simply: 'The ultimate lesson of psychoanalysis is that human life is never "just life": humans are not simply alive, they are possessed by the strange drive to enjoy life to excess, passionately attached to a surplus which sticks out and derails the ordinary run of things.'[43] Of course, the surplus that 'sticks out' is, in Žižek's Freudian terms, the phallus.

At the heart of Žižek's Lacanian turn from both postmodern and modernist approaches is thus a distinctive and, ultimately, quite disturbing theory of the subject. Against poststructuralist and postmodernist deconstructionists, who typically reduce the subject to a merely derivative status as a by-product of 'subjectifying' regimes of discourse or power, Žižek regards the subject as the necessary basis of social critique and radical politics. The subject is the indispensable source of negation, the essential pivot that gives us some critical purchase on existing social arrangements and values: '[T]he subject exists as an eternal dimension of resistance-excess towards all forms of subjectivation (or what Althusser would call interpellation).'[44] At the same time, Žižek takes his stand against overly self-confident, humanist philosophies, which view the subject as the potentially *consistent* and *stable* foundation of sound judgement and valid knowledge. The subject – whether in the form of the isolated consciousness of post-Cartesian philosophy or Habermas's normatively regulated and irreducibly intersubjective communication community – cannot guarantee reliable access to truth, objectivity and morality. Žižek's position is *anti*-humanist, because he insists on the subject's fundamentally alienated, fractured and so unreliable nature. He draws here on the German Idealist Friedrich Schelling and an idiosyncratic reading of Hegelian 'negation' to characterize the foundational 'madness' of the subject's existence in the world. 'Man is – Hegel *dixit* – "an animal sick unto death", an animal extorted by an insatiable parasite (reason, *logos*, language).'[45] The subject exists (*pace* postmodernism), but only (*pace* modernism) as irredeemably flawed.

An apparent advantage of Žižek's approach is its ability to make sense of such virulent ideological formations as xenophobia, nationalism, fascism and anti-Semitism. These ideologies are so resistant to rational argument and so often popular because they provide a deep but unacknowledged (and, like the repressed material of the unconscious mind, unacknowledgeable) source of *jouissance* to their adherents. One of Žižek's recurring examples is the 'ideological dream' of anti-Semitism, which illustrates the futility of attempting to set aside our 'ideological spectacles' in order to see reality as it actually is. To set out to investigate the 'facts' about the behaviour and character of Jews is, in fact, just another manifestation of the same 'paranoid construction' of anti-Semitism. Why do we need to investigate this category of people and not others? Even when the facts tend to contradict anti-Semitic prejudices, the outcome is the same. So in the case of an anti-Semite who happens to have a Jewish neighbour – who is 'a good man to chat with in the evenings, whose children play with his' and so on – these facts will, paradoxically, only reinforce his prejudice:

> An ideology is really 'holding us' only when we do not feel any opposition between it and reality – that is, when the ideology succeeds in determining the mode of our everyday experience of reality itself. How then would our poor German, if he were a good anti-Semite, react to this gap between the ideological figure of the Jew (schemer, wire-puller, exploiting our brave men and so on) and the common everyday experience of his good neighbour, Mr Stern? His answer would be to turn this gap, this discrepancy itself, into an argument for anti-Semitism: 'You see how dangerous they really are? It is difficult to recognize their real nature. They hide behind the mask of everyday appearance – and it is exactly this hiding of one's real nature, this duplicity, that is a basic feature of the Jewish nature.' An ideology really succeeds when even the facts which at first sight contradict it start to function as arguments in its favour.[46]

Well-meaning appeals to tolerance and humanitarian sympathy evidently stand little chance in the face of the perverse enjoyments of anti-Semitism and similar ideological formations such as multiculturalism, which also (inevitably) fail to engage adequately with the 'Real kernel' of human desire. Multiculturalism too can be seen as a symptom 'bringing to light the inherent contradiction of the liberal-democratic ideological project.'[47] The only promising strategy left is a psychoanalytic one. Subjects must 'traverse the fantasy' that holds them in its thrall, because (as psychoanalysis teaches) only the dream offers access to the 'Real' of our desire. Žižek's often entertaining analyses of popular culture, jokes, opera and film, even, it has been suggested, his playful, indirect and disjointed mode of argument, are designed to contribute to this essentially therapeutic goal.[48] Significantly, though, in contrast to Frankfurt School thinkers like Marcuse and Fromm – whose theories assume an originally or, at least, potentially healthy human psychology that is manipulated and distorted by capitalism and other manifestations of instrumental rationality – Žižek believes that there can be no final or absolute redemption from the subject's irretrievable 'madness'.

Despite his overtly political and polemical discourse, Žižek's 'ontological-transcendental' view of the human subject as *intrinsically* and *irredeemably* flawed is difficult to reconcile with historical analysis and the prospects of political action. As Judith Butler puts it: 'If the subject always meets its limit in the selfsame place, then the subject is fundamentally exterior to the history in which it finds itself: there is no historicity to the subject, its limits, its articulability.'[49] If every ideology is a symptom of the same essential dislocation and 'nothingness' of the subject, how can one ideology be judged better or worse than another? If we can never dispense with ideology altogether, what motivates our political attempts to replace one ideology with another? Recognizing these problems, Žižek has distanced himself in more recent writings from his 'quasi-transcendental reading' of Lacan which, he admits, 'focused on the notion of the Real as the impossible Thing-in-itself' and so 'opens the way to the celebration of failure: to the idea that every act ultimately misfires, and that the proper ethical stance is heroically to accept this failure'.[50] He seeks, instead, to adopt a more actively political register, even if politics is still often described in psychoanalytic and therapeutic terms. The change of emphasis relies on regarding the Lacanian 'Real' not as *impossible* – which implies a 'transcendental' and timeless logic – but rather *impossible to sustain*. The latter interpretation supposedly lends itself more easily to an *historical* critique of ideology and hence to the possibility of a meaningful political response. Žižek's political turn is accompanied by renewed emphasis on capitalism and the necessity of a systemic alternative to it. He makes no attempt, however, to supply the concrete analysis that any serious resumption of the Marxist project would require. Instead, he pays attention to what, from the perspective of post-Marxist and postmodern liberal democracy, are the irrevocably 'lost causes' of revolutionary politics. The familiar excesses and pathologies of the French and Russian Revolutions – the expedient abandonment of conventional morality, political prison camps, paranoid purges, violence and popular justice – are re-examined with a conspicuously open mind. Well taken (if not particularly original) is his point that, beyond the visible 'subjective' violence of those who resist exploitation and oppression, we should also recognize the 'objective' violence implicit in the inequalities and injustice of the prevailing economic and political order.[51]

More interesting than Žižek's qualified rehabilitation of the revolutionary morality of Robespierre and the Jacobins of the French Revolution is his exploration of the political act. In this context, he refers approvingly to Lenin's understanding of the decisive intervention of political will and Lukács's notion of the decisive 'moment' (*Augenblick*), contrasting them with the evolutionary, developmental and deterministic accounts of history that have dominated the Marxist tradition.[52] Revolution should not be seen as the predictable outcome of social processes but rather as an always unprecedented event. In this context, Žižek appeals – in a way very reminiscent of Hannah Arendt – to Walter Benjamin's 'theses on history' which, in terse and elliptical terms, intimate an alternative view of the present as that point 'between past and future' when it is possible to act, to intervene. What Žižek calls the 'real act' is not determined by the past and may, contrary to our fatalistic tendencies, effect a significant change in the future.[53] The act potentially changes the matrix of historical conditions because, in the absence of any simple objectivity, the social totality is always subject to redefinition at the hands of political agents:

> This is why, for Benjamin, revolution is not part of continuous historical evolution but, on the contrary, a moment of 'stasis' when the continuity is broken, when the texture of previous history, that of the winners, is annihilated, and when, retroactively, through the success of the revolution, each abortive act, each slip, each past failed attempt which functioned in the reigning Text as an empty and meaningless trace, will be 'redeemed', will receive its signification. In this sense, revolution is strictly a *creationist* act, a radical intrusion of the 'death drive': erasure of the reigning Text, creation *ex nihilo* of a new Text by means of which the stifled past 'will have been'.[54]

At the same time, the act is somehow supposed to take advantage of the 'inner self-fissure' or 'out-of-jointness' of the historical subject.[55] But the subject's location beyond any straightforward societal rationality provides, at best, a narrow and precarious foothold for revolutionary optimism. It is precarious, because the disjointedness of the subject offers (as we have seen) a similar foothold for ideologies of fascist *jouissance* and consumerist excess. How can a movement against capitalism, a movement for socialism, manoeuvre to outbid the malevolent and so deeply rooted appeal of such ideologies?

In the event of Alain Badiou

Marking out a strikingly different path, Alain Badiou (1937–) is one of the few Marxists from the 1960s who has not renounced militant politics. Although Badiou does now reject the claims of 'scientific Marxism' and even the label 'Marxist', his consistent allegiance to militant politics is reflected in respectful discussion of revolutionary figures from Robespierre and Saint-Just to Lenin and Mao. He is correspondingly contemptuous of anti- and sometime ex-Marxist, usually liberal and pro-Enlightenment, 'new philosophers' (*nouveaux philosophes*) such as Bernard-Henri Lévy, André Glucksmann and Alain Finkielkraut. But he is equally hostile to the radically sceptical, anti-modernist but still determinedly post-Marxist thought of post-structuralists, postmodernists and others inspired by Heidegger. Badiou's distinctive philosophical position can be accessed, however, only with considerable effort. His serious writings are often dauntingly impenetrable, his writings for 'beginners' are merely difficult. In addition to the challenges of his philosophical language, Badiou deploys a fascinatingly diverse range of discursive elements. The philosophy of mathematics, logic and axiomatizations of set theory, with extensive discussion of figures like Cantor, Cohen, Gödel, Zermelo and Fraenkel, play a central role. But so too does Lacanian psychoanalysis, the poetry of Hölderlin, Mallarmé, Celan and Mandelstam, the theatre of Brecht and Pirandello and other expressions of artistic surrealism and modernism. It is thus not easy to assess Badiou's frank claim to have 'written a "great" book of philosophy' and to have 'inscribed [his] name . . . in the history of those philosophical systems which are the subject of interpretations and commentaries throughout the centuries'.[56] It would be unwise, even for someone who has thoroughly mastered every peak and crevasse of Badiou's thought, to attempt a succinct summary of his entire oeuvre. What follows is merely a brief survey of some of its intellectual foothills.

At the heart of Badiou's anti-Heideggerian project is his insistence on a radical disjunction between ontology and history, between truth and politics. This, combined with his avowed Platonism, might raise suspicions of a relapse into metaphysics or what Derrida criticized as 'logocentrism'. But crucially (and to postmodern sensibilities shockingly), Badiou aligns truth not with ontology or 'Being', but with history and politics, with the 'subject' and the 'Event'. He nevertheless defends a Platonic conception of philosophy as concerned with truths which have, despite their association with subjects and events, universal validity. At the same time, he reverses the Platonic relationship between philosophy and truth, seeing philosophy not as the *source* of these universal truths but as dependent on them as its 'conditions' of possibility: 'Thus, philosophy operates on the basis of multiple truths, and certainly does not generate them itself.'[57] Badiou's rehabilitation of a strong conception of universal truth is best understood in terms of his vigorous antagonism to everything associated with postmodernism and, more broadly, Heideggerian approaches in philosophy. He maintains a strict opposition to what he calls 'antiphilosophies', which in various ways deny the possibility of universal truth, leaving us with no recourse other than to mere convention, for the later Wittgenstein and Lyotard, or meaning in the case of phenomenology, hermeneutics and deconstruction. Equally objectionable is any subordination of philosophy to religion or ethics – or both in the case of Levinas's ethical injunction to respond to the ineffable and infinite demands of the Other. The ethical absolutism of Levinas's invocation of responsibility to 'the *absolutely* (divinely) other' is, as Badiou's parenthesis suggests, thinly disguised religion.[58] In any case, infinite responsiveness to the particularity or difference of an 'other' can support no rigorous or specific moral implications, which always depend, for Badiou, on the recognition of some 'sameness' or equality.[59]

Badiou's commitment to universal truth is reinforced, at least ostensibly, by his use of mathematics and, in particular, set theory as the basis of an austerely abstract ontology of 'multiples' and 'multiples of multiples'. He locates his own rigorous description of the ultimate nature of reality, of 'what there is', in terms of the ancient philosophical opposition between partisans of 'the one' and 'the many'. His hostility to any version of 'the one' of traditional ontology reflects his rejection of all 'anti-philosophies' and, indeed, any theological, religious, Heideggerian or poetic conception of ultimate reality as unified 'Being'. Set theory suits Badiou's austere ontological purposes, because it offers a fundamental categorial framework stripped of all unnecessary and unjustifiable assumptions. There are sets or 'multiples' of things and 'multiples of multiples', including the limit case of the 'null' or 'empty set'. That's all. This approach has the additional advantage that, as Hallward puts it, '[o]nly set theory can present inconsistency'.[60] The multiples of multiples must be posited without any assumption of overall consistency, because consistency would in turn imply a kind of metaphysical oneness. In any case, Kurt Gödel's incompleteness theorems have demonstrated that the consistency of formal axiomatic systems can never be proven.[61]

With his mathematical ontology Badiou also signals an apparent break from the anti-Enlightenment and anti-scientific animus of many continental philosophers. Indeed, he is contemptuous of any such distinction: 'I would like to mark an obvious fact: the nullity of the opposition between analytic thought and continental thought.'[62] Notwithstanding such pronouncements, Badiou's commitment to universal truth and science is given a distinctly 'continental' twist. As his association of truth with 'subjects' and 'events' might have led us to suspect, he is less interested in accumulated scientific findings or facts, opinions and 'common sense' than he is in those 'truths' that disrupt and renew accepted 'knowledges'. Truth, in Badiou's special sense, is always innovative or revolutionary in its relation to established bodies of knowledge and states of affairs. Truths represent a break from current assumptions and, in political terms, a threat to prevailing relations of power. The special status of truth is made apparent through its pairing with the notion of 'event'. A truth is always the product of an event, which is something that is necessarily unpredictable and inexplicable from the perspective of existing knowledge: 'A truth is solely constituted by rupturing with the order which supports it, never as an effect of that order. I have named this type of rupture which opens up truths "the event".'[63] So contrary to the traditionally empiricist or inductive focus on the slow accumulation of 'experience', 'observations' or 'data', science is of interest to Badiou only as the site of the revolutionary innovation – for example, the 'discoveries' of Galileo, Newton and Einstein in the physical sciences, and those of Cantor, Gödel, Zermelo-Fraenkel and Paul Cohen in mathematics and set theory.

Subsequent scientists and mathematicians demonstrate their 'fidelity' to such decisive intellectual 'ruptures' as they elaborate their implications in the course of what Badiou terms a scientific 'truth procedure'. Within *analytical* philosophy of science, Karl Popper's emphasis on the discontinuity of 'scientific conjectures' and Kuhn's account of paradigm-shifting scientific revolutions sparked debates about the 'incommensurability' of different paradigms, with the underlying aim of rescuing some objective criteria of scientific progress and the accumulation of knowledge.[64] By contrast, Badiou enthusiastically endorses a subjective and even 'decisionist' understanding of truth. Although truths are universal in their address – they demand, though they may never attain, the universal fidelity of investigators in a particular field – there can be no permanent and objective criteria of their validity. This follows, for Badiou, simply from the fact that, by definition, the scientific event transcends the existing body of knowledge and opinion. Truths are *made* rather than *discovered* by subjects. What is more, both truths and events are subjective in the additional sense that they serve to *constitute* genuine subjects in the first place – in the present case, subjects of science. It is only through fidelity to particular events that human beings transcend their merely animal individuality in order to become true subjects: 'A subject is nothing other than an active fidelity to the event of truth. This means that a subject is a militant of truth.'[65]

The subjective nature of truth comes into sharper focus when we consider the other 'truth procedures', which provide further conditions for Badiou's philosophy. In all, there are just four kinds of truth procedure in art, love, science and politics, corresponding to four kinds of subject, 'the artistic, amorous, scientific' and 'political'.[66] The implications of these abstract categories are most telling (or, perhaps, less counterintuitive) in the area of politics. Whereas scientists might be disconcerted to find themselves described as 'militants of truth', it is less surprising that Badiou, as a former Maoist, should describe the *political* subject in this way.[67] What is more, his focus on the political event as something that is always innovative in relation to the current state of affairs has the effect of aligning him, at least superficially, with other theorists of 'the political'. They also see genuine politics as more than the administration of everyday affairs, more than the mediation of existing conflicts of interest through the parliamentary institutions of liberal democracy. Political 'truth', in Badiou's terms, only occurs in a radical break from existing states of affairs and – for Badiou the term is almost synonymous – the state. Genuine politics breaks new ground, for example, by recognizing a previously ignored and excluded constituency or by politicizing new issues of contestation. Badiou's own political organization, *L'Organisation politique*, has been most involved with the case of France's 'illegal aliens' (*sans papiers*) and immigrants.

Badiou's militant conception of politics promises to reinforce political commitment and activism in two ways. In the first place, it is diametrically opposed to any kind of social or historical determinism. As a result, there is no foothold for fatalism and apathy on the basis of the supposedly 'inevitable' futility of action. Far from being the predictable outcome of the present situation, the political event always transcends it, and in ways that can never be foreseen. In the absence of political action, on the other hand, there is only the endless reproduction of the status quo or its evolution in directions that have nothing to do with human will. It might be objected that the political intervention must, on Badiou's account, always be unreasonable or irrational as well, since, by definition, it transcends the present state of affairs and any possible grounds or reasons that might be derived from that. The political act is always the product of what amounts to a 'leap of faith'.[68] From another perspective, however, this might also be seen as reinforcing political engagement. The 'unreasonable' nature of the political act is a corollary of its essentially creative role. To insist always on justifications and guarantees of success for political action represents, for Badiou, a kind of category mistake – a mistake that serves to entrench conformity to the prevailing social order.

What differentiates Badiou's stance from other theorists of the political is thus the uncompromising activism of his 'metapolitical' approach.[69] This stance aligns Badiou most closely with 'voluntarist' strands of revolutionary politics, which emphasize the decisive role of will and discipline in effecting change – a stance associated with Lenin, Mao and even such usually reviled figures of the French Revolution as Saint-Just and Robespierre. Other approaches fall short, because they neglect the militant as 'the central subjective figure of politics'.[70] On the other hand, Badiou no longer calls himself a Marxist. The Leninist and Maoist 'sequence' culminating in the upsurge of Maoist activism and the events of May 1968 in France is no longer operative. After the failure of revolutionary Marxism, these interventions may be worthy of study, but 'at the level of practical politics they have become unworkable'. More generally, Badiou is not willing to countenance the authority of any 'master-science' to guide political intervention.[71] To do so would be to deny the 'evental' character of political truth and the ethical dimension of the militant's fidelity to that truth. Nor is Badiou troubled by some of the familiar side effects of political activism and revolutionary upheavals. He defends the 'politico-historical heroism' which sometimes involves the sacrifice of individuals: '[T]he imposition of a heroism of discontinuity onto vital continuity finds its (political) resolution in the necessity of terror.'[72] Reflex horror at the violence associated with both the French and the Russian Revolutions, the automatic assumption that terror is always 'unintelligible and unthinkable', is just the other face of what Badiou derides as the 'humanitarian preaching' of human rights.[73] It is important to add, though, that Badiou, like Agamben and Nancy, acknowledges the ever-present risk that the 'we' of political intervention will metamorphose into a brutal collectivism.[74]

Badiou is perhaps on stronger ground when he argues that the current almost mandatory rejection of any kind of radical politics for the sake of the merely negative goal of avoiding evil is itself neither neutral nor without risk. The accelerating technical transformation of humanity and the world at the hands of capitalism and science is a quasi-automatic process whose future consequences, for all their unintended nature, may be just as bad as past (and similarly unintended) political disasters. At stake is nothing less than the future of 'man' as a potential subject, who is being reduced by this process to the status of a domesticated species of merely animal humanity.[75] These stakes are illuminated by Badiou's provocative discussion of ethics. Ethics is not itself a 'truth procedure' but concerns the ways in which subjects relate to, and are constituted through, their relation to the four truth procedures already named. It is crucial for the survival of an activist, fully subjective and human orientation that ethics is not reduced to the merely negative task of preventing evil. In contemporary discourse, the latter approach translates into an advocacy of multiculturalism and human rights, which is otherwise agnostic about what is good. Against these popular but ultimately anti-philosophical positions, Badiou insists on the more demanding and 'interventionist' implications of the subject's fidelity to truth procedures. The indispensable ethical demand is that we overcome the 'merely animal' self-interest of our individual natures for the sake of the subject's 'disinterested interest' in, and pursuit of, truths. Whether in pursuit of scientific truth, in loving devotion or as a political militant, the subject of truth always transcends mere 'perseverance-of-self'.[76]

It has been suggested that the ultimate basis of Badiou's philosophy is religious.[77] It would be more accurate to say that, like Hegel, Badiou propounds an atheism with religious characteristics. Illuminating, in this regard, is his discussion of the seventeenth-century French philosopher and Christian apologist Blaise Pascal. Badiou begins by referring to Lacan's judgement 'that if no religion were true, Christianity, nevertheless, was the religion which came closest to the question of truth'.[78] For Badiou, Pascal is exemplary because, although he fully understood the corrosive force of scientific reason, he boldly aims his arguments for religious belief not at the doubter or 'lukewarm believer' but at the 'resolute unbeliever'.[79] What is more, the 'evental' character of Christian belief is reflected in Pascal's famous wager and his emphasis on the role of miracles as 'the emblem of the pure event as resource of truth'.[80] If such remarks are reminiscent of Kierkegaard, Badiou himself is well aware of his philosophical affinities with existentialism. The dependence of truth on subjects and events bears some resemblance to Sartre's doctrine of radical freedom, which implies that for human beings 'existence' precedes 'essence'.[81] But Sartre's existentialism is, unapologetically, still a form of 'humanism'. The denial of God's role in creation is taken to imply that humanity's 'essential' project is to create itself or, in Badiou's words, 'Man is what man must invent'.[82] Badiou himself is closer to the radical *anti*-humanism of Nietzsche's 'overman' (*Übermensch*) and Foucault's related celebration of the disappearance of the 'figure of man'. The creation of a worthwhile humanity of 'subjects' (rather than mere animals) is, for Badiou, a project manifestly beyond the capabilities of mere humans. The 'programme of the Godless man' must rely instead on 'the man of inhuman beginning, who installs his thought in what happens and abides in the discontinuity of his arrival'.[83] Mathematics is once again called upon to provide an inspiring model for this kind of beginning. Mathematics is, after all, an impressive human creation which derives a remarkable body of truths from an austere set of axioms with few traces of their human-all-too-human origins. Whether the 'independent creativity of axiomatic decision itself' can be relied upon in other less rigorous domains of life is more questionable.[84] According to Badiou's own criteria of truth, the answer may depend on the fidelity of others to his novel and self-consciously counterintuitive philosophical system.

Further Reading

If the most accessible and timely introduction to Agamben's work is *State of Exception*, most influential is probably *Homo Sacer: Sovereign Power and Bare Life*. For Jean-Luc Nancy, *The Inoperative Community* and *Being Singular Plural* offer direct (but never easy) paths into the heart of his philosophy. For Žižek, *The Sublime Object of Ideology*, *In Defense of Lost Causes* and *The Žižek Reader* give some idea of the range and broad trajectory of his prolific writings. More immediately entertaining (and less off-putting) are *Conversations with Žižek*, *Violence: Six Sideways Reflections* and *Welcome to the Desert of the Real: Five Essays on September 11 and Related Dates*. The best points of entry to Alain Badiou's innovative philosophy are the selection of his writings in *Infinite Thought: Truth and the Return to Philosophy*, *Ethics: An Essay on the Understanding of Evil* and *The Century*. His most ambitious works are *Being and Event* and *Logics of Worlds (Being and Event, 2)*.

The secondary literature on the thinkers discussed in this chapter is mostly quite recent. For Agamben, see Leland de la Durantaye, *Giorgio Agamben: A Critical Introduction*, Catherine Mills, *The Philosophy of Agamben*, the essays collected in M. Calarco and S. DeCaroli's *Giorgio Agamben: Sovereignty and Life* and C. Norris's edited *Politics,*

Metaphysics, and Death: Essays on Giorgio Agamben's 'Homo Sacer'. On Jean-Luc Nancy, try Ian James, *The Fragmentary Demand: An Introduction to the Philosophy of Jean-Luc Nancy* and *On Jean-Luc Nancy: The Sense of Philosophy* (ed. S. Sparks et al.). Sarah Kay manages a coherent and critical reading in *Žižek: A Critical Introduction.* Ed Pluth, *Alain Badiou*, provides an impressively lucid and succinct introduction to Badiou; Peter Hallward's *Badiou: A Subject to Truth* is longer and more difficult.

Notes

Chapter 1 Introduction: What is Continental Philosophy?

1 If reference is nevertheless made to 'a' or 'the' continental tradition, this term should always be understood as an abbreviation for a more complex constellation of thinkers and ideas.

2 Thus, although the eighteenth-century Scottish philosopher David Hume casts doubt even on our knowledge of relations of cause and effect, which underpins all scientific knowledge concerning matters of fact, at the same time he defines his whole project as an attempt to apply the methods of natural science to the 'sciences of man': D. Hume, *A Treatise of Human Nature*, p. xx.

3 The main themes of modern European philosophy, the Enlightenment and its continental critics will be discussed in the following chapter.

4 At this point some readers may wish to proceed directly to chapter 2.

5 See W. Kirk, 'The Introduction and Critical Reception of Hegelian Thought in Britain, 1830–1900', and P. M. Kennedy, 'Idealists and Realists: British Views of Germany, 1864–1939'.

6 For a classic history of recent analytical and continental philosophy, see J. Passmore, *A Hundred Years of Philosophy*. The second edition contains useful additional material on continental philosophy.

7 D. Hume, *Enquiry Concerning Human Understanding*, Book IV, part I, sections 20–1, pp. 25–6.

8 Michael Dummett, quoted in D. E. Cooper, 'The Presidential Address: Analytical and Continental Philosophy', p. 11.

9 See S. Critchley, *Continental Philosophy: A Very Short Introduction*, ch. 1.

10 A. J. Ayer, *Language, Truth and Logic*, pp. 59–61.
11 See ch. 4.
12 Of course, Wittgenstein's philosophy was also significantly influenced by continental currents of thought. Members of the Vienna Circle included Moritz Schlick and Rudolf Carnap.
13 J. Derrida, 'The Ends of Man', in *Margins of Philosophy*, p. 114.

Chapter 2 Modernity, Enlightenment and their Continental Critics

1 See M. Weber, *Economy and Society*, vol. 1, pp. 85–6 and passim. For an accessible account of Weber, see J. Keane, *Public Life and Late Capitalism*, ch. 2, or D. G. MacRae, *Weber*. See also S. Lash and S. Whimster, eds, *Max Weber, Rationality and Modernity*.
2 Weber, *Economy and Society*, vol. 2, pp. 882–9. On Roman law, see also, e.g., M. P. Gilmore, *Arguments from Roman Law in Political Thought, 1200–1600*, and P. Sigmund, *Natural Law in Political Thought*, or A. D. E. Lewis and D. J. Ibbetson, eds, *The Roman Law Tradition*.
3 In fact, Harold Berman argues that the popes of the eleventh and twelfth centuries were responsible for the spread of Roman law, when they adapted it for the reform of canon law. See H. J. Berman, *Law and Revolution*.
4 Even when religious belief is retained, it tends to be reinterpreted so as to be compatible with more rational procedures.
5 See, e.g., M. Bloch, *Feudal Society*. On some of the developments occurring during the medieval period, see M. Oakeshott, 'The Masses in Representative Democracy', in *Rationalism in Politics, and Other Essays*, R. Tuck, *Natural Rights Theories* and Q. Skinner, *The Foundations of Modern Political Thought*.
6 See J. Habermas, *Philosophical Discourse of Modernity*.
7 Ibid., p. 5.
8 Ibid. Here Habermas also draws on the work of R. Koselleck, *Critique and Crisis: Enlightenment and the Pathogenesis of Modern Society*. Compare Skinner, Tuck and Oakeshott (see note 5), who locate this transition somewhat earlier, from around the thirteenth century.
9 See, e.g., Daniel Defoe's novel *Robinson Crusoe* (1719) or some of the *contes* or stories of Voltaire.
10 On these developments in art, see E. H. Gombrich, *Symbolic Images: Studies in the Art of the Renaissance* and D. Hockney, *Secret Knowledge: Rediscovering the Lost Techniques of the Old Masters*.
11 F. Bacon, *The Advancement of Learning*, p. 8; see also the third essay in M. Oakeshott, *On Human Conduct*, esp. p. 288.

12 Bacon, quoted by M. Oakeshott, 'Rationalism in Politics', in *Rationalism in Politics*, p. 15.

13 Ironically Nicolaus Copernicus (1473–1543) was inspired to propose heliocentrism by his enthusiasm for sun-worship. It was Johannes Kepler (1571–1630) who, in his *Astronomia Nova* of 1609, was able to simplify calculations of these movements with his assumption that the motion of planets is elliptical rather than circular.

14 See B. Brecht, *Life of Galileo*, and G. Galilei, *Dialogue on Two World Systems* (1632).

15 This view of the world supports the 'argument from design' for the existence of God. See, e.g., Aquinas' arguments for the existence of God, which relied heavily on newly discovered texts of Aristotle: M. T. Clark, ed., *An Aquinas Reader*, pp. 115–27. Contemporary ecology manifests a rather different appreciation of the order in nature.

16 C. Taylor, *Hegel*, p. 4.

17 On Descartes see, e.g., B. Williams, *Descartes*, J. Rée, *Descartes* or T. M. Schmaltz, ed., *Receptions of Descartes: Cartesianism and Anti-Cartesianism in Early Modern Europe*.

18 R. Descartes, 'Meditations on First Philosophy', pp. 151–2. Of course, even the claim that the occurrence of a thought implies the existence of an 'I' which thinks would be doubted, most notably by Hume (see below, p. 281, note 38); and see Rée, *Descartes*, ch. 6.

19 Taylor, *Hegel*, pp. 8ff.

20 Bacon, *The Advancement of Learning*, p. 35.

21 It is also worth noting that Newton spent a considerable portion of his later life studying alchemy, astrology and theology.

22 See Christopher Marlowe's play *Doctor Faustus* (1592), Goethe's *Faust* (1808, 1832) and Mary Shelley's *Frankenstein* (1818).

23 Descartes, 'Meditations', VI, esp. pp. 172ff.

24 Bacon, *Advancement of Learning*; J. Locke, *Essay Concerning Human Understanding*, pp. 6ff, 296.

25 I. Kant, 'An Answer to the Question: What is Enlightenment?', p. 41.

26 In fact, similar views had already been advanced, albeit in cautious or veiled terms, by earlier modern philosophers such as Thomas Hobbes. See Hobbes, *Leviathan*; cf. the Introduction to this edition by K. R. Minogue, esp. pp. xxi ff.

27 For Hume's analysis of causality, see *A Treatise of Human Nature*, Book I, part III or *Enquiry Concerning Human Understanding*, section VII.

28 Hume, *Treatise of Human Nature*, pp. xix ff.

29 Hume, *Enquiry Concerning Human Understanding*, section X, and *Dialogues Concerning Natural Religion*.

30 Hume, *Treatise of Human Nature*, p. 470.

31 Ibid., p. 299.

32 Ibid., p. 471. Significantly, this view allows no clear distinction between aesthetic and ethical experience. For Hume, the distinction rests only on the kinds of object valued – objects or things in the world may be beautiful; virtues, characters and actions are good or bad.

33 On Kant's moral philosophy, see the following section.

34 For a concise account of Kant's philosophy, see R. Scruton, *Kant*. An important study is H. E. Allison, *Kant's Transcendental Idealism*. See also C. D. Broad, *Kant: An Introduction* and D. Garber and B. Longuenesse, eds, *Kant and the Early Moderns*.

35 Kant, *Critique of Pure Reason*, p. 7.

36 On the debate between rationalism and empiricism, see R. Scruton, *A Short History of Modern Philosophy*, parts I–II, or B. Aune, *Rationalism, Empiricism, and Pragmatism*.

37 Plato, *Phaedo*, 72B, pp. 120ff.

38 See Plato, *Meno*, 82, pp. 130ff.

39 Kant, *Critique of Pure Reason*, p. 93.

40 Kant, *Critique of Pure Reason*, pp. 22–3. On Copernicus and Galileo, see above, p. 13. Ironically, the effect of Kant's revolution is, in a sense, to reinstate the human subject at the centre of its world.

41 On phenomenalism, see A. J. Ayer, *The Foundations of Empirical Knowledge*.

42 Allison, *Kant's Transcendental Idealism*, p. 7.

43 Ibid., p. 8. A fuller account is provided in ibid., chs 1–3.

44 Ibid., p. 7.

45 Ibid., ch. 2, section B.

46 Ibid., p. 38. See ibid., ch. 3, for a useful discussion of the cosmological argument.

47 For a detailed discussion of the transcendental deduction see ibid., ch. 7.

48 The latter seems to be the strategy of P. F. Strawson, *The Bounds of Sense*; cf. his 'Sensibility, Understanding, and the Doctrine of Synthesis'.

49 Kant, *Critique of Pure Reason*, quoted above, p. 18.

50 D. Henrich, 'Kant's Notion of a Transcendental Deduction and the Methodological Background of the First *Critique*', p. 41.

51 Kant, 'What is Enlightenment?' p. 41.

52 Ibid., pp. 41, 46.

53 See J. O. de la Mettrie, *Man a Machine*.

54 See above, p. 17.

55 Kant, *Critique of Pure Reason*, p. 29; cf. Scruton, *Kant*, ch. 2.

56 I. Kant, *Groundwork of the Metaphysic of Morals*, pp. 88, 95.

57 S. Hampshire, 'The Social Spirit of Mankind', p. 145.

58 Ibid., p. 152.

59 R. Brandt, 'The Deductions in the *Critique of Judgment*', p. 186.

60 F. Schiller, *Über die ästhetische Erziehung des Menschen*, pp. 56–7; translated as F. Schiller, *On the Aesthetic Education of Man*.

61 See I. Berlin, 'The Counter-Enlightenment', in *Against the Current*.

62 Indeed, the terms 'conservative' (earlier 'conservatory') and 'reaction' only capture distinct political positions on the assumption of an established direction of history as 'progress' or 'improvement'. The notion of progress as an 'evident or discoverable general movement of history' was first apparent in the 'Universal histories of the Enlightenment': see R. Williams, *Keywords*, p. 206. 'Reactionary' was first used in its modern political sense during the French Revolution of 1789 to describe those 'wishing to re-establish a pre-revolutionary state of affairs': ibid., p. 215.

63 J.-J. Rousseau, 'Discourse on the Origin of Inequality', p. 104. For helpful guides to Rousseau, see T. O'Hagan, *Rousseau*, C. Bertram, *Rousseau and the Social Contract* and G. Dart, *Rousseau, Robespierre and English Romanticism*.

64 Rousseau, 'Discourse on the Origin of Inequality', p. 64.

65 Ibid., p. 66n.

66 Ibid.

67 Ibid., p. 81.

68 This is despite his famous intention of 'laying all facts aside', a pledge which in context refers to the 'facts' of religion: ibid., p. 45.

69 Ibid., pp. 112–13.

70 This is not to deny that some of Rousseau's remarks lend support to such an interpretation, e.g. the first sentence of Rousseau's *Émile*, according to which 'God makes all things good; man meddles with them and they become evil': p. 35.

71 Rousseau, 'Discourse on the Origin of Inequality', p. 45.

72 See T. Hobbes, *Leviathan*, ch. 17, pp. 87ff. 'Leviathan', in Hebrew a kind of monster, is Hobbes's term for the sovereign collective entity created by the social contract or, in effect, the state.

73 Rousseau, 'Discourse on the Origin of Inequality', p. 45.

74 Ibid., pp. 177–8.

75 See above, pp. 25–7.

76 Rousseau, *Social Contract*, Book I, ch. VII, p. 177. For a classic account of the dangers of 'positive' as opposed to 'negative' freedom, see I. Berlin, *Four Essays on Liberty*, ch. 3, 'Two Concepts of Liberty'.

77 In John Keane's words, Rousseau describes 'an individualism of cooperation and uniqueness (*Einzigkeit*) compared with that of mere singleness (*Einzelheit*)': J. Keane, *Public Life and Late Capitalism*, p. 254.

78 For an illuminating account, see F. C. Beiser, *The Fate of Reason: German Philosophy from Kant to Fichte*. The following discussion of Jacobi and Hamann is indebted to this work. A broad collection of relevant essays is collected in E. Hammer, ed., *German Idealism: Contemporary Perspectives*.

79 Kant, *Critique of Pure Reason*, p. 29 (emphasis in original).
80 See Beiser, *Fate of Reason*, pp. 44–8, 81–3. On Hume, see above, pp. 17–18.
81 Beiser, *Fate of Reason*, ch. 1, p. 36. *Aesthetica in nuce* might be translated as 'aesthetics in a nut-shell'.
82 J. G. Herder, *Discourse on the Origin of Language*. See R. T. Clark, *Herder: His Life and Thought*.
83 See I. Berlin, *The Crooked Timber of Humanity*, p. 39.
84 Ibid., p. 210.
85 Ibid., p. 37.
86 R. C. Solomon, *Continental Philosophy Since 1750*, p. 13.
87 Sentiment figures prominently in novels like Henry Fielding's *Tom Jones* (1749).
88 Berlin, *The Crooked Timber of Humanity*, p. 215.
89 Taylor, *Hegel*, pp. 15–16.
90 Ibid., p. 17. See also C. Taylor, *Sources of the Self*, ch. 21.
91 For the subsequent development of German Romanticism and its relation to German Idealism, see M. Frank, *The Philosophical Foundations of Early German Romanticism*.
92 For useful guides to Hegel's sometimes difficult writings, see P. Singer, *Hegel: A Very Short Introduction*, Charles Taylor, *Hegel*, J. N. Findlay, *Hegel: A Re-examination* and Richard Norman, *Hegel's Phenomenology: An Introduction*.
93 This remains, of course, a disputed claim. Some Kantians argue that the universalization principle is capable of supporting a determinate moral conclusion: e.g., Lucien Goldman, *Immanuel Kant*. More conventionally, T. C. Williams, *The Concept of the Categorical Imperative*, defends the assumption that 'reason can be "practical" and can, of itself alone, be the motive of actions' (p. 4); and see esp. ch. 9.
94 Kant, *Groundwork of the Metaphysic of Morals*, pp. 57–8.
95 G. W. F. Hegel, *The Phenomenology of Mind*, pp. 601–2. The translation of this work by A. V. Miller, *Hegel's Phenomenology of Spirit*, is generally clearer than J. B. Baillie's translation, cited here.
96 Ibid., p. 604.
97 G. W. F. Hegel, *The Philosophy of Right*, para. 139, p. 92.
98 In the terms of a later tradition, the Kantian reconstruction is based on a process which is purely 'monological' rather than 'dialogical'. Although universalization involves considering what would happen if all subjects were to adopt a particular maxim, the process of deliberation can in principle be carried out by a single subject in isolation. There is no genuine recognition of the other. On this distinction in relation to Habermas, see T. McCarthy, *The Critical Theory of Jürgen Habermas*, pp. 326ff. As we shall see, this requirement also implies the importance of history. If individuals must always be understood as members of a concrete community and culture, then they must also be understood historically.
99 Hegel, *The Philosophy of Right*, p. 23.

100 In terms more often used by Fichte and subsequent commentators than by Hegel himself, the contradictions within a particular 'thesis' lead to an opposing thesis or 'antithesis'. The antithesis in turn gives way to a new position, which preserves the 'truth' of both thesis and antithesis and so represents a higher 'synthesis'. Hegel speaks rather of the 'negation' of a 'truth' leading to its 'sublation' or 'transcendence' (*Aufheben*). In fact, Hegel's use of the dialectic is far less mechanical than some descriptions suggest.

101 G. W. F. Hegel, *The Philosophy of History*, p. 19.

102 See ibid. For a succinct account of Hegel's philosophy of history, see P. Singer, *Hegel*, ch. 2 or Taylor, *Hegel*, part IV.

103 Singer, *Hegel*, p. 51. See also the Preface to Hegel's *The Phenomenology of Mind*.

104 R. Norman, *Hegel's Phenomenology*, p. 14. See also Taylor, *Hegel*, part II.

105 Hegel, quoted by Norman, *Hegel's Phenomenology*, p. 17.

106 Taylor, *Hegel*, pp. 109–10.

107 J. N. Findlay, *Hegel: A Re-examination*, p. 23.

108 Other aspects of Hegel's many-sided philosophy will be introduced in the context of these responses.

Chapter 3 Dialectics of Emancipation: Marx, the Frankfurt School and Habermas

1 Hegel saw America as a new moment in the unfolding of history. See W. Kaufmann, 'The Hegel Myth and its Method'.

2 See above, ch. 1, n. 7 and ch. 2, p. 44.

3 On the Frankfurt School and Habermas, see the second and third sections of this chapter, pp. 60–84. On the relationship of Marxism and postmodernism, see ch. 7, pp. 212–14.

4 David McLellan, *Karl Marx: His Life and Thought*, p. 128.

5 Some, such as Michael Oakeshott, have argued that Marx fundamentally misunderstands Hegel as a result: see M. Oakeshott, 'Michael Oakeshott on Marx on Hegel'. For accounts of Feuerbach, see V. A. Harvey, *Feuerbach and the Interpretation of Religion* and E. Kamenka, *The Philosophy of Ludwig Feuerbach*.

6 Compare the atheist conservatism of David Hume with the defiant immorality of the Marquis de Sade (1740–1814).

7 Voltaire, *Épîtres*, no. 96, 'À l'Auteur du livre des trois imposteurs', in *Oxford Dictionary of Quotations*, p. 716.

8 L. Feuerbach, *Essence of Christianity*, p. 14.

9 Ibid., p. 26.

10 Ibid., p. 13.

11 Ibid.

12 E. Kamenka, *The Philosophy of Ludwig Feuerbach*, p. 39. The allusion to psychoanalysis here is appropriate, since Feuerbach,

who also describes religion as 'the dream of the human mind', provides a model for Freud's subsequent 'demystification' of dreams and other aberrations from the self-transparency of the conscious mind (see below, ch. 6, pp. 177–9).

13 L. Feuerbach, *Principles of the Philosophy of the Future* (1843).
14 Feuerbach quoted by Kamenka, *The Philosophy of Ludwig Feuerbach*, pp. 78, 80.
15 Ibid., p. 76.
16 K. Marx, 'Critique of Hegel's Doctrine of the State' (1843) and 'On the Jewish Question' (1843). Apart from the many works on Marx by D. McLellan, see D. Leopold, *The Young Karl Marx: German Philosophy, Modern Politics, and Human Flourishing* and S. Avineri, *The Social and Political Thought of Karl Marx*.
17 See K. Marx, *The Civil War in France* and *Critique of the Gotha Programme*. Cf. B. Jessop, *The Capitalist State* and *State Theory*.
18 Marx, 'On the Jewish Question', pp. 218, 217.
19 D. McLellan, *Marx*, p. 29.
20 Marx, 'On the Jewish Question', pp. 227, 229 (emphasis in original).
21 Marx, 'Hegel's Doctrine of the State', p. 191 (emphasis in original).
22 Adam Smith, *The Wealth of Nations* (1776), vol. 1, IV, ii, 9, p. 456. There were, of course, also substantial disagreements between the classical political economists, e.g. over the degree of compatibility of the interests of landowners, wage-labourers and capitalists. See, e.g., M. Blaug, *Economic Theory in Retrospect*, B. Burkitt, *Radical Political Economy* and M. C. Howard and J. E. King, *The History of Marxian Economics*.
23 Engels famously described the miserable conditions endured by the working classes at the height of the industrial revolution in England in *The Condition of the Working Class in England in 1844*.
24 Marx, 'On the Jewish Question', p. 233.
25 Marx, 'Economic and Philosophical Manuscripts', p. 333.
26 Ibid., pp. 328–9. For some, like Louis Althusser, this notion reflects an early 'essentialist' or 'humanist' Marx, superseded in the writings of the mature Marx.
27 Ibid., pp. 325–31.
28 McLellan, *Marx*, p. 39.
29 K. Marx and F. Engels, *The German Ideology*, p. 62.
30 Marx, 'Theses on Feuerbach', p. 423.
31 Marx and Engels, *The German Ideology*, p. 48.
32 The dialectic of lordship and bondage is discussed in Hegel, *Phenomenology of Mind*, pp. 228–40, and see R. Norman, *Hegel's Phenomenology*, ch. 3, and A. Kojève, *Introduction to the Reading of Hegel*.
33 Marx and Engels, *The German Ideology*, p. 58.
34 Ibid., p. 64.
35 Ibid., p. 57.

36 K. Marx, *Critique of the Gotha Programme*, p. 16.
37 See K. Marx and F. Engels, *The Communist Manifesto*, p. 16.
38 Marx, *Critique of the Gotha Programme*, p. 17.
39 Marx and Engels, *The Communist Manifesto*, p. 17.
40 See in particular K. Marx, *Grundrisse* and *Capital*. I discuss the economic and sociological theory here only in so far as it helps to clarify what Marx and Engels understood by 'scientific' as opposed to 'utopian' socialism. This also helps to understand what Frankfurt School theorists would later mean by a 'critical theory' of society (see following section).
41 Marx, 'Theses on Feuerbach', pp. 421–3.
42 This view is in fact much closer to Feuerbach than to Marx.
43 McLellan, *Marx*, p. 75.
44 An early use of this term was in Engels's article 'On Historical Materialism'. See T. Carver, *Engels*, p. 38. B. Ollman, *Alienation*, offers a rather different interpretation of Engels's role.
45 On Comte and positivism, see below, pp. 63–4.
46 T. Carver, *Friedrich Engels: His Life and Thought*, p. 238. The text referred to is F. Engels, 'The Part Played by Labour in the Transition from Ape to Man' (1896).
47 F. Engels, letter to J. Bloch, 21 September 1890, quoted in *Fontana Dictionary of Modern Thought*, p. 285.
48 It is worth noting, however, that Marx himself did not have a fixed opinion on this question, recognizing the possibility of revolutionary transformations in the less developed regions of Europe including Russia. See McLellan, *Marx*, pp. 62ff.
49 See F. Fukuyama, *The End of History*; cf. E. J. Hobsbawm et al., *The Forward March of Labour Halted*. On the recent 'resumption' of history, see below, ch. 8.
50 On Althusser see G. Elliott, *Althusser*, T. Benton, *The Rise and Fall of Structural Marxism*, and see below, ch. 6, pp. 187–8. On Sartre's Marxism see M. Poster, *Sartre's Marxism* and below, ch. 5, pp. 167–8. In contrasting style, the 'analytical Marxism' of J. Elster and G. Cohen is closely related to the analytical tradition in philosophy. See, e.g., J. Elster, *An Introduction to Karl Marx*, G. A. Cohen, *Karl Marx's Theory of History: A Defence* and A. H. Carling, *Social Division*.
51 Marx's *Economic and Philosophical Manuscripts* was first published in 1932. The *German Ideology*, written in 1846, was also published posthumously.
52 M. Horkheimer and T. Adorno, *Dialectic of Enlightenment*, p. x.
53 For a detailed history of the Frankfurt School see R. Wiggershaus, *The Frankfurt School*. See also M. Jay, *The Dialectical Imagination: A History of the Frankfurt School and the Institute for Social Research, 1923–1950* and D. Held, *Introduction to Critical Theory: Horkheimer to Habermas*. A less sympathetic account is presented in T. B. Bottomore, *The Frankfurt School*.

54 See Held, *Introduction to Critical Theory*, ch. 2. On some interpretations, though, these developments are not really incompatible
with Marx's theory of crisis: see, e.g. S. Clarke, *Marx's Theory of
Crisis*.

55 M. Horkheimer, *Critical Theory*, p. vi.

56 See H. Marcuse, *Soviet Marxism*.

57 Marx, 'Theses on Feuerbach', p. 423 (quoted above).

58 G. Lukács, *History and Class Consciousness*, p. 1.

59 For an alternative account, see P. Dunne, *Quantitative Marxism*
and Clarke, *Marx's Theory of Crisis*.

60 For a critique of this conception from a Trotskyist point of view,
see C. Harman and A. Callinicos, *The Changing Working Class*.

61 The inability of the working class to get beyond merely 'trade
union consciousness' without the leadership of the 'vanguard party'
is alleged in V. I. Lenin, *What is to be Done?*, esp. parts II–IV.

62 R. Williams, *Keywords*, p. 200.

63 Hume, *Treatise*, p. xx.

64 R. Geuss, *The Idea of a Critical Theory*, p. 2. Geuss provides, more
generally, an excellent analysis of the notion of critical theory.

65 M. Horkheimer, 'Traditional and Critical Theory' (1937), in *Critical Theory* and see T. Adorno et al., *The Positivist Dispute in
German Sociology*.

66 Marcuse, *Soviet Marxism*.

67 Compare the similar analysis of C. Castoriadis in *The Imaginary
Institution of Society*, part I.

68 See S. Lukes, *Marxism and Morality*, ch. 6.

69 See above, pp. 55–6.

70 Marcuse, quoted by Held, *Introduction to Critical Theory*, p. 85.

71 H. Marcuse, *Counterrevolution and Revolt*, p. 107.

72 See T. W. Adorno, *Aesthetic Theory* and *The Culture Industry*.
See also L. Zuidervaart, *Adorno's Aesthetic Theory*.

73 H. Marcuse, *One-Dimensional Man*, p. 155.

74 In their more favourable evaluation of 'bourgeois' art and philosophy, Frankfurt theorists are closer to Marx's *Economic and
Philosophical Manuscripts*, with its extensive quotation from
Shakespeare, than the 'socialist realism' and 'agitprop' of Soviet
communism. Their relationship to contemporary artistic movements attempting to combine politics and art was a complex one.
See Jay, *The Dialectical Imagination*, ch. 6.

75 Horkheimer, *Critical Theory*, p. 218.

76 Ibid., p. 213.

77 See Held, *Introduction to Critical Theory*, p. 178.

78 Ibid., pp. 205, 181–2. In this respect, Horkheimer and Adorno
anticipate the warnings about 'totalizing theories' of theorists like
Foucault and Deleuze (see below, ch. 6).

79 T. W. Adorno, *Negative Dialectics*. See Held, *Introduction to
Critical Theory*, ch. 7, G. Rose, *The Melancholy Science*, J. M.

Bernstein, *Disenchantment and Ethics* and S. Jarvis, *Adorno: A Critical Introduction.*

80 At the same time, Frankfurt theorists were critical of what they saw as Nietzsche's elitist, anti-democratic and even anti-political philosophy. For a fuller account of Nietzsche, see below, ch. 5.

81 Habermas, *Philosophical Discourse of Modernity*, p. 108. See Horkheimer and Adorno, *Dialectic of Enlightenment.*

82 Ibid., p. 5.

83 Adorno cited in Held, *Introduction to Critical Theory*, p. 151.

84 Horkheimer and Adorno, *Dialectic of Enlightenment*, p. 12.

85 Ibid., pp. 4, 9.

86 Ibid., pp. 25 and ff.

87 Habermas, *Philosophical Discourse of Modernity*, p. 110.

88 Horkheimer and Adorno, *Dialectic of Enlightenment*, p. 86.

89 On Weber's account of the rationalization of society, see above, ch. 2, pp. 9–11.

90 On the distinction between formal and substantive rationality see M. Weber, *Economy and Society*, vol. 1, pp. 85–6.

91 For a fuller account of Freud, see below, pp. 177–9.

92 S. Freud, *Civilization and its Discontents.*

93 H. Marcuse, *Eros and Civilization*; cf. Wilhelm Reich, *The Invasion of Compulsory Sex-Morality*. On Marcuse, see V. Geoghegan, *Reason and Eros: The Social Theory of Herbert Marcuse*, D. Kellner, *Herbert Marcuse and the Crisis of Marxism* and J. Bokina et al., eds, *Marcuse: From the New Left to the Next Left.*

94 W. Benjamin, 'The Work of Art in the Age of Mechanical Reproduction', in *Illuminations*, p. 223.

95 Ibid., p. 225.

96 Ibid., p. 236.

97 Ibid., pp. 243–4. Benjamin committed suicide in 1940 while attempting to escape Nazi persecution.

98 On Benjamin's aesthetics, see S. Buck-Morss, *The Origin of Negative Dialectics*. 'Agitprop' was originally the Department of Agitation and Propaganda of the Communist Party of the Soviet Union, set up in 1920.

99 T. W. Adorno, 'Culture Industry Reconsidered', in *The Culture Industry*, p. 85. Cf. R. W. Witkin, *Adorno on Popular Culture.*

100 Held, *Introduction to Critical Theory*, pp. 94–6; cf. T. W. Adorno, 'How to Look at Television', in *The Culture Industry.*

101 P. Connerton, *Tragedy of Enlightenment*, ch. 3, esp. pp. 55ff.

102 Adorno, quoted by J. M. Bernstein in his 'Introduction' to Adorno's *The Culture Industry*, p. 13.

103 Adorno, *The Culture Industry*, p. 43.

104 Ibid., p. 52.

105 Ibid., p. 85.

106 See Marcuse, *One-Dimensional Man.*

107   Connerton, *Tragedy of Enlightenment*, pp. 58–9; cf. J. Habermas, *The Structural Transformation of the Public Sphere*.
108   Marcuse, *One-Dimensional Man*, pp. 199–200.
109   Connerton, *Tragedy of Enlightenment*, p. 102.
110   The phrase derives originally from R. Rolland. See A. Gramsci, *Selections from the Prison Notebooks*, p. 175 and note.
111   Habermas diverges from the earlier Frankfurt School in ways which reflect, among other things, his less sympathetic attitude to Nietzsche. For useful introductions to the ideas of Habermas, see U. Steinhoff, *The Philosophy of Jürgen Habermas: A Critical Introduction*, W. Outhwaite, *Habermas*, Held, *Introduction to Critical Theory*, part II, T. McCarthy, *The Critical Theory of Jürgen Habermas* and S. K. White, ed., *The Cambridge Companion to Habermas*.
112   Labour corresponds to the concept of instrumental rationality as used by earlier members of the Frankfurt School and Weber's notion of formal rationalization.
113   J. Habermas, 'Technology and Science as "Ideology"', in *Toward a Rational Society*, p. 92.
114   Ibid., p. 87.
115   Ibid., p. 92 (emphasis in original).
116   See above, pp. 54–9.
117   See J. Habermas, 'Modernity: An Incomplete Project', in M. P. d'Entrèves and S. Benhabib, eds, *Habermas and the Unfinished Project of Modernity*; cf. R. J. Bernstein, *Habermas and Modernity*.
118   Habermas, *The Structural Transformation of the Public Sphere*, pp. 25–6.
119   Decisionism is the view that, in the absence of objective criteria, moral values can be nothing more than the product of arbitrary decisions. A notable exponent of this position was Carl Schmitt (see below, pp. 127–9). For the concept of 'economic rationalism', see M. Pusey, *Economic Rationalism in Canberra*, passim.
120   Habermas, *Toward a Rational Society*, p. 90; cf. *The Structural Transformation of the Public Sphere*, parts V–VI.
121   J. Habermas, *Knowledge and Human Interests*, p. 309.
122   A classic exposition of the hypothetico-deductive account of science is provided by C. G. Hempel, *Aspects of Scientific Explanation*. The confirmation of theories by experiment and observation is, of course, not straightforward: see, e.g., K. Popper, *Conjectures and Refutations*.
123   Habermas, *Knowledge and Human Interests*, p. 91 and see below, ch. 5 passim.
124   Ibid., p. 93.
125   Habermas quoted by Held, *Introduction to Critical Theory*, p. 303.

126   Habermas, *Knowledge and Human Interests*, ch. 7. On Dilthey, see below, ch. 4, pp. 87–95.
127   Ibid., p. 313.
128   Ibid., p. 175.
129   Habermas, *Knowledge and Human Interests*, p. 310. On Habermas's debates with positivism and hermeneutics, see R. C. Holub, *Jürgen Habermas: Critic in the Public Sphere*, chs 2 and 3. For Habermas's relationship to the hermeneutic phenomenology of Paul Ricoeur, see J. B. Thompson, *Critical Hermeneutics: A Study in the Thought of Paul Ricoeur and Jürgen Habermas*.
130   On Freudian psychoanalysis, see below, pp. 177–9.
131   See J. Habermas, 'A Postscript to *Knowledge and Human Interests*'.
132   Habermas, *Communication and the Evolution of Society*, pp. 96–7.
133   Habermas, *Knowledge and Human Interests*, p. 314. The theory is developed in J. Habermas, *The Theory of Communicative Action*, vol. 1, esp. ch. III, pp. 273 ff.
134   McCarthy, *The Critical Theory of Jürgen Habermas*, p. 7. In fact, this 'linguistic turn' is paralleled in much twentieth-century analytical and continental philosophy.
135   Habermas, *Communication and the Evolution of Society*, pp. 2–3. On the three world relations, see *Theory of Communicative Action*, vol. 1, ch. I, section 3, esp. pp. 99–101.
136   J. Habermas, *Über Sprachtheorie*, p. 17 (my translation).
137   Habermas, *Knowledge and Human Interests*, p. 314 (quoted above).
138   J. Habermas, 'Wahrheitstheorien', p. 226 (my translation). The American pragmatist C. S. Peirce is an important source of Habermas's consensus theory of truth.
139   For Habermas's relationship with postmodernism, see below, ch. 7, pp. 220–2, 238–40. For critical discussion of Habermas's theory of communicative rationality, see T. McCarthy, *The Critical Theory of Jürgen Habermas*, ch. 4, S. Benhabib and F. Dallmayr, *The Communicative Ethics Controversy* and J. Thompson and D. Held, eds, *Habermas: Critical Debates*.
140   See J. Habermas, 'Discourse Ethics' and 'Morality and Ethical Life', in *Moral Consciousness and Communicative Action* and J. Habermas, *Justification and Application*, chs 1–2; cf. P. Dews, Introduction to J. Habermas, *Autonomy and Solidarity*, pp. 18ff.
141   Habermas, *Philosophical Discourse of Modernity*, p. 312.
142   See S. Benhabib and F. Dallmayr, *The Communicative Ethics Controversy*. For an overview, see J. Bohman, 'Discourse Theory'.
143   See J. Bohman, *Public Deliberation: Pluralism, Complexity, and Democracy*. For an overview, see J. S. Dryzek, 'Democratic Political Theory'.
144   Cf. M. Rosenfeld and A. Arato, *Habermas on Law and Democracy: Critical Exchanges*.

145 Also Hegelian, of course, is Habermas's indefatigable commitment to theoretical synthesis, even if Habermas has constructed his synthesis in very different ways.

146 See J. Habermas, *The New Conservatism*, *The Postnational Constellation* and *The Future of Human Nature*. For an overview of Habermas's debates on a variety of issues, see R. C. Holub, *Jürgen Habermas: Critic in the Public Sphere*.

147 J. Habermas, *Religion and Rationality: Essays on Reason, God, and Modernity*, *Between Naturalism and Religion: Philosophical Essays* and *An Awareness of What is Missing: Faith and Reason in a Post-Secular Age*.

148 See J. Habermas and J. Derrida, *Philosophy in a Time of Terror*.

149 J. Habermas, *An Awareness of What is Missing*, p. 16.

150 J. Habermas, *Between Naturalism and Religion*, ch. 8, 'The Boundary Between Faith and Knowledge'.

151 The tradition of critical theory is continued by A. Honneth: e.g. *The Critique of Power: Reflective Stages in a Critical Social Theory* and *Disrespect: The Normative Foundations of Critical Theory*; and A. Wellmer, *The Persistence of Modernity: Essays on Aesthetics, Ethics and Postmodernism* and *Endgames: The Irreconcilable Nature of Modernity*.

Chapter 4 Historicism, Hermeneutics and Phenomenology

1 Historicism in the sense discussed here should not be confused with Karl Popper's somewhat eccentric use of the term to refer to philosophies of history that are committed to a belief in overall laws of historical development: see *The Poverty of Historicism*. The Enlightenment was also associated with significant contributions to the writing of history, notably Edward Gibbon (1737–94), *The History of the Decline and Fall of the Roman Empire* (1776–88), as well as works of Herder, Fichte and the Grimm brothers.

2 See ch. 2, pp. 41–2.

3 See Hegel, *Philosophy of Right*, para. 348, p. 218; cf. para. 344, p. 217. Related assumptions are made by the 'Whig interpretation of history', classically expressed in Herbert Butterfield, *The Whig Interpretation of History*.

4 This development is associated with the German nineteenth-century 'critical historians' Leopold von Ranke (1795–1886) and Theodor Mommsen (1817–1903), among others.

5 See Taylor, *Hegel*, pp. 34ff. On Romanticism, see above, pp. 34–5.

6 On Kierkegaard and the development of existentialism, see below, ch. 5.

7 Bollnow, quoted in Richard E. Palmer, *Hermeneutics*, p. 101.

8 Thus, for historians like Ranke and Droysen the category of life plays a similar role to the concept of spirit in Hegelianism.

9   On the meaning of speculative idealism, see above, p. 38.
10   This possibility finds some confirmation in the writings of Schopenhauer. See pp. 145–7 below.
11   The German word *Geisteswissenschaften*, literally the systematic study of spirit or mind (*Geist*), signals the connection with the ideas of both Herder and Hegel. For discussion of Dilthey, see J. de Mul, *The Tragedy of Finitude: Dilthey's Hermeneutics of Life*, R. A. Makkreel, *Dilthey: Philosopher of Human Studies*, H. P. Rickman, *Wilhelm Dilthey: Pioneer of the Human Studies* and H. A. Hodges, *The Philosophy of Wilhelm Dilthey*.
12   Dilthey in *W. Dilthey: Selected Writings*, from 'Introduction to the Human Studies', pp. 161–2. Dilthey uses the word *Erlebnis* as opposed to *Erfahrung* to refer to experience which is not merely intellectual or cognitive but also affective, a part of life in the fullest sense. This emphasis, characteristic of life philosophy, is reflected in the etymological relationship between *Erlebnis* and *Leben* (life).
13   Rickman, in Introduction to *W. Dilthey: Selected Writings*, p. 17.
14   This phrase is the subtitle of W. Dilthey, *Introduction to the Human Sciences*.
15   Dilthey, from 'Ideas about a Descriptive and Analytical Psychology', in *W. Dilthey: Selected Writings*, p. 88.
16   Dilthey, 'The Development of Hermeneutics', in *W. Dilthey: Selected Writings*, p. 248.
17   Ibid.
18   Quoted by Palmer, *Hermeneutics*, p. 115.
19   Rickman, Introduction, *W. Dilthey: Selected Writings*, p. 20.
20   Dilthey, 'The Rise of Hermeneutics', in H. A. Hodges, *Wilhelm Dilthey*, pp. 125–6.
21   As Foucault helpfully remarks, Hermes is also reputed to have taught human beings how to masturbate – through the good offices of Pan – 'And the shepherds seem to have learned it subsequently from Pan': M. Foucault, *The Care of the Self*, p. 140.
22   Foucault, *The Care of the Self*, p. 6.
23   Palmer, *Hermeneutics*, pp. 35ff.
24   There was a related growth at this time in the comparative and historical study of languages, or philology. For an account of the development of philology in the nineteenth century see H. Pedersen, *The Discovery of Language*.
25   D. E. Linge, Introduction to H.-G. Gadamer, *Philosophical Hermeneutics*, p. xiii.
26   Dilthey, 'Development of Hermeneutics', p. 259.
27   E.g., see David Wootton's scholarly Introduction to Locke's *Political Writings* on their relationship to the 'Glorious Revolution' of 1688.
28   David Boucher, *Texts in Context*, p. 21.
29   Dilthey, 'Development of Hermeneutics', p. 258.

30 Rickman, Introduction, *W. Dilthey: Selected Writings*, p. 15.
31 Habermas, *Knowledge and Human Interests*, p. 147.
32 H. A. Hodges, *The Philosophy of Wilhelm Dilthey*, pp. 141–2.
33 E. Husserl, 'Philosophy as Rigorous Science', p. 81. For an intro-
    duction to Husserl and phenomenology, see D. Moran, *Introduc-
    tion to Phenomenology*, chs 1–5, or E. Pivčević, *Husserl and
    Phenomenology*.
34 Dilthey quoted by Husserl, 'Philosophy as Rigorous Science', p.
    124. Incidentally, Dilthey returns the favour, describing Husserl as
    'A true Plato, who first of all fixes in concepts things that become
    and flow and then supplements the fixed concept with a concept
    of flowing' (ibid., p. 124, editor's note 62).
35 P. Dews, *Logics of Disintegration*, p. 6.
36 Husserl, 'Philosophy as Rigorous Science', p. 72.
37 Ibid., pp. 145–6. One of Husserl's major later works is entitled
    Cartesian Meditations (1929); cf. A. D. Smith's helpful commen-
    tary, *Husserl and the 'Cartesian Meditations'*.
38 See above, ch. 2. For Descartes it is at least certain that I exist as
    a thing which thinks and perceives. For the even more persistent
    scepticism of Hume, we can be certain only that there are sensa-
    tions – and then only at the time of their occurrence. What we
    cannot be sure of is that these sensations provide us with indubi-
    table knowledge of an external reality or even that 'I' exist as an
    enduring subject of experience.
39 E. Husserl, *Cartesian Meditations*, para. 10, pp. 23–5.
40 For a more detailed account of Kant's philosophy, see above,
    ch. 2.
41 See E. Husserl, *Ideas*, para. 62, p. 166.
42 E. Husserl, *Logical Investigations*, vol. 1, p. 42.
43 Cited by Pivčević, *Husserl and Phenomenology*, p. 149.
44 While much of Frege's critique is arguably based on misunder-
    standing, he rightly points out that in this work Husserl fails to
    distinguish between describing what number is and describing
    what it is for us to understand number concepts. This is something
    Husserl himself had begun to appreciate by the time the *Philosophy
    of Arithmetic* appeared. On Husserl's early work, see J. Mohanty,
    Edmund Husserl's Theory of Meaning and D. Willard, *Logic and
    the Objectivity of Knowledge*. For a contrasting view, see D.
    Føllesdal, *Husserl und Frege* or H. L. Dreyfus and H. Hall, *Husserl,
    Intentionality and Cognitive Science*. It was Frege's criticism of
    Husserl that helped to inspire Russell and Whitehead's account of
    the foundations of mathematics and so contributed to the birth
    of contemporary analytical philosophy (see above, ch. 1).
45 Husserl, 'Philosophy as Rigorous Science', p. 86.
46 Pivčević, *Husserl and Phenomenology*, p. 42.
47 Passmore, *A Hundred Years of Philosophy*, p. 176.
48 Husserl, 'Philosophy as Rigorous Science', p. 104.

49 Passmore, *A Hundred Years of Philosophy*, p. 178. See also H.-G. Gadamer, 'The Phenomenological Movement', in *Philosophical Hermeneutics*, pp. 155–6.

50 F. Brentano, *Psychology from an Empirical Standpoint*, pp. 88–9. Husserl acknowledges the importance of Brentano's criterion of the mental in *Ideas*, para. 85, p. 229. Cf. Moran, *Introduction to Phenomenology*, ch. 1.

51 Brentano, *Psychology from an Empirical Standpoint*, pp. 93ff. Within the analytical tradition in philosophy the relation between intentionality in Brentano's sense and the 'intensionality' of certain kinds of sentence, including those describing mental states (e.g. 'I believe that . . .', 'I imagine that . . .' in contrast to 'I stroked (the dog)' etc.) has been shown to be a complex one. See D. Carr, 'Intentionality' and J. L. Mackie, 'Problems of Intentionality', in E. Pivčević, ed., *Phenomenology and Philosophical Understanding*.

52 This concern also preoccupied another of Brentano's students, Alexius von Meinong (1853–1928).

53 Pivčević, *Husserl and Phenomenology*, p. 76.

54 The term has been used in German philosophy in a variety of different senses, e.g. by J. H. Lambert (in 1764), Herder, Kant, Fichte, Hegel and others. See J. Hoffmeister, *Wörterbuch der philosophischen Begriffe*, pp. 463ff.

55 Husserl, *Ideas*, para. 32, pp. 99–100.

56 Husserl, *Cartesian Meditations*, para. 34, p. 70.

57 Husserl, 'Philosophy as Rigorous Science', pp. 110, 112. Of course, the distinction between essence and existence also plays a crucial role both for Heidegger and for existentialism (see following section and below, ch. 5).

58 Husserl, *Ideas*, para. 53, pp. 150–1.

59 Husserl, 'Philosophy as Rigorous Science', p. 111.

60 Whether phenomenology can really *explain* this achievement is, of course, more controversial.

61 Husserl, 'Philosophy as Rigorous Science', p. 89.

62 See Husserl, *Ideas*, para. 62, p. 166 and *The Crisis of European Sciences*, pp. 87–8; cf. Passmore, *A Hundred Years of Philosophy*, p. 189.

63 Husserl, *The Crisis of European Sciences*, pp. 5–6.

64 Pivčević, *Husserl and Phenomenology*, p. 88, and compare the very similar concerns of members of the Frankfurt School (see above, ch. 3).

65 Husserl, *The Crisis of European Sciences*, pp. 104–5. Compare Habermas's notion of the 'life-world' in *Theory of Communicative Action*.

66 It also seems to be no coincidence that Husserl's language begins to show signs of the influence of Heidegger, who provides something close to a phenomenological analysis of the life-world. Compare Husserl's discussion of intersubjectivity and his attempt

to resist solipsism in the Fifth of the *Cartesian Meditations*, paras. 42–62, pp. 89–151.

67 R. Bubner, *Modern German Philosophy*, p. 21. Indeed, in his predilection for technical terms as well as in many of his philosophical concerns, Husserl has much in common with philosophical contemporaries and successors who, despite their 'continental' origins, are now regarded as securely within the analytical tradition, e.g. Frege, Carnap and Wittgenstein.

68 E.g. M. Merleau-Ponty, *The Structure of Behaviour* and *The Phenomenology of Perception*.

69 See A. Schütz, *The Phenomenology of the Social World*.

70 For a helpful guide to the phenomenological tradition, see D. Moran, *Introduction to Phenomenology*.

71 Clear and readable introductions to Heidegger's philosophy are provided by S. Critchley and R. Schürmann, *On Heidegger's 'Being and Time'*, H. L. Dreyfus, *Being-in-the-World: A Commentary on Heidegger's 'Being and Time', Division I*, J. Macquarrie, *Martin Heidegger*, and G. Steiner, *Heidegger*.

72 But compare Gadamer's defence of philosophical etymology as necessary to provide a 'firm foundation' for the etymologies of linguistic science which are 'not proofs but achievements preparatory to conceptual analysis', in *Truth and Method*, p. 103 and n. 195.

73 This notion of substance is much stronger than the merely formal or logical notion of substance as that which has properties or that of which things can be predicated – the equivalent of the 'x' in 'x is green and made of glass'.

74 On Descartes, see above, ch. 2, pp. 14–15.

75 For a fuller exposition of Kierkegaard and existentialism see below, ch. 5.

76 M. Heidegger, *Being and Time*, p. 494, n. vi to Division Two, section 45 (my emphasis).

77 Ibid., p. 33.

78 Ibid., pp. 454, 72.

79 Gadamer, 'On the Problem of Self-Understanding' (1962), in *Philosophical Hermeneutics*, pp. 48–9.

80 Macquarrie, *Martin Heidegger*, p. 5.

81 Heidegger, *Being and Time*, p. 455.

82 Ibid. Husserl too was concerned to explore the distinctive 'being' of mental or psychic phenomena as the clue to a general understanding of truth and being, including the being of nature, more adequate to human life and culture. See previous section.

83 Macquarrie, *Martin Heidegger*, p. 8. There are analogies (though clearly also important differences) between Heidegger's project and Descartes's method of radical doubt, which sets out from the perspective of the doubting subject. Heidegger's 'Dasein' is accordingly the equivalent of the Cartesian 'ego'.

84   See Heidegger, *Being and Time*, p. 27 and n. 1. In German *da* can mean both 'there' and 'here'. As 'Dasein' is so closely associated in English with Heidegger's philosophy, I leave it untranslated and treat it as an English word.

85   Kant uses this distinction to refute the 'ontological' argument for the existence of God. According to this argument, the concept of God is the concept of a perfect being. A perfect being cannot lack any attribute, otherwise it would not be perfect. Therefore God cannot lack existence. This argument does not work in the same way, if existence cannot be treated as a predicate. See Kant, *Critique of Pure Reason*, pp. 500–7.

86   Heidegger, *Being and Time*, pp. 83–4.

87   Ibid., pp. 96–8. For this reason Heidegger's views have been compared to the philosophical pragmatism of Charles Sanders Peirce and Jürgen Habermas (see above, ch. 3, section on Habermas).

88   Heidegger, *Being and Time*, p. 225.

89   Ibid., pp. 153–5.

90   Ibid., p. 155.

91   Ibid., p. 164. In German '*man*' is the third person indefinite pronoun equivalent to 'one' or 'they' used in a non-specific sense. '*Das Man*' is a Heideggerian neologism.

92   Ibid., pp. 33–4.

93   Ibid., p. 220.

94   Ibid., p. 378.

95   Ibid., pp. 294, 298.

96   On this distinction, see above, p. 107.

97   See H.-G. Gadamer, 'Heidegger's Later Philosophy', in *Philosophical Hermeneutics*. Gadamer sees the later philosophy as a continuous development of themes already present in the earlier work.

98   M. Heidegger, 'Letter on Humanism' (1947), in M. Heidegger, *Basic Writings*, p. 210. Compare M. Heidegger, *Discourse on Thinking*.

99   Heidegger, 'Letter on Humanism', p. 193.

100   Heidegger, 'On the Essence of Truth' (1961), in *Basic Writings*, p. 127.

101   Heidegger, 'The Origin of the Work of Art' (1936), in *Basic Writings*, p. 185.

102   Ibid., p. 186. The poetry of Hölderlin, also greatly admired by Hegel, 'still confronts the Germans as a test to be stood' (ibid., p. 187).

103   Gadamer, *Truth and Method*, pp. 490–1: the concluding remarks. For an account of Gadamer see J. Grondin, *The Philosophy of Gadamer* or G. Warnke, *Gadamer: Hermeneutics, Tradition and Reason*.

104   Palmer, *Hermeneutics*, p. 163. An alternative continuation of hermeneutics and phenomenology, which shares the influence of Heidegger, Hegel and Aristotle, can be found in the work of the French philosopher and religious thinker, Paul Ricoeur

(1913–2005). See, e.g., P. Ricoeur, *Oneself as Another* and *Memory, History, Forgetting*. For commentary on Ricoeur, see B. P. Dauenhauer, *Paul Ricoeur: The Promise and Risk of Politics* and K. Simms, *Paul Ricoeur*.

105 Bubner, *Modern German Philosophy*, pp. 53, 54 (emphasis in original).
106 Cf. M. Heidegger, 'The Question Concerning Technology', in *Basic Writings*.
107 Linge, Introduction to Gadamer, *Philosophical Hermeneutics*, p. l.
108 Gadamer, 'The Phenomenological Movement' (1963), in *Philosophical Hermeneutics*, esp. pp. 163ff. On the concept of the life-world see above, pp. 103–4.
109 Gadamer, 'The Science of the Life-World' (1969), in *Philosophical Hermeneutics*, p. 196.
110 Gadamer, *Truth and Method*, p. 7.
111 Ibid., p. 491, quoted above.
112 Linge, Introduction to Gadamer, *Philosophical Hermeneutics*, p. xxii.
113 Gadamer, *Truth and Method*, p. 491, quoted above.
114 Ibid.
115 Ibid., p. 302.
116 Ibid., p. 300.
117 Ibid., p. 301.
118 Ibid., pp. 300–1.
119 Ibid., p. 297.
120 Ibid., p. 298.
121 On Kant's notion of the thing-in-itself or noumenon, see above, pp. 22–3.
122 I am grateful to Bruin Christensen for this interpretation of Gadamer's account of meaning as well as for many other helpful suggestions.
123 Gadamer, *Truth and Method*, p. 104. Cf. Warnke, *Gadamer*, pp. 48ff.
124 Gadamer, *Truth and Method*, p. 327.
125 Ibid., pp. 340–1.
126 Ibid., p. 328.
127 Ibid., pp. 326–7.
128 Application in this sense is very different from the theoretical application of a scientific law to make a prediction or to test an hypothesis.
129 Gadamer, *Truth and Method*, p. 21. Beyond this, moral knowledge also presupposes a 'direction of the will – i.e., moral being (*hexis*)' (ibid., p. 22). Cf. R. Beiner, *Political Judgment*, esp. pp. 19ff.
130 Gadamer, *Truth and Method*, pp. 328–9.
131 'Dialectic' derives from the Greek '*dialektike*' meaning '(art) of debate': see *Concise Oxford English Dictionary*, p. 322.
132 Boucher, *Texts in Context*, p. 26.
133 Gadamer, *Truth and Method*, p. 491, quoted above.

134 Ibid., p. 279.

135 Ibid., p. 490, quoted above.

136 On the historicity of truth see R. Campbell, *Truth and Historicity*.

137 For the debate between Gadamer and Habermas, see J. Habermas, 'On Systematically Distorted Communication', H.-G. Gadamer, 'On the Scope and Function of Hermeneutical Reflection' and J. Habermas, 'Summation and Response'; cf. above, ch. 3, pp. 78–9. The debate is discussed in R. C. Holub, *Jürgen Habermas*, ch. 3.

138 Linge, Introduction to Gadamer, *Philosophical Hermeneutics*, pp. xxxvi–xxxvii. On the concept of language-game, see L. Wittgenstein, *Philosophical Investigations*, para. 7, p. 5 and passim.

139 Gadamer, *Truth and Method*, p. 491, quoted above.

140 See below, ch. 5.

141 See below, pp. 181–2.

142 On Arendt's life and relationship with Heidegger, see E. Ettinger, *Hannah Arendt/Martin Heidegger* and E. Young-Bruehl, *Hannah Arendt: For Love of the World*.

143 H. Arendt, *Men in Dark Times*, pp. 205–6, referring to Shakespeare's *The Tempest*. '*Urphänomene*' means 'original phenomena'.

144 H. Arendt, *The Human Condition* (1958) was first published in German as *Vita Activa, oder vom tätigen Leben*, 'on the active life'. For helpful accounts of Arendt's philosophy, see M. Canovan, *Hannah Arendt: A Reinterpretation of Her Political Thought*, D. R. Villa, *Arendt and Heidegger: The Fate of the Political* and M. P. d'Entrèves, *The Political Philosophy of Hannah Arendt*.

145 Arendt, *Human Condition*, pp. 83–4.

146 Ibid., p. 136.

147 Ibid., p. 144.

148 Ibid., p. 177.

149 H. Arendt, *The Promise of Politics*, pp. 5–13.

150 H. Arendt, *On Revolution*, esp. ch. 6.

151 Ibid., p. 114.

152 Rousseau, *Social Contract*, Bk. I, ch. 7, p. 177. Cf. I. Berlin, 'Two Concepts of Liberty'; cf. above, ch. 2, pp. 32–3.

153 C. Schmitt, *The Concept of the Political*, Foreword, p. xii.

154 Ibid, p. 26. *Agōn* is the ancient Greek word for contest, struggle or battle.

155 Cf. above, p. 109.

156 See below, p. 162.

157 C. Schmitt, *The Leviathan in the State Theory of Thomas Hobbes*.

158 C. Schmitt, *The Crisis of Parliamentary Democracy*. He ignores other possible explanations of the collapse of the Weimar Republic, such as the consequences of military occupation and the crushing terms of the Versailles Treaty.

159 Schmitt, *Leviathan*, esp. chs V-VI.
160 Arendt, *Promise of Politics*, p. 93.
161 H. Arendt, *The Origins of Totalitarianism*, p. 326.
162 Ibid., pp. 464–6.
163 Ibid., p. 438. On Giorgio Agamben's related account of 'the camp' see below, ch. 8, pp. 247–8.
164 H. Arendt, *Between Past and Future*, pp. 77–8; cf. above, p. 56.
165 Ibid., pp. 79–80.
166 Arendt, *Promise of Politics*, p. 95.
167 Arendt, *Human Condition*, pp. 184, 192. For Dilthey's similar view of history, see above, pp. 93–4.
168 See H. Arendt, *Essays in Understanding*, 'Frank Kafka: A Revaluation', pp. 74–5.
169 W. Benjamin, 'Theses on the Philosophy of History', in *Illuminations*, pp. 259–64.
170 Arendt, *Between Past and Future*, p. 11.
171 See G. Kateb, *Hannah Arendt: Politics, Conscience, Evil* and H. Pitkin, *The Attack of the Blob*, esp. ch. 8. Cf. Judith Butler's comments in *Who Sings the Nation-State* on the tensions between Arendt's *Human Condition* and *Origins of Totalitarianism*: esp. pp. 12ff, 55ff.
172 Arendt, *Between Past and Future*, p. 153. There are interesting parallels between Arendt's approach and that of Paul Ricoeur, particularly his discussion of action, narrative and history, and his related view of politics: for references, see note 104 above.

Chapter 5 Beyond Theory: Kierkegaard, Nietzsche, Existentialism

1 P. Rohde, *Kierkegaard*, p. 31. For guides to the life and thought of Kierkegaard, see A. Hannay, *Kierkegaard* and *Kierkegaard: A Biography*, P. Rohde, *Kierkegaard: An Introduction to His Life and Philosophy*.
2 See above, ch. 2 on Hegel and ch. 3 on Feuerbach and Marx.
3 Fideism is 'the doctrine that all or some knowledge depends on faith or revelation': *Concise Oxford English Dictionary*, p. 434.
4 B. Pascal, *The Provincial Letters*, p. 85.
5 In retrospect humanist theology is risky in another way. By subordinating religious to scientific truth, it renders religion permanently vulnerable to future scientific developments. This possibility was confirmed later in the nineteenth century by developments such as Darwin's theory of evolution and new geological estimates of the age of the earth.
6 Hume, *Enquiries*, p. 131. Kierkegaard was influenced by Hamann and Jacobi's criticisms of Kant's rationalism: see above, ch. 2, pp. 33–4.

7 Aristotle, *Aristotle's Ethics*, p. 122. See also Habermas, *Knowledge and Human Interests*, p. 301.

8 By contrast, for Aristotle *techne*, as the 'workmanlike skill' required for the production of 'useful or beautiful artefacts', is associated with the distinct category of productive activity or *poiesis*; see T. McCarthy, *The Critical Theory of Jürgen Habermas*, p. 3.

9 Kierkegaard, quoted in Translators' Preface to S. Kierkegaard, *Either/Or*, vol. 1, p. xi.

10 Rohde, *Kierkegaard*, p. 149.

11 The notion of subjective truth is developed most extensively in S. Kierkegaard, *Concluding Unscientific Postscript*, vol. 1, pp. 189ff.

12 S. Kierkegaard, *The Concept of Irony*, p. 9.

13 L. M. Hollander, Introduction to Kierkegaard, *Selections from the Writings of Kierkegaard*, p. 7.

14 Kierkegaard, *Either/Or*.

15 For the relation of Kierkegaard's thought and life, see Rohde, *Kierkegaard*.

16 On Descartes, see above, ch. 2, pp. 14–15.

17 In a related way, in Christian theology goodness could not exist without the possibility of sin.

18 Cf. Sartre's notion of 'bad faith' as a prime object of moral condemnation; also see below, pp. 162–3.

19 S. Kierkegaard, *The Concept of Dread*, p. 40. It is, of course, this 'existential' sense of anxiety or dread that is now usually referred to as *angst*.

20 Ibid., p. 38.

21 Rohde, *Kierkegaard*, pp. 55, 102, 66.

22 S. Kierkegaard, *The Sickness unto Death*, p. 43.

23 Rohde, *Kierkegaard*, p. 66.

24 Hannay, Introduction to Kierkegaard, *The Sickness unto Death*, p. 4.

25 Kierkegaard, *The Sickness unto Death*, p. 71.

26 Ibid., p. 55.

27 Ibid., p. 75.

28 Ibid., p. 112.

29 Ibid., p. 115.

30 Kierkegaard, *Either/Or*, vol. 1, p. 26.

31 Ibid., p. 28.

32 H. J. Blackham, *Six Existentialist Thinkers*, p. 9.

33 Kierkegaard, *Either/Or*, vol. 2, p. 28.

34 Ibid., pp. 149, 37. These possibilities are personified, for the aesthete of the first volume, by Don Juan. Vol. 1 contains a lengthy discussion of 'the musical erotic' in relation to Mozart's opera *Don Giovanni*.

35 S. Kierkegaard, *Fear and Trembling*, p. 65. Sartre provides a rather different reading of the story of Isaac in *Existentialism and Humanism*, pp. 31ff.

36 Kierkegaard, *Fear and Trembling*, p. 82.
37 The phrase derives from Jacobi: see Hoffmeister, *Wörterbuch der philosophischen Begriffe*, p. 532 and on Jacobi, see above, pp. 33–4. Kierkegaard takes the expression from Lessing: see Kierkegaard, *Philosophical Fragments*; cf. Hannay, *Kierkegaard*, pp. 97–9.
38 Of course, a significant tradition of existentialist theology, including Martin Buber and Gabriel Marcel, also draws inspiration from Kierkegaard's writings. For a brief account of 'theistic existentialism', see F. Copleston, *Contemporary Philosophy*, ch. 10. A concise introduction to existentialism more generally is provided by J. Macquarrie, *Existentialism*.
39 The following is a brief and confessedly systematic account of Nietzsche's thought. For general guides to Nietzsche, see W. Kaufmann, *Nietzsche: Philosopher, Psychologist, Antichrist*, R. Schacht, *Nietzsche* or R. J. Hollingdale, *Nietzsche*. It should be said that, according to another view, the essayistic and aphoristic form and paradoxical style of Nietzsche's writing reflect the essentially unsystematic nature of his thought. This view of Nietzsche is emphasized, e.g., by A. C. Danto, *Nietzsche as Philosopher*. Some 'postmodern' readings of Nietzsche are presented in D. B. Allison, ed., *The New Nietzsche: Contemporary Styles of Interpretation*.
40 F. Nietzsche, *Beyond Good and Evil*, p. 57. In fact, Nietzsche has a much more nuanced attitude to both Christianity and Jesus Christ than this quotation might suggest.
41 See his extended polemic against the rational religion of 'David Strauss, the confessor and the writer', the first of Nietzsche's *Untimely Meditations*. There he remarks that 'the new religion is not a new faith, but precisely on a par with modern science, and thus not religion at all' (p. 41).
42 On Kaufmann's interpretation, Nietzsche is not as hostile to Hegel as others, such as Deleuze, suppose. See W. Kaufmann, *Nietzsche*, pp. 235–46 and G. Deleuze, *Nietzsche and Philosophy*, ch. 5.
43 Quoted by Kaufmann, *Nietzsche*, p. 204.
44 See above, ch. 3, pp. 48–9.
45 See Nietzsche, *Gay Science*, 347, pp. 287–90.
46 Nietzsche quoted by Kaufmann, *Nietzsche*, p. 122.
47 See C. Darwin, *The Origin of Species*, esp. ch. 14. Nietzsche, though, is critical of Darwin's 'incomprehensibly onesided doctrine of the "struggle for existence"' in *Gay Science*, 349, p. 292.
48 A. Schopenhauer, *The World as Will and Representation*, vols I–II (1818, 1844); cf. F. Nietzsche, 'Schopenhauer as Educator' (1874) in *Untimely Meditations*. For introductory guides to Schopenhauer, see P. Gardiner, *Schopenhauer* and B. Magee, *The Philosophy of Schopenhauer*. On Kant, see above, ch. 2, esp. pp. 22–3.
49 Schopenhauer, *World as Will and Representation*, vol. I, esp. bk. II, §§17 et seq., pp. 95ff.

50 Ibid., vol. II, ch. 44, p. 535. On Romanticism, see above, ch. 2, p. 34.

51 Ibid., chs 46–50.

52 Nietzsche, quoting Schopenhauer, in *Birth of Tragedy*, p. 16; also see para. 1, pp. 14–16.

53 Kaufmann, *Nietzsche*, p. 128.

54 Nietzsche, *Birth of Tragedy*, p. 16.

55 See F. Schopenhauer, *The World as Will and Representation*.

56 Nietzsche, *Birth of Tragedy*, p. 17.

57 Kaufmann, *Nietzsche*, p. 128.

58 Compare Thomas Mann's novella *Death in Venice*, which was influenced by Nietzsche, in which artistic achievement is understood as the result of a fragile victory over disorder and disease.

59 Nietzsche quoted by Kaufmann, *Nietzsche*, p. 131. Nietzsche also admires the Greek obsession with the contest (or *agon*) and sees conflict as the crucible in which culture is formed.

60 Nietzsche, *Birth of Tragedy*, 12, pp. 59ff.

61 Ibid., 7, p. 40.

62 F. Nietzsche, *Human, All Too Human*, 18, p. 22.

63 Nietzsche, *Twilight of the Idols*, p. 36.

64 Ibid.

65 Nietzsche, *Beyond Good and Evil*, 11, p. 24. On Kant's Copernican revolution see above, pp. 20–1. For an interpretation of Nietzsche as something close to a positivist, see H. Schnädelbach, *Philosophy in Germany 1831–1933* and M. Clark, *Nietzsche on Truth and Philosophy*.

66 On Hume's empiricism, see above, pp. 17ff.

67 Nietzsche, *Beyond Good and Evil*, 2, pp. 15ff and *Twilight of the Idols*, p. 37.

68 For Rousseau, as for many other Enlightenment thinkers, woman was not necessarily as naturally good as man. See J.-J. Rousseau, *Émile* and W. Godwin, *Enquiry concerning Political Justice*.

69 Hume, *Enquiry Concerning the Principles of Morals*, para. 184, p. 227.

70 A notorious exception, of course, is the Marquis de Sade.

71 F. Nietzsche, *On the Genealogy of Morals* (1887), p. 26. For an account of Nietzsche's 'genealogical' method, see M. Foucault, 'Nietzsche, Genealogy, History', pp. 149–64 and below, p. 191.

72 Nietzsche, *On the Genealogy of Morals*, p. 20.

73 On Freud, see below, ch. 6, pp. 177–9.

74 'L'amour-propre est plus habile que le plus habile homme du monde': maxim 4 in Duc de la Rochefoucauld (1613–80), *Maximes et réflexions diverses*, p. 25 (my translation).

75 Nietzsche, *Human, All Too Human*, vol. 1, 50, pp. 38–9; cf. *The Anti-Christ*, 7, p. 118.

76 Nietzsche, *Human, All Too Human*, vol. 1, 44, p. 42.

77 Ibid., vol. 1, 92, p. 49.

78 Ibid., vol. 1, 99, p. 53.
79 Nietzsche, *The Anti-Christ*, 2, p. 115.
80 Nietzsche on a postcard to Overbeck quoted in Kaufmann, *Nietzsche*, p. 140.
81 'Le moi est haïssable' (my translation), from B. Pascal, *Pensées*, para. 136, p. 82.
82 Compare Deleuze, *Nietzsche and Philosophy* and his account of Spinozist 'ethics' as opposed to Kantian 'morality' in *Spinoza: Practical Philosophy*, ch. 2.
83 Kaufmann, *Nietzsche*, p. 196; cf. F. Nietzsche, *Thus Spake Zarathustra*, 'Of Self-Overcoming', p. 138.
84 Nietzsche also explicitly denies that sex is the most basic motive of human action, seeing it instead as a special case of the will to power. On the other hand, Nietzsche objects to Christianity's negative attitude toward sexuality. See Kaufmann, *Nietzsche*, p. 222.
85 See R. J. Hollingdale, *Nietzsche*, pp. 186ff.
86 Nietzsche, *Twilight of the Idols*, 'Morality as Anti-Nature', 1, p. 42.
87 Nietzsche, *The Anti-Christ*, 52, p. 169.
88 Kaufmann, *Nietzsche*, pp. 230, 232; cf. Hollingdale, *Nietzsche*, ch. 4.
89 See Deleuze, *Nietzsche and Philosophy*, ch. 5.
90 Nietzsche, 'On the Uses and Disadvantages of History for Life', in *Untimely Meditations*, p. 111.
91 My translation of 'Genug des werdens, lass mich sein', from Richard Wagner, *Five Songs by Mathilde Wesendonck*.
92 Kaufmann, *Nietzsche*, p. 147.
93 F. Nietzsche, from 'Ecce Homo', in *On the Genealogy of Morals and Ecce Homo*, p. 295.
94 Nietzsche, *Thus Spake Zarathustra*, p. 332. Nietzsche's notion of eternal recurrence has parallels with Kierkegaard's 'repetition'. See S. Kierkegaard, *Repetition*; cf. Hannay, *Kierkegaard*, pp. 66–72.
95 Nietzsche, *Untimely Meditations*, p. 120.
96 Kaufmann, *Nietzsche*, p. 418. This interpretation of Nietzsche has been challenged recently by K. Ansell-Pierson, *Nietzsche contra Rousseau* and M. Warren, *Nietzsche and Political Thought*.
97 See J. P. Stern, *Nietzsche* and J. A. Bernstein, *Nietzsche's Moral Philosophy*.
98 Kaufmann, *Nietzsche*, p. 303.
99 For Nietzsche's attitude to women, see Paul Patton, ed., *Nietzsche, Feminism and Political Theory*.
100 F. Dostoyevsky, *The Brothers Karamazov*, p. 69.
101 M. Heidegger, *Nietzsche*, and see above, p. 106.
102 G. Deleuze, 'Nomad Thought', p. 149; cf. Deleuze, *Nietzsche and Philosophy*.
103 Deleuze, 'Nomad Thought', p. 149.

104   J.-P. Sartre, *Being and Nothingness*. Heidegger rejected Sartre's interpretation of his ideas: M. Heidegger, 'Letter on Humanism', in *Basic Writings*. For a guide to Sartre's philosophy, see R. Aronson, *Jean-Paul Sartre: Philosophy in the World*, Arthur C. Danto, *Sartre* and C. Howells, ed., *The Cambridge Companion to Sartre*.

105   On the distinction between essence and existence, see above, p. 109.

106   Sartre, 'Une idée', quoted in Aronson, *Jean-Paul Sartre*, p. 97.

107   Aronson quoting Sartre in *Jean-Paul Sartre*, pp. 90–1.

108   Cf. Sartre, *Being and Nothingness*, pp. 3–4.

109   J.-P. Sartre, *Imagination: A Psychological Critique* (1936) and *L'Imaginaire* (1939).

110   Sartre quoted by Aronson, *Jean-Paul Sartre*, p. 41.

111   Aronson, *Jean-Paul Sartre*, p. 41. In fact, Sartre describes a range of mental states, which become increasingly negative ('creative' and 'spontaneous') as they approach the status of pure imagination.

112   Sartre quoted by Aronson, *Jean-Paul Sartre*, p. 42.

113   Sartre, *Being and Nothingness*, p. xxvii.

114   Ibid., p. xxviii.

115   Ibid., p. xxix.

116   Ibid., p. xxvii.

117   See Berkeley, *The Principles of Human Knowledge*.

118   Sartre, *Being and Nothingness*, p. xxxi.

119   Ibid.

120   Ibid., p. xxxii.

121   Ibid., p. xxii.

122   Ibid., p. xxxvii.

123   Ibid., pp. xxii.

124   Ibid., pp. xlii, xl, xli.

125   J.-P. Sartre, *Nausea* (1938), p. 183.

126   Sartre, *Being and Nothingness*, p. 18.

127   Ibid., p. 5.

128   Compare Saussure's account of 'language' as a system of differential oppositions. See below, pp. 184–5.

129   Sartre, *Being and Nothingness*, p. 7.

130   Ibid., p. 8.

131   Ibid., pp. 24–5.

132   Ibid., p. 25.

133   Danto, *Sartre*, p. 74.

134   Sartre, *Being and Nothingness*, pp. 48ff and *Existentialism and Humanism*, pp. 28–9.

135   Sartre, *Being and Nothingness*, pp. 55–63. For a sceptical discussion of these examples, see M. Le Doeuff, *Hipparchia's Choice*, pp. 70ff.

136   Sartre, *Being and Nothingness*, pp. 63–4.

137   Ibid., p. 64.

138 Sartre, *Being and Nothingness*, p. 65. Sartre's attitude to the emotions as a deliberate orientation to the world is developed in *Sketch for a Theory of the Emotions*.

139 Aronson, *Jean-Paul Sartre*, p. 81.

140 Sartre, *Being and Nothingness*, p. 397.

141 Ibid., p. 394.

142 Ibid., p. 79.

143 Ibid., p. 305.

144 Ibid., p. 326. The notion of the world as an instrumental complex is borrowed directly from Heidegger (see above, p. 110).

145 Sartre, *Being and Nothingness*, pp. 252–6.

146 Ibid., pp. 262–3.

147 Here, Sartre expresses, albeit in rhetorically heightened terms, an insight similar to that of Hegel's dialectic of master and bondsman. See above, ch. 3, pp. 54–5 and note 32.

148 Compare Heidegger's discussion of the 'everyday' and the 'they' (*das Man*) and Kierkegaard's disdain for conformity to the masses: see pp. 111, 139 above.

149 J.-P. Sartre, *The Age of Reason*, p. 195. Paradoxically, as several commentators have noted, there is a parallel here with Kant's very different view of moral duty, which implies that only actions bearing no relation to the agent's desires or inclinations can safely be regarded as ones performed 'for the sake of duty alone'.

150 Sartre would later distance himself from this essay's not very convincing arguments.

151 On Kant's categorical imperative and its problems, see above, pp. 27f, 38–9.

152 Cf. Sartre, 'A Plea for Intellectuals', in *Between Existentialism and Marxism*. See also Aronson, *Jean-Paul Sartre*, pp. 142ff, 310.

153 Aronson, *Jean-Paul Sartre*, p. 157 and passim. See also G. Elliott, 'Further Adventures of the Dialectic' for a useful review of Sartre's political and intellectual context.

154 'Childhood of a Leader' is translated in J.-P. Sartre, *Intimacy*.

155 See P. Thody, *Jean-Paul Sartre*.

156 J.-P. Sartre, *Critique of Dialectical Reason*, vol. 1, p. 113.

157 M. Poster, *Sartre's Marxism*, p. 43.

158 Sartre, *Critique of Dialectical Reason*, pp. 256–342.

159 Poster, *Sartre's Marxism*, p. 86.

160 S. de Beauvoir, *The Second Sex*, p. 29. On de Beauvoir, see P. Deutscher, *The Philosophy of Simone de Beauvoir: Ambiguity, Conversion, Resistance*, E. Fullbrook and K. Fullbrook, *Simone de Beauvoir: A Critical Introduction*, D. Bair, *Simone de Beauvoir: A Biography*; on *The Second Sex*, see E. Lundgren-Gothlin, *Simone de Beauvoir's 'The Second Sex'*.

161 de Beauvoir, *The Second Sex*, p. 736; cf. p. 734.

162 On the philosophical relationship between Sartre and de Beauvoir, see Le Doeuff, *Hipparchia's Choice*, pp. 135ff and passim. Another

attempt to provide a more situated account of freedom and the self is provided by P. Ricoeur, *Freedom and Nature: The Voluntary and the Involuntary* and *Fallible Man*.

163 F. Fanon, *The Wretched of the Earth*; also see D. Caute, *Fanon*, pp. 34ff on Fanon's relationship to Sartrian philosophy.

164 See Sartre, *Critique of Dialectical Reason* and *Saint Genet*.

165 Sartre, quoted by M. Gatens, *Feminism and Philosophy*, p. 56.

166 Beauvoir, *The Second Sex*, p. 66.

167 Gatens, *Feminism and Philosophy*, p. 57.

168 See below, ch. 7, pp. 232–5.

169 See S. E. Bronner, *Camus: Portrait of a Moralist*, J. Cruickshank, *Albert Camus and the Literature of Revolt*, C. C. O'Brien, *Camus* and E. J. Hughes, ed., *The Cambridge Companion to Camus*.

170 A. Camus, *The Myth of Sisyphus*, pp. 26, 31–2.

171 My translation of '*Mais qu'est ce que ça veut dire, la peste? C'est la vie et voilà tout*', in Camus, *La Peste* (1947), p. 246, translated as *The Plague*.

172 Camus, *The Myth of Sisyphus*, p. 11.

173 Ibid., p. 111.

174 A. Camus, *The Rebel*, p. 22.

175 Cf. Simone de Beauvoir, *The Ethics of Ambiguity*.

176 H. Marcuse, 'Sartre's Existentialism', p. 174. On the Frankfurt School, see above, ch. 3.

Chapter 6 Beyond the Subject: Structuralism and Poststructuralism

1 A useful discussion of humanism and anti-humanism is provided by K. Soper, *Humanism and Anti-humanism*.

2 On Kierkegaard, see above, ch. 5.

3 Of course, the notion of the individual has undergone significant transformations since the onset of the modern period. Women, servants and the propertyless were not, at first, regarded as individuals in their own right but as the property of particular men, who represented them. See C. Pateman, 'The Fraternal Social Contract' and her *The Sexual Contract*, esp. ch. 1.

4 See above, ch. 2.

5 See above, ch. 3.

6 K. Marx and F. Engels, *The German Ideology*, pp. 58–9, 64–5.

7 See R. Thompson, *The Pelican History of Psychology*, part I and ch. 14. On Freud, see J. Lear, *Freud*, R. Wollheim, *Freud*, esp. ch. 1, and P. Rieff, *The Triumph of the Therapeutic*, esp. ch. 1. The assumptions of both experimental and introspectionist psychology were, as we have already seen, questioned by Brentano and Husserl (see above, pp. 99ff). The description and classification of 'abnormal' sexual behaviour has a long history, including the

eighteenth-century works of the Marquis de Sade, particularly his *The 120 Days of Sodom* (lost in 1789, first published in Berlin, 1904), and R. von Krafft-Ebing (1840–1902), *Psychopathia Sexualis* (1893).

8   The word 'hysteria' derives from the Greek '*husterikos*' meaning 'of the womb': *Concise Oxford English Dictionary*, p. 582.

9   See Wollheim, *Freud*, p. 23.

10   See, e.g. J. Breuer and S. Freud, *Studies on Hysteria*, esp. part II.

11   See S. Freud, *Psychopathology of Everyday Life* and *The Interpretation of Dreams*.

12   The notion of the unconscious was not itself new. It is implicit in the thought of La Rochefoucauld, Schopenhauer and Nietzsche among others.

13   Norris describes this demotion of the conscious ego in favour of the unconscious as Freud's 'Copernican revolution': C. Norris, *Derrida*, p. 207. On Deleuze's interpretation, this revolution was already achieved by Spinoza in the seventeenth century: see *Spinoza: Practical Philosophy*, ch. 2.

14   See C. MacCabe, ed., *The Talking Cure*.

15   A. Lorenzer, *Kritik des psychoanalytischen Symbolbegriffs* and J. Habermas, *Knowledge and Human Interests*, ch. 10.

16   In effect, Freud's interpretations of unconscious mental states and phenomena extend hermeneutic principles beyond their traditional concern with deliberate expressions of mental life. Beneath the surface meaning of text and utterance, mental categories of interpretation or understanding are applied to unconscious, unintentional and hidden meanings.

17   See S. Freud, 'Analysis Terminable and Interminable' and 'Civilization and its Discontents', in *Civilization, Society and Religion*. In fact, some of Freud's collaborators and successors came closer to breaking with his ultimately individualistic assumptions. Carl Gustav Jung (1875–1961) uses the notion of a '*collective unconscious*' to refer to the accumulated past experiences of humanity. These experiences are supposedly preserved as collective memories available to each individual. Dreams and myths are analysed in similar terms as manifestations of universal human 'archetypes', explaining symbols (phallic being only the most familiar) commonly encountered in Freud's case histories. However, even with Jung the fundamental human striving is towards individual wholeness and fulfilment. See C. G. Jung, *The Integration of the Personality*, F. Fordham, *An Introduction to Jung's Psychology* and Rieff, *Triumph of the Therapeutic*, ch. 5.

18   On hermeneutics, see above, ch. 4.

19   Sartre, *Existentialism and Humanism*, p. 17. Compare Heidegger, 'The Question Concerning Technology' and 'Letter on Humanism', in *Basic Writings*; also see above, ch. 4. For Heidegger's

understanding of humanity, see F. A. Olafson, *What is a Human Being? A Heideggerian View.*

20 Heidegger, 'Letter on Humanism', p. 230.

21 Ibid., pp. 225, 228.

22 Nietzsche, *Gay Science*, para. 346, quoted in D. B. Allison, *The New Nietzsche*, p. xix.

23 Heidegger, 'The Question Concerning Technology', pp. 297, 299 and passim. Compare the Frankfurt School's critique of instrumental rationality (above, ch. 3). Cf. Andrew Feenberg, *Heidegger and Marcuse: The Catastrophe and Redemption of History.*

24 On Heidegger's associations with the Nazis, see P. Lacoue-Labarthe, *Heidegger: Art and Politics*, J.-F. Lyotard, *Heidegger and the Jews* and H. Ott, *Martin Heidegger: A Political Life.*

25 Lyotard, *Heidegger and the Jews*, p. 64.

26 R. E. Palmer, *Hermeneutics*, p. 163; also see above, ch. 4.

27 R. A. Cohen, Introduction to E. Levinas, *Time and the Other*, pp. 14–15. Cohen's introduction provides a clear overview of the development of Levinas's thought. See E. Levinas, *The Levinas Reader*, for a useful collection of his writings. See also D. T. Awerkamp, *Emmanuel Levinas* and R. Bernasconi and S. Critchley, *Re-reading Levinas.*

28 Cohen, in Levinas, *Time and the Other*, p. 16.

29 Ibid., p. 15.

30 Z. Bauman, *Modernity and the Holocaust*, p. 183.

31 S. Hand, Introduction to Levinas, *The Levinas Reader*, p. 6.

32 Levinas, *The Levinas Reader*, p. 158.

33 Ibid., p. 183.

34 Ibid. There are obvious affinities between Levinas and Derrida. See, e.g., J. Derrida, 'Violence and Metaphysics', in *Writing and Difference*; on logocentrism, see below, pp. 198–9.

35 See F. de Saussure, *Course in General Linguistics*. Appropriately enough for someone who is credited with dislodging both subject and author from their pre-eminent positions, Saussure's major work was in fact compiled from lecture notes by his students and published only posthumously. Cf. J. Culler, *Saussure.*

36 Culler, *Saussure*, p. 29. The term 'speech act' is associated with the work of J. L. Austin and John Searle. Cf. J. R. Searle, *Speech Acts: An Essay in the Philosophy of Language.*

37 In Piaget's terms, Saussure explains language in terms of 'equilibrium laws' rather than 'developmental laws'. See J. Piaget, *Structuralism*, ch. 5, section 14.

38 Even so, different languages typically have different (though recognizably similar) onomatopes for the same thing – e.g. 'quack' in English, 'couin-couin' in French.

39 Culler, *Saussure*, p. 36.

40 See Piaget, *Structuralism*, chs 2–3.

41 H. L. Dreyfus and P. Rabinow, *Michel Foucault*, pp. xv–xvi. See also P. Pettit, *The Concept of Structuralism.*

42   Sociology in the collectivist style of Émile Durkheim (1858–1917) has similar implications for the position of the subject. See É. Durkheim, *The Rules of Sociological Method* and S. Lukes, *Émile Durkheim*.

43   Roman Jakobson (1896–1982), a member of the Prague School of linguistics, applied a structural method similar to Saussure's to the phonological analysis of language. Jakobson analysed the sound systems of languages in terms of contrasting sets of 'phonemes', which are defined as 'the smallest unit in the sound-system capable of indicating contrasts in meaning': *Fontana Dictionary of Modern Thought*, p. 470.

44   C. Lévi-Strauss, *Structural Anthropology*, p. 18; also see C. Lévi-Strauss, *The Elementary Structures of Kinship*. On Lévi-Strauss's debt to Freud, Marx and Saussure, see I. Rossi, 'Intellectual Antecedents of Lévi-Strauss' Notion of Unconscious'. On Lévi-Strauss, see B. Wiseman, *Lévi-Strauss, Anthropology, and Aesthetics*.

45   C. Lévi-Strauss, *The Savage Mind*; cf. J. Sturrock, *Structuralism*, p. 48.

46   Sturrock, *Structuralism*, p. 41. In a similar way, Noam Chomsky posits a 'universal grammar' common to speakers of all languages. In psychology, Piaget claims to identify invariant and universal sequences in the child's development of intellectual capacities. Lawrence Kohlberg has applied Piaget's approach to moral development: see L. Kohlberg et al., *Moral Stages*.

47   See L. Althusser and E. Balibar, *Reading Capital*, and Althusser, *For Marx*. Cf. P. Anderson, *In the Tracks of Historical Materialism*, ch. 2 and G. Elliott, ed., *Althusser: A Critical Reader*.

48   The revival of Hegelianism in France has been attributed to Alexandre Kojève's lectures on Hegel, 1933–9. Some of these lectures are published as A. Kojève, *Introduction to the Reading of Hegel*; also see V. Descombes, *Modern French Philosophy*, ch. 1.

49   See I. Meszaros, *Lukács' Concept of Dialectic*.

50   L. Althusser, 'Marxism and Humanism', in *For Marx*, pp. 237–9.

51   See E. P. Thompson, *The Poverty of Theory* and the response by P. Anderson, *Considerations on Western Marxism*.

52   In order to avoid unnecessary confusion, the following brief account of Foucault will not attempt to recount every stage in his intellectual development, but rather to present his most influential ideas in something like their final form. There are many commentaries on Foucault, including H. L. Dreyfus and P. Rabinow, *Michel Foucault*, B. Smart, *Foucault, Marxism, Critique*, A. Sheridan, *Michel Foucault: The Will to Truth*, C. Falzon, *Foucault and Social Dialogue: Beyond Fragmentation* and L. McNay, *Foucault: A Critical Introduction*.

53   This is Eribon's gloss on a tribute by Deleuze; Foucault had written in 1970 that 'Some day this will be a Deleuzian century.' See D. Eribon, *Michel Foucault*, p. 4.

54   M. Foucault, 'Afterword: The Subject and Power', p. 208.
55   Dreyfus and Rabinow, *Michel Foucault*, p. 28.
56   Foucault, 'Afterword', p. 212.
57   Other examples are judicial practices and 'practices of the self': see M. Foucault, *Discipline and Punish* and *The Care of the Self*.
58   According to Eribon, Foucault left the Communist Party no later than 1955: see *Michel Foucault*, p. 57. In particular M. Foucault's *The Archaeology of Knowledge* was criticized as idealist because of its apparently exclusive concern with 'discourse'.
59   M. Foucault, *Discipline and Punish*, p. 27. On the other hand, Foucault rejects any easy identification of the two to the effect that 'power *is* knowledge'.
60   Smart, *Foucault, Marxism, Critique*, p. 84.
61   Ibid., p. 80.
62   See M. Foucault, 'Nietzsche, Genealogy, History' and Nietzsche, *On the Genealogy of Morals*. In *The Archaeology of Knowledge* Foucault refers approvingly to the model of Nietzsche's 'genealogy' of morality (pp. 13–14).
63   Foucault, 'Nietzsche, Genealogy, History', pp. 76, 81.
64   Foucault, 'Afterword', p. 219.
65   Smart, *Foucault, Marxism, Critique*, p. 83.
66   A. Sheridan, *Michel Foucault*, p. 83.
67   As some critics have pointed out, Foucault's periodization follows quite closely the conventions of French historiography.
68   M. Foucault, *History of Sexuality*, vol. 1, *An Introduction*, p. 86.
69   Ibid., pp. 137, 143.
70   E.g. A. Gobineau, *The Inequality of the Human Races*; cf. Foucault's lectures in *Society Must be Defended*.
71   See M. Foucault, 'Governmentality' and C. Gordon, 'Governmental Rationality: An Introduction', both in G. Burchell et al., *The Foucault Effect*.
72   Foucault, 'Afterword', p. 214.
73   Ibid.
74   Ibid., p. 215.
75   Ibid.
76   The term 'statistics' derives from the French, '*statistique*', originally the 'doctrine of the state': Hoffmeister, *Wörterbuch der philosophischen Begriffe*, p. 579.
77   Foucault, *Discipline and Punish*, p. 24. The quotation marks around 'scientific' reflect a problem not explicitly thematized in Foucault's thought. Although he is clearly sceptical of the scientific pretensions of the human sciences, he apparently accepts the genuinely scientific status of such natural sciences as astronomy, physics and chemistry. This raises the question whether the mutual implication of knowledge and power is, as he usually presents it, a feature of knowledge generally or only within the human sciences.

On this question see G. Gutting, *Michel Foucault's Archaeology of Scientific Reason*, esp. final chapter.

78   See M. Foucault, *The Birth of the Clinic* and *History of Madness*. An abridged translation of the original French edition of the latter work (*Folie et déraison: Histoire de la folie à l'âge classique*) was first published in English as *Madness and Civilization* in 1967.

79   Foucault, *Discipline and Punish*, p. 138.

80   Smart, *Foucault, Marxism, Critique*, p. 113.

81   Foucault, *Discipline and Punish*, pp. 200–1.

82   Smart, *Foucault, Marxism, Critique*, p. 111. Cf. E. Goffman, *Asylums*, for an alternative account of these 'closed institutions'.

83   Foucault's volumes on the history of sexuality have influenced both a plethora of historical studies and 'queer theories' of sex, gender and sexuality. For the latter, see, in particular, the work of Judith Butler, who provides constructive criticism of Foucault in *Gender Trouble: Feminism and the Subversion of Identity*, esp. pp. 91ff. Less critical is D. Halperin's avowedly 'hagiographic' *Saint Foucault: Towards a Gay Hagiography*.

84   See M. Foucault, 'Intellectuals and Power'.

85   Sheridan, *Michel Foucault*, pp. 139–40.

86   Foucault, 'Intellectuals and Power', p. 208.

87   G. Deleuze in Foucault, 'Intellectuals and Power', p. 209.

88   Cf. Foucault, 'Afterword', p. 212. Note also the influence of Foucault on contemporary gay or 'queer' politics: see D. Halperin, *Saint Foucault*.

89   Foucault, 'Afterword', p. 210.

90   See Habermas, *Philosophical Discourse of Modernity*. Foucault is, in fact, closer to earlier Frankfurt theorists Horkheimer and Adorno, whose *Dialectic of Enlightenment* is criticized by Habermas on similar grounds.

91   E.g. Smart, *Foucault, Marxism, Critique*, p. 87.

92   M. Foucault, 'Polemics, Politics, and Problematizations', pp. 381–2.

93   Derrida, *Writing and Difference*, p. 59.

94   J. Derrida, *Speech and Phenomena*, *Of Grammatology* and *Writing and Difference*. Helpful guides to Derrida's thought are provided by C. Norris, *Derrida*, J. Culler, *On Deconstruction*, R. Gasché, *The Tain of the Mirror: Derrida and the Philosophy of Reflection*; cf. D. Wood, ed., *Derrida: A Critical Reader*.

95   One result of this difficult stance is that in the case of Derrida the usual disclaimers regarding attempts to provide a brief and clear guide to a complex body of thought must be considerably amplified. It is not only that with Derrida the terrain is uncompromisingly difficult and unforgiving (explorers may be lost without trace or return strangely changed), it is also that normal map-making conventions no longer apply. In fact, like a hall of mirrors or the well-designed labyrinth, the environment has been designed to defy

such simple representational devices. At best one can warn of obvious pitfalls, recommend some useful conceptual equipment and preach the virtues of independent exploration from a safe distance.

96 Sturrock, *Structuralism*, p. 137; also see above, pp. 184–8.

97 In that sense, it differs from the usual contrast between modernism and postmodernism.

98 E. Grosz, *Sexual Subversions*, p. xix. 'Logos' is Greek for 'the word', 'discourse' or 'reason' and a cognate of '*legein*', 'to speak'. It is both the etymological root of our word 'logic' and a suffix of words denoting particular branches of knowledge, such as 'geology', 'theology' or 'physiology'.

99 Habermas, *Philosophical Discourse of Modernity*, p. 176.

100 Ibid., pp. 174–5.

101 Sturrock, *Structuralism*, pp. 139–40.

102 J. Derrida, '*Différance*', in *Margins of Philosophy*, p. 11. Peter Dews has pointed to the similarities between this Derridean term of art and a pervading theme of nineteenth-century German speculative idealism. Both *différance* and the 'absolute I' of Schelling's 'philosophy of identity' affirm 'the identity of identity and non-identity' as the basis of a theory of representation: Dews, *Logics of Disintegration*, pp. 28, 159.

103 Sturrock, *Structuralism*, p. 159.

104 Ibid., p. 138.

105 Habermas, *Philosophical Discourse of Modernity*, p. 171.

106 Ibid., p. 165.

107 Derrida, *Of Grammatology*, pp. 30ff (esp. pp. 35, 41); cf. Norris, *Derrida*, pp. 90–1.

108 Derrida quoted by Norris, *Derrida*, p. 95.

109 Derrida, *Of Grammatology*, p. 51.

110 Norris, *Derrida*, p. 23.

111 It is also a feature of 'other-worldly' Eastern religions, for which wisdom or truth is approached only to the extent that the material world, the body and its desires are left behind: see M. Weber, *Sociology of Religion*.

112 In Christianity this relationship can be seen in the role of the direct encounter with the truth of the 'word of God', e.g. in the conversion of the apostles after meeting Christ or 'doubting Thomas' after he sees Christ's wounds or in the power attributed to miracles.

113 Derrida quoted by Norris, *Derrida*, p. 33.

114 Derrida, 'Plato's Pharmacy', in *Dissemination*, p. 103.

115 Ibid., p. 146.

116 Norris, *Derrida*, p. 33.

117 Ibid., pp. 35–6.

118 Derrida, *Dissemination*, p. 129.

119 Norris, *Derrida*, p. 19.

120 Grosz, *Sexual Subversions*, p. xv.

121 Derrida, in R. Mortley, *French Philosophers in Conversation*, p. 97.
122 J. Derrida, *Positions*, p. 45.
123 T. McCarthy, 'The Politics of the Ineffable', p. 148.
124 R. Rorty, 'Is Derrida a Transcendental Philosopher?', p. 240.
125 Derrida, quoted by Norris, *Derrida*, p. 113.
126 Derrida, *Writing and Difference*, p. 32.
127 Derrida, *Positions*, pp. 40–1, where *'relève'* is Derrida's translation of Hegel's *'Aufhebung'* ('sublation' or 'transcendence').
128 Ibid., pp. 41–2.
129 On the comparison between Derrida and Gadamer, see D. P. Michelfelder and R. E. Palmer, *Dialogue and Deconstruction*.
130 Dews, *Logics of Disintegration*, p. 34. On Derrida's political thought, see R. Beardsworth, *Derrida and the Political*.
131 McCarthy, quoting Derrida in 'The Politics of the Ineffable', pp. 153–4.
132 See J. Derrida, 'The Laws of Reflection: Nelson Mandela, in Admiration'.
133 M. Ryan, *Marxism and Deconstruction*, pp. 219, 215.
134 Derrida, quoted by McCarthy, 'The Politics of the Ineffable', p. 157.
135 McCarthy, 'The Politics of the Ineffable', p. 156. See R. Boyne, *Foucault and Derrida*, for a more positive view of Derrida's influence on politics.
136 Boyne, *Foucault and Derrida*, p. 217.
137 Norris, *Derrida*, p. 214.
138 Rorty, on the other hand, sees Derrida as closer to his own postmodern or 'post-metaphysical' position. Rorty optimistically sums up Derrida's complex notions as 'merely abbreviations for the familiar Peircean-Wittgensteinian anti-Cartesian thesis that meaning is a function of context, and that there is no theoretical barrier to an endless sequence of recontextualizations': R. Rorty, 'Is Derrida a Transcendental Philosopher?', p. 240.
139 Derrida, *Writing and Difference*, p. 59.

Chapter 7 Postmodernism

1 See Marshall Berman, *All that is Solid Melts into Air*. This phrase is used by Marx to describe the 'bourgeois epoch' in K. Marx and F. Engels, *The Communist Manifesto*, p. 16 and derives from Shakespeare, *The Tempest*, IV, 1: 'Are melted into air, into thin air'.
2 See J.-F. Lyotard, *The Postmodern Condition*, discussed below. The definition of postmodernism is itself controversial. The term is used here to refer to currents of thought which acknowledge, in some way, the usefulness of the concepts of 'postmodernity' or 'postmodern' and their cognates.

3 '. . . you must go on, I can't go on, I'll go on', the last words of S. Beckett, *The Unnamable*, p. 414.

4 Zygmunt Bauman, *Modernity and the Holocaust*, p. xiv.

5 This phrase was coined by Rudolf Bahro as the subtitle of his book, *The Alternative in Eastern Europe*, to mark the difference between these regimes and the *ideal* of socialism or communism.

6 The question whether Marxist theory should be held responsible for the defects of actually existing socialism has a long history within Marxism: see, e.g., G. Lukács, 'What is Orthodox Marxism?' in *History and Class Consciousness* and C. Castoriadis, *The Imaginary Institution of Society*, part I, ch. 1.

7 Essentially, the problem of practice concerns the realization of communism. It is a particularly acute problem for Marxist theory, which sets out to overcome the gap between theory and practice characteristic of 'bourgeois idealism'. See above, ch. 3, esp. p. 58.

8 See G. Elliott, 'Further Adventures of the Dialectic' and P. Dews, *Logics of Disintegration*, Introduction. The exceptions are Italy and Spain.

9 See R. Williams, *Keywords*, p. 174.

10 The term was also used to describe a late nineteenth-century movement of modernizing Roman Catholic theologians.

11 S. Gaggi, *Modern/Postmodern*, p. 18.

12 In retrospect, though, both surrealism and Dadaism display recognizably postmodern themes.

13 D. Harvey, *The Condition of Postmodernity*, p. 36.

14 See H. Foster, 'Introduction' in *Postmodern Culture*, p. xv.

15 B. Smart quoting M. Calinescu in *Postmodernity*, p. 19. Smart's first chapter provides a useful account of the history and variety of uses of 'postmodernism' and its cognates.

16 F. Jameson, *Postmodernism, or, The Cultural Logic of Late Capitalism*, p. 17.

17 In W. Benjamin, *Illuminations*; cf. above, pp. 69–70.

18 In this context, he cites such works as *Las Meninas* of Velasquez, Cervantes's *Don Quixote*, Sterne's *Tristram Shandy*, Shakespeare's *Hamlet* and *The Tempest*, Caldéron de la Barca's *Life is a Dream* and the theatrical works of Pirandello and Brecht: Gaggi, *Modern/Postmodern*, p. 13. Gaggi suggests that scepticism contributes to the intellectual background of modernism as well.

19 See, e.g. R. Barthes, *S/Z*.

20 See T. Kuhn, *The Structure of Scientific Revolutions* and P. Feyerabend, *Against Method*.

21 Smart, *Postmodernity*, pp. 25–6.

22 Foster, *Postmodern Culture*, pp. xi–xii.

23 Still, despite these radical intentions, postmodernist ideas have been taken by some to lead fairly directly to conventionally liberal or even conservative conclusions. This interpretation finds support in the political and philosophical stance of Richard Rorty, who

explicitly defends a version of 'postmodernist bourgeois liberalism'. See R. Rorty, 'Postmodernist Bourgeois Liberalism'.

24 Lyotard, *The Postmodern Condition*, p. 8. On Lyotard, see
S. Malpas, *Jean-François Lyotard* and A. Benjamin, ed., *Judging
Lyotard*.

25 Lyotard, *The Postmodern Condition*, p. xxiii.

26 Ibid., p. 37.

27 Some critics suggest that Lyotard is entangled in his own metanarrative of modernity and postmodernity – an impression reinforced
by his association of postmodernity with a stage of postindustrial
society.

28 A. Touraine, 'Introduction to the Study of Social Movements', p.
781; cf. *The Voice and the Eye*. The term was used earlier by
Daniel Bell in *The Coming of Post-Industrial Society*.

29 Lyotard, *The Postmodern Condition*, pp. 45–6; cf. Marcuse's
similar use of the term 'performance principle' in *Eros and Civilization*, pp. 50ff and passim.

30 Lyotard, *The Postmodern Condition*, p. xxiv.

31 On totalizing theory see above, pp. 195–6.

32 Lyotard, *The Postmodern Condition*, pp. xxiv–xxv. 'Language-
game' is a term derived from L. Wittgenstein, *Philosophical Investigations*, para. 7, p. 5 and passim.

33 D. Hoy, 'Foucault – Modern or Postmodern?', p. 34.

34 Lyotard, *The Postmodern Condition*, p. 66; also see the discussion
of Habermas above, pp. 81–2.

35 Ibid., p. 64.

36 Ibid., p. 79.

37 Ibid., p. 78. Compare D. Hebdige on the notion of the aesthetic
sublime in contemporary theory: cited by S. Connor, *Postmodernist Culture*, pp. 212ff. Cf. Heidegger's conception of the role of
poetry, above, p. 113.

38 Lyotard, *The Postmodern Condition*, p. 66.

39 J. Keane, in A. Benjamin, *Judging Lyotard*, pp. 84, 91.

40 Ibid., pp. 89, 92, 94.

41 Ibid., pp. 96, 95.

42 Habermas, *Philosophical Discourse of Modernity*, p. 86.

43 Ibid., p. 94.

44 Ibid., pp. 136–40.

45 Ibid., p. 205.

46 Ibid., pp. 276, 278.

47 D. M. Rasmussen, *Reading Habermas*, p. 26.

48 Habermas, *Philosophical Discourse of Modernity*, p. 296; cf. his
'Modernity – An Incomplete Project' in Foster, *Postmodern Culture*.

49 For discussion of Habermas's views on modernity, see R. J.
Bernstein, ed., *Habermas and Modernity*.

50 See D. Kellner, *Jean Baudrillard*. On situationism, see C. Gray, ed.,
Leaving the 20th Century and G. Debord, *Society of the Spectacle*.

51 Baudrillard makes his final break with Marxism in *The Mirror of Production*.
52 J. Baudrillard, 'Consumer Society', in *Jean Baudrillard: Selected Writings*, p. 29.
53 Ibid., p. 48.
54 Ibid., p. 47.
55 Connor, *Postmodernist Culture*, p. 51.
56 'Simulacra and Simulations', in *Jean Baudrillard: Selected Writings*, p. 166.
57 Ibid., pp. 171ff.
58 Baudrillard, quoted by Z. Bauman, *Intimations of Postmodernity*, p. 151.
59 J. Baudrillard, 'The Ecstasy of Communication', p. 127.
60 'Consumer Society', in *Jean Baudrillard: Selected Writings*, p. 29.
61 Baudrillard, 'The Ecstasy of Communication', pp. 130–1.
62 Ibid., pp. 132–3.
63 Ibid., p. 129. The distinction between 'hot' and 'cold' universes recalls Marshall McLuhan's distinction between 'hot' and 'cool' media in *The Gutenberg Galaxy*.
64 See above, pp. 167–8.
65 'The Masses', in *Jean Baudrillard: Selected Writings*, p. 219.
66 Bauman, *Intimations of Postmodernity*, p. 153.
67 See above, ch. 6.
68 *Jean Baudrillard: Selected Writings*, p. 219.
69 As we have already seen, Lyotard assigns postmodern culture to the contemporary stage of 'postindustrial' society.
70 This kind of postmodernist Marxism is very different from the position of more orthodox Marxists like A. Callinicos in *Against Postmodernism*. For him, although postmodern thought and culture do indeed reflect objective features of contemporary capitalism, in the end they must be demystified as ideological diversions so that they do not distort unduly either theoretical analysis or class struggle.
71 For a parallel account of contemporary society, see S. Lash and J. Urry, *The End of Organised Capitalism*.
72 'Fordism' is associated with the domination of industrial society by the assembly-line production of more or less identical commodities for a mass market. It is named after Henry Ford, the American car manufacturer, whose 'Model T Ford' transformed the industry after 1912.
73 See, e.g., E. Laclau and C. Mouffe, *Hegemony and Socialist Strategy* and J. Habermas, 'New Social Movements'.
74 E.g., Frankfurt School theorists, but also E. Mandel, *Late Capitalism*.
75 Cf. above, note 28 on Touraine.
76 Jameson, *Postmodernism*, p. xii.

77 Ibid., Introduction and ch. 1, section IV. Jameson also explicitly refers to Adorno and Horkheimer's account of late capitalism (Introduction, pp. xvii–xviii).
78 Ibid., p. 2.
79 Ibid., p. xi.
80 Ibid., p. 25.
81 Ibid., p. 48.
82 Jameson, quoted by Gaggi, *Modern/Postmodern*, pp. 180–1.
83 Gaggi, *Modern/Postmodern*, p. 180.
84 Jameson, *Postmodernism*, p. 319.
85 Ibid., pp. 329ff, 408ff. For a rather different attempt to pursue the socialist project in the face of postmodernism's sceptical prohibitions, see M. Ryan, *Marxism and Deconstruction*.
86 Bauman, *Intimations of Postmodernity*, p. 167.
87 Ibid., p. 168.
88 Smart, *Postmodernity*, p. 63.
89 Ibid., pp. 41–2.
90 See Smart, *Postmodernity*, p. 41 and A. Giddens, *Social Theory and Modern Sociology*.
91 Smart, *Postmodernity*, p. 106.
92 Grosz, *Sexual Subversions*, p. 231.
93 See M. Le Doeuff, *The Philosophical Imaginary*. See also M. Morris, 'Operative Reasoning'.
94 Grosz, *Sexual Subversions*, p. 227.
95 Ibid., p. 233.
96 Le Doeuff, in R. Mortley, *French Philosophers in Conversation*, ch. 5, pp. 86ff.
97 R. Tong, *Feminist Thought*, p. 227. On Irigaray, see M. Whitford, *Luce Irigaray: Philosophy in the Feminine*. On Kristeva, see J. Lechte, *Julia Kristeva*.
98 Grosz, *Sexual Subversions*, p. 231. See, e.g. J. Kristeva, *The Kristeva Reader*.
99 Ibid., p. xxiii.
100 Tong, *Feminist Thought*, p. 231.
101 Grosz, *Sexual Subversions*, p. 97; cf. Nietzsche's notions of the Apolline and the Dionysiac, above, pp. 146–7.
102 Tong, *Feminist Thought*, p. 226.
103 Ibid. See, e.g., L. Irigaray, *This Sex Which is Not One* and *The Irigaray Reader*.
104 Grosz, *Sexual Subversions*, p. 179.
105 Tong, *Feminist Thought*, pp. 226–8.
106 Grosz, *Sexual Subversions*, pp. 179, 181.
107 I. M. Young, 'The Ideal of Community and the Politics of Difference', in L. J. Nicholson, ed., *Feminism/Postmodernism*, p. 301; cf. Young, *Justice and the Politics of Difference*.
108 See, e.g., J. Flax's and A. Yeatman's contributions to L. J. Nicholson, ed., *Feminism/Postmodernism*.

109 Said, quoted by Connor, *Postmodernist Culture*, p. 233; also see E. Said, *Orientalism*.
110 Connor, *Postmodernist Culture*, pp. 233–4.
111 Ibid.
112 'Flight' is a term used by G. Deleuze and F. Guattari, *A Thousand Plateaus*, esp. Introduction.
113 Connor, *Postmodernist Culture*, p. 243.
114 Cf. S. White, *Political Theory and Postmodernism*, p. 122.
115 Rorty, 'Postmodernist Bourgeois Liberalism'.
116 Quoted by White, *Political Theory and Postmodernism*, p. 16.
117 Gaggi, *Modern/Postmodern*, p. 175.
118 Quoted by Gaggi, *Modern/Postmodern*, p. 174. Eagleton does recognize a limited role for deconstruction and poststructuralist critique as political tools to be deployed against the ideology of Western societies. See T. Eagleton, *Literary Theory: An Introduction*, esp. pp. 143–5.
119 Oakeshott, *Rationalism in Politics*, esp. pp. 22ff.
120 Mussolini, quoted by Gaggi, *Modern/Postmodern*, p. 177. Mussolini's admirer Pirandello, whose plays are considered to have made an important contribution to the postmodern sensibility, was also apparently aware of the connection.
121 Hebdige, quoted by Connor, *Postmodernist Culture*, p. 213.
122 Connor, *Postmodernist Culture*, p. 18.
123 See F. Schiller, *On the Aesthetic Education of Man* and above, p. 28.
124 White, *Political Theory and Postmodernism*, p. 3.
125 William Connolly, quoted by White, *Political Theory and Postmodernism*, pp. 19–20.
126 White, *Political Theory and Postmodernism*, p. 22. Another influential thinker who emphasizes recognition of otherness is Emmanuel Levinas – see above, ch. 6, pp. 182–3.
127 White, *Political Theory and Postmodernism*, pp. 60, 61, 66.
128 Ibid., p. 67.
129 Ibid., pp. 68–9.
130 Ibid., p. 33.
131 Ibid., p. 72.
132 Ibid., p. 22.
133 Ibid., p. 83.
134 Ibid., ch. 6.

Chapter 8 Radical Departures

1 F. Fukuyama, *The End of History and the Last Man*.
2 For some philosophical responses to the events of 9/11 see G. Borradori, *Philosophy in a Time of Terror: Dialogues with Habermas and Jacques Derrida*, S. Žižek, *Welcome to the Desert of the Real:*

Five Essays on September 11 and Related Dates. For the dubious and potentially self-fulfilling prophecy of a 'clash of civilizations', see S. P. Huntington, *The Clash of Civilizations and the Remaking of World Order.*

3   P. Virilio: *The Original Accident*, p. 11; cf. J. Diamond, *Collapse: How Societies Choose to Fail or Survive.*

4   See above, esp. ch. 3.

5   See above, ch. 4, pp. 125–31.

6   On the controversy concerning Heidegger's relationship with National Socialism, see above, ch. 6, pp. 181–2.

7   On Arendt and Schmitt, see above, ch. 4, pp. 127–8.

8   See, for example, G. Agamben, *Stanzas.* For critical discussion of Agamben, see L. de la Durantaye, *Giorgio Agamben: A Critical Introduction*, M. Calarco et al., eds, *Giorgio Agamben: Sovereignty and Life*, A. Ross, *The Agamben Effect* and C. Norris, ed., *Politics, Metaphysics, and Death: Essays on Giorgio Agamben's 'Homo Sacer'.*

9   Agamben edited Benjamin's complete works for an Italian edition published between 1979 and 1994.

10   G. Agamben, *State of Exception.*

11   Ibid., ch. 1.

12   Ibid., pp. 11–19.

13   See G. Agamben, *Homo Sacer: Sovereign Power and Bare Life* and *Means Without End.*

14   See Agamben, *Means Without End*, ch. 4 'What is a camp?' and *Homo Sacer*, Part III.

15   Agamben, *Homo Sacer*, pp. 166–71; cf. Arendt, *Origins of Totalitarianism*, ch. 9 and above, ch. 4, p. 129. See also J. Butler, *Who Sings the Nation–State*, esp. pp. 36–43.

16   Agamben, *Homo Sacer*, pp. 71–2.

17   Ibid., p. 83.

18   Ibid., p. 6. For Foucault, see *Society Must be Defended* and M. Foucault, *The Birth of Bio-Politics*, esp. p. 317; cf. above, p. 193.

19   G. Agamben, *The Coming Community*, esp. XII–XVIII; cf. G. Debord, *Society of the Spectacle.*

20   Agamben, *Means Without End*, p. 84; cf. *Coming Community*, pp. 47–50.

21   Agamben, *Coming Community*, pp 1–2, 65 and *passim.*

22   Agamben, 'Notes on Gesture', in *Means Without End*, pp. 56–60 and *passim.* On Arendt's distinction, see above, ch. 4, pp. 125–6.

23   See, e.g., P. Lacoue-Labarthe and J.-L. Nancy, *Retreating the Political.* On Nancy, see I. James, *The Fragmentary Demand: An Introduction to the Philosophy of Jean-Luc Nancy* and S. Sparks et al., eds, *On Jean-Luc Nancy: The Sense of Philosophy.*

24   J.-L. Nancy, *The Inoperative Community*, p. 11.

25   Nancy, cited by P. Connor, Preface, *Inoperative Community*, p. xxxviii.

26 Lacoue-Labarthe and Nancy, *Retreating the Political*, p. 111.
27 On Arendt, see above, pp. 125–6.
28 Nancy, *Inoperative Community*, pp. 6–7.
29 Ibid., p. 19.
30 Ibid., pp. 32–3.
31 Ibid., pp. 36–40.
32 Ibid., pp. 25–6.
33 On Badiou, see below.
34 See above, ch. 3, pp. 60–72. For critical guides to Žižek, see S. Kay, *Žižek: A Critical Introduction*, I. Parker, *Slavoj Žižek: A Critical Introduction* and M. Sharpe, *Slavoj Žižek: A Little Piece of the Real.*
35 S. Žižek, 'The Obscene Object of Postmodernity', in *The Žižek Reader*, p. 40.
36 For an anti-essentialist account of the 'articulation' of different subject positions, see, e.g., E. Laclau and C. Mouffe, *Hegemony and Socialist Strategy.*
37 S. Žižek, 'The Spectre of Ideology', in *Žižek Reader*, pp. 56–7.
38 S. Žižek, *The Universal Exception*, pp. 170–1.
39 For introductory guides to Lacan's difficult oeuvre, see, e.g., M. Bowie, *Lacan* and S. Homer, *Jacques Lacan*. For Žižek's reading of Lacan, see S. Žižek, *How to Read Lacan, Everything You Always Wanted to Know about Lacan* or *Enjoy Your Symptom! Jacques Lacan in Hollywood and Out.*
40 Žižek, 'The Spectre of Ideology', pp. 60–1. A similar view is implicit in Ernst Bloch's affirmation of utopian thinking in *Principle of Hope* and the Frankfurt School's various views of the emancipatory potential of art.
41 S. Žižek, *The Sublime Object of Ideology*, p. 45.
42 Ibid., pp. 4–5.
43 S. Žižek, *In Defense of Lost Causes*, p. 395.
44 S. Žižek, *Conversations with Žižek*, p. 4.
45 Žižek, *Sublime Object of Ideology*, pp. 4–5; cf. *The Abyss of Freedom*, p. 9: 'In short, the ontological necessity of "madness" resides in the fact that it is not possible to pass directly from the purely "animal soul" immersed in its natural life-world to "normal" subjectivity dwelling in its symbolic universe – the vanishing mediator between the two is the "mad" gesture of radical withdrawal from reality that opens up the space for its symbolic (re)constitution.'
46 Žižek, *Sublime Object of Ideology*, pp. 48–9.
47 Žižek, *Abyss of Freedom*, p. 27.
48 See Kay, *Žižek*, ch. 1.
49 J. Butler, in J. Butler et al., *Contingency, Hegemony, Universality: Contemporary Dialogues on the Left*, p. 13. Marcuse's critique of Sartrean existentialism offers a different version of this complaint: see above, p. 171.

50 S. Žižek, *For They Know Not What They Do*, p. xii; cf. *Conversations with Žižek*, pp. 70–5. Cf. Žižek's contributions to J. Butler et al., *Contingency, Hegemony, Universality*.

51 S. Žižek, *Violence: Six Sideways Reflections*, p. 1 and ch. 1 *passim*.

52 Žižek, *Universal Exception*, pp. 104–6; cf. *Defense of Lost Causes*, ch. 4.

53 Žižek, *Sublime Object of Ideology*, pp. 136–45, 216–17. On Arendt, see above, pp. 126, 130.

54 Ibid., pp. 143–4; cf. *Universal Exception*, pp. 106–7.

55 Žižek, *Universal Exception*, pp. 108ff.

56 A. Badiou, *Being and Event*, p. xi. On Badiou, see E. Pluth, *Alain Badiou*, P. Hallward, *Badiou: A Subject to Truth*, J. Barker, *Alain Badiou: A Critical Introduction* and G. Riera, ed., *Alain Badiou: Philosophy and its Conditions*.

57 A. Badiou, *Metapolitics*, p. xxxi.

58 A. Badiou, *Ethics*, pp. 19–23; cf. P. Hallward, Introduction to *Ethics*, pp. xxii–xxiii. On Levinas, see above, pp. 182–3.

59 Badiou, *Ethics*, pp. 26–7.

60 Hallward, *Badiou*, p. 90.

61 See P. Smith, *An Introduction to Gödel's Theorems*.

62 Badiou, *Being and Event*, p. xiv.

63 Ibid., p. xii.

64 See, e.g., K. Popper, *Conjectures and Refutations*, T. Kuhn, *The Structure of Scientific Revolutions* and P. Feyerabend, *Against Method*.

65 Badiou, *Being and Event*, p. xiii.

66 Ibid., pp. 16–7.

67 Ibid., p. xiii, cited above.

68 Hallward, *Badiou*, pp. 125–6.

69 Badiou, *Metapolitics*, p. xxxix.

70 Ibid., p. 122.

71 A. Badiou, 'The Communist Hypothesis', p. 37; cf. J. Barker's Introduction to *Metapolitics*, pp. xxi–xxiii.

72 A. Badiou, *The Century*, p. 16.

73 Badiou, *Metapolitics*, p. 138. Žižek's similarly militant political stance and qualified defence of 'subjective' violence is discussed above, p. 257.

74 Badiou, *The Century*, p. 97.

75 Ibid., p. 175; cf. Habermas's concerns about genetic technology in *The Future of Human Nature*.

76 Badiou, *Ethics*, p. 46. Badiou's approach to ethics has some affinities with Kant's account of morality: see above, pp. 26–7.

77 S. Žižek, *The Ticklish Subject*, ch. 3. For a thoughtful discussion of Badiou's atheist deployment of religious categories, see Pluth, *Alain Badiou*, esp. Conclusion, pp. 175ff.

78 Badiou, *Being and Event*, p. 212.

79 Ibid., p. 215.
80 Ibid., p. 216.
81 J.-P. Sartre, *Existentialism and Humanism*, pp. 27–8; also see above, ch. 5, esp. pp. 162–3. Of course, Sartre is primarily concerned with human freedom, morality and politics rather than with science.
82 Badiou, *The Century*, p. 170.
83 Ibid., pp. 171–4.
84 Hallward, *Badiou*, p. 77. A. Badiou, *Logics of Worlds* (the sequel to *Being and Event*) offers more concrete analyses of 'faithful, 'reactive' and 'obscure' subjects: cf. Pluth, *Alain Badiou*, pp. 142ff.

References

Adorno, T. W.: *Negative Dialectics* (1966), trans. E. B. Ashton (Routledge, London, 1973).

Adorno, T. W.: *Minima Moralia: Reflections from Damaged Life*, trans. E. F. N. Jephcott (Verso, London and New York, 1974).

Adorno, T. W.: *Aesthetic Theory* (Routledge & Kegan Paul, London and Boston, 1984).

Adorno, T. W.: *The Culture Industry: Selected Essays on Mass Culture*, ed. J. M. Bernstein (Routledge, London, 1991).

Adorno, T. W. et al., eds: *The Positivist Dispute in German Sociology*, trans. G. Adey and D. Frisby (Heinemann Educational Books, London, 1976).

Agamben, G.: *Stanzas: Word and Phantasm in Western Culture*, trans. R. L. Martinez (University of Minnesota Press, Minneapolis, 1993).

Agamben, G.: *The Coming Community*, trans. M. Hardt (University of Minnesota Press, Minneapolis and London, 1993).

Agamben, G.: *Homo Sacer: Sovereign Power and Bare Life*, trans. D. Heller-Roazen (Stanford University Press, Stanford, 1998).

Agamben, G.: *Means Without End: Notes on Politics*, trans. V. Binetti and C. Casarino (University of Minnesota Press, Minneapolis and London, 2000).

Agamben, G.: *State of Exception*, trans. K. Attell (University of Chicago Press, Chicago and London, 2005).

Allison, D. B., ed.: *The New Nietzsche: Contemporary Styles of Interpretation* (Delta, New York, 1977).

Allison, H. E.: *Kant's Transcendental Idealism: An Interpretation and Defense* (Yale University Press, New Haven and London, 1983).

Althusser, L.: *For Marx*, trans. B. Brewster (Verso, London, 1977).

Althusser, L. and Balibar, E.: *Reading Capital*, trans. B. Brewster (New Left Books, London, 1970).

Anderson, P.: *Considerations on Western Marxism* (New Left Books, London, 1976).

Anderson, P.: *In the Tracks of Historical Materialism* (Verso, London, 1983).

Ansell-Pierson, K.: *Nietzsche contra Rousseau: A Study of Nietzsche's Moral and Political Thought* (Cambridge University Press, Cambridge and New York, 1991).

Arendt, H.: *The Origins of Totalitarianism*, 2nd edn (Allen & Unwin, London, 1951/1958).

Arendt, H.: *The Human Condition* (University of Chicago Press, Chicago and London, 1958).

Arendt, H.: *Between Past and Future: Six Exercises in Political Thought* (Faber & Faber, London, 1961).

Arendt, H.: *Men in Dark Times* (Harcourt, Brace, New York and London, 1968).

Arendt, H.: *Essays in Understanding: 1930–54*, ed. J. Kohn (Harcourt, Brace, New York, 1994).

Arendt, H.: *The Promise of Politics*, ed. J. Kohn (Schocken Books, New York, 2005).

Aristotle: *Aristotle's Ethics*, trans. J. Warrington (Dent & Dutton, London and New York, 1963).

Aronson, R.: *Jean-Paul Sartre: Philosophy in the World* (Verso, London, 1980).

Aune, B.: *Rationalism, Empiricism, and Pragmatism: An Introduction* (Random House, New York, 1970).

Avineri, S.: *The Social and Political Thought of Karl Marx* (Cambridge University Press, Cambridge, 1968).

Awerkamp, D. T.: *Emmanuel Levinas: Ethics and Politics* (Revisionist Press, New York, 1977).

Ayer, A. J.: *The Foundations of Empirical Knowledge* (Macmillan, Basingstoke, 1940).

Ayer, A. J.: *Language, Truth and Logic* (1936) (Penguin Books, Harmondsworth and New York, 1971).

Bacon, F.: *The Advancement of Learning* (1605), ed. G. W. Kitchen (Dent, London, 1973).

Badiou, A.: *Manifesto for Philosophy*, trans. N. Madarasz (State University of New York Press, Albany, 1999).

Badiou, A.: *Ethics: An Essay on the Understanding of Evil*, trans. P. Hallward (Verso, London and New York, 2001).

Badiou, A.: *Infinite Thought: Truth and the Return to Philosophy*, trans. O. Feltham and J. Clemens (Continuum, London and New York, 2005).

Badiou, A.: *Being and Event*, trans. O. Feltham (Continuum, London and New York, 2006).

Badiou, A.: *Metapolitics*, trans. J. Barker (Verso, London and New York, 2006).

Badiou, A.: *The Century*, trans. A. Toscano (Polity, Cambridge and Malden, MA, 2007).

Badiou, A.: 'The Communist Hypothesis', *NLR* 49, Jan/Feb 2008, pp. 29–42.

Badiou, A.: *Logics of Worlds (Being and Event, 2)*, trans. A. Toscano (Continuum, London and New York, 2009).

Bahro, R.: *The Alternative in Eastern Europe*, trans. D. Fernbach (New Left Books, London, 1978).

Bair, D.: *Simone de Beauvoir: A Biography* (Cape, London, 1990).

Bakunin, M. A.: *Marxism, Freedom and the State*, trans. and ed. K. J. Kenafick (Freedom Press, London, 1950).

Barker, J.: *Alain Badiou: A Critical Introduction* (Pluto Press, London and Sterling, VA, 2002).

Barthes, R.: *S/Z*, trans. R. Miller (Cape, London, 1975).

Baudrillard, J.: *The Mirror of Production*, trans. M. Poster (Telos Press, St Louis, 1975).

Baudrillard, J.: 'The Ecstasy of Communication', in H. Foster, ed., *Postmodern Culture* (Pluto Press, London, 1985).

Baudrillard, J.: *Jean Baudrillard: Selected Writings*, ed. M. Poster (Polity, Cambridge, 1988).

Bauman, Z.: *Modernity and the Holocaust* (Polity, Cambridge, 1989).

Bauman, Z.: *Intimations of Postmodernity* (Routledge, London and New York, 1992).

Beardsworth, R.: *Derrida and the Political* (Routledge, London and New York, 1996).

Beauvoir, S. de: *The Ethics of Ambiguity*, trans. B. Frechtman (Citadel Press, Secaucus, NJ, 1972).

Beauvoir, S. de: *The Second Sex* (1949), trans. H. M. Parshley (Penguin Books, Harmondsworth, 1972).

Beckett, S.: *The Unnamable*, in *Three Novels by Samuel Beckett: Molloy, Malone Dies, The Unnamable* (Grove Press, New York, 1965).

Beiner, R.: *Political Judgment* (Methuen, London, 1983).

Beiser, F. C.: *The Fate of Reason: German Philosophy from Kant to Fichte* (Harvard University Press, Cambridge, MA, and London, 1987).

Bell, D.: *The Coming of Post-industrial Society* (Basic Books, New York, 1978).

Benhabib, S. and Dallmayr, F.: *The Communicative Ethics Controversy* (MIT Press, Cambridge, MA, and London, 1990).

Benjamin, A., ed.: *Judging Lyotard* (Routledge, London and New York, 1992).

Benjamin, W.: *Illuminations*, trans. H. Zohn (Fontana/Collins, London, 1968).

Benso, S. and Schroeder, B., eds: *Contemporary Italian Philosophy: Crossing the Borders of Ethics, Politics, and Religion* (State University of New York Press, New York, 2007).

Benton, T.: *The Rise and Fall of Structural Marxism: Althusser and his Influence* (Macmillan, London, 1984).

Berkeley, G.: *The Principles of Human Knowledge*, ed. G. J. Warnock (Collins, London, 1962).

Berlin, I.: *Four Essays on Liberty* (Oxford University Press, Oxford and New York, 1969).

Berlin, I.: *Against the Current: Essays in the History of Ideas*, ed. H. Hard (Hogarth Press, London, 1979).

Berlin, I.: *The Crooked Timber of Humanity: Chapters in the History of Ideas*, ed. H. Hardy (John Murray, London, 1990).

Berman, H. J.: *Law and Revolution: The Formation of the Western Legal Tradition* (Harvard University Press, Cambridge, MA, 1983).

Berman, M.: *All that is Solid Melts into Air* (Verso, London, 1982).

Bernasconi, R. and Critchley, S., eds: *Re-reading Levinas* (Athlone Press, London, 1991).

Bernstein, J. A.: *Nietzsche's Moral Philosophy* (Fairleigh Dickinson University Press, Rutherford, NJ, 1987).

Bernstein, J. M.: *Adorno: Disenchantment and Ethics* (Cambridge University Press, Cambridge and New York, 2001).

Bernstein, R. J., ed.: *Habermas and Modernity* (Polity, Cambridge, 1985).

Bertram, C.: *Rousseau and the Social Contract* (Routledge, London and New York, 2004).

Blackham, H. J.: *Six Existentialist Thinkers* (Routledge & Kegan Paul, London, 1961).

Blaug, B.: *Economic Theory in Retrospect*, 4th edn (Cambridge University Press, Cambridge and New York, 1985).

Bloch, E.: *Principle of Hope*, trans. N. Plaice et al. (Blackwell, Oxford, 1986).

Bloch, M.: *Feudal Society* (Routledge & Kegan Paul, London, 1961).

Bohman, J.: *Public Deliberation: Pluralism, Complexity, and Democracy* (MIT Press, Cambridge, MA, 1996).

Bohman, J.: 'Discourse Theory', in G. F. Gaus and C. Kukathas, *Handbook of Political Theory* (Sage, London and Thousand Oaks, CA, 2004), ch. 12, pp. 155–66.

Bokina, J. and Lukes, T. J., eds: *Marcuse: From the New Left to the Next Left* (University Press of Kansas, Lawrence, 1994).

Bollnow, O. F.: *Die Lebensphilosophie* (Springer, Berlin, 1958).

Borradori, G.: *Philosophy in a Time of Terror: Dialogues with Jürgen Habermas and Jacques Derrida* (University of Chicago Press, Chicago and London, 2003).

Bottomore, T. B.: *The Frankfurt School* (E. Horwood, London and Tavistock, NY, 1984).

Boucher, D.: *Texts in Context: Revisionist Methods for Studying the History of Ideas* (Nijhoff, Dordrecht and Boston, 1985).

Bowie, A.: *Introduction to German Philosophy: From Kant to Habermas* (Polity, Cambridge and Malden, MA, 2003).

Bowie, M.: *Lacan* (Fontana, London, 1991).

Boyne, R.: *Foucault and Derrida* (Unwin Hyman, London, 1990).

Brandt, R.: 'The Deductions in the *Critique of Judgment*: Comments on Hampshire and Horstmann', in E. Förster, ed., *Kant's Transcendental Deductions: The Three* Critiques *and the* Opus postumum (Stanford University Press, Stanford, 1989), pp. 177–90.

Brecht, B.: *Life of Galileo*, trans. D. Vesey (Methuen, London, 1965).

Brentano, F.: *Psychology from an Empirical Standpoint* (1874), trans. A. C. Rancurello, D. B. Terrell and L. L. McAlister (Routledge & Kegan Paul, London, 1973).

Breuer, J. and Freud, S.: *Studies on Hysteria*, trans. J. and A. Strachey (Penguin Books, Harmondsworth, 1974).

Broad, C. D.: *Kant: An Introduction* (Cambridge University Press, Cambridge, 1978).

Bronner, S. E.: *Camus: Portrait of a Moralist* (University of Minnesota Press, Minneapolis, 1999).

Bubner, R.: *Modern German Philosophy*, trans. E. Matthews (Cambridge University Press, Cambridge and New York, 1981).

Buck-Morss, S.: *The Origin of Negative Dialectics: Theodor W. Adorno, Walter Benjamin and the Frankfurt School* (Harvester, Brighton, 1977).

Burchell, G., Gordon, C. and Miller, P., eds: *The Foucault Effect: Studies in Governmentality* (Chicago University Press, Chicago, 1991).

Burkitt, B.: *Radical Political Economy: An Introduction to the Alternative Economics* (Wheatsheaf, Brighton, 1984).

Butler, J.: *Gender Trouble: Feminism and the Subversion of Identity* (Routledge, London and New York, 1990).

Butler, J. and Spivak, G. C.: *Who Sings the Nation-State: Language, Politics, Belonging* (Seagull Books, London and New York, 2007).

Butler, J., Laclau, E. and Žižek, S.: *Contingency, Hegemony, Universality: Contemporary Dialogues on the Left* (Verso, London and New York, 2000).

Butterfield, H.: *The Whig Interpretation of History* (G. Bell, London, 1950).

Calarco, M. and DeCaroli, S., eds: *Giorgio Agamben: Sovereignty and Life* (Stanford University Press, Stanford, 2007).

Callinicos, A.: *Against Postmodernism: A Marxist Critique* (Polity, Cambridge, 1989).

Campbell, R.: *Truth and Historicity* (Clarendon Press, Oxford, 1992).

Camus, A.: *The Plague* (Alfred A. Knopf, New York, 1948).

Camus, A.: *La Peste* (1947) (Livre de Poche/Gallimard, Paris, 1962).

Camus, A.: *The Myth of Sisyphus* (1942) (Penguin Books, Harmondsworth, 1975).

Camus, A.: *The Rebel: An Essay on Man in Revolt*, trans. A. Bower (Alfred A. Knopf, New York, 1978).

Canovan, M.: *Hannah Arendt: A Reinterpretation of Her Political Thought* (Cambridge University Press, Cambridge, 1992).

Carling, A. H.: *Social Division* (Verso, London and New York, 1991).

Carver, T.: *Engels* (Oxford University Press, Oxford, 1981).

Carver, T.: *Friedrich Engels: His Life and Thought* (Macmillan, London, 1989).

Castoriadis, C.: *The Imaginary Institution of Society*, trans. K. Blamey (Polity, Cambridge, 1987).

Caute, D.: *Fanon* (Fontana/Collins, London, 1970).

Clark, M.: *Nietzsche on Truth and Philosophy* (Cambridge University Press, New York, 1990).

Clark, M. T., ed.: *An Aquinas Reader: Selections from the Writings of Thomas Aquinas* (Hodder & Stoughton, London, 1972).

Clark, R. T.: *Herder: His Life and Thought* (University of California Press, Berkeley, 1955).

Clarke, S.: *Marx's Theory of Crisis* (St Martin's Press, New York, 1993).

Cohen, G. A.: *Karl Marx's Theory of History: A Defence* (Clarendon Press, Oxford, 1978).

Colletti, L., ed.: *Karl Marx: Early Writings*, trans. R. Livingstone and G. Benton (Penguin Books, Harmondsworth, 1976).

Concise Oxford English Dictionary, ed. R. E. Allen (Clarendon Press, Oxford, 1990).

Connerton, P.: *Tragedy of Enlightenment* (Cambridge University Press, Cambridge and New York, 1980).

Connor, S.: *Postmodernist Culture: An Introduction to Theories of the Contemporary* (Blackwell, New York, 1989).

Cooper, D. E.: 'The Presidential Address: Analytical and Continental Philosophy', *Proceedings of the Aristotelian Society*, 94 (1994), pp. 1–18.

Copleston, F.: *Contemporary Philosophy: Studies of Logical Positivism and Existentialism* (Search Press, London, 1972).

Critchley, S.: *Continental Philosophy: A Very Short Introduction* (Oxford University Press, Oxford and New York, 2001).

Critchley, S. and Schürmann, R.: *On Heidegger's 'Being and Time'* (Routledge, London and New York, 2008).

Cruickshank, J.: *Albert Camus and the Literature of Revolt* (Oxford University Press, New York, 1960).

Culler, J.: *Saussure* (Fontana/Collins, London, 1976).

Culler, J.: *On Deconstruction: Theory and Criticism after Structuralism* (Cornell University Press, Ithaca, 1982).

Cutrofello, A.: *Continental Philosophy: A Contemporary Introduction* (Routledge, London and New York, 2005).

Danto, A. C.: *Nietzsche as Philosopher* (Macmillan, New York, 1965).

Danto, A. C.: *Sartre* (Fontana/Collins, London, 1975).

Dart, G.: *Rousseau, Robespierre, and English Romanticism* (Cambridge University Press, New York and London, 1999).

Darwin, C.: *The Origin of Species by Means of Natural Selection* (1859), ed. J. W. Burrow (Penguin Books, Harmondsworth, 1968).

Dauenhauer, B. P.: *Paul Ricoeur: The Promise and Risk of Politics* (Rowman & Littlefield, Lanham, MD, 1998).

Debord, G.: *Society of the Spectacle* (Black and Red, Detroit, 1977).

Deleuze, G.: 'Nomad Thought', in D. B. Allison, ed., *The New Nietzsche: Contemporary Styles of Interpretation* (Delta, New York, 1977), pp. 142–9.

Deleuze, G.: *Nietzsche and Philosophy*, trans. H. Tomlinson (Athlone Press, London, 1983).

Deleuze, G.: *Spinoza: Practical Philosophy*, trans. R. Hurley (City Light Books, San Francisco, 1988).

Deleuze, G. and Guattari, F.: *A Thousand Plateaus: Capitalism and Schizophrenia*, trans. B. Massumi (Athlone Press, London, 1988).

Deleuze, G. and Guattari, F.: *What is Philosophy?*, trans. H. Tomlinson and G. Burchell (Columbia University Press, New York, 1994).

Derrida, J.: *Speech and Phenomena* (Northwestern University Press, Evanston, 1973).

Derrida, J.: *Of Grammatology* (Johns Hopkins University Press, Baltimore, 1976).

Derrida, J.: 'The Question of Style', in D. B. Allison, ed., *The New Nietzsche: Contemporary Styles of Interpretation* (Delta, New York, 1977), pp. 176–89.

Derrida, J.: *Writing and Difference*, trans. A. Bass (Routledge & Kegan Paul, London, 1978).

Derrida, J.: *Dissemination* (1972), trans. B. Johnson (Chicago University Press, Chicago, 1981).

Derrida, J.: *Positions*, trans. A. Bass (Chicago University Press, Chicago, 1981).

Derrida, J.: *Margins of Philosophy* (1972), trans. A. Bass (Harvester Wheatsheaf, New York and London, 1982).

Derrida, J.: 'The Laws of Reflection: Nelson Mandela, in Admiration', in J. Derrida and M. Tlili, eds., *For Nelson Mandela* (Seaver, New York, 1987).

Descartes, R.: 'Meditations on First Philosophy' (1641), in *The Philosophical Works of Descartes*, vol. 1, trans. E. S. Haldane and G. R. T. Ross (Dover, London and New York, 1931).

Descombes, V.: *Modern French Philosophy*, trans. L. Scott-Fox and J. M. Harding (Cambridge University Press, Cambridge and New York, 1980).

Deutscher, P.: *The Philosophy of Simone de Beauvoir: Ambiguity, Conversion, Resistance* (Cambridge University Press, Cambridge and New York, 2008).

Dews, P.: *Logics of Disintegration* (Verso, London and New York, 1987).

Diamond, J.: *Collapse: How Societies Choose to Fail or Survive* (Allen Lane, London and New York, 2005).

Dilthey, W.: *Selected Writings*, ed. H. P. Rickman (Cambridge University Press, Cambridge and New York, 1976).

Dilthey, W.: *Introduction to the Human Sciences*, trans. R. J. Betanzos (Wayne State University Press, Detroit, 1988).

Dostoyevsky, F.: *The Brothers Karamazov*, trans. R. Pevear and L. Volokhonsky (Vintage Books, London, 1990).

Dreyfus, H. L.: *Being-in-the-World: A Commentary on Heidegger's 'Being and Time', Division I* (MIT Press, Cambridge, MA, and London, 1991).

Dreyfus, H. L. and Hall, H.: *Husserl, Intentionality and Cognitive Science* (MIT Press, Cambridge, MA, 1982).

Dreyfus, H. L. and Rabinow, P.: *Michel Foucault: Beyond Structuralism and Hermeneutics* (Harvester, Brighton, 1982).

Dryzek, J. S.: 'Democratic Political Theory', in G. F. Gaus and C. Kukathas, *Handbook of Political Theory* (Sage, London and Thousand Oaks, CA, 2004), ch. 11, pp. 143–54.

Dummett, M.: 'Can Analytical Philosophy be Systematic, and Ought it to be?' in *Truth and Other Enigmas* (Duckworth, London, 1978).

Dunne, P.: *Quantitative Marxism* (Blackwell, Cambridge, MA, 1991).

Durantaye, L. de la: *Giorgio Agamben: A Critical Introduction* (Stanford University Press, Stanford, 2009).

Durkheim, E.: *The Rules of Sociological Method* (1895), trans. S. A. Solovaye and J. H. Mueller (Free Press, New York, 1965).

Eagleton, T.: *Literary Theory: An Introduction* (University of Minnesota Press, Minneapolis, 1983).

Elliott, G.: *Althusser: The Detour of Theory* (Verso, London and New York, 1987).

Elliott, G.: 'Further Adventures of the Dialectic', in A. Phillips Griffiths, ed., *Contemporary French Philosophy* (Cambridge University Press, Cambridge and New York, 1987).

Elliott, G., ed.: *Althusser: A Critical Reader* (Blackwell, Oxford, 1994).

Elster, J.: *An Introduction to Karl Marx* (Cambridge University Press, Cambridge and New York, 1986).

Engels, F.: 'On Historical Materialism', in *Anti-Dühring* (Lawrence & Wishart, London, 1947).

Engels, F.: *The Condition of the Working Class in England in 1844* (1845), trans. F. K. Wischnewetzky (Allen & Unwin, London, 1950).

d'Entrèves, M. P.: *The Political Philosophy of Hannah Arendt* (Routledge, London and New York, 1994).

d'Entrèves, M. P. and Benhabib, S., eds: *Habermas and the Unfinished Project of Modernity: Critical Essays on the Philosophical Discourse of Modernity* (MIT Press, Cambridge, MA, 1997).

Eribon, D.: *Michel Foucault*, trans. B. Wing (Harvard University Press, Cambridge, MA, 1991).

Ettinger, E.: *Hannah Arendt/ Martin Heidegger* (Yale University Press, New Haven and London, 1995).

Falzon, C.: *Foucault and Social Dialogue: Beyond Fragmentation* (Routledge, London and New York, 1998).

Fanon, F.: *The Wretched of the Earth*, trans. C. Farrington (Penguin Books, Harmondsworth, 1969).

Feenberg, A.: *Heidegger and Marcuse: The Catastrophe and Redemption of History* (Routledge, New York and London, 2005).

Feuerbach, L.: *Essence of Christianity* (1841), trans. G. Eliot (Harper & Row, New York and London, 1957).

Feuerbach, L.: *Principles of the Philosophy of the Future*, trans. Manfred U. Vogel (Bobbs-Merrill, Indianapolis, 1966).

Feyerabend, P.: *Against Method* (Verso, London and New York, 1988).

Findlay, J. N.: *Hegel: A Re-examination* (Allen & Unwin, London, and Macmillan, New York, 1958).

Føllesdal, D.: *Husserl und Frege* (I kommisjon hos Aschehoug, Oslo, 1958).

Fontana Dictionary of Modern Thought, ed. A. Bullock and O. Stally-brass (Fontana/Collins, London, 1977).

Fordham, F.: *An Introduction to Jung's Psychology* (Penguin Books, Harmondsworth, 1953).

Foster, H., ed.: *Postmodern Culture* (Pluto Press, London, 1985).

Foucault, M.: *The Archaeology of Knowledge* (1969), trans. A. M. Sheridan Smith (Tavistock Publications, London, 1972).

Foucault, M.: 'Intellectuals and Power', in *Language, Counter-memory, Practice*, trans. D. F. Bouchard and S. Simon (Blackwell, Oxford, and Cornell University Press, Ithaca, 1977).

Foucault, M.: 'Nietzsche, Genealogy, History', in *Language, Counter-memory, Practice*, trans. D. F. Bouchard and S. Simon (Blackwell, Oxford, and Cornell University Press, Ithaca, 1977).

Foucault, M.: *History of Sexuality*, vol. 1: *An Introduction*, trans. R. Hurley (Penguin Books, Harmondsworth, 1978).

Foucault, M.: *Discipline and Punish* (Penguin Books, Harmondsworth and New York, 1979).

Foucault, M.: 'Afterword: The Subject and Power', in H. L. Dreyfus and P. Rabinow, *Michel Foucault: Beyond Structuralism and Hermeneutics* (Harvester, Brighton, 1982).

Foucault, M.: 'Polemics, Politics, and Problematizations', in P. Rabinow, ed., *A Foucault Reader* (Penguin Books, Harmondsworth, 1984).

Foucault, M.: *The Care of the Self: The History of Sexuality*, vol. 3, trans. R. Hurley (Penguin Books, Harmondsworth and New York, 1986).

Foucault, M.: *Madness and Civilization: A History of Insanity in the Age of Reason* (Routledge, London, 1989).

Foucault, M.: *The Birth of the Clinic: An Archaeology of Medical Perception* (Vintage Books, New York, 1994).

Foucault, M.: *Society Must be Defended*, trans. D. Macey (Penguin Books, London and New York, 2004).

Foucault, M.: *The Birth of Bio-Politics: Lectures at the Collège de France, 1978–79*, trans. G. Burchell (Palgrave Macmillan, New York and London, 2008).

Foucault, M.: *History of Madness* (Routledge, London and New York, 2009).

Frank, M.: *The Philosophical Foundations of Early German Romanticism*, trans. E. Millán-Zaibert (State University of New York Press, Albany, 2004).

Freud, S.: *Psychopathology of Everyday Life* (Penguin Books, Harmondsworth, 1975).

Freud, S.: *The Interpretation of Dreams*, trans. J. Strachey (Penguin Books, Harmondsworth, 1976).

Freud, S.: *Civilization, Society and Religion: Group Psychology, Civilization and its Discontents and Other Works* (Penguin Books, Harmondsworth, 1985).

Freud, S.: 'Analysis Terminable and Interminable', in S. Freud, *On Freud's 'Analysis Terminable and Interminable'* (Yale University Press, New Haven, 1991).

Fukuyama, F.: *The End of History and the Last Man* (Free Press, New York and Oxford, 1992).

Fullbrook, E. and Fullbrook, K.: *Simone de Beauvoir: A Critical Introduction* (Polity, Cambridge and Malden, MA, 1998).

Gadamer, H.-G.: 'On the Scope and Function of Hermeneutical Reflection', *Continuum*, 8 (1970), pp. 77–95.

Gadamer, H.-G.: *Philosophical Hermeneutics*, ed. D. E. Linge (University of California Press, Berkeley, 1976).

Gadamer, H.-G.: *Truth and Method*, 2nd rev. edn, trans. J. Weinsheimer and D. G. Marshall (Continuum, New York, 1989).

Gaggi, S.: *Modern/Postmodern: A Study in Twentieth-Century Arts and Ideas* (University of Pennsylvania Press, Philadelphia, 1989).

Garber, C. and Longuenesse, B., eds: *Kant and the Early Moderns* (Princeton University Press, Princeton, 2008).

Gardener, P.: *Schopenhauer* (Penguin Books, Harmondsworth, 1963).

Gasché, R.: *The Tain of the Mirror: Derrida and the Philosophy of Reflection* (Harvard University Press, Cambridge, MA, 1986).

Gasché, R.: *Inventions of Difference: On Jacques Derrida* (Harvard University Press, Cambridge, MA, and London, 1994).

Gatens, M.: *Feminism and Philosophy* (Polity, Cambridge, 1991).

Geoghegan, V.: *Reason and Eros: The Social Theory of Herbert Marcuse* (Pluto Press, London, 1981).

Geuss, R.: *The Idea of a Critical Theory: Habermas and the Frankfurt School* (Cambridge University Press, Cambridge and New York, 1981).

Giddens, A.: *Social Theory and Modern Sociology* (Stanford University Press, Stanford, and Polity, Cambridge, 1987).

Gilmore, M. P.: *Arguments from Roman Law in Political Thought, 1200–1600* (Harvard University Press, Cambridge, MA, 1971).

Glendinning, S.: *The Idea of Continental Philosophy: A Philosophical Chronicle* (Edinburgh University Press, Edinburgh, 2006).

Gobineau, A.: *The Inequality of the Human Races* (1853–5) (Noontide Press, Los Angeles, 1966).

Godwin, W.: *Enquiry concerning Political Justice* (1793), ed. I. Kramnick (Penguin Books, Harmondsworth, 1976).

Goffman, E.: *Asylums: Essays on the Social Situation* (Penguin Books, Harmondsworth, 1974).

Goldman, L.: *Immanuel Kant*, trans. R. Black (New Left Books, London, 1971).

Gombrich, E. H.: *Symbolic Images: Studies in the Art of the Renaissance* (Phaidon, London, 1972).

Gramsci, A.: *Selections from the Prison Notebooks*, trans. Q. Hoare and G. Nowell Smith (Lawrence & Wishart, London, 1971).

Gray, C., ed.: *Leaving the 20th Century: The Incomplete Work of the Situationist International* (Free Fall, London, 1974).

Grondin, J.: *The Philosophy of Gadamer*, trans. K. Plant (McGill-Queen's University Press, New York, 2003).

Grosz, E.: *Sexual Subversions* (Allen & Unwin, Sydney, 1989).

Gutting, G.: *Michel Foucault's Archaeology of Scientific Reason* (Cambridge University Press, Cambridge and New York, 1989).

Gutting, G.: *French Philosophy in the Twentieth Century* (Cambridge University Press, Cambridge and New York, 2001).

Habermas, J.: 'On Systematically Distorted Communication', *Inquiry*, 13 (1970), pp. 205–18.

Habermas, J.: 'Summation and Response', *Continuum*, 8 (1970), pp. 123–33.

Habermas, J.: *Über Sprachtheorie: Vorbereitende Bemerkungen zu einer Theorie der kommunikativen Kompetenz* (Handblume, Vienna, 1970).

Habermas, J.: *Toward a Rational Society*, trans. J. J. Shapiro (Heinemann, London, 1971).

Habermas, J.: *Knowledge and Human Interests*, trans. J. J. Shapiro (Heinemann, London, 1972).

Habermas, J.: 'A Postscript to *Knowledge and Human Interests*', *Philosophy of the Social Sciences*, 3 (1973), pp. 157–89.

Habermas, J.: 'Wahrheitstheorien', in *Wirklichkeit und Reflexion: Walter Schulz zum 60. Geburtstag* (Neske, Pfullingen, 1973).

Habermas, J.: 'New Social Movements', *Telos*, 49 (1981), pp. 33–7.

Habermas, J.: *Communication and the Evolution of Society*, trans. T. McCarthy (Polity, Cambridge, 1984).

Habermas, J.: *Theory of Communicative Action*, 2 vols, trans. T. McCarthy (Beacon Press, Boston, and Polity, Cambridge, 1984/1987).

Habermas, J.: *Autonomy and Solidarity: Interviews with Jürgen Habermas*, ed. P. Dews (Verso, London, 1986).

Habermas, J.: *The Structural Transformation of the Public Sphere*, trans. T. Burger (MIT Press, Cambridge, MA, and Polity, Cambridge, 1989).

Habermas, J.: *The New Conservatism: Cultural Criticism and the Historians' Debate*, ed. S. W. Nicholson (MIT Press, Cambridge, MA, 1989).

Habermas, J.: *Moral Consciousness and Communicative Action*, trans. C. Lenhardt and S. W. Nicholson (MIT Press, Cambridge, MA, and Polity, Cambridge, 1990).

Habermas, J.: *Philosophical Discourse of Modernity* (Polity, Cambridge, 1990).

Habermas, J.: *Justification and Application: Remarks on Discourse Ethics*, trans. C. Cronin (Polity, Cambridge, 1993).

Habermas, J.: *Between Facts and Norms: Contributions to a Discourse Theory of Law and Democracy*, trans. W. Rehg (Polity, Cambridge, 1996).

Habermas, J.: *The Postnational Constellation: Political Essays*, trans. M. Pensky (MIT Press, Cambridge, MA, 2001).

Habermas, J.: *Religion and Rationality: Essays on Reason, God, and Modernity* (MIT Press, Cambridge, MA, 2002).

Habermas, J.: *The Future of Human Nature* (Polity, Cambridge and Malden, MA, 2003).

Habermas, J.: *Between Naturalism and Religion: Philosophical Essays*, trans. C. Cronin (Polity, Cambridge and Malden, MA, 2008).

Habermas, J. and Derrida, J.: *Philosophy in a Time of Terror: Dialogues with Jürgen Habermas and Jacques Derrida*, ed. G. Borradori (University of Chicago Press, Chicago, 2003).

Habermas, J. et al.: *An Awareness of What is Missing: Faith and Reason in a Post-Secular Age* (Polity, Cambridge and Malden, MA, 2010).

Hallward, P.: *Badiou: A Subject to Truth* (University of Minnesota Press, Minneapolis and London, 2003).

Halperin, D.: *Saint Foucault: Towards a Gay Hagiography* (Oxford University Press, Oxford and New York, 1995).

Hammer, E., ed.: *German Idealism: Contemporary Perspectives* (Routledge, London and New York, 2007).

Hampshire, S.: 'The Social Spirit of Mankind', in E. Förster, ed., *Kant's Transcendental Deductions: The Three* Critiques *and the* Opus postumum (Stanford University Press, Stanford, 1989), pp. 145–56.

Hannay, A.: *Kierkegaard* (Routledge, London and New York, 1991).

Hannay, A.: *Kierkegaard: A Biography* (Cambridge University Press, Cambridge and New York, 2001).

Hannay, A. and Marino, G. D., eds: *The Cambridge Companion to Kierkegaard* (Cambridge University Press, Cambridge and New York, 1998).

Harman, C. and Callinicos, A.: *The Changing Working Class* (Bookmarks, London, 1987).

Harvey, D.: *The Condition of Postmodernity: An Inquiry into the Origins of Cultural Change* (Blackwell, Oxford, 1990).

Harvey, V. A.: *Feuerbach and the Interpretation of Religion* (Cambridge University Press, Cambridge and New York, 1995).

Hegel, G. W. F.: *The Philosophy of Right* (1821), trans. T. M. Knox (Oxford University Press, Oxford and New York, 1952).

Hegel, G. W. F.: *Lectures on the History of Philosophy*, 3 vols, trans. E. S. Haldane and F. H. Simson (Routledge, London, 1955).

Hegel, G. W. F.: *The Phenomenology of Mind* (1807), trans. J. B. Baillie (Harper & Row, New York and London, 1967).

Hegel, G. W. F.: *Phenomenology of Spirit* (1807), trans. A. V. Miller (Oxford University Press, Oxford and New York, 1977).

Hegel, G. W. F.: *Introduction to the Lectures on the Philosophy of History*, trans. T. M. Knox and A. V. Miller (Oxford University Press, Oxford and New York, 1985).

Hegel, G. W. F.: *The Philosophy of History* (1822), trans. J. Sibree (Prometheus, New York, 1991).

Heidegger, M.: *Discourse on Thinking: A Translation of* Gelassenheit (1955), trans. J. M. Anderson and E. H. Freund (Harper Torchbooks, New York and London, 1966).

Heidegger, M.: *Being and Time*, trans. J. Macquarrie and E. Robinson (Blackwell, Oxford, 1967).

Heidegger, M.: *Basic Writings*, ed. D. Farrell Krell (Harper, San Francisco, 1977).

Heidegger, M.: *Nietzsche*, 4 vols, trans. D. Farrell Krell (Harper & Row, San Francisco, 1979).

Held, D.: *Introduction to Critical Theory: Horkheimer to Habermas* (University of California Press, Berkeley and Los Angeles, 1980; and Polity, Cambridge, 1990).

Hempel, C. G.: *Aspects of Scientific Explanation, and Other Essays in the Philosophy of Science* (Free Press, New York, 1965).

Henrich, D.: 'Kant's Notion of a Transcendental Deduction and the Methodological Background of the First *Critique*', in E. Förster, ed., *Kant's Transcendental Deductions: The Three* Critiques *and the* Opus postumum (Stanford University Press, Stanford, 1989), pp. 29–46.

Herder, J. G.: *Discourse on the Origin of Language* (1772), ed. J. H. Moran (F. Unger, New York, 1967).

Hobbes, T.: *Leviathan* (Dent, London, 1973).

Hobsbawm, E. J. et al., eds: *The Forward March of Labour Halted* (New Left Books, London, 1981).

Hockney, D.: *Secret Knowledge: Rediscovering the Lost Techniques of the Old Masters* (Thames and Hudson, London, 2001).

Hodges, H. A.: *Wilhelm Dilthey: An Introduction* (Kegan Paul, Trench and Trubner, London, 1944).

Hodges, H. A.: *The Philosophy of Wilhelm Dilthey* (Routledge, London, 1952).

Hoffmeister, J.: *Wörterbuch der philosophischen Begriffe*, 2nd edn (Felix Meiner, Hamburg, 1955).

Hollingdale, R. J.: *Nietzsche* (Routledge & Kegan Paul, London and Boston, 1973).

Holub, R. C.: *Jürgen Habermas: Critic in the Public Sphere* (Routledge, London and New York, 1991).

Homer, S.: *Jacques Lacan* (Routledge, London and New York, 2005).

Honneth, A.: *The Critique of Power: Reflective Stages in a Critical Social Theory*, trans. K. Baynes (MIT Press, Cambridge, MA, 1991).

Honneth, A.: *Disrespect: The Normative Foundations of Critical Theory* (Polity, Cambridge and Malden, MA, 2007).

Horkheimer, M.: *Eclipse of Reason* (Continuum, New York, 1974).

Horkheimer, M.: *Critical Theory: Selected Essays*, trans. M. J. O'Connell et al. (Continuum, New York, 1992).

Horkheimer, M. and Adorno, T. W.: *Dialectic of Enlightenment* (1944), trans. John Cumming (Verso, London and New York, 1979).

Howard, M. C. and King, J. E.: *The History of Marxian Economics* (Macmillan, Basingstoke, 1989–92).

Howells, C., ed.: *The Cambridge Companion to Sartre* (Cambridge University Press, Cambridge and New York, 1992).

Hoy, D.: 'Foucault – Modern or Postmodern?' in J. Arac, ed., *After Foucault: Humanistic Knowledge, Postmodern Challenge* (Rutgers University Press, New Brunswick, 1988).

Hughes, E. J., ed.: *The Cambridge Companion to Camus* (Cambridge University Press, Cambridge and New York, 2007).

Hume, D.: *A Treatise of Human Nature*, ed. L. A. Selby-Bigge (Clarendon Press, Oxford, 1888).

Hume, D.: *Enquiries Concerning Human Understanding and Concerning the Principles of Morals*, ed. L. A. Selby-Bigge (Clarendon Press, Oxford, 1902).

Hume, D.: *Dialogues Concerning Natural Religion*, ed. M. Bell (Penguin Books, Harmondsworth and New York, 1990).

Huntington, S. P.: *The Clash of Civilizations and the Remaking of World Order* (Simon and Schuster, New York, 1996).

Husserl, E.: *Cartesian Meditations: An Introduction to Phenomenology*, trans. D. Cairns (Nijhoff, The Hague, 1960).

Husserl, E.: *Ideas: General Introduction to Phenomenology*, trans. W. R. Boyce Gibson (London, Collier-Macmillan, 1962).

Husserl, E.: 'Philosophy as Rigorous Science', in *Phenomenology and the Crisis of Philosophy*, trans. Q. Lauer (Harper Torchbooks, New York and London, 1965).

Husserl, E.: *Logical Investigations*, 2 vols, trans. J. N. Findlay (Humanities Press, New York, 1970).

Husserl, E.: *Philosophy of Arithmetic: Psychological and Logical Investigations*, in *Edmund Husserl's Collected Works*, vol. 10, trans. D. Willard (Kluwer Academic Publishing, Dordrecht, 2003).

Husserl, E.: *The Crisis of European Sciences and Transcendental Phenomenology*, trans. D. Carr (Northwestern University Press, Evanston, 1970).

Inwood, M.: *A Hegel Dictionary* (Blackwell, Oxford and Cambridge, MA, 1992).

Irigaray, L.: *This Sex which is Not One*, trans. C. Porter and C. Burke (Cornell University Press, Ithaca, 1985).

Irigaray, L.: *The Irigaray Reader*, ed. M. Whitford (Blackwell, Oxford, and Cambridge, MA, 1991).

James, I.: *The Fragmentary Demand: An Introduction to the Philosophy of Jean-Luc Nancy* (Stanford University Press, Stanford, 2006).

Jameson, F.: *Postmodernism, or, The Cultural Logic of Late Capitalism* (Duke University Press, Durham, NC, 1991).

Jarvis, S.: *Adorno: A Critical Introduction* (Polity, Cambridge, 1998).

Jay, M.: *The Dialectical Imagination: A History of the Frankfurt School and the Institute for Social Research, 1923–1950* (Little, Brown, Boston and London, 1973).

Jessop, B.: *The Capitalist State: Marxist Theories and Methods* (New York University Press, New York, and M. Robertson, Oxford, 1982).

Jessop, B.: *State Theory: Putting the Capitalist State in its Place* (Polity, Cambridge, 1990).

Jung, C. G.: *The Integration of the Personality*, trans. S. M. Dell (Farrar & Rinehart, New York, 1939).

Kamenka, E.: *The Philosophy of Ludwig Feuerbach* (Routledge & Kegan Paul, London, 1970).

Kant, I.: *Critique of Pure Reason* (1781/1787), trans. N. Kemp-Smith (Macmillan, London and New York, 1933).

Kant, I.: *Critique of Judgement* (1790), trans. J. C. Meredith (Clarendon Press, Oxford, 1952).

Kant, I.: *Critique of Practical Reason* (1788), trans. L. White Beck (Bobbs-Merrill, Indianapolis, 1956).

Kant, I.: *Groundwork of the Metaphysic of Morals*, ed. H. J. Paton (Harper & Row, New York, 1965).

Kant, I.: 'An Answer to the Question: What is Enlightenment?' in *Perpetual Peace and Other Essays*, trans. T. Humphrey (Hackett, Indianapolis, and Cambridge, 1983).

Kant, I.: *Critique of the Power of Judgment* (1790), trans. P. Guyer and E. Matthews (Cambridge University Press, Cambridge and New York, 2000).

Kant, I.: *Groundwork for the Metaphysics of Morals*, trans. A. W. Wood (Yale University Press, New Haven, 2002).

Kateb, G.: *Hannah Arendt: Politics, Conscience, Evil* (Rowman and Allanheld, Totowa, NJ, 1983).

Kaufmann, W.: 'The Hegel Myth and its Method', *Philosophical Review*, 60 (1951), pp. 459–86.

Kaufmann, W.: *Nietzsche: Philosopher, Psychologist, Antichrist*, 4th edn (Princeton University Press, Princeton, 1974).

Kay, S.: *Žižek: A Critical Introduction* (Polity, Cambridge and Malden, MA, 2003).

Keane, J.: *Public Life and Late Capitalism* (Cambridge University Press, London and New York, 1984).

Kellner, D.: *Herbert Marcuse and the Crisis of Marxism* (Macmillan, London, 1984).

Kellner, D.: *Jean Baudrillard: From Marxism to Postmodernism and Beyond* (Stanford University Press, Stanford, and Polity, Cambridge, 1989).

Kennedy, P. M.: 'Idealists and Realists: British Views of Germany, 1864–1939', *Transactions of the Royal Historical Society*, 5th series, 25 (1975), pp. 137–56.

Kierkegaard, S.: *The Concept of Dread*, trans. W. Lowrie (Princeton University Press, Princeton, 1946).

Kierkegaard, S.: *Repetition*, trans. W. Lowrie (Oxford University Press, London, 1946).

Kierkegaard, S.: *Either/Or*, 2 vols, trans. D. F. Swenson and L. M. Swenson (vol. 1) and W. Lowrie (vol. 2) (Princeton University Press, Princeton, 1959).

Kierkegaard, S.: *Selections from the Writings of Kierkegaard*, ed. L. M. Hollander (Doubleday, New York, 1960).

Kierkegaard, S.: *Philosophical Fragments or a Fragment of Philosophy*, trans. D. F. Swenson (Princeton University Press, Princeton, 1962).

Kierkegaard, S.: *Fear and Trembling: Dialectical Lyric by Johannes de Silentio*, trans. A. Hannay (Penguin Books, Harmondsworth and New York, 1985).

Kierkegaard, S.: *The Concept of Irony, with Continual Reference to Socrates*, trans. H. V. Hong and E. H. Hong (Princeton University Press, Princeton, 1989).

Kierkegaard, S.: *The Sickness unto Death: A Christian Psychological Exposition for Edification and Awakening by Anti-Climacus*, trans. A. Hannay (Penguin Books, Harmondsworth and New York, 1989).

Kierkegaard, S.: *Concluding Unscientific Postscript to Philosophical Fragments*, vol. 1, trans. H. V. Hong and E. H. Hong (Princeton University Press, Princeton, 1992).

Kirk, W.: 'The Introduction and Critical Reception of Hegelian Thought in Britain, 1830–1900', *Victorian Studies*, 32, 1 (Fall 1988), pp. 85–111.

Kohlberg, L., Levine, C. and Hewer, A.: *Moral Stages: A Current Formulation and a Response to Critics* (Karger, Basle and New York, 1983).

Kojève, A.: *Introduction to the Reading of Hegel: Lectures on the Phenomenology of Spirit*, trans. J. H. Nichols (Basic Books, New York, 1969).

Koselleck, R.: *Critique and Crisis: Enlightenment and the Pathogenesis of Modern Society* (MIT Press, Cambridge, MA, 1998).

Kristeva, J.: *The Kristeva Reader*, ed. T. Moi (Blackwell, Oxford, 1986).

Kuhn, T.: *The Structure of Scientific Revolutions* (Chicago University Press, Chicago, 1970).

Laclau, E. and Mouffe, C.: *Hegemony and Socialist Strategy* (Verso, London, 1985).

Lacoue-Labarthe, P.: *Heidegger: Art and Politics*, trans. C. Turner (Blackwell, Oxford, 1990).

Lacoue-Labarthe, P. and Nancy, J.-L.: *Retreating the Political*, ed. S. Sparks (Routledge, London and New York, 1997).

Lash, S. and Urry, J.: *The End of Organised Capitalism* (Polity, Cambridge, 1987).

Lash, S. and Whimster, S., eds: *Max Weber, Rationality and Modernity* (Allen & Unwin, London and Boston, 1987).

Lear, J.: *Freud* (Routledge, London and New York, 2005).

Lechte, J.: *Julia Kristeva* (Routledge, London and New York, 1990).

Le Doeuff, M.: *The Philosophical Imaginary* (Athlone Press, London, 1989).

Le Doeuff, M.: *Hipparchia's Choice: An Essay concerning Women, Philosophy etc.*, trans. T. Selous (Blackwell, Oxford, 1991).

Lenin, V. I.: *What is to be Done? Burning Questions of Our Movement* (Foreign Languages Press, Peking, 1975).

Leopold, D.: *The Young Karl Marx: German Philosophy, Modern Politics, and Human Flourishing* (Cambridge University Press, Cambridge and New York, 2007).

Levinas, E.: *Time and the Other, and Additional Essays*, trans. R. A. Cohen (Duquesne University Press, Pittsburgh, 1987).

Levinas, E.: *The Levinas Reader*, ed. S. Hand (Blackwell, Oxford and Cambridge, MA, 1989).

Lévi-Strauss, C.: *The Savage Mind* (Chicago University Press, Chicago, 1966).

Lévi-Strauss, C.: *Structural Anthropology*, trans. C. Jacobson and B. G. Schoepf (Penguin Books, Harmondsworth, 1968).

Lévi-Strauss, C.: *The Elementary Structures of Kinship*, trans. J. H. Bell et al. (Eyre & Spottiswoode, London, 1969).

Lewis, A. D. E. and Ibbetson, D. J., eds: *The Roman Law Tradition* (Cambridge University Press, Cambridge and New York, 1994).

Locke, J.: *Essay Concerning Human Understanding*, 2 vols, ed. J. W. Yolton (Dent, London and New York, 1965).

Locke, J.: *Political Writings*, ed. D. Wootton (Penguin Books, Harmondsworth and New York, 1993).

Lorenzer, A.: *Kritik des psychoanalytischen Symbolbegriffs* (Suhrkamp, Frankfurt, 1970).

Lukács, G.: *History and Class Consciousness*, trans. R. Livingstone (Merlin Press, London, 1971).

Lukes, S.: *Émile Durkheim: His Life and Work, a Historical and Critical Study* (Harper & Row, New York, 1972).

Lukes, S.: *Marxism and Morality* (Oxford University Press, Oxford, 1987).

Lundgren-Gothlin, E.: *Simone de Beauvoir's 'The Second Sex'* (Athlone Press, London, 1996).

Lyotard, J.-F.: *The Postmodern Condition: A Report on Knowledge*, trans. G. Bennington and B. Massumi (Manchester University Press, Manchester, 1984).

Lyotard, J.-F.: *The Lyotard Reader*, ed. A. Benjamin (Blackwell, Oxford and New York, 1989).

Lyotard, J.-F.: *Heidegger and the Jews*, trans. A. Michel and M. S. Roberts (University of Minnesota Press, Minneapolis, 1990).

MacCabe, C., ed.: *The Talking Cure: Essays in Psychoanalysis and Language* (Macmillan, London, 1981).

McCarthy, T.: *The Critical Theory of Jürgen Habermas* (Polity, Cambridge, 1984).

McCarthy, T.: 'The Politics of the Ineffable: Derrida's Deconstructionism', *Philosophical Forum*, 21 (1989–90), pp. 146–68.

Machiavelli, N.: *The Prince* (Penguin Books, Harmondsworth and New York, 1961).

McLellan, D.: *Karl Marx: His Life and Thought* (Macmillan, London, 1973).

McLellan, D.: *Marx* (Fontana, London, 1975).

McLuhan, M.: *The Gutenberg Galaxy* (Routledge & Kegan Paul, London, 1962).

McNay, L.: *Foucault: A Critical Introduction* (Polity, Cambridge, 1994).

Macquarrie, J.: *Martin Heidegger* (Lutterworth Press, London, and John Knox Press, Richmond, VA, 1968).

Macquarrie, J.: *Existentialism* (Penguin Books, Harmondsworth, 1973).

MacRae, D. G.: *Weber* (Fontana/Collins, London, 1987).

Magee, B.: *The Philosophy of Schopenhauer*, 2nd edn (Clarendon Press, Oxford and New York, 1997).

Makkreel, R. A.: *Dilthey: Philosopher of Human Studies* (Princeton University Press, Cambridge, MA, 1992).

Malpas, S.: *Jean-François Lyotard* (Routledge, London and New York, 2003).

Mandel, E.: *Late Capitalism*, trans. J. De Bres (New Left Books, London, 1975).

Marcuse, H.: *One-Dimensional Man* (Sphere Books, London, 1968).

Marcuse, H.: *An Essay on Liberation* (Allen Lane, London, 1969).

Marcuse, H.: *Eros and Civilization* (1956) (Sphere Books, London, 1969).

Marcuse, H.: *Soviet Marxism* (Penguin Books, Harmondsworth and New York, 1971).

Marcuse, H.: *Counterrevolution and Revolt* (Allen Lane, London, 1972).

Marcuse, H.: 'Sartre's Existentialism', in *Studies in Critical Philosophy* (New Left Books, London, 1972, and Beacon Press, Boston, 1973).

Marx, K.: *Critique of the Gotha Programme* (Foreign Languages Press, Peking, 1972).

Marx, K.: *Grundrisse* (Penguin Books, Harmondsworth, 1973).

Marx, K.: *The Civil War in France* (Progress Publishers, Moscow, 1974).

Marx, K.: *Capital: A Critique of Political Economy*, vol. 1 (1867), trans. B. Fowkes (Penguin Books, Harmondsworth and New York, 1976).

Marx, K.: 'Critique of Hegel's Doctrine of the State', in *Karl Marx: Early Writings*, trans. R. Livingstone and G. Benton (Penguin Books, Harmondsworth, 1976).

Marx, K.: 'Economic and Philosophical Manuscripts' (1844), in *Karl Marx: Early Writings*, trans. R. Livingstone and G. Benton (Penguin Books, Harmondsworth, 1976).

Marx, K.: 'On the Jewish Question', in *Karl Marx: Early Writings*, trans. R. Livingstone and G. Benton (Penguin Books, Harmondsworth, 1976).

Marx, K.: 'Theses on Feuerbach', in *Karl Marx: Early Writings*, trans. R. Livingstone and G. Benton (Penguin Books, Harmondsworth, 1976).

Marx, K. and Engels, F.: *The Communist Manifesto*, in *Essential Works of Marxism* (Bantam Books, New York and London, 1961).

Marx, K. and Engels, F.: *The German Ideology*, ed. C. J. Arthur (Lawrence & Wishart, London, 1977).

Merleau-Ponty, M.: *The Phenomenology of Perception*, trans. C. Smith (Routledge & Kegan Paul, London, 1962).

Merleau-Ponty, M.: *The Structure of Behaviour*, trans. A. L. Fisher (Beacon Press, Boston, 1963).

Meszaros, I.: *Lukács' Concept of Dialectic* (Merlin Press, London, 1972).

Mettrie, J. O. de la: *Man a Machine*, ed. G. C. Bussey (Open Court, Chicago, 1927).

Michelfelder, D. P. and Palmer, R. E., eds: *Dialogue and Deconstruction: The Gadamer–Derrida Encounter* (State University of New York Press, Albany, 1989).

Mill, J. S.: *A System of Logic, Ratiocinative and Inductive*, 2 vols, 10th edn (Longmans Green, London, 1879).

Mills, C.: *The Philosophy of Agamben* (Acumen, Durham, 2008, and McGill-Queen's University Press, Montreal, 2009).

Mohanty, J.: *Edward Husserl's Theory of Meaning* (Nijhoff, The Hague, 1964).

Moore, G. and Brobjer, T. H., eds: *Nietzsche and Science* (Ashgate, Aldershot and Burlington, VT, 2004).

Moran, D.: *Introduction to Phenomenology* (Routledge, London and New York, 2000).

Morris, M.: 'Operative Reasoning: Michèle Le Doeuff, Philosophy and Feminism', *Ideology and Consciousness*, 9 (Winter, 1981/2), pp. 71–101.

Mortley, R.: *French Philosophers in Conversation: Levinas, Schneider, Serres, Irigaray, Le Doeuff, Derrida* (Routledge, London and New York, 1991).

Mul, J. de: *The Tragedy of Finitude: Dilthey's Hermeneutics of Life*, trans. T. Burrett (Yale University Press, New Haven, 2004).

Nancy, J.-L.: *The Inoperative Community*, ed. P. Connor (University of Minnesota Press, Minneapolis, 1991).

Nancy, J.-L.: *Being Singular Plural*, trans. R. D. Richardson and A. E. O'Byrne (Stanford University Press, Stanford, 2000).

Nicholson, L. J., ed.: *Feminism/Postmodernism* (Routledge, New York and London, 1990).

Nietzsche, F.: *Twilight of the Idols and The Anti-Christ*, trans. R. J. Hollingdale (Penguin Books, Harmondsworth, 1968).

Nietzsche, F.: *On the Genealogy of Morals and Ecce Homo*, trans. W. Kaufmann and R. J. Hollingdale (Vintage Books, New York, 1969).

Nietzsche, F.: *Thus Spake Zarathustra*, trans. R. J. Hollingdale (Penguin Books, Harmondsworth, 1969).

Nietzsche, F.: *Beyond Good and Evil*, trans. R. J. Hollingdale (Penguin Books, Harmondsworth and New York, 1973).

Nietzsche, F.: *Gay Science*, trans. W. Kaufmann (Vintage Books, New York, 1974).

Nietzsche, F.: *Untimely Meditations*, trans. R. J. Hollingdale (Cambridge University Press, Cambridge and New York, 1983).

Nietzsche, F.: *Human, All Too Human* (Cambridge University Press, Cambridge and New York, 1986).

Nietzsche, F.: *Birth of Tragedy*, trans. S. Whiteside (Penguin Books, Harmondsworth and New York, 1993).

Norman, R.: *Hegel's Phenomenology: A Philosophical Introduction* (St Martin's Press, New York, 1976).

Norris, C.: *Derrida* (Fontana, London, 1987).

Norris, C., ed.: *Politics, Metaphysics, and Death: Essays on Giorgio Agamben's 'Homo Sacer'* (Duke University Press, Durham, 2005).

Norris, C.: *Badiou's 'Being and Event': A Reader's Guide* (Continuum, New York, 2009).

Oakeshott, M.: *Experience and its Modes* (Cambridge University Press, Cambridge, 1933).

Oakeshott, M.: *Rationalism in Politics, and Other Essays* (Methuen, London, 1962).

Oakeshott, M.: 'Michael Oakeshott on Marx on Hegel', *Spectator* (6 February 1971), pp. 192–3.

Oakeshott, M.: *On Human Conduct* (Clarendon Press, Oxford, 1975).

O'Brien, C. C.: *Camus* (Fontana/Collins, London, 1970).

O'Hagan, T.: *Rousseau* (Routledge, London and New York, 2003).

Olafson, F. A.: *What is a Human Being? A Heideggerian View* (Cambridge University Press, Cambridge and New York, 1995).

Ollman, B.: *Alienation: Marx's Conception of Man in Capitalist Society* (Cambridge University Press, Cambridge, 1971).

Ott, H.: *Martin Heidegger: A Political Life*, trans. A. Blunden (Harper Collins, London, 1993).

Outhwaite, W.: *Habermas: A Critical Introduction*, 2nd edn (Polity, Cambridge, 2009).

Oxford Dictionary of Quotations, 4th edn (Oxford University Press, Oxford and New York, 1992).

Palmer, R. E.: *Hermeneutics: Interpretation Theory in Schleiermacher, Dilthey, Heidegger, and Gadamer* (Northwestern University Press, Evanston, 1969).

Parker, I.: *Slavoj Žižek: A Critical Introduction* (Pluto Press, London and Sterling, VA, 2004).

Pascal, B.: *Pensées*, ed. J. Chevalier (Gallimard, Paris, 1962).

Pascal, B.: *The Provincial Letters*, trans. A. J. Krailsheimer (Penguin Books, Harmondsworth, 1967).

Passmore, J.: *A Hundred Years of Philosophy*, 2nd edn (Penguin Books, Harmondsworth and New York, 1978).

Passmore, J.: *Recent Philosophers* (Duckworth, London, 1985).

Pateman, C.: 'The Fraternal Social Contract', in J. Keane, ed., *Civil Society and the State* (Verso, London, 1988).

Pateman, C.: *The Sexual Contract* (Polity, Cambridge, 1988).

Patton, P., ed.: *Nietzsche, Feminism and Political Theory* (Routledge, London and New York, 1993).

Patton, P.: *Deleuze and the Political* (Routledge, London and New York, 2000).

Pedersen, H.: *The Discovery of Language: Linguistic Science in the Nineteenth Century*, ed. J. W. Spargo (Indiana University Press, Bloomington, 1967).

Pettit, P.: *The Concept of Structuralism* (University of California Press, Berkeley, 1975).

Piaget, J.: *Structuralism*, trans. C. Maschler (Routledge & Kegan Paul, London, 1971).

Pitkin, H. F.: *The Attack of the Blob: Hannah Arendt's Concept of the Social* (University of Chicago Press, Chicago, 1998).

Pivčević, E.: *Husserl and Phenomenology* (Hutchinson University Library, London and Sydney, 1970).

Pivčević, E., ed.: *Phenomenology and Philosophical Understanding* (Cambridge University Press, Cambridge, 1975).

Plato: *Meno*, in *Protagoras and Meno*, trans. W. K. C. Guthrie (Penguin Books, Harmondsworth, 1956).

Plato: *Phaedo*, in *The Last Days of Socrates: Euthyphro, The Apology, Crito, Phaedo*, trans. H. Tredennick (Penguin Books, Harmondsworth, 1969).

Pluth, E.: *Alain Badiou* (Polity, Cambridge and Malden, MA, 2010).

Popper, K.: *The Poverty of Historicism* (Routledge & Kegan Paul, London, 1957).

Popper, K.: *Conjectures and Refutations: The Growth of Scientific Knowledge* (Routledge & Kegan Paul, London, 1963).

Poster, M.: *Sartre's Marxism* (Pluto Press, London, 1979).

Pusey, M.: *Economic Rationalism in Canberra: A Nation Building State Changes its Mind* (Cambridge University Press, Cambridge and New York, 1991).

Rasmussen, D. M.: *Reading Habermas* (Blackwell, Oxford, 1990).

Rée, J.: *Descartes* (Allen Lane, London, 1974).

Reich, W.: *The Invasion of Compulsory Sex-Morality* (Souvenir Press, London, 1972).

Rickman, H. P.: *Wilhelm Dilthey: Pioneer of the Human Studies* (Paul Elek, London, 1979).

Ricoeur, P.: *Freedom and Nature: The Voluntary and the Involuntary*, trans. E. V. Kohak (Northwestern University Press, Evanston, IL, 1966).

Ricoeur, P.: *Fallible Man*, trans. C. A. Kelbley, rev. edn (Fordham University Press, New York, 1986).

Ricoeur, P.: *Oneself as Another*, trans. K. Blamey (University of Chicago Press, Chicago, 1992).

Ricoeur, P.: *Memory, History, Forgetting*, trans. K. Blamey and D. Pellauer (University of Chicago Press, Chicago, 2004).

Rieff, P.: *The Triumph of the Therapeutic: Uses of Faith after Freud* (Penguin Books, Harmondsworth, 1973).

Riera, G., ed.: *Alain Badiou: Philosophy and its Conditions* (State University of New York Press, Albany, 2005).

Rochefoucauld, F. de la, Duc de: *Maximes et réflexions diverses*, ed. J.-P. Caput (Larousse, Paris, 1975).

Rohde, P.: *Kierkegaard: An Introduction to His Life and Philosophy* (Allen & Unwin, London, 1959).

Rosenfeld, M. and Arato, A., eds: *Habermas on Law and Democracy: Critical Exchanges* (University of California Press, Berkeley, CA, 1998).

Rorty, R.: 'Postmodernist Bourgeois Liberalism', *Journal of Philosophy*, 80/10 (1983), pp. 583–9.

Rorty, R.: 'Is Derrida a Transcendental Philosopher?' in David Wood, ed., *Derrida: A Critical Reader* (Blackwell, Oxford and Cambridge, MA, 1992).

Rose, G.: *The Melancholy Science: An Introduction to the Thought of Theodor W. Adorno* (Macmillan, London, 1978).

Ross, A.: *The Agamben Effect: The South Atlantic Quarterly 107:1 Winter 2008* (Duke University Press, Durham, NC, 2007).

Rossi, I.: 'Intellectual Antecedents of Lévi-Strauss' Notion of Unconscious', in *The Unconscious in Culture: The Structuralism of Claude Lévi-Strauss in Perspective*, ed. I. Rossi (Dutton, New York, 1974).

Rousseau, J.-J.: 'Discourse on the Origin of Inequality' (1754), in *The Social Contract and Discourses*, trans. G. D. H. Cole (Dent, London, 1973).

Rousseau, J.-J.: *Émile*, trans. B. Foxley (Dent, London, 1974).

Ryan, M.: *Marxism and Deconstruction* (Johns Hopkins University Press, Baltimore, 1982).

Ryle, G.: *The Concept of Mind* (Penguin Books, Harmondsworth, 1976).

Said, E.: *Orientalism* (Routledge & Kegan Paul, London, 1978).

Sartre, J.-P.: *What is Literature?* trans. B. Frechtman (Methuen, London, 1950).

Sartre, J.-P.: *Existentialism and Humanism*, trans. P. Mairet (Methuen, London, 1952).

Sartre, J.-P.: *Being and Nothingness*, trans. H. E. Barnes (Routledge, London, 1958).

Sartre, J.-P.: *The Age of Reason*, Book I of *The Roads to Freedom* (Penguin Books, Harmondsworth, 1961).

Sartre, J.-P.: *Imagination: A Psychological Critique*, trans. F. Williams (University of Michigan Press, Ann Arbor, 1962).

Sartre, J.-P.: *Sketch for a Theory of the Emotions*, trans. P. Mairet (Methuen, London, 1962).

Sartre, J.-P.: *Saint Genet: Actor and Martyr*, trans. B. Frechtman (George Braziller, New York, 1963).

Sartre, J.-P.: *Nausea*, trans. R. Baldick (Penguin Books, Harmondsworth, 1965).

Sartre, J.-P.: *L'Imaginaire* (Methuen, London, 1972).

Sartre, J.-P.: *Between Existentialism and Marxism*, trans. J. Matthews (NLB, London, 1974).

Sartre, J.-P.: *The Wall (Intimacy) and Other Stories*, trans. L. Alexander (New Directions, New York, 1975).

Sartre, J.-P.: *Critique of Dialectical Reason*, vol. 1, trans. A. Sheridan-Smith (Verso, London and New York, 1991).

Sartre, J.-P.: *Existentialism is a Humanism*, trans. C. Macomber (Yale University Press, New Haven, 2007).

Saussure, F. de: *Course in General Linguistics*, trans. W. Baskin (McGraw-Hill, New York and London, 1959).

Schacht, R.: *Nietzsche* (Routledge, London and New York, 1983).

Schiller, F.: *Über die ästhetische Erziehung des Menschen*, in E. Ackerknecht, ed., *Schillers Werke*, vol. 2 (Knaur Klassiker, Munich, 1953).

Schiller, F.: *On the Aesthetic Education of Man* (1794), ed. and trans. E. M. Wilkinson and L. A. Willoughby (Clarendon Press, Oxford, 1967).

Schmaltz, T. M., ed.: *Receptions of Descartes: Cartesianism and Anti-Cartesianism in Early Modern Europe* (Routledge, London and New York, 2005).

Schmitt, C.: *The Crisis of Parliamentary Democracy*, trans. E. Kennedy (MIT Press, Cambridge, MA, and London, 1985).

Schmitt, C.: *The Leviathan in the State Theory of Thomas Hobbes: Meaning and Failure of a Political Symbol*, trans. G. Schwab and E. Hilfstein (Greenwood Press, Westport, CN, 1996).

Schmitt, C.: *The Concept of the Political*, trans. G. Schwab (University of Chicago Press, Chicago and London, 2007).

Schnädelbach, H.: *Philosophy in Germany 1831–1933*, trans. E. Matthews (Cambridge University Press, Cambridge and New York, 1984).

Schopenhauer, A.: *The World as Will and Representation*, 2 vols, trans. E. F. J. Payne (Dover, New York, 1966).

Schroeder, W. R.: *Continental Philosophy: A Critical Approach* (Blackwell, Oxford and Malden, MA, 2005).

Schütz, A.: *The Phenomenology of the Social World*, trans. G. Walsh and F. Lehnert (Northwestern University Press, Evanston, 1967).

Scruton, R.: *Kant* (Oxford University Press, Oxford and New York, 1982).

Scruton, R.: *A Short History of Modern Philosophy: From Descartes to Wittgenstein* (Routledge, London, 1984).

Searle, J. R.: *Speech Acts: An Essay in the Philosophy of Language* (Cambridge University Press, Cambridge, 1969).

Sharpe, M.: *Slavoj Žižek: A Little Piece of the Real* (Ashgate, Aldershot and Burlington, VT, 2004).

Sheridan, A.: *Michel Foucault: The Will to Truth* (Routledge & Kegan Paul, London, 1990).

Sigmund, P.: *Natural Law in Political Thought* (Winthrop, Cambridge, MA, 1971).

Simms, K.: *Paul Ricoeur* (Routledge, London and New York, 2003).

Singer, P.: *Hegel* (Oxford University Press, Oxford and New York, 1983).

Singer, P.: *Hegel: A Very Short Introduction* (Oxford University Press, Oxford and New York, 2001).

Skinner, Q.: *The Foundations of Modern Political Thought*, 2 vols (Cambridge University Press, Cambridge, 1978).

Smart, B.: *Foucault, Marxism, Critique* (Routledge & Kegan Paul, London, 1983).

Smart, B.: *Postmodernity* (Routledge, London and New York, 1993).

Smith, A.: *An Inquiry into the Nature and Causes of the Wealth of Nations*, ed. R. H. Campbell and A. S. Skinner, 2 vols (Clarendon Press, Oxford, 1976).

Smith, A. D.: *Husserl and the 'Cartesian Meditations'* (Routledge, London and New York, 2003).

Smith, P.: *An Introduction to Gödel's Theorems* (Cambridge University Press, Cambridge and New York, 2007).

Solomon, R. C.: *Continental Philosophy Since 1750: The Rise and Fall of the Self* (Oxford University Press, Oxford and New York, 1988).

Soper, K.: *Humanism and Anti-humanism* (Hutchinson, London, 1986).

Sparks, S., D. Sheppard and C. Thomas, eds: *On Jean-Luc Nancy: The Sense of Philosophy* (Routledge, London and New York, 1997).

Steiner, G.: *Heidegger* (Fontana/Collins, London, 1992).

Steinhoff, U.: *The Philosophy of Jürgen Habermas: A Critical Introduction* (Oxford University Press, Oxford and New York, 2009).

Stern, J. P.: *Nietzsche* (Fontana/Collins, London, 1978).

Stirk, P. M. R.: *Max Horkheimer: A New Interpretation* (Harvester Wheatsheaf, Hemel Hempstead and Lanham, MD, 1992).

Strawson, P. F.: *The Bounds of Sense: An Essay on Kant's* Critique of Pure Reason (Methuen, London, 1966).

Strawson, P. F.: 'Sensibility, Understanding, and the Doctrine of Synthesis', in E. Förster, ed., *Kant's Transcendental Deductions: The Three Critiques and the* Opus postumum (Stanford University Press, Stanford, 1989), pp. 69–77.

Strawson, P. F.: *Analysis and Metaphysics: An Introduction to Philosophy* (Oxford University Press, Oxford, 1992).

Sturrock, J.: *Structuralism*, 2nd edn (Fontana, London, 1993).

Taylor, C.: *Hegel* (Cambridge University Press, Cambridge and New York, 1975).

Taylor, C.: *Sources of the Self: The Making of the Modern Identity* (Cambridge University Press, Cambridge and New York, 1989).

Thody, P.: *Jean-Paul Sartre: A Literary and Political Study* (Hamish Hamilton, London, 1960).

Thompson, E. P.: *The Poverty of Theory* (Merlin Press, London, 1978).

Thompson, J. B.: *Critical Hermeneutics: A Study in the Thought of Paul Ricoeur and Jürgen Habermas* (Cambridge University Press, Cambridge, 1981).

Thompson, J. B. and Held, D., eds: *Habermas: Critical Debates* (Macmillan, London, 1982).

Thompson, R.: *The Pelican History of Psychology* (Penguin Books, Harmondsworth, 1968).

Tong, R.: *Feminist Thought: A Comprehensive Introduction* (Westview Press, Boulder, 1989).

Touraine, A.: *The Voice and the Eye: An Analysis of Social Movements*, trans. A. Duff (Cambridge University Press, Cambridge, 1981).

Touraine, A.: 'Introduction to the Study of Social Movements', *Social Research*, 52 (Winter, 1985), pp. 749–87.

Tuck, R.: *Natural Rights Theories: Their Origin and Development* (Cambridge University Press, Cambridge, 1979).

Villa, D. R.: *Arendt and Heidegger: The Fate of the Political* (Princeton University Press, Princeton, 1996).

Virilio, P.: *The Original Accident* (Polity, Cambridge and Malden, MA, 2007). First published as *L'Accident originel*, 2005.

Warnke, G.: *Gadamer: Hermeneutics, Tradition and Reason* (Polity, Cambridge, 1987).

Warren, M.: *Nietzsche and Political Thought* (MIT Press, Cambridge, MA, 1988).

Weber, M.: *Sociology of Religion* (Methuen, London, 1965).

Weber, M.: *Economy and Society: An Outline of Interpretive Sociology*, ed. G. Roth and C. Wittich, 2 vols (University of California Press, Berkeley, 1978).

Wellmer, A.: *The Persistence of Modernity: Essays on Aesthetics, Ethics and Postmodernism*, trans. D. Midgley (Polity, Cambridge, 1991).

Wellmer, A.: *Endgames: The Irreconcilable Nature of Modernity: Essays and Lectures*, trans. D. Midgley (MIT Press, Cambridge, MA, 2000).

White, S. K.: *Political Theory and Postmodernism* (Cambridge University Press, Cambridge and New York, 1991).

White, S. K., ed.: *The Cambridge Companion to Habermas* (Cambridge University Press, Cambridge and New York, 1995).

Whitehead, A. N. and Russell, B.: *Principia Mathematica*, 2nd edn, 3 vols (Cambridge University Press, Cambridge and New York, 1950).

Whitford, M.: *Luce Irigaray: Philosophy in the Feminine* (Routledge, London and New York, 1991).

Wiggershaus, R.: *The Frankfurt School*, trans. M. Robertson (Polity, Cambridge, 1994).

Willard, D.: *Logic and the Objectivity of Knowledge: A Study in Husserl's Early Philosophy* (Ohio University Press, Athens, 1984).

Williams, B.: *Descartes: The Project of Pure Enquiry* (Penguin Books, Harmondsworth, 1978).

Williams, B.: *In the Beginning Was the Deed: Realism and Moralism in Political Argument*, ed. G. Hawthorn (Princeton University Press, Princeton and Oxford, 2005).

Williams, R.: *The Long Revolution* (Penguin Books, Harmondsworth and New York, 1961).

Williams, R.: *Keywords* (Fontana/Collins, London, 1976).

Williams, T. C.: *The Concept of the Categorical Imperative* (Clarendon Press, Oxford, 1968).

Wiseman, B.: *Lévi-Strauss, Anthropology, and Aesthetics* (Cambridge University Press, Cambridge and New York, 2007).

Witkin, R. W.: *Adorno on Popular Culture* (Routledge, London and New York, 2003).

Wittgenstein, L.: *Philosophical Investigations*, trans. G. E. M. Anscombe (Blackwell, Oxford, 1974).

Wollheim, R.: *Freud* (Fontana/Collins, London, 1971).

Wood, D., ed.: *Derrida: A Critical Reader* (Blackwell, Oxford and Cambridge, MA, 1992).

Woodcock, G.: *Anarchism: A History of Libertarian Ideas and Movements* (Penguin Books, Harmondsworth, 1975).

Young, I. M.: *Justice and the Politics of Difference* (Princeton University Press, Princeton, 1990).

Young, I. M.: 'The Ideal of Community and the Politics of Difference', in L. J. Nicholson, ed., *Feminism/Postmodernism* (Routledge, New York and London, 1990).

Young-Bruehl, E.: *Hannah Arendt: For Love of the World*, 2nd edn (Yale University Press, New Haven and London, 2004).

Žižek, S.: *The Sublime Object of Ideology* (Verso, London and New York, 1989).

Žižek, S.: *Everything You Always Wanted to Know about Lacan (But Were Afraid to Ask Hitchcock)* (Verso, London and New York, 1992).

Žižek, S.: *Enjoy Your Symptom! Jacques Lacan in Hollywood and Out* (Routledge, London and New York, 1992).

Žižek, S.: *The Abyss of Freedom* (University of Michigan Press, Ann Arbor, 1997).

Žižek, S.: *The Ticklish Subject: The Absent Centre of Political Ontology* (Verso, London and New York, 1999).

Žižek, S.: *The Žižek Reader*, ed. Elizabeth Wright and Edmond Wright (Blackwell, Oxford and Malden, MA, 1999).

Žižek, S.: *Welcome to the Desert of the Real: Five Essays on September 11 and Related Dates* (Verso, London and New York, 2002).

Žižek, S.: *How to Read Lacan* (Norton, New York, 2007).

Žižek, S.: *The Universal Exception*, ed. R. Butler and S. Stephens (Continuum, London and New York, 2007).

Žižek, S.: *For They Know Not What They Do: Enjoyment as a Political Factor*, 2nd edn (Verso, London and New York, 2008).

Žižek, S.: *In Defense of Lost Causes* (Verso, London and New York, 2008).

Žižek, S.: *Violence: Six Sideways Reflections* (Profile Books, London, 2008).

Žižek, S. and Daly, G.: *Conversations with Žižek* (Polity, Cambridge and Malden, MA, 2004).

Zuidervaart, L.: *Adorno's Aesthetic Theory* (MIT Press, Cambridge, MA, 1991).

Index

Gadamer, H.-G.
  application 121–2
  authority 123
  hermeneutics 114–15, 118–24,
    182, 206
  history of effect 118–19
  humanism 182
  human sciences 114–16
  interpretation 114, 116–22
  life-world 115–16
  meaning 119–20
  subjectivism 115–16
  tradition 122–3
  Truth and Method 114–15
  understanding 115, 116–19
Gaggi, Silvio 215–16, 237
Galilei, Galileo 13
Geist (worldview) 41, 175–6,
  280n11
Geisteswissenschaften (human
  sciences) 77–8, 90, 114–15,
  280n11
genealogy 149, 191, 195, 211,
  221, 239
Gentile, Giovanni 44
Geuss, Raymond 63–4
Giddens, Anthony 230
Gilligan, Carol 240
globalization 83, 230
God 14, 16, 23, 33–4, 48–9, 135,
  139–42, 143–4, 154, 219,
  284–85, 300–112
Goethe, J. W. von 36
Gramsci, Antonio 55, 60, 63, 72,
  213
Greek tragedies 146–7
Green, T. H. 44
Grosz, Elizabeth 198, 232–4
Grünberg, Carl 61
Guattari, F. 225

Habermas, Jürgen 11, 68, 179
  communicative action 73–5,
    76–7
  communicative rationality 80–2
  critical theory 74–5
  Derrida 84, 199

discourse ethics 82–3, 220,
  221–2, 240
historical materialism 73–4
instrumental rationality
  73–6
knowledge 76–8
*Knowledge and Human
  Interests* 76–9
postmodernism 221–2
public sphere 71, 75, 83
purposive-rational action 73–4,
  76–7
speech 80–2
truth, consensus theory 81–2,
  220
values 79–80
Hamann, Johann Georg 34
Hampshire, Stuart 26
Hannay, A. 139
Harvey, D. 215
Hegel, Georg Wilhelm Friedrich
  dialectical method 41–2, 66,
    285n131, 134
  Enlightenment 37–8, 44
  ethical life 39–40
  freedom 41, 254–5
  history 40–2, 66, 87–8
  idealism 43–4, 53–4
  Kant 38–40
  lordship and bondage
    54–5
  modernism 211
  morality 38–40, 87–88,
    134–5
  Phenomenology of Mind 42–3,
    54
  philosophy 2–3, 3–4, 42–4
  Philosophy of Right 39–40, 47,
    50–1
  reason (*Vernunft*) 38, 74
  Romantics 37–8
  spirit (*Geist*) 41, 87
  subject 54–5, 175–6
  understanding 38
  world spirit 87, 175–6
Hegelianism 44, 47, 49–50, 53, 55,
  66–7, 87–9, 135, 176